CALIFORNIA REAL ESTATE PRACTICE

Third Edition

Anthony Schools®

Anthony Schools®
Real Estate
College Level Series

Escrows and Title Insurance
Legal Aspects of Real Estate
Real Estate Appraisal
Real Estate Economics
Real Estate Finance
Real Estate Office Administration
Real Estate Practice
Real Estate Principles
Real Estate Property Management

EDITORIAL AND EXECUTIVE OFFICES
Anthony Schools Corporation
15942 Foothill Blvd., Suite 100
San Leandro, CA 94578

INDEPENDENT STUDY OFFICES
Anthony Schools Corporation
POB 18827
Irvine, CA 92713-8827

California Real Estate Practice, Third Edition
Published by Anthony Schools Corporation
San Leandro, California

© 1990, 1988, 1987 by Anthony Schools Corporation

ISBN 0-941833-31-3

DISCLAIMER
This material is for educational purposes only. In no way should any statements or summaries be used as a substitute for legal or tax advice.

10 9 8 7 6 5 4 3

Printed in China

CONTENTS

Chapter 1
The Real Estate Profession

THE REAL ESTATE INDUSTRY

There are many strata or levels of activities within the real estate industry. Many kinds of activities are a part of the industry, and many kinds of persons participate. The entire construction industry is, in fact, a part of the larger real estate industry. Owners, sellers and buyers, lenders and borrowers, landlords and tenants, contractors, builders, attorneys, as well as real estate licensees all participate in the many activities that make up this many-faceted industry.

Real Estate Licenses By completing specified education and registration requirements an individual may be licensed to conduct a variety of real estate activities. Here again we see a stratified industry. Some real estate licensees specialize only in single-family residential property, others in residential income property such as apartment buildings, some in office buildings, some in retail commercial space, or industrial property, farm, ranch, or agricultural property. Some licensees specialize in dealing in mortgage loans, some in property management. Career opportunities are varied and extensive.

Who May Be Licensed. A natural person (individual) or a legal entity (corporation) may be licensed as a broker. However, only a natural person may be licensed as a salesperson.

Broker and Salesperson. If an activity requires a real estate license, it requires a broker's license, but a salesperson may perform these tasks for and in the name of the broker.

Mineral, Oil, and Gas. An MOG broker's license authorizes a person to engage in the business, act in the capacity of, or advertise as a mineral, oil and gas broker.

Corporation. A corporation may be licensed as a real estate broker provided at least one officer of the corporation is a duly qualified real estate broker willing to act as the corporation's responsible designated broker-officer.

Partnership. While no formal partnership licenses have been issued since 1968 when a change in the law was made, partnerships may be formed under the general partnership law and engage in real estate business. For ownership of the business enterprise, a broker may be partner with:

- □ Another broker,
- □ A non-licensee, provided the non-licensee performs no acts or services for which a license is required, or
- □ A sales licensee provided the broker is responsible for supervision of the licensed activities of the salesperson.

Real Property Securities Endorsement. Generally this endorsement to a broker's license allows the real property securities dealer to act as a principal or agent in real property securities transactions.

Loan Brokerage. Loan brokerage can be a natural and profitable adjunct to real estate sales. However, caution should be exercised to avoid a conflict of interest when the broker is handling both the sale and the loan in a single transaction.

Business Practices The real estate professional will need to develop a knowledge of real estate business practices, office operations, and the attributes for success in the profession of real estate.

The Real Estate Office. Considerations include type of ownership and methods of operation, office site location and office layout, selection and training of personnel, and the details of the broker-salesperson relationship, company policy manual, and sales meetings.

Professional Skills and Practices. These include a knowledge of the listing process and types of listings, marketing and advertising techniques, prospecting for listings and buyers, successful selling techniques, and financing the sale.

Specialized Fields There are many specialized activities which support each real estate transaction, and many specialized types of transactions. A general knowledge of each of these fields is necessary for the professional real estate licensee; they also offer opportunities for specialized careers.

Appraisal. Real estate appraising is a specialized field in which many real estate licensees pursue careers. This field is becoming ever more specialized now that real estate appraisers are required to be licensed, as covered in detail in Chapter 5.

Title and Escrow. Work in the title and escrow field is attracting more and more professionals. All real estate licensees, however, need some knowledge of this specialized field.

Income Tax. The jobs of the tax attorney and the tax accountant are quite different from those of the real estate broker and salesperson. However, the real estate licensee knows that clients and customers give great weight to tax consequences of their real estate decisions.

Property Management. Since all real estate should be managed, and since many investors do not desire personally to manage the properties in which they invest, the field of income-property management has become a profession unto itself, and many real estate licensees pursue careers in this licensed specialization. With some exceptions, a broker's license is required for property management.

Subdivision Sales. Subdivision development and marketing are specialized activities somewhat different from general real estate brokerage. For example, real estate licensees are familiar with the applications and requirements of the three subdivision laws—(1) the Subdivision Map Act, which requires approval of local government, (2) the Subdivided Lands Act, which requires approval of state government, and (3) the Interstate Land Sales Full Disclosure Act, which in some cases requires approval of the federal government.

Business Opportunities. Many years ago a special license was required for a person acting as an agent in the marketing of a business. Now only a real estate license is required, but it is an area of specialization in which some real estate licensees pursue careers. A later chapter addresses this special activity, Chapter 15.

REAL ESTATE IN THE U.S. ECONOMY

The real estate industry in our economy is both vast and complex. Defined to include contract construction, real estate services, and related financial services, it is the third largest industry in the United States. As such, it offers unlimited career opportunities.

Size of Market Approximately three-fourths of the wealth of the nation is held in the form of real estate, and about one-eighth of the U.S. national income is generated in the real estate industry.

GNP. Since 1971, the real estate industry has produced about 11.5 percent of the annual gross national product (GNP). Since 1974, real estate GNP has been responsible for an average of 3.5 percent of the increases recorded by the total private business sector.

Ups and Downs. The downturn of the real estate industry from 1979 to 1982 resulted in a $248.4 billion loss in GNP because of the ripple or multiplier effect on the overall economy of the U.S. The recovery of the industry since 1982 has contributed significantly to the growth of prosperity that has continued into the 1990s.

Foreign Investment. Foreign investment in real estate has become an important factor in California and the U.S. An estimated seven-fold increase ($1 billion to $7 billion) in the decade 1970-79 resulted because of political and economic instability abroad. The decade 1979-1989 was characterized by massive foreign investment in U.S. real estate. Licensees should keep abreast of foreign investment patterns in the rural, urban and suburban areas in which they operate.

Constant Market. Twenty percent of U.S. households, California included, move each year. National data show on an average that one household in five is contemplating buying or selling every day of the year.

Market Opportunities Real estate markets may be divided into residential and nonresidential. A licensee's practice will usually be concentrated in one field or another.

Residential. The residential market includes all the various forms of housing units: single-family residences, townhomes, condominiums, planned unit developments, mobilehomes, and residential income properties such as apartment houses.

Nonresidential. Nonresidential real estate may be divided into several major categories, and often highly specialized subcategories. It includes commercial or business space (stores, shopping centers), office space, industrial and warehouse space of many types and sizes, and agricultural and recreational land.

Commercial or Business Space. Commercial property is classified according to its location and trading area.

☐ The central business district is the concentration of commercial, retail, financial and other business activities at the center or heart of a city.

☐ Regional shopping centers typically include at least one department store of 100,000 square feet or more as the "anchor." A center of this type requires a site of 35 to 100 acres, and a trading area of approximately 200,000 in population to support it.

- A community shopping center may center on a smaller department store and/or a supermarket of 25,000 to 35,000 square feet. This type of center typically requires 15 to 40 acres, and a trade area population of 35,000 to 100,000 to support it.

- A neighborhood shopping center may consist of a smaller supermarket or convenience store up to 20,000 square feet, and typically requires a site area of 5-20 acres and trade area population of 15,000 to 20,000.

- Business streets, "string" or "strip" centers include a variety of business, professional and other goods and service firms located parallel to the street. The nature of the uses depends on the extent to which the street is a main vehicular artery or core of a residential area.

Office Space. Owner occupied space is often a privately owned building with almost 100 percent occupancy by its single tenant owner. Non-owner occupied space may be a privately owned structure available for rental occupancy by tenants other than the owner.

Industrial and Warehouse Space. Topography, configuration, accessibility, transportation and utilities are all important features in determining industrial and warehouse locations. Access to labor force, housing, and transportation systems are requisites for heavy and light manufacturing sites or industrial parks. Categories include:

- *Heavy Manufacturing.* Requires extensive area of land.

- *Light Manufacturing.* May be housed in buildings and areas devoted in part to other uses.

- *Loft Space.* May be provided in structures originally built for either heavy or light manufacturing activities. Loft space requires large unobstructed areas of covered space.

- *Public Warehousing.* Requires large covered areas of well-secured space adaptable to a variety of configurations for enclosed spaces.

- *Private Warehousing.* Requires physical characteristics similar to a public warehouse, but differs in that the principal occupant is usually one business entity and the building is generally not open to the public or other tenants.

- *Mini-Storage.* A large number of covered cubicles in a variety of sizes within a secured perimeter area. Public tenants rent varying sizes of space on a month-to-month or longer basis. Access to the individually locked spaces is usually limited to specific times.

Farm and Ranch Land. The corporate farm is owned and operated by and for a corporate entity. The family farm is owned and operated by an individual or family.

Recreation Land may be water-oriented, mountain, desert, etc.

A Real Estate Career A real estate career offers attractive opportunities but requires self-discipline and careful planning.

Independence. As a business person, the real estate licensee enjoys independence and opportunity beyond that of many jobs. There is great freedom of choice as to employer, type of career, geographic location, working hours and schedule, and changing from one real estate activity or specialization to another.

Income Opportunities. Earnings are generally related to experience, education, product knowledge, effective effort, available affordable financing, and luck. Income is not guaranteed; most licensees work on some type of incentive or commission basis. A California Association of Realtors® survey indicated that the average work week for both brokers and salespersons was 49.7 hours. Services must often be performed to fit clients schedules. Weekend and evening work may mean personal and family sacrifice for the licensee.

Satisfying Work. The licensee enjoys personal satisfaction as a result of assisting buyers and sellers in important decisions, serving people well–resulting in more referral and repeat business, and working in an expanding field with opportunities for learning and diversification. Not everyone has the necessary attributes to be successful in real estate, but most people can learn success-oriented behaviors.

THE REAL ESTATE PROFESSION

United States Supreme Court Justice Brandeis defined a profession as "an occupation requiring extensive preliminary intellectual training; pursued primarily for others and not merely for oneself; and accepting as the measure of achievement one's contributions to society rather than individual financial reward." For the real estate professional, this means high individual responsibility, service to the client as the primary motive, and conscious recognition of social service, including the sharing of knowledge with other members of the profession.

Ethics Ethics may be broadly defined as the study of the general nature of morals, and more specifically the duties which a member of a profession or craft owes to the public, to the client or patron, and to the fellow members of the profession. "Professional ethics" are the rules or standards by which the members of a profession govern the conduct of the profession.

California Code. In order to enhance the professionalism of the California real estate industry, and to maximize protection for members of the public dealing with the real estate licensees, Article 11, Section 2785, of the Regulations of the Real Estate Commissioner, discussing ethics and professional conduct, was adopted as part of the California Administrative Code (now the California Code of Regulations). The licensee should be familiar with those provisions (see page 14-17).

Relation of Law and Ethics. Ethics extend beyond strict legal limitations and regulations to include our attitudes toward others, and our social and business conduct. Thus the Commissioner's Code of Ethics outlines categories of "unethical" and "beneficial" conduct, as well as prohibiting the strictly unlawful.

Private Codes. Professional organizations commonly establish their own codes of ethics for their members, paralleling and supplementing governmental regulations. The National Association of Realtors® has such a code (page 17-26), as do many of its affiliates and other organizations.

Education The professional growth of the real estate industry and its members is enhanced by professional education. The educational requirements for licensing and license renewal reflect this fact. Experience alone will not insure success in real estate because of the increasingly complex nature of the transactions and relationships. The successful licensee needs to be familiar with:

Social Sciences. Practical knowledge of finance, law, economics, sociology, and psychology.

Housing and Development. An understanding of business conditions, engineering, architecture, construction, landscaping, planning, and taxation.

Urban Planning. Familiarity with city growth and trends, transportation systems, energy, and consumer expenditure patterns.

Global Trends. Awareness of national and international affairs and their effect on real estate.

Industry Self-Regulation All trade, business, and professional groups seek recognition, respect, and acceptance by the public. Professional status, in theory, means that an industry will police itself in addition to being supervised by the appropriate regulatory agency. Members of recognized professional organizations are expected to conform to professional standards with a minimum of supervision, while promoting progress, enhancing service to clients and the public, and seeking solutions to the industry's problems.

Standards of Success Success is a personal concept. The most important aspect of success is what it means to the licensee. However, the ultimate "success" is determined by the number and quality of satisfied clients.

Career Planning. Successful career planning requires a systematic approach to the development of career goals and objectives. This begins with determined answers to the questions:

> "What do I really want to do with my life?"
>
> "What do I need to be happy and fulfilled in life?"
>
> "What are my plans for personal development?"

A comparison of occupational interests and personal characteristics to those of successful real estate practitioners is another way of looking at these questions. The prospective licensee will need to get the necessary education and experience to attain competence, and apply for membership in various professional real estate organizations (page 11).

Goal Setting Career planning is based on goals. A goal must be capable of definition; it must be a concrete measurable objective. For example: "I want to earn $75,000 this year," "I want to own my own company in 5 years," "I want to retire in 10 years." Goals should refer to specific time periods, and can be classified by length of time involved.

☐ Time scheduling tasks—goals sought during a 12 month period

☐ Short-range goals—within 1 to 5 years

☐ Medium-range goals—within 10 years

☐ Long-range goals—within 15 years

> **Earnings Goal**
>
> My goal this year is an average of two escrows per month. If my personal commission is 1 1/2%* of the average selling price of $200,000, I will earn a gross of $72,000 (.015 x 200,000 x 24 = 72,000).
>
> *1 1/2 % is a typical beginning salesperson's beginning commission split for cooperating transactions through an MLS.

In Writing. Written goals have the effect of visual impact. Unreasonable goals become more apparent when reduced to writing. Priorities can be assigned to written goals, and low-priority goals will not be forgotten. Written goals may be evaluated every month and new priorities can be established, new goals may be added, or certain goals may be dropped or revised to become more realistic.

Time Management. Allocation or budgeting of time on a daily basis will help insure achievement of written short and long-term goals. One method is outlined below.

At the end of each day list 15 goals to be accomplished the following day.

☐ Select the five highest priority items which must be done

☐ Select five lower priority items which should be done

☐ The remaining items are lowest priority, and may be done tomorrow.

Screen top priority items to find the least desirable or most disagreeable items, to be done first; completing the others will then seem easier.

At the end of the day, note which goals were actually completed. The remaining items may be given priority ranking for the following day if they are still important.

LICENSING

The basic purpose of the Real Estate Law is to protect the public against fraud and other dishonest practices, by regulating those persons engaged in real estate activities.

When a Real Estate License is Required
A real estate license is required when any activity in a real estate transaction is performed for another or others for a fee, commission, compensation, or in expectation of any remuneration.

Unlicensed Practice. An unlicensed person who receives payment for a real estate transaction, in violation of the law, is subject to a fine of $10,000 and/or 6 months in the county jail. A corporation is subject to a $50,000 fine.

Employing Unlicensed Person. It is also a misdemeanor, punishable by a fine of up to $100, to pay compensation to a nonlicensee for performing services for which a license is required.

License Law History
Before the License Law was passed by the California legislature in 1919, anyone could operate as a real estate agent. There was no control over the agent's activities in handling transactions involving valuable properties and large sums of money belonging to others, except for the general laws permitting an injured party to sue for damages or prosecute the wrongdoer.

The License Law. The License Law is now contained in the Business and Professions Code. The Real Estate Commissioner has the power to make reasonable regulations to supplement the License Law as long as they do not conflict with the License Law enacted by the legislature. Real estate licensees are also subject to the general laws applicable to all persons, particularly the Law of Agency in the Civil Code.

STATE REGULATORY AUTHORITIES

California state laws and regulatory bodies have been established to provide maximum protection for buyers and sellers of real estate, real estate lenders and borrowers, and others involved in transactions with real estate licensees.

California Department of Real Estate

The DRE was first created by the California Legislature in 1917. This statute, the first of its kind in the United States, provided for the licensing and regulation of real estate agents. As amended in 1919 to delete portions found unconstitutional, the law remained in effect until 1943. The Real Estate Law was codified and merged into the Business and Professions Code in 1943.

Purpose and Methods. The primary purpose of the Real Estate Law is to protect the public against fraud and incompetence in real estate transactions. The Real Estate Law establishes and regulates education requirements, qualifying examinations, licensing, standards, and practices. It has been instrumental in moving the real estate industry toward professional standards and acceptance by the public.

Real Estate Commissioner

The chief executive officer of the Department of Real Estate is the Real Estate Commissioner who is appointed by the governor. The Commissioner's primary responsibility is to determine department administrative policy and enforce the provisions of the Real Estate Law.

Duties. The Commissioner's specific responsibilities under the law include:

☐ Screening and qualifying license applicants

☐ Investigation of complaints against licensees

☐ Regulation of certain aspects of subdivision sales

☐ Regulation of nonexempt franchises

☐ Regulation of certain real property securities

☐ Investigation of nonlicensees alleged to be performing acts for which a license is required.

Disciplinary Procedure. The Administrative Procedure Act provides the Commissioner with the authority to hold formal hearings for determination of actions involving licensees, license applicants, or subdividers. After a formal hearing, the Commissioner may suspend, revoke, or deny a license, or halt sales in a subdivision. The Commissioner may delegate to the Department the power to hear and decide certain disciplinary matters.

Jurisdiction. The Commissioner does not assume the role of a court of law nor give legal advice. There are definite limitations of the Commissioner's authority. For example, the Commissioner does not have the authority to settle commission disputes or determine who is legally entitled to a deposit claim.

Real Estate Advisory Commission The Real Estate Advisory Commission meets, consults, and advises the Commissioner on functions and policies of the Department, as they affect the public, the licensees, and the industry.

Establishment. On January 1, 1977, this committee replaced the State Real Estate Commission, which was established by legislative act in 1937 as the State Real Estate Board. The name was changed from Board to Commission in 1957.

Membership. The Commission consists of ten commissioners who are all appointed members, serving at the Real Estate Commissioner's pleasure. Six of the members are California licensed real estate brokers, and four are public members. The members are not employees of the state, and each receives only $100 compensation per meeting, plus reimbursement of actual and necessary expenses.

Meetings. The Real Estate Commissioner is required to call at least four Advisory Commission meetings a year. Ten-day advance written notice must be sent to the Commission members and others who have requested notification.

Continuing Education Advisory Committee In January 1987, a Real Estate Continuing Education Advisory Committee was created by the Real Estate Commissioner pursuant to Business and Professions Code §10170.2. Members are licensees and persons with expertise in real estate education, who advise the Commissioner with respect to continuing education requirements.

PROFESSIONAL REAL ESTATE ORGANIZATIONS

No broker or salesperson licensed by the California Department of Real Estate is required by law to join any business, trade, or professional association, though many do. Licensees may join local boards, state or national associations, or independent boards at their discretion.

The National Association of Realtors® NAR is a national voluntary organization whose members are engaged in some phase of the real estate business and is one of the largest trade associations in the world. Because the real estate business is so diversified, a number of specialized groups, or "affiliates," have been founded within the framework of NAR.

Structure. Each member of NAR must be in good standing with a local realty board, real estate board, or Board of Realtors® (which also must be in good standing with its individual statewide board or association of Realtors®). In California, the California Association of Realtors® (CAR) is the statewide agency.

Purposes. CAR's constitution sets forth its objectives and purposes as follows: to unite its members; to promote high standards; to safeguard the land-buying public; to foster legislation for the benefit and protection of real estate; and to cooperate in the economic growth and development of the state.

United Interests. The basic goals and objectives of NAR are generally the same as those of the local and state boards while uniting and unifying the organized real estate interests throughout the country. NAR presents a common cause and national legislative program regarding real estate.

Realtor.® The term Realtor® may be used only by those licensees engaged in the real estate business who are members of a local board or individual members of NAR. They are subject to NAR's rules and regulations, observe its standards of conduct, and are entitled to its benefits.

Code of Ethics. Every Realtor® must agree to abide by NAR's Code of Ethics, which was first adopted in 1913. This Code covers certain practical situations not included in the Commissioner's Code (e.g. placing a sign on an owner's property without permission, professional courtesies and controversies among Realtors®). The full text of this code begins on page 17.

NAR Affiliates The affiliated councils, institutes, and societies of NAR, which require membership in the national association, are listed here, followed by the designations they award:

- American Chapter of the International Real Estate Federation

- American Institute of Real Estate Appraisers

  MAI - Member Appraisal Institute

  RM - Residential Member

- American Society of Real Estate Counselors (ASREC)

  CRE - Counselor in Real Estate

- Institute of Real Estate Management (IREM)

  CPM - Certified Property Manager

  ARM - Accredited Resident Manager

  AMO - Accredited Management Organization

- Farm and Land Institute (FLI)

  AFLM - Accredited Farm and Land Member

- Real Estate Securities and Syndication Institute (RESSI)

  CRSS - Certified Real Estate Securities Sponsor

  CRSM - Certified Real Estate Securities Marketer

- □ Realtors® National Marketing Institute (RNMI)
    - CRB - Certified Residential Broker
    - CCIM - Certified Commercial Investment Member
- □ Society of Industrial Realtors® (SIR)
- □ Women's Council of Realtors® (WCR)

CAR Affiliates The affiliated professional divisions of CAR, which require membership in the statewide association, include:

- □ Graduate, Realtors® Institute (GRI)
- □ Industrial-Commercial Division (ICD)
- □ Investment Division
- □ Property Management Division (PMD)
- □ Real Estate Certificate Institute (RECI)
- □ Real Estate Syndication Division (RESD)

Other Real Estate Associations There are other professional organizations parallel to NAR, and organizations of persons in peripheral fields such as construction and finance.

The National Association of Real Estate Brokers. NAREB is an organization of predominantly black real estate brokers using the trade name Realtist, with chapters in major cities and states throughout the country. Both local chapter and national memberships are required of Realtists. The code of ethics, goals, and purpose include working for better housing in the communities served.

California Affiliates of NAREB. The California Association of Real Estate Brokers is affiliated with NAREB and has several associated boards including Associated Real Property Brokers in Oakland; Consolidated Real Estate Brokers in Sacramento; Consolidated Realty Board in Los Angeles; and the San Diego Board of Realtists.

The International Society of Real Estate Appraisers. SREA is an independent association of practicing appraisers and other industry-related individuals. SREA members agree to abide by a professional code of ethics and may, through education, examination, and experience, earn the right to use such professional designations as SRPA—Senior Real Property Analyst, SREA—Senior Real Estate Appraiser, and SRA—Senior Residential Appraiser.

Construction, Management, and Maintenance Related Associations. These include:

- □ National Association of Home Builders (NAHB)
- □ Building Owners and Managers Association (BOMA)

Finance and Related Associations. These include the banking, title, and escrow fields, and such organizations as: American Bankers Association; Mortgage Bankers Association; The U.S. League of Savings Associations; American Savings and Loan Institute; National Association of Mutual Savings Banks; California Escrow Association; American Escrow Association; American Land Title Association

Multiple Listing Services (MLS) These are sponsored and operated by local real estate boards or other organizations in California. A multiple listing service is a cooperative listing service conducted by a group of brokers who may or may not belong to a local board. The group distributes listings submitted by MLS members to all other MLS members. All MLS members have the right to work on MLS listings. The greater market exposure and large number of licensees working on each listing provide better, more efficient service to clients and the public. Distribution of listings to MLS members is in the form of a multiple listing book which is usually copyrighted, or through access to a central computer system

---

CODE OF PROFESSIONAL CONDUCT
COMMISSIONER'S REGULATION 2785

EFFECTIVE JUNE 9, 1990

Commissioner's Regulation 2785. PROFESSIONAL CONDUCT

In order to enhance the professionalism of the California real estate industry, and maximize protection for members of the public dealing with real estate licensees, whatever their area of practice, the following standards of professional conduct and business practices are adopted:

(a) Unlawful Conduct in Sale, Lease and Exchange Transactions. Licensees when performing acts within the meaning of Section 10131 (a) of the Business and Professions Code shall not engage in conduct which would subject the licensee to adverse action, penalty or discipline under Sections 10176 and 10177 of the Business and Professions Code including, but not limited to, the following acts and omissions:

Comm. Reg. 2785. (a)(1)

Knowingly making a substantial misrepresentation of the likely value of real property to:
(A) Its owner either for the purpose of securing a listing or for the purpose of acquiring an interest in the property for the licensee's own account.
(B) A prospective buyer for the purpose of inducing the buyer to make an offer to purchase the real property.

Comm. Reg. 2785. (a)(2)

Representing to an owner of real property when seeking a listing that the licensee has obtained a bona fide written offer to purchase the property, unless at the time of the representation the licensee has possession of a bona fide written offer to purchase.

Comm. Reg. 2785. (a)(3)

Stating or implying to an owner of real property during listing negotiations that the licensee is precluded by law, by regulation, or by the rules of any organization, other than the broker firm seeking the listing, from charging less than the commission or fee quoted to the owner by the licensee.

Comm. Reg. 2785. (a)(4)

Knowingly making substantial misrepresentations regarding the licensee's relationship with an individual broker, corporate broker, or franchised brokerage company or that entity's/person's responsibility for the licensee's activities.

Comm. Reg. 2785. (a)(5)

Knowingly underestimating the probable closing costs in a communication to the prospective buyer or seller of real property in order to induce that person to make or to accept an offer to purchase the property.

Comm. Reg. 2785. (a)(6)

Knowingly making a false or misleading representation to the seller of real property as to the form, amount and/or treatment of a deposit toward the purchase of the property made by an offeror.

Comm. Reg. 2785. (a)(7)

Knowingly making a false or misleading representation to a seller of real property, who has agreed to finance all or part of a purchase price by carrying back a loan, about a buyer's ability to repay the loan in accordance with its terms and conditions.

Comm. Reg. 2785. (a)(8)

Making an addition to or modification of the terms of an instrument previously signed or initialed by a party to a transaction without the knowledge and consent of the party.

Comm. Reg. 2785. (a)(9)

A representation made as a principal or agent to a prospective purchaser of a promissory note secured by real property about the market value of the securing property without a reasonable basis for believing the truth and accuracy of the representation.

Comm. Reg. 2785. (a)(10)

Knowingly making a false or misleading representation or representing, without a reasonable basis for believing its truth, the nature and/or condition of the interior or exterior features of a property when soliciting an offer.

Comm. Reg. 2785. (a)(11)

Knowingly making a false or misleading representation or representing, without a reasonable basis for believing its truth, the size of a parcel, square footage of improvements or the location of the boundary lines of real property being offered for sale, lease or exchange.

Comm. Reg. 2785. (a)(12)

Knowingly making a false or misleading representation or representing to a prospective buyer or lessee of real property, without a reasonable basis to believe its truth, that the property can be used for certain purposes with the intent of inducing the prospective buyer or lessee to acquire an interest in the real property.

Comm. Reg. 2785. (a)(13)

When acting in the capacity of an agent in a transaction for the sale, lease or exchange of real property, failing to disclose to a prospective purchaser or lessee facts known to the licensee materially affecting the value or desirability of the property, when the licensee has reason to believe that such facts are not known to nor readily observable by a prospective purchaser or lessee.

Comm. Reg. 2785. (a)(14)

Willfully failing, when acting as a listing agent, to present or cause to be presented to the owner of the property any written offer to purchase received prior to the closing of a sale, unless expressly instructed by the owner not to present such an offer, or unless the offer is patently frivolous.

Comm. Reg. 2785. (a)(15)

When acting as the listing agent, presenting competing written offers to purchase real property to the owner in such a manner as to induce the owner to accept the offer which will provide the greatest compensation to the listing broker without regard to the benefits, advantages and/or disadvantages to the owner.

Comm. Reg. 2785. (a)(16)

Failing to explain to the parties or prospective parties to a real estate transaction for whom the licensee is acting as an agent the meaning and probable significance of a contingency in an offer or contract that the licensee knows or reasonably believes may affect the closing date of the transaction, or the timing of the vacating of the property by the seller or its occupancy by the buyer.

Comm. Reg. 2785. (a)(17)

Failing to disclose to the seller of real property in a transaction in which the licensee is an agent for the seller the nature and extent of any direct or indirect interest that the licensee expects to acquire as a result of the sale. The prospective purchase of the property by a person related to the licensee by blood or marriage, purchase by an entity in which the licensee has an ownership interest, or purchase by any other person with whom the licensee occupies a special relationship where there is a reasonable probability that the licensee could be indirectly acquiring an interest in the property shall be disclosed to the seller.

Comm. Reg. 2785. (a)(18)

Failing to disclose to the buyer of real property in a transaction in which the licensee is an agent for the buyer the nature and extent of a licensee's direct or indirect ownership interest in such real property. The direct or indirect ownership interest in the property by a person related to the licensee by blood or marriage, by an entity in which the licensee has an ownership interest, or by any other person with whom the licensee occupies a special relationship shall be disclosed to the buyer.

Comm. Reg. 2785. (a)(19)

Failing to disclose to a principal for whom the licensee is acting as an agent any significant interest the licensee has in a particular entity when the licensee recommends the use of the services or products of such entity.

Comm. Reg. 2785. (a)(20)

The refunding by a licensee, when acting as an agent for seller, all or part of an offeror's purchase money deposit in a real estate sales transaction after the seller has accepted the offer to purchase, unless the licensee has the express permission of the seller to make the refund.

(b) Unlawful Conduct When Soliciting, Negotiating or Arranging a Loan Secured by Real Property or the Sale of a Promissory Note Secured by Real Property. Licensees when performing acts within the meaning of subdivision (d) or (e) of Section 10131 of the Business and Professions Code shall not violate any of the applicable provisions of subdivision (a), or act in a manner which would subject the licensee to adverse action, penalty or discipline under Sections 10176 and 10177 of the Business and Professions Code including, but not limited to, the following acts and omissions:

Comm. Reg. 2785. (b)(1)

Knowingly misrepresenting to a prospective borrower of a loan to be secured by real property or to an assignor/endorser of a promissory note secured by real property that there is an existing lender willing to make the loan or that there is a purchaser for the note, for the purpose of inducing the borrower or assignor/endorser to utilize the services of the licensee.

Comm. Reg. 2785. (b)(2)

(a) Knowingly making a false or misleading representation to a prospective lender or purchaser of a loan secured directly or collaterally by real property about a borrower's ability to repay the loan in accordance with its terms and conditions;

(b) Failing to disclose to a prospective lender or note purchaser information about the prospective borrower's identity, occupation, employment, income and credit data as represented to the broker by the prospective borrower.

(c) Failing to disclose information known to the broker relative to the ability of the borrower to meet his or her potential or existing contractual obligations under the note or contract including information known about the borrower's payment history on an existing note, whether the note is in default or the borrower in bankruptcy.

Comm. Reg. 2785. (b)(3)

Knowingly underestimating the probable closing costs in a communication to a prospective borrower or lender of a loan to be secured by a lien on real property for the purpose of inducing the borrower or lender to enter into the loan transaction.

Comm. Reg. 2785. (b)(4)

When soliciting a prospective lender to make a loan to be secured by real property, falsely representing or representing without a reasonable basis to believe its truth, the priority of the security, as a lien against the real property securing the loan, i.e. a first, second or third deed of trust.

Comm. Reg. 2785. (b)(5)

Knowingly misrepresenting in any transaction that a specific service is free when the licensee knows or has a reasonable basis to know that it is covered by a fee to be charged as part of the transaction.

Comm. Reg. 2785. (b)(6)

Knowingly making a false or misleading representation to a lender or assignee/endorsee of a lender of a loan secured directly or collaterally by a lien on real property about the amount and treatment of loan payments, including loan payoffs, and the failure to account to the

lender or assignee/endorsee of a lender as to the disposition of such payments.

Comm. Reg. 2785. (b)(7)

When acting as a licensee in a transaction for the purpose of obtaining a loan, and in receipt of an "advance fee" from the borrower for this purpose, the failure to account to the borrower for the disposition of the "advance fee."

Comm. Reg. 2785. (b)(8)

Knowingly making a false or misleading representation or representing, without a reasonable basis for believing its truth, when soliciting a lender or negotiating a loan to be secured by a lien on real property about the market value of the securing real property, the nature and/or condition of the interior or exterior features of the securing real property, its size or the square footage of any improvements on the securing real property.
Authority: Business and Professions Code Section 10080. Reference: Business and Professions Code Sections 10176 and 10177.

SUGGESTIONS FOR PROFESSIONAL CONDUCT

Note: The Real Estate Commissioner has issued Suggestions for Professional Conduct in Sale, Lease and Exchange Transactions and Suggestions for Professional Conduct When Negotiating or Arranging Loans Secured by Real Property or Sale of a Promissory Note Secured by Real Property.

The Purpose of the Suggestions is to encourage real estate licensees to maintain a high level of ethics and professionalism in their business practices when performing acts for which a real estate license is required.

The Suggestions are not intended as statements of duties imposed by law nor as grounds for disciplinary action by the Department of Real Estate, but as suggestions for elevating the professionalism of real estate licensees.

Copies of the suggestions may be obtained from the Department.

As a part of the effort to promote ethical business practices of real estate licensees, the Real Estate commissioner has issued the following Suggestions for Professional Conduct as a companion to the Code of Professional Conduct (Section 2785, Title 10, California Code of Regulation):

(a) Suggestions for Professional Conduct in Sale, Lease and Exchange Transactions. In order to maintain a high level of ethics and professionalism in their business practices, real estate licensees are encouraged to adhere to the following suggestions in conducting their business activities:

(1) Aspire to give a high level of competent, ethical and quality service to buyers and sellers in real estate transactions.

(2) Stay in close communication with clients or customers to ensure that questions are promptly answered

and all significant events or problems in a transaction are conveyed in a timely manner.

(3) Cooperate with the California Department of Real Estate's enforcement of, and report to that Department evident violations of, Real Estate Law.

(4) Use care in the preparation of any advertisement to present an accurate picture or message to the reader, viewer or listener.

(5) Submit all written offers in a prompt and timely manner.

(6) Keep oneself informed and current on factors affecting the real estate market in which the licensee operates as an agent.

(7) Make a full, open and sincere effort to cooperate with other licensees, unless the principal has instructed the licensee to the contrary.

(8) Attempt to settle disputes with other licensees through mediation or arbitration.

(9) Advertise or claim to be an expert in an area of specialization in real estate brokerage activity, e.g., appraisal, property management, industrial siting, mortgage loan, etc., only if the licensee has had special training, preparation or experience.

(10) Strive to provide equal opportunity for quality housing and a high level of service to all persons regardless of race, color, sex, religion, ancestry, physical handicap, marital status or national origin.

(11) Base opinions of value, whether for the purpose of advertising or promoting real estate brokerage business, upon documented objective data.

(12) Make every attempt to comply with these Suggestions for Professional Conduct and the Code of Professional Conduct and the Code of Ethics of any organized real estate industry group of which the licensee is a member.

(b) <u>Suggestions for Professional conduct When Negotiating or Arranging Loans Secured by Real Property or Sale of a Promissory Note Secured by Real Property</u>. In order to maintain a high level of ethics and professionalism in their business practices when performing acts within the meaning of subdivisions (d) and (e) of Section 10131 and Sections 10131.1 and 10131.2 of the Business and Professions Code, real estate licensees are encouraged to adhere to the following suggestions, in addition to any applicable provisions of subdivision (a), in conducting their business activities:

(1) Aspire to give a high level of competent, ethical and quality service to borrowers and lenders in loan transactions secured by real estate.

(2) Stay in close communication with borrowers and lenders to ensure that reasonable questions are promptly answered and all significant events or problems in a loan transaction are conveyed in a timely manner.

(3) Keep oneself informed and current on factors affecting the real estate loan market in which the licensee acts as an agent.

(4) Advertise or claim to be an expert in an area of specialization in real estate mortgage loan transactions only if the licensee has had special training, preparation or experience in such area.

(5) Strive to provide equal opportunity for quality mortgage loan services and a high level of service to all borrowers or lenders regardless of race, color, sex, religion, ancestry, physical handicap, marital status or national origin.

(6) Base opinions of value in a loan transaction, whether for the purpose of advertising or promoting real estate mortgage loan brokerage business, on documented objective data.

(7) Respond to reasonable inquiries of a principal as to the status or extent of efforts to negotiate the sale of an existing loan.

(8) Respond to reasonable inquiries of a borrower regarding the net proceeds available from a loan arranged by the licensee.

(9) Make every attempt to comply with the standards of professional conduct and the code of ethics of any organized mortgage loan industry group of which the licensee is a member.

The conduct suggestions set forth in subsections (a) and (b) are not intended as statements of duties imposed by law nor as grounds for disciplinary action by the Department of Real Estate, but as guidelines for elevating the professionalism of real estate licensees.

Commissioner's Regulation 2785, formerly known as "Code of Ethics and Professional Conduct," was revised as of 1990 as a "Code of Professional Conduct." The new "Code" consists of two major parts: essentially a review of unlawful activities as decreed by the Real Estate Law, and, secondly, a statement of "Suggestions for Professional Conduct" to "encourage real estate licenses to maintain a high level of ethics and professionalism in their business practices."

NATIONAL ASSOCIATION OF REALTORS® CODE OF ETHICS AND STANDARDS OF PRACTICE

An important source of rules of ethical behavior is the Code of Ethics of the National Association of Realtors®. Every Realtor® must agree to abide by this Code of Ethics as a condition of membership in a Realtors'® organization. While a licensee who is not a Realtor®

is not compelled to abide by these provisions, which are not also contained in the laws or regulations, the Real Estate Commissioner nevertheless encourages all licensees to abide by this Code of Ethics.

Where the word REALTORS® is used in this Code and Preamble, it shall be deemed to include REALTOR-ASSOCIATE®s.

While the Code of Ethics establishes obligations that may be higher than those mandated by law, in any instance where the Code of Ethics and the law conflict, the obligations of the law must take precedence.

Preamble . . .

Under all is the land. Upon its wise utilization and widely allocated ownership depend the survival and growth of free institutions and of our civilization. REALTORS® should recognize that the interests of the nation and its citizens require the highest and best use of the land and the widest distribution of land ownership. They require the creation of adequate housing, the building of functioning cities, the development of productive industries and farms, and the preservation of a healthful environment.

Such interests impose obligations beyond those of ordinary commerce. They impose grave social responsibility and a patriotic duty to which REALTORS® should dedicate themselves, and for which they should be diligent in preparing themselves. REALTORS®, therefore, are zealous to maintain and improve the standards of their calling and share with their fellow REALTORS® a common responsibility for its integrity and honor. The term REALTOR® has come to connote competency, fairness, and high integrity resulting from adherence to a lofty ideal of moral conduct in business relations. No inducement of profit and no instruction from clients ever can justify departure from this ideal.

In the interpretation of this obligation, REALTORS® can take no safer guide than that which has been handed down through the centuries, embodied in the Golden Rule, "Whatsoever ye would that others should do to you, do ye even so to them."

Accepting this standard as their own, REALTORS® pledge to observe its spirit in all of their activities and to conduct their business in accordance with the tenets set forth below.

Articles 1 through 5 are aspirational and establish ideals REALTORS® should strive to attain.

Article 1

In justice to those who place their interests in a real estate professional's care, REALTORS® should endeavor to become and remain informed on matters affecting real estate in their community, the state, and nation. (Amended 11/92)

Article 2

In the interest of promoting cooperation and enhancing their professional image, REALTORS® are encouraged to refrain from unsolicited criticism of other real estate practitioners and, if an opinion is sought about another real estate practitioner, their business or their business practices, any opinion should be offered in an objective, professional manner. (Amended 11/92)

Article 3

REALTORS® should endeavor to eliminate in their communities any practices which could be damaging to the public or bring discredit to the real estate profession. REALTORS® should assist the governmental agency charged with regulating the practices of brokers and sales licensees in their states. (Amended 11/87)

Article 4

To prevent dissension and misunderstanding and to assure better service to the owner, REALTORS® should urge the exclusive listing of property unless contrary to the best interest of the owner. (Amended 11/87).

Article 5

In the best interests of society, of their associates, and their own businesses, REALTORS® should willingly share with other REALTORS® the lessons of their experience and study for the benefit of the public, and should be loyal to the Board of REALTORS® of their community and active in its work.

Articles 6 through 23 establish specific obligations. Failure to observe these requirements subject REALTORS® to disciplinary action.

Article 6

REALTORS® shall seek no unfair advantage over other REALTORS® and shall conduct their business so as to avoid controversies with other REALTORS®. (Amended 11/87)

- **Standard of Practice 6-1**

  REALTORS® shall not misrepresent the availability of access to show or inspect a listed property. (Cross-reference Article 22.) (Amended 11/87)

- **Standard of Practice 6-2**

  Article 6 is not intended to prohibit otherwise ethical, aggressive or innovative business practices. "Controversies," as used in Article 6, does not relate to disputes over commissions or divisions of commissions. (Adopted 4/92)

Article 7

When representing a buyer, seller, landlord, tenant, or other client as an agent, REALTORS® pledge themselves to protect and promote the interests of their client. This obligation of absolute fidelity to the client's interests is primary, but it does not relieve REALTORS® of their obligation to treat all parties honestly. When serving a buyer, seller, landlord, tenant or other party in a nonagency capacity, REALTORS® remain obligated to treat all parties honestly. (Amended 11/92)

- **Standard of Practice 7-1(a)**

  REALTORS® shall submit offers and counter-offers as quickly as possible. (Adopted 11/92)

- **Standard of Practice 7-1(b)**

  When acting as listing brokers, REALTORS® shall continue to submit to the seller/landlord all offers and counter-offers until closing or execution of a lease unless the seller/landlord has waived this obligation in writing. REALTORS® shall not be obligated to continue to market the property after an offer has been accepted by the seller/landlord. REALTORS® shall recommend that sellers/landlords obtain the advice of legal counsel prior to acceptance of a subsequent offer except where the acceptance is contingent on the termination of the pre-existing purchase contract or lease. (Cross-reference Article 17.) (Amended 11/92)

- **Standard of Practice 7-1(c)**

  REALTORS® acting as agents of buyers/tenants shall submit to buyers/tenants all offers and counter-offers until acceptance but have no obligation to continue to show properties to their clients after an offer has been accepted unless otherwise agreed in writing. REALTORS® acting as agents of buyers/tenants shall recommend that buyers/tenants obtain the advice of legal counsel if there is a question as to whether a pre-existing contract has been terminated. (Adopted 11/92)

- **Standard of Practice 7-2**

  REALTORS®, when seeking to become a buyer/tenant representative, shall not mislead buyers or tenants as to savings or other benefits that might be realized through use of the REALTOR®'s services. (Amended 11/92)

- **Standard of Practice 7-3**

  REALTORS®, in attempting to secure a listing, shall not deliberately mislead the owner as to market value.

- **Standard of Practice 7-4**

  (Refer to Standard of Practice 22-1, which also relates to Article 7, Code of Ethics.)

- **Standard of Practice 7-5**

  (Refer to Standard of Practice 22-2, which also relates to Article 7, Code of Ethics.)

- **Standard of Practice 7-6**

  REALTORS®, when acting as principals in a real estate transaction, remain obligated by the duties imposed by the Code of Ethics. (Amended 11/92)

- **Standard of Practice 7-7**

  REALTORS® may represent the seller/landlord and buyer/tenant in the same transaction only after full disclosure to and with informed consent of both parties. (Cross-reference Article 9) (Adopted 11/92)

- **Standard of Practice 7-8**

  The obligation of REALTORS® to preserve confidential information provided by their clients continues after the termination of the agency relationship. REALTORS® shall not knowingly, during or following the termination of a professional relationship with their client:

  1) reveal confidential information of the client; or

2) use confidential information of the client to the disadvantage of the client; or

3) use confidential information of the client for the REALTORS®' advantage or the advantage of a third party unless the client consents after full disclosure unless:

   a) required by court order; or

   b) it is the intention of the client to commit a crime and the information is necessary to prevent the crime; or

   c) necessary to defend the REALTOR® or the REALTOR®'s employees or associates against an accusation of wrongful conduct. (Cross-reference Article 9) (Adopted 11/92)

Article 8

In a transaction, REALTORS® shall not accept compensation from more than one party, even if permitted by law, without disclosure to all parties and the informed consent of the REALTOR®'s client or clients. (Amended 11/92)

Article 9

REALTORS® shall avoid exaggeration, misrepresentation, or concealment of pertinent facts relating to the property or the transaction. REALTORS® shall not, however, be obligated to discover latent defects in the property, to advise on matters outside the scope of their real estate license, or to disclose facts which are confidential under the scope of agency duties owed to their clients. (Amended 11/92)

- **Standard of Practice 9-1**

  REALTORS® shall not be parties to the naming of a false consideration in any document, unless it be the naming of an obviously nominal consideration.

- **Standard of Practice 9-2**

  (Refer to Standard of Practice 21-3, which also relates to Article 9, Code of Ethics.)

- **Standard of Practice 9-3**

  (Refer to Standard of Practice 7-3, which also relates to Article 9, Code of Ethics.)

- **Standard of Practice 9-4**

  REALTORS® shall not offer a service described as "free of charge" when the rendering of a service is contingent on the obtaining of a benefit such as a listing or commission.

- **Standard of Practice 9-5**

  REALTORS® shall, with respect to the subagency of another REALTOR®, timely communicate any change of compensation for subagency services to the other REALTOR® prior to the time such REALTOR® produces a prospective buyer who has signed an offer to purchase the property for which the subagency has been offered through MLS or otherwise by the listing agency.

- **Standard of Practice 9-6**

  REALTORS® shall disclose their REALTOR® status and contemplated personal interest, if any, when seeking information from another REALTOR® concerning real property. (Cross-reference to Article 12) (Amended 11/92)

- **Standard of Practice 9-7**

  The offering of premiums, prizes, merchandise discounts or other inducements to list, sell, purchase, or lease is not, in itself, unethical even if receipt of the benefit is contingent on listing, purchasing, or leasing through the REALTOR® making the offer. However, REALTORS® must exercise care and candor in any such advertising or other public or private representations so that any party interested in receiving or otherwise benefiting from the REALTOR®'s offer will have clear, thorough, advance understanding of all the terms and conditions of the offer. The offering of any inducements to do business is subject to the limitations and restrictions of state law and the ethical obligations established by Article 9, as interpreted by any applicable Standard of Practice. (Amended 11/92)

- **Standard of Practice 9-8**

  REALTORS® shall be obligated to discover and disclose adverse factors reasonably apparent to someone with expertise in only those areas required by their real estate licensing authority. Article 9 does not impose upon the REALTOR® the obligation of expertise in other professional or technical disciplines. (Cross-reference Article 11.) (Amended 11/86)

- **Standard of Practice 9-9**

  REALTORS®, acting as listing brokers, have an affirmative obligation to disclose the existence of dual or variable rate commission arrangements (i.e., listings where one amount of commission is payable if the listing broker's firm is the procuring cause of sale and a different amount of commission is payable if the sale results through the efforts of the seller or a cooperating broker). The listing broker shall, as soon as practical, disclose the existence of such arrangements to potential cooperating brokers and shall, in response to inquiries from cooperating brokers, disclose the differential that would result in a cooperative transaction or in a sale that results through the efforts of the seller. (Amended 11/91)

- **Standard of Practice 9-10(a)**

  When entering into listing contracts, REALTORS® must advise sellers/landlords of:

  1) the REALTOR®'s general company policies regarding cooperation with subagents, buyer/tenant agents, or both;

  2) the fact that buyer/tenant agents, even if compensated by the listing broker, or by the seller/landlord will represent the interests of buyers/tenants; and

  3) any potential for the listing broker to act as a disclosed dual agent, e.g. buyer/tenant agent. (Adopted 11/92)

- **Standard of Practice 9-10(b)**

  When entering into contracts to represent buyers/tenants, REALTORS® must advise potential clients of:

  1) the REALTOR®'s general company policies regarding cooperation with other firms; and

  2) any potential for the buyer/tenant representative to act as a disclosed dual agent, e.g. listing broker, subagent, landlord's agent, etc. (Adopted 11/92)

- **Standard of Practice 9-11**

  Factors defined as "non-material" by law or regulation or which are expressly referenced in law or regulation as not being subject to disclosure are considered not "pertinent" for purposes of Article 9. (Adopted 11/92)

Article 10

REALTORS® shall not deny equal professional services to any person for reasons of race, color, religion, sex, handicap, familial status, or national origin. REALTORS® shall not be parties to any plan or agreement to discriminate against a person or persons on the basis of race, color, religion, sex, handicap, familial status, or national origin. (Amended 11/89)

Article 11

REALTORS® are expected to provide a level of competent service in keeping with the standards of practice in those fields in which the REALTOR® customarily engages.

REALTORS® shall not undertake to provide specialized professional services concerning a type of property or service that is outside their field of competence unless they engage the assistance of one who is competent on such types of property or service, or unless the facts are fully disclosed to the client. Any persons engaged to provide such assistance shall be so identified to the client and their contribution to the assignment should be set forth.

REALTORS® shall refer to the Standards of Practice of the National Association as to the degree of competence that a client has a right to expect the REALTOR® to possess, taking into consideration the complexity of the problem, the availability of expert assistance, and the opportunities for experience available to the REALTOR®.

- **Standard of Practice 11-1**

  Whenever REALTORS® submit an oral or written opinion of the value of real property for a fee, their opinion shall be supported by a memorandum in the file or an appraisal report, either of which shall include as a minimum the following:

  1. Limiting conditions
  2. Any existing or contemplated interest
  3. Defined value
  4. Date applicable
  5. The estate appraised
  6. A description of the property
  7. The basis of the reasoning including applicable market data and/or capitalization computation

  This report or memorandum shall be available to the Professional Standards Committee for a period of at least two years (beginning subsequent to final determination of the court if the appraisal is involved in litigation) to ensure compliance with Article 11 of the Code of Ethics of the NATIONAL ASSOCIATION OF REALTORS®.

- **Standard of Practice 11-2**

  REALTORS® shall not undertake to make an appraisal when their employment or fee is contingent upon the amount of appraisal.

- **Standard of Practice 11-3**

  REALTORS® engaged in real estate securities and syndications transactions are engaged in an activity subject to regulations beyond those governing real estate transactions generally, and therefore have the affirmative obligation to be informed of applicable federal and state laws, and rules and regulations regarding these types of transactions.

Article 12

REALTORS® shall not undertake to provide professional services concerning a property or its value where they have a present or contemplated interest unless such interest is specifically disclosed to all affected parties.

- **Standard of Practice 12-1**

  (Refer to Standards of Practice 9-4 and 16-1, which also relate to Article 12, Code of Ethics.) (Amended 5/84)

Article 13

REALTORS® shall not acquire an interest in or buy or present offers from themselves, any member of their immediate families, their firms or any member thereof, or any entities in which they have any ownership interest, any real property without making their true position known to the owner or the owner's agent. In selling property they own, or in which they have any interest, REALTORS® shall reveal their ownership or interest in writing to the purchaser or the purchaser's representative. (Amended 11/90)

- **Standard of Practice 13-1**

  For the protection of all parties, the disclosures required by Article 13 shall be in writing and provided by REALTORS® prior to the signing of any contract. (Adopted 2/86)

Article 14

In the event of a controversy between REALTORS® associated with different firms, arising out of their relationship as REALTORS® the REALTORS® shall submit the dispute to arbitration in accordance with the regulations of their Board or Boards rather than litigate the matter.

In the event clients of REALTORS® wish to arbitrate contractual disputes arising out of real estate transactions, REALTORS® shall arbitrate those disputes in accordance with the regulations of their Board, provided the clients agree to be bound by the decision. (Amended 11/92)

- **Standard of Practice 14-1**

  The filing of litigation and refusal to withdraw from it by REALTORS® in an arbitrable matter constitutes a refusal to arbitrate. (Adopted 2/86)

- **Standard of Practice 14-2**

  Article 14 does not require REALTORS® to arbitrate in those circumstances when all parties to the dispute advise the Board in writing that they choose not to arbitrate before the Board. (Amended 11/92)

Article 15

If charged with unethical practice or asked to present evidence or to cooperate in any other way, in any disciplinary proceeding or investigation, REALTORS® shall place all pertinent facts before the proper tribunals of the Member Board or affiliated institute, society, or council in which membership is held and shall take no action to disrupt or obstruct such processes. (Amended 11/89)

- **Standard of Practice 15-1**

  REALTORS® shall not be subject to disciplinary proceedings in more than one Board of REALTORS® with respect to alleged violations of the Code of Ethics relating to the same transaction.

- **Standard of Practice 15-2**

  REALTORS® shall not make any unauthorized disclosure or dissemination of the allegations, findings, or decision developed in connection with an ethics hearing or appeal or in connection with an arbitration hearing or procedural review. (Amended 11/91)

- **Standard of Practice 15-3**

  REALTORS® shall not obstruct the Board's investigative or disciplinary proceedings by instituting or threatening to institute actions for libel, slander or defamation against any party to a professional standards proceeding or their witnesses. (Adopted 11/87)

- **Standard of Practice 15-4**

  REALTORS® shall not intentionally impede the Board's investigative or disciplinary proceedings by filing multiple ethics complaints based on the same event or transaction. (Adopted 11/88)

Article 16

When acting as agents, REALTORS® shall not accept any commission, rebate, or profit on expenditures made for their principal, without the principal's knowledge and consent. (Amended 11/91)

- **Standard of Practice 16-1**

  REALTORS® shall not recommend or suggest to a client or a customer the use of services of another organization or business entity in which they have a direct interest without disclosing such interest at the time of the recommendation or suggestion. (Amended 5/88)

- **Standard of Practice 16-2**

  When acting as agents or subagents, REALTORS® shall disclose to a client or customer if there is any financial benefit or fee the REALTOR® or the REALTOR®'s firm may receive as a direct result of having recommended real estate products or services (e.g., homeowner's insurance, warranty programs, mortgage financing, title insurance, etc.) other than real estate referral fees. (Adopted 5/88)

Article 17

REALTORS® shall not engage in activities that constitute the unauthorized practice of law and shall recommend that legal counsel be obtained when the interest of any party to the transaction requires it.

Article 18

REALTORS® shall keep in a special account in an appropriate financial institution, separated from their own funds, monies coming into their possession in trust for other persons, such as escrows, trust funds, client's monies, and other like items.

Article 19

REALTORS® shall be careful at all times to present a true picture in their advertising and representations to the public. REALTORS® shall also ensure that their professional status (e.g., broker, appraiser, property manager, etc.) or status as REALTORS® is clearly identifiable in any such advertising. (Amended 11/92)

- **Standard of Practice 19-1**

  REALTORS® shall not offer for sale/lease or advertise property without authority. When acting as listing brokers or as subagents. REALTORS® shall not quote a price different from that agreed upon with the seller/landlord. (Amended 11/92)

- **Standard of Practice 19-2**

  (Refer to Standard of Practice 9-4, which also relates to Article 19, Code of Ethics.)

- **Standard of Practice 19-3**

  REALTORS® when advertising unlisted real property for sale/lease in which they have an ownership interest, shall disclose their status as both owners/landlords and as REALTORS® or real estate licensees. (Amended 11/92)

- **Standard of Practice 19-4**

  REALTORS® shall not advertise nor permit any person employed by or affiliated with them to advertise listed property without disclosing the name of the firm. (Adopted 11/86)

- **Standard of Practice 19-5**

  Only REALTORS® as listing brokers, may claim to have "sold" the property, even when the sale resulted through the cooperative efforts of another broker. However, after transactions have closed, listing brokers may not prohibit successful cooperating brokers from advertising their "cooperation," "participation," or "assistance" in the transaction, or from making similar representations.

  Only listing brokers are entitled to use the term "sold" on signs, in advertisements, and in other public representations. (Amended 11/89)

REALTORS®, for the protection of all parties, shall see that financial obligations and commitments regarding real estate transactions are in writing, expressing the exact agreement of the parties. A copy of each agreement shall be furnished to each party upon their signing such agreement.

- **Standard of Practice 20-1**

  At the time of signing or initializing, REALTORS® shall furnish to each party a copy of any document signed or initialed. (Adopted 5/86)

- **Standard of Practice 20-2**

  For the protection of all parties, REALTORS® shall use reasonable care to ensure that documents pertaining to the purchase, sale, or lease of real estate are kept current through the use of written extensions or amendments. (Amendments 11/92)

REALTORS® shall not engage in any practice or take any action inconsistent with the agency of other REALTORS®.

- **Standard of Practice 21-1**

  Signs giving notice of property for sale, rent, lease, or exchange shall not be placed on property without consent of the seller/landlord. (Amended 11/92)

- **Standard of Practice 21-2**

  REALTORS® acting as subagents or as buyer/tenant agents, shall not attempt to extend a listing broker's offer of cooperation and/or compensation to other brokers without the consent of the listing broker. (Amended 11/92)

- **Standard of Practice 21-3**

  REALTORS® shall not solicit a listing which is currently listed exclusively with another broker. However, if the listing broker, when asked by the REALTOR®, refuses to disclose the expiration date and nature of such listing; i.e., an exclusive right to sell, an exclusive agency, open listing, or other form of contractual agreement between the listing broker and the client, the REALTOR® may contact the owner to secure such information and may discuss the terms upon which the REALTOR® might take a future listing or, alternatively, may take a listing to become effective upon expiration of any existing exclusive listing. (Amended 11/86)

- **Standard of Practice 21-4**

  REALTORS® shall not use information obtained by them from the listing broker, through offers to cooperate received through Multiple Listing Services or other sources authorized by the listing broker, for the purpose of creating a referral prospect to a third broker, or for creating a buyer/tenant prospect unless such use is authorized by the listing broker. (Amended 11/92)

- **Standard of Practice 21-5**

  The fact that an agency agreement has been entered into with a REALTOR® shall not preclude or inhibit any other REALTOR® from entering into a similar agreement after the expiration of the prior agreement. (Amended 11/92)

- **Standard of Practice 21-6**

  The fact that a client has retained a REALTOR® as an agent in one or more past transactions does not preclude other REALTORS® from seeking such former client's future business. (Amended 11/92)

- **Standard of Practice 21-7**

  REALTORS® shall be free to list property which is "open listed" at any time, but shall not knowingly obligate the seller to pay more than one commission except with the seller's knowledgeable consent. (Cross-reference Article 7.) (Amended 5/88)

- **Standard of Practice 21-8**

  When REALTORS® are contacted by the client of another REALTOR® regarding the creation of an agency relationship to provide the same type of service, and REALTORS® have not directly or indirectly initiated such discussions, they may discuss the terms upon which they might enter into a future agency agreement or, alternatively, may enter into an agency agreement which becomes effective upon expiration of any existing exclusive agreement. (Amended 11/92)

- **Standard of Practice 21-9**

  In cooperative transactions REALTORS® shall compensate cooperating REALTORS® (principal brokers) and shall not compensate nor offer to compensate, directly or indirectly, any of the sales licensees employed by or affiliated with other REALTORS® without the prior express knowledge and consent of the cooperating broker.

- **Standard of Practice 21-10**

  Article 21 does not preclude REALTORS® from making general announcements to prospective clients describing their services and the terms of their availability even though some recipients may have entered into agency agreements with another REALTOR®. A general telephone canvass, general mailing or distribution addressed to all prospective clients in a given geographical area or in a given profession, business, club, or organization, or other classification or group is deemed "general" for purposes of this standard.

  Article 21 is intended to recognize as unethical two basic types of solicitations:

  First, telephone or personal solicitations of property owners who have been identified by a real estate sign, multiple listing compilation, or other information service as having exclusively listed their property with another REALTOR®; and

  Second, mail or other forms of written solicitations of prospective clients whose properties are exclusively listed with another REALTOR® when such solicitations are not part of a general mailing but are directed specifically to property owners identified through compilations of current listing, "for sale" or "for rent" signs, or other sources of information required by Article 22 and Multiple Listing Service rules to be made available to other REALTORS® under offers of subagency or cooperation. (Amended 11/92)

- **Standard of Practice 21-11**

  REALTORS®, prior to entering into an agency agreement, have an affirmative obligation to make reasonable efforts to determine whether the client is subject to a current, valid exclusive agreement to provide the same types of real estate service. (Amended 11/92)

- **Standard of Practice 21-12**

  REALTORS®, acting as agents of buyers or tenants, shall disclose that relationship to the seller/landlord's agent at first contact and shall provide written confirmation of that disclosure to the seller/landlord's agent not later than execution of a purchase agreement or lease. (Cross-reference Article 7.) (Amended 11/92)

- **Standard of Practice 21-13**

  On unlisted property, REALTORS® acting as buyer/tenant agents shall disclose that relationship to the seller/landlord at first contact for that client and shall provide written confirmation of such disclosure to the seller/landlord not later than execution of any purchase or lease agreement.

  REALTORS® shall make any request for anticipated compensation from the seller/landlord at first contact. (Cross-reference Article 7.) (Amended 11/92)

- **Standard of Practice 21-14**

  REALTORS®, acting as agents of sellers/landlords or as subagents of listing brokers, shall disclose that relationship to buyers/tenants as soon as practicable and shall provide written confirmation of such disclosure to buyers/tenants not later than execution of any purchase or lease agreement. (Amended 11/92)

- **Standard of Practice 21-15**

  Article 21 does not preclude REALTORS® from contacting the client of another broker for the purpose of offering to provide, or entering into a contract to provide, a different type of real estate service unrelated to the type of service currently being provided (e.g., property management as opposed to brokerage). However, information received through a Multiple Listing Service or any other offer of cooperation may not be used to target clients of other REALTORS® to whom such offers to provide services may be made. (Amended 11/92)

- **Standard of Practice 21-16**

  REALTORS®, acting as subagents or buyer/tenant agents, shall not use the terms of an offer to purchase/lease to attempt to modify the listing broker's offer of compensation to subagents or buyer's agents nor make the submission of an executed offer to purchase/lease contingent on the listing broker's agreement to modify the offer of compensation. (Amended 11/92)

- **Standard of Practice 21-17**

  Where property is listed on an open listing basis, REALTORS® acting as buyer/tenant agents may deal directly with the seller/landlord. (Adopted 11/92)

- **Standard of Practice 21-18**

  All dealings concerning property exclusively listed, or with buyer/tenants who are exclusively represented shall be carried on with the client's agent, and not with the client, except with the consent of the client's agent. (Adopted 11/92)

Article 22

REALTORS® shall cooperate with other brokers except when cooperation is not in the client's best interest. (Amended 11/92)

- **Standard of Practice 22-1**

  It is the obligation of subagents to promptly disclose all pertinent facts to the principal's agent prior to as well as after a purchase or lease agreement is executed. (Cross-reference to Article 9) (Amended 11/92)

- **Standard of Practice 22-2**

  REALTORS® shall submit offers and counter-offers, in an objective manner. (Amended 11/92)

- **Standard of Practice 22-3**

  REALTORS® shall disclose the existence of an accepted offer to any broker seeking cooperation. (Adopted 5/86)

- **Standard of Practice 22-4**

  REALTORS®, acting as exclusive agents of sellers, establish the terms and conditions of offers to cooperate. Unless expressly indicated in offers to cooperate made through MLS or otherwise, a cooperating broker may not assume that the offer of cooperation includes an offer of compensation. Entitlement to compensation in a cooperative transaction must be agreed upon between a listing and cooperating broker prior to the time an offer to purchase the property is produced. (Adopted 11/88)

Article 23

REALTORS® shall not knowingly or recklessly make false or misleading statements about competitors, their businesses, or their business practices. (Amended 11/91)

The Code of Ethics was adopted in 1913. Amended at the Annual Convention in 1924, 1928, 1950, 1951, 1952, 1955, 1956, 1961, 1962, 1974, 1982, 1986, 1987, 1989, 1990, 1991, and 1992.

EXPLANATORY NOTES (Amended 11/88)

The reader should be aware of the following policies which have been approved by the Board of Directors of the National Association:

In filing a charge of an alleged violation of the Code of Ethics by a REALTOR®, the charge shall read as an alleged violation of one or more Articles of the Code. A Standard of Practice may only be cited in support of the charge.

The Standards of Practice are not an integral part of the Code but rather serve to clarify the ethical obligations imposed by the various Articles. The Standards of Practice supplement, and do not substitute for, the Case *Interpretations in Interpretations of the Code of Ethics.*

Modifications to existing Standards of Practice and additional new Standards of Practice are approved from time to time. The reader is cautioned to ensure that the most recent publications are utilized.

Articles 1 through 5 are aspirational and establish ideals that a REALTOR® should strive to attain. Recognizing their subjective nature, these Articles shall not be used as the bases for charges of alleged unethical conduct or as the bases for disciplinary action.

1. The real estate industry includes:

   (A) Single family home sales
   (B) Loan brokerage
   (C) Construction
   ✓(D) All of the above

2. A professional real estate licensee's knowledge should include the areas of:

   (A) Escrow
   (B) Appraisal
   (C) Property management
   ✓(D) All of the above

3. Approximately _____ of the wealth of the nation is held in the form of real estate:

   (A) 10%
   (B) 50%
   ✓(C) 75%
   (D) 85%

4. Shopping centers requiring a trade area population of 35,000 to 100,000 to support them, built on 15 to 40 acres, and with a supermarket of 25,000 to 35,000 square feet, are identified as:

   (A) Regional shopping centers
   (B) Neighborhood shopping centers
   ✓(C) Community shopping centers
   (D) None of the above

5. Advantages of a professional real estate career include:

   (A) Personal satisfaction from serving people well
   (B) Good income opportunities
   (C) A high level of independence and freedom of choice
   ✓(D) All of the above

6. The basic purpose of the Real Estate Law is to:

   (A) Regulate real property securities
   ✓(B) Protect the public against fraud
   (C) Provide the Commissioner with the authority to hold hearings affecting the licensees
   (D) None of the above

7. With certain exceptions, a real estate license is required when any activity in a real estate transaction is performed for another or others for a:

   (A) Fee
   (B) Commission
   (C) Compensation
   ✓(D) Any of the above

8. The chief executive officer of the Department of Real Estate is the Real Estate Commissioner who is:

   (A) Elected by residents of California
   (B) Appointed by the California Association of Realtors®
   ✓(C) Appointed by the governor
   (D) Appointed for a designated term of six years

9. The Real Estate Commissioner does *not*:

   (A) Screen and qualify license applicants
   (B) Investigate complaints against licensees
   (C) Regulate certain real property securities
   ✓(D) Assume the role of a court of law

10. The Real Estate Advisory Commission consists of _____ members.

    ✓(A) 10
    (B) 6
    (C) 4
    (D) 12

Chapter 2
The Real Estate Office

OPENING THE REAL ESTATE OFFICE

The attraction of higher commissions has led many successful salespersons to obtain their broker licenses and open their own offices. However, many licensees do not foresee the complexity of operating a real estate business or have the necessary specialized knowledge, capital, and managerial skills to succeed on their own. Once the licensee has determined to open an office, many decisions must be made.

Preopening Decisions

Type of Business Entity. Even before a broker candidate makes application to the Department of Real Estate for the broker's license, the candidate must make decisions about the organization of this future brokerage company. For example, is the company to be incorporated? If so, the broker's license will be issued to the corporation. The corporation must, therefore, be formed in advance, and a Certificate of Status, obtained from the California Secretary of State, must be submitted with the license application.

Name of the Company. If the company is to operate under a fictitious name or dba (doing business as), the broker's license must identify that dba in the license itself. The license applicant must submit a copy of the Fictitious Business Name Statement filed with the county clerk's office.

Physical Aspects of Office Site and Layout. Selection of the office location and layout should be made as soon as possible after selecting the market area of the company. The broker's license is issued for the broker to operate at a specific approved location. If the broker is to maintain more than one place of business, an additional license is required for each branch location.

Office Operations

Office Procedural Policies. An office policy and procedures manual is a useful tool for any size real estate office. Policies and procedures should be planned before any business is conducted. A good office procedures manual will, of course, be subject to modification as experience and growing wisdom will indicate.

Interviewing, Selecting, and Training Salespersons. Hiring a staff will of necessity follow the issue of a broker's license, but the *plans* for hiring of a staff should be a part of the planning of the business. Some key persons may actually be hired before opening the office, even though licensed personnel are licensed to the licensed employing broker.

Role of the Broker. A broker planning the opening of an office must be aware of B&P Code Section 10177(h) which provides that the Real Estate Commissioner may suspend or revoke the license of a broker who has "... failed to exercise reasonable supervision over the activities of his salespersons; or, as the officer designated by a corporate broker licensee, failed to exercise reasonable supervision and control of the activities of the corporation for which a real estate license is required."

Broker-Salesperson Relationship. Commissioner's Regulation 2726 requires that there be a written contract between a broker and " ...each of his salesmen, whether licensed as a salesman or as a broker under a broker-salesman arrangement ... and shall cover material aspects of the relationships ... including supervision of licensed activities, duties and compensation." The salesperson may be an independent contractor under IRS regulations, permitting the broker to avoid withholding income tax and social security contributions from the salesperson's commissions. However, under California Real Estate Law, the salesperson is an *employee* of the broker who acts only as the agent of the employing broker.

BUSINESS ENTITIES AND METHODS OF OPERATION

Like any business, the real estate office may be legally organized as a sole proprietorship, partnership, or corporation. Franchise affiliations have also become widespread.

Individual Proprietorship

The individual proprietorship can be any size company from a one-person operation to a large firm with specialized brokerage departments. The majority of real estate offices in the United States today are relatively small single owner operations. A nationwide survey of real estate firms by NAR in 1985 revealed that more than 6 of every 10 small firms (sales forces of 5 or less) use this form of legal organization. Over 60% of the firms surveyed had five or fewer salespersons.

Advantages. Formation and organization is simple. The owner enjoys independence of action, freedom in management, and has full control and responsibility for the firm. Profits are the owner's alone.

Disadvantages. Operations are limited by the extent of the broker/owner's initial capital. The proprietor assumes unlimited personal liability and ownership cannot be shared with others. Limited provisions are available for business continuity in the event of illness or death and limited talent is on hand to develop and expand the business. The business requires continuous personal attention of the owner and financial losses are the owner's alone.

Partnership   A partnership consists of two or more persons pooling their efforts, time, or capital to form a business for profit. The partnership law of the state governs the rights and duties of each partner to the other and to the public. A written Statement of Partnership sets forth the names of the partners and, when recorded, means that one partner alone cannot sell the partnership rights. Recording gives constructive notice that other parties have legal interests or rights in the partnership. Brokers contemplating the formation of a partnership for a real estate business should consult an attorney.

Limited or Special Partnership. A limited partnership can be formed for a single, specific transaction or investment. Limited partners are not able to participate in management, but have limited liability. Generally, this is not practical in an ongoing real estate brokerage business.

General Partnership. A general partnership can be created to conduct a business in which all partners have a voice in management, and have unlimited liability. According to the NAR survey, 8% of firms in 1985 used this form of organization.

Advantages. The partners pool their expertise, capital, and business contacts and share responsibility and liability. Continuity of the business may be provided for in the partnership agreement. The partnership entity is not taxed as such by the federal government. The partnership files an "information return" and the individual partners pay taxes on the individual profits from the partnership. Net profit taken out of the partnership by each partner is taxed as ordinary income.

Disadvantages. Each partner is bound by the actions of the other partners when acting within the scope of the partnership. Liability for partnership debts is held jointly and severally. Therefore, the personal assets of each partner may be attached by creditors and others due to judgments involving injury, damage, trespassing, assault, or tort.

The Partnership Agreement. A written partnership agreement, although not required by law, is extremely important in defining composition, continuity, rights, and other organizational matters. Past or present personal, financial, or social problems of any partner can adversely affect the business. Without a carefully drawn contract, partners may have disagreements over responsibilities, amount of work to be accomplished by each partner, the type of business services to be offered by the company, and personal or business philosophical differences.

Corporation   The corporation is artificial, invisible, intangible, and exists only as a "legal person" in the eyes of the law. It is an entity separate and apart from its stockholders, officers, or directors. While not a complete escape from personal liability, the important characteristics of a corporation include its separate capacity to deal with property independently from its members, and its centralized control in a board of directors. The larger the firm, the more likely that it will be organized as a corporation.

Types of Corporations. The formation process, including choice of a corporate form, should be guided by a corporation attorney.

☐ The general or normal form of corporation is that of an entity owned by its stockholders. It has officers, and a board of directors.

☐ A "thin corporation" is one with relatively few stockholders and is often closely held.

☐ A tax-option corporation (S corporation) is a corporation formed to avoid double taxation of profits. S corporations are subject to tax reporting rules similar to those applied to partnerships. However, shareholders who work for the corporation are treated as employees for social security purposes. Each stockholder reports his share of corporate items of income and loss, deductions, and credits. The election may be made for a domestic corporation which is not a member of an affiliated group which meets all of the following qualifications:

• There can be no more than 35 stockholders, and all must agree to the election.

• All of the stockholders must be U.S. citizens.

• There can be only one class of stock; the company cannot issue both common and preferred stock.

Authority to Conduct Real Estate Business. Under the California Business and Professions Code, a corporation may conduct a real estate brokerage business if licensed through officers of the corporation. The corporation must apply for and maintain licenses for each active officer qualifying as a broker. The license issued for the corporation entitles the qualified officer to transact business only for, and on behalf of, the corporation. A separate license must be secured to enable the officer to transact business as an individual or for another firm.

Advantages. Liability of each stockholder is limited to the amount of investment in the corporation by the shareholder, unless the entity is used as a "corporate veil," i.e., incorporation merely as a shield for an individual who is undercapitalized. Greater credibility is possible with customers, other professionals, and potential employees, and a corporation may obtain capital with greater ease for initial organization or expansion. Shares of stock are freely transferable, and anonymity of ownership exists.

☐ *Continuity*. The corporation has life in perpetuity, regardless of death or retirement of its shareholders, an important protection for the continuity of a real estate brokerage. If the real estate license is issued to a sole proprietor and that person dies, the license is cancelled, all listings terminate, and all employed salespersons' licenses are cancelled.

☐ *Taxes*. Tax advantages include: lower tax rates; lower tax consequences for heirs of corporation assets; and tax advantages of retirement plans.

Disadvantages. There are some costs for incorporation, including legal fees. Incorporation may not provide complete limited liability; a principal may still have to personally guarantee debt. To help minimize personal liability the corporation should have adequate capitalization, maintain a proper debt to equity ratio, avoid "milking" the corporate money, observe corporate formalities, and obtain good legal and accounting advice.

☐ *Double Taxation*. A corporation is subject to federal and state income taxes on its net income, without deduction for dividends paid to stockholders. The stockholders are then subject to income taxes on dividends paid. This creates a double taxation, because dividends are taxed against the corporation and against the stockholder.

☐ *Rules and Regulations*. There is less management freedom because of corporate formalities, which include the obligations to issue shares, hold regular meetings, and maintain a minute book. There also are limitations on investing corporate assets. Officers of the corporation must guard against commingling corporate and personal funds.

Franchise A franchisee is granted the right to engage in the business of offering, selling, or distributing certain goods or services. This is accomplished through a marketing system which is substantially designed, developed, and monitored by a franchisor, and which usually involves a trademark.

Structure. A franchise operation involves a contract or agreement, express or implied, oral or written, by which use of the franchisor's trademark name, logo, service mark, and advertising program is permitted in the operation of the franchisee's business, while operating under the specified plan or system. The franchisee pays the franchisor or designee, directly or indirectly, a franchise fee.

Real Estate Franchise Business. A number of national and regional firms operate real estate franchises. In 1985, 19% of all firms were affiliated with franchise organizations.

Advantages. Immediate name identification is possible through national, regional, or local advertising programs. The franchisor may provide resources for training salespersons and for purchasing signs, supplies, and equipment. A common referral system may be available among franchises and more uniform management systems and procedures are utilized. Ownership and control of individual firms is retained.

Disadvantages to Franchisees. There is an initial franchise fee, and there are continuing fees, usually based on gross sales volume. Loss of local name identity may occur, the franchisor may go out of business, or the franchisor might place a competing franchisee in the same market area.

Rent-a-Desk (100% Commission) Some brokers offer rent-a-desk or 100% commission operations. This type of office usually requires a flat rental fee for desk space which may or may not include limited telephone, advertising, or secretarial services. This plan is not a business organization form, but is a form of commission split agreement. A real estate commission cannot lawfully be paid directly from a client to a salesperson; it must be paid directly to the employing licensed broker, then split between the broker and salesperson in accordance with their written employment contract. In the rent-a-desk plan, all of the commission brought into the office by the salesperson is passed through to the salesperson except the portion which the broker retains in accordance with the rent-a-desk agreement.

Rationale. Many successful salespersons may feel their broker is receiving a disproportionate share of the commission split; however, they may not want to open their own brokerage firm because of managerial responsibilities and operating expenses.

Advantages. The high-producing licensee may retain a larger portion of commissions. The licensee may maintain independent contractor status under tax laws and the desk fee may provide a relatively low overhead to the licensee, without responsibilities of ownership.

Disadvantages. Inequity of advertising or floor time may occur and the licensee may have limited control over office appearance. Salespersons must be highly organized and motivated to work totally on their own and generally have limited access to training programs.

Employment Status. A real estate salesperson cannot truly be an independent contractor under the Real Estate Law because the Real Estate Law holds a broker responsible for the supervision of associate licensees, even if the salespersons qualify as independent contractors under tax laws.

OFFICE LOCATION AND LAYOUT

The physical setting is important to the business in many ways, including marketing, efficient operation, and morale.

Site Selection

One of the most important requisites for a successful real estate office is accessibility and proximity to potential clients and customers. Market area characteristics which should be considered are:

Neighborhood. The broker planning to open an office must give first consideration to the "neighborhood" which the broker hopes to serve, whether that neighborhood be a geographic residential neighborhood or a business or investment "community."

Focus. The broker's target market must be identified to promote concentration of effort and area expertise.

Strategic Locations. Shopping centers and other high traffic areas are good for offices which expect some drop-in business. A corner location provides maximum visibility. Adequate and accessible parking is essential for almost every type of operation. A street level location is usually convenient, although specialized operations may be successfully located above street level.

Office Layout

The optimum size, shape, layout, furniture, and design is that which allows the owner-broker and associates to conduct their duties in the most efficient manner. Company image, budget, and personal preference must all be considered.

Adequate Floor Space. Whether an office is large or small, the comfortable level of space utilization is approximately 125-135 square feet per desk or 50-300 square feet per person.

Office Arrangement. The open office layout is most prevalent in use at the present time. Combinations of open and closed arrangements are also possible.

☐ *Open.* An open plan, with individual desks and telephones, allows communication among associates. Access to a conference room or private office is desirable when working with clients or customers. Clients may be impressed with an environment of many active associates. However, noise and distractions may interfere with some activities.

☐ *Closed.* A closed plan, with separate offices or cubicles, allows privacy at the associate's desk where all pertinent data, forms, and information may be located. Sales associates may enjoy a feeling of security and privacy at the expense of communication with other associates. Commercial-industrial brokerages utilize the closed office layout more often than residential offices.

Common Areas. Provision is typically made for common areas such as a reception area, multipurpose room (conference, meeting, training, lounge area), supply-storage area, and reference area.

Equipment and Furnishings. Properly equipped and furnished offices contribute to better performance by the firm's workers. Office equipment and furnishings should be efficient and comfortable, reflecting a professional image. Furnishings should enhance a pleasant atmosphere with effective color coordination. Wall coverings, carpeting, and draperies are important for noise control, a warm feeling, and lower maintenance costs. Many real estate companies adopt a color trademark to promote their name.

Work Stations The larger the staff, the more planning this will require.

Sales Associates. Each associate licensee should have a desk, chair, and client/customer seating area. An individual telephone and access to a typewriter are essential tools of each sales associate. Most newer offices provide for computer access from each desk to a multiple listing service.

Secretarial. Secretarial services, space and equipment should be planned. Computer, copy machines, and other equipment should be located conveniently with regard to their users and usage. The same applies to reference materials, files, records, office supplies, custodial equipment, and maintenance supplies.

Reception. For most businesses a reception area should be conveniently located for clients' and customers' access and inquiries.

ROLE OF THE BROKER

As owner-manager or managing broker, the former salesperson encounters new responsibilities in planning, administration, and leadership.

Definition of Management Four basic functions included in the concept of management are planning, organizing, directing, and controlling.

Planning. The tasks of selecting the firm's objectives, goals, and programs and determining methods to achieve them are the responsibilities of the managing broker. The owner-broker must first determine the form of business entity of the enterprise. The broker will then set up immediate goals, such as:

☐ To have a profitable operation within two years from starting

☐ To specialize in residential real estate brokerage

☐ To capture 15 percent of the market in the area.

Long-range planning might look to the lifespan of the enterprise, considering such options as:

☐ Incorporating and having the estate or its heirs continue operation

☐ Selling or merging upon retirement

☐ Closing the operation in 10 years

Management formulates plans through market research and analysis for:

☐ Establishing boundaries of the desired market area

☐ Determining number of associates necessary to achieve objectives

☐ Estimating the necessary working capital

☐ Establishing budgets and pro forma statements for short and long-term financial planning

☐ Determining staff selection and training procedures

☐ Determining office location, layout, and furnishings.

Organizing. Management's responsibilities include implementation of the formulated plans, allocation of the required resources, and assignment of responsibilities for achieving the desired objectives. Examples include:

☐ Preparation of office policy manual

☐ Identifying individuals responsible for preparing ads

☐ Identifying specific media and other providers of services.

Directing. Directing the operation means providing the leadership necessary for selection, supervision, and administration of the program and individuals who will help the broker achieve the planned objectives. Examples include:

☐ Establishing the specific criteria to be used in the sales associate selection process

☐ Providing appropriate job descriptions for office staff

☐ Providing necessary and appropriate training of all personnel.

Controlling. Guidance of activity toward the goal. The broker is responsible for measuring and comparing results with the planned objectives and, when necessary, making changes to achieve the desired results. Examples include:

☐ Establishing criteria by which performance may be evaluated

☐ Preparing strategies for improving performance.

Broker Qualities The broker should have the ability to plan, organize, lead, use good judgment, and relate well with people. Professional appearance should project tasteful grooming and dress, as well as a healthy attitude and physical condition.

Abilities. The broker must have the ability to set objectives, follow through, exercise self-discipline, delegate responsibility, motivate others to achieve results, give credit where and when warranted, and discipline impartially.

Knowledge. The broker must have knowledge of business development, financial management, real estate law, the real estate industry, the community the market and products, the competition, and management techniques.

STAFF SELECTION AND TRAINING

Proper selection of both sales and nonsales personnel is necessary to achieve maximum efficiency for the firm and succeed in reaching goals and objectives.

Sales Manager Employment of a sales manager may be considered necessary when there are eight or more sales associates in an office. In smaller offices, the owner-broker usually fills the role of the sales manager.

Function. The sales manager's duties and responsibilities typically include recruiting sales associates; screening, selecting, and training sales associates; and assessing sales potential of each sales associate.

Qualifications. A productive sales associate does not necessarily make a successful transition into management responsibilities. Qualifications and capabilities should be considered carefully when selecting the sales manager.

- ☐ Unquestioned integrity, personal and moral
- ☐ Unquestioned loyalty and ability to enforce policy in an effective, impartial manner
- ☐ Knowledge of business and financial management
- ☐ Good health and work habits
- ☐ Good appearance and grooming
- ☐ Having the confidence and respect of associates
- ☐ Ability to pay close attention to details
- ☐ Patience and understanding
- ☐ Ability to discipline oneself and others impartially
- ☐ Ability to delegate responsibility and give credit

☐ Ability to generate enthusiasm and motivate others.

Compensation. The sales manager's compensation may be based on several methods:

☐ Minimum salary plus an override on all business income, with no selling by the sales manager

☐ Percentage override on all business income plus the sales manager's own sales commissions

☐ Straight salary

☐ Any combination of methods.

Sales Associates   Associate licensees are the core of the real estate office.

Sales Associate Selection. The broker-manager will need to pursue a process of outreach and screening, looking for both general sales promise and compatibility with the office's particular focus.

Recruiting. The search for successful sales associates may include advertising, providing a job description, and collecting resumes and application forms from interested applicants.

Screening. Evaluation of the applicants' resumes and application forms for qualifications, experience, and education should precede the interview when possible. A person to person meeting between the broker-owner and the applicant is essential to further evaluate personality, education, experience, and potential for success in that particular office.

Qualifications. The broker will want to hire the best applicant(s) for the job. Desired qualities for a successful sales associate include:

☐ Unquestioned integrity and loyalty

☐ Self-discipline and determined goals and objectives

☐ Motivation to achieve own goals and objectives

☐ Career-minded and cooperative attitude

☐ Consistency as a producer

☐ Outlook compatible with company policy and management

☐ Enthusiasm for product, people, and firm

☐ Ability to relate to clients, customers, associates, and firm

☐ Willingness to give friendly assistance to associates, clients, customers, and others

☐ Capacity for learning

☐ Good health, appearance, grooming, and attire.

Sales Associate Training. Either the broker (owner-manager or managing broker) or the sales manager may have the responsibility of training the sales associates. Associates should learn a sense of pride in their work, their firm, and their community. A well-rounded training program combines individual on-the-job training and staff meetings, and professional and academic seminars, workshops and courses. The real estate industry and proprietary schools offer such courses both for self-improvement and for meeting continuing education requirements.

Non-Sales Staff Depending on the size of the real estate office, various nonsales personnel may be hired. Typical jobs to be filled include receptionist, secretary, accountant, escrow specialist, and custodian. The real estate office must be an equal opportunity employer, that is, it must not discriminate on the basis of race, national origin, sex, or age.

BROKER-SALES ASSOCIATE AGREEMENT

Commissioner's Regulation 2726 requires every real estate broker to have a written agreement with each salesperson (Exhibit 1), whether licensed as a salesperson or as a broker working subject to a broker-salesperson relationship, and whether the associates are employees or independent contractors.

Content The agreement must be dated and signed by both parties, and must express the material aspects of the relationship between the parties including:

- ☐ Duties and responsibilities
- ☐ Compensation or commission
- ☐ Supervision of licensed activities.

Recordkeeping The agreement must be available for inspection by the Commissioner or authorized representative upon request. A copy must be retained by each party for at least three years after the termination date of the agreement.

POLICY MANUAL

A policy manual is a requisite and integral tool for a productive brokerage operation. It stands as a necessary form of communication from management to all other firm personnel, and may serve as a reference and training manual.

Characteristics The manual should be written in a concise, simple manner, easy to read, using simple language. It should be consistent with the work status of sales associates, whether employees or independent contractors. A loose leaf binder arrangement, with numbered pages, allows for flexibility, as it is easy to add or remove material.

Contents Depending on the size and nature of the firm, the policy manual should cover most or all of the following:

General. Policies which should be spelled out include company policies about:

☐ Association agreement/contract–employee or independent contractor

☐ Appearance, conduct, and dress code

☐ Automobile usage, liabilities, insurance, and reimbursable expenses

☐ Advertising and public relations procedures

☐ Signs, supplies, name riders, and business cards

☐ Personal real estate transactions of the associate licensee

☐ Telephone usage and telephone protocol

☐ Client protection

☐ Correspondence procedures

☐ Hours of operation

☐ Assignment of "floor time."

Agency. Policies should be adopted and published concerning agency legislation compliance. The California Association of Realtors® Legal Department has published a series of sample office policies applying to listing agents, selling agents, subagents, dual agents, in-house sales, and cooperating sales. (Major portions of this complete *Agency Legislation Compliance Manual* are included in Chapter 3 of this text.)

Listing. Policies might be stated regarding prospects, ownership of listings, servicing of listings, expired listings, acceptable types of listings, cancellation of listings, and commissions, compensation, and bonuses.

Selling. Policies should exist about contract writing, handling of buyers' deposits, buyer protection, presentation of offers, commissions, compensation, bonuses, reporting procedures, and escrow procedures.

Other. Policy statements might address property ownership, disputes and arbitration procedures, transfers, terminations, leaves of absence, vacations, benefits of association, and real estate board affiliation.

SALES MEETINGS

Carefully planned sales meetings are valuable sales and training aids. They can be one of the most popular means of communication with the sales associates.

Agenda Each meeting should have an agenda. The following are helpful guidelines in arranging the meeting agenda:

Purpose. Decide the purpose of the meeting.

Program. Establish a definite program which explores the best methods of achieving the purpose of the meeting.

Schedule. Stick to the agenda; all scheduled meetings should be held on time—begun on time, and ended on time.

Topics of Discussion. Frequent topics in many offices are goals and objectives of the firm and the sales associates, policy manual items, (to keep the manual current or clarify certain points), successful listing, selling, and closing techniques, current financing techniques, current listings and problem properties, advertising, "want/need" problems, referral services, brainstorming, new laws, law compliance, unlawful discrimination, and plans for the firm's future.

Discussion Leaders Generally the broker will open the meeting by reviewing the agenda and introducing the discussion leader for the specific topic. Frequently individuals with expertise will be invited to discuss their field of specialization. These individuals may be members of the firm or outside experts, such as mortgage bankers, title company representatives, and escrow officers.

BROKER—SALESPERSON CONTRACT

(INDEPENDENT CONTRACTOR)

CALIFORNIA ASSOCIATION OF REALTORS® STANDARD FORM

THIS AGREEMENT, made this _____ day of _____ , 19 ____ , by and between

_____ hereinafter referred to as Broker and _____

_____ hereinafter referred to as Salesperson,

WITNESSETH:

WHEREAS, Broker is duly licensed as a real estate broker by the State of California, and

WHEREAS, Broker maintains an office, properly equipped with furnishings and other equipment necessary and incidental to the proper operation of business, and staffed suitably to serving the public as a real estate broker, and

WHEREAS, Salesperson is now engaged in business as a real estate licensee, duly licensed by the State of California.

NOW, THEREFORE, in consideration of the premises and the mutual agreements herein contained, it is understood and agreed as follows:

1. Broker agrees, at Salesperson's request, to make available to Salesperson all current listings in the office, except such as Broker may choose to place in the exclusive possession of some other Salesperson. In addition, at Salesperson's discretion and at Salesperson's request Broker may, from time to time, supply Salesperson with prospective listings; Salesperson shall have absolute discretion in deciding upon whether to handle and the method of handling any such leads suggested by Broker. Nothing herein shall be construed to require that Salesperson accept or service any particular listing or prospective listing offered by Broker; nor shall Broker have any right or authority to direct that Salesperson see or service particular parties, or restrict Salesperson's activities to particular areas. Broker shall have no right, except to the extent required by law, to direct or limit Salesperson's activities as to hours, leads, open houses, opportunity or floor time, production, prospects, reports, sales, sales meetings, schedule, services, inventory, time off, training, vacation, or other similar activities.

At Salesperson's request and at Salesperson's sole discretion Broker agrees to furnish such advice, information and full cooperation as Salesperson shall desire. Broker agrees that thereby Broker obtains no authority or right to direct or control Salesperson's actions except as specifically required by law (including Business and Professions Code Section 10177 (h)) and that Salesperson assumes and retains discretion for methods, techniques and procedures in soliciting and obtaining listings and sales, rentals, or leases of listed property.

2. Broker agrees to provide Salesperson with use, equally with other Salespersons, of all of the facilities of the office now operated by Broker in connection with the subject matter of this contract, which office is now maintained at _____

3. Until termination hereof, Salesperson agrees to work diligently and with Salesperson's best efforts to sell, lease or rent any and all real estate listed with Broker, to solicit additional listings and customers, and otherwise promote the business of serving the public in real estate transactions to the end that each of the parties hereto may derive the greatest profit possible, provided that nothing herein shall be construed to require that Salesperson handle or solicit particular listings, or to authorize Broker to direct or require that Salesperson to do so. Salesperson assumes and agrees to perform no other activities in association with Broker, except to solicit and obtain listings and sales, rentals, or leases of property for the parties' mutual benefit, and to do so in accordance with law and with the ethical and professional standards as required in paragraph 4 below.

4. Salesperson agrees to commit no act of a type for which the Real Estate Commissioner of the State of California is authorized by Section 10176 of the California Business & Professions Code to suspend or to revoke license.

5. Broker's commissions as set forth in the attached schedule, marked "Exhibit A" and hereby incorporated by reference, shall be charged to the parties for whom services are performed except that Broker may agree in writing to other rates with such parties.

Broker will advise all Salespersons associated with Broker of any special commission rates made with respect to listings as provided in this paragraph.

When Salesperson shall have performed any work hereunder whereby any commission shall be earned and when such commission shall have been collected, Salesperson shall be entitled to a share of such commission as determined by the attached commission schedule, marked "Exhibit B" and hereby incorporated by reference, except as may otherwise be agreed in writing by Broker and Salesperson before completion of any particular transaction.

6. In the event that two or more Salespeople participate in such work, Salesperson's share of the commission shall be divided between the participating Salespersons according to agreement between them or by arbitration.

7. In compliance with Section 10138 of the California Business and Professions Code, all commissions will be received by Broker; Salesperson's share of such commissions, however, shall be payable to Salesperson immediately upon collection or as soon thereafter as practicable.

8. In no event shall Broker be personally liable to Salesperson for Salesperson's share of commissions not collected, nor shall Salesperson be entitled to any advance or payment from Broker upon future commissions, Salesperson's only renumeration being Salesperson's share of the commission paid by the party or parties for whom the service was performed. Nor shall Salesperson be personally liable to Broker for any commission not collected.

9. Broker shall not be liable to Salesperson for any expenses incurred by Salesperson or for any of his acts except as specifically required by law, nor shall Salesperson be liable to Broker for office help or expense. Salesperson shall have no authority to bind Broker by any promise or representation unless specifically authorized in writing in a particular transaction. Expenses which must by reason of some necessity be paid from the commissions, or are incurred in the collection of, or in the attempt to collect the commission, shall be paid by the parties in the same proportion as provided for herein in the division of commissions.

Salesperson agrees to provide and pay for all necessary professional licenses and dues. Broker shall not be liable to reimburse Salesperson therefor.

In the event Broker elects to advance sums with which to pay for the account of Salesperson professional fees or other items, Salesperson will repay the same to Broker on demand and Broker may deduct such advances from commissions otherwise payable to Salesperson.

To order, contact—California Association of Realtors®
525 S. Virgil Avenue, Los Angeles, California 90020

FORM I-14

Exhibit 1.1

10. This agreement does not constitute a hiring by either party. It is the parties' intention that so far as shall be in conformity with law the Salesperson be an independent contractor and not Broker's employee, and in conformity therewith that Salesperson retain sole and absolute discretion and judgment in the manner and means of carrying out Salesperson's selling and soliciting activities. Therefore, the parties hereto are and shall remain independent contractors bound by the provisions hereof. Salesperson will not be treated as an employee with respect to the service performed by such salesperson as a real estate agent for state tax and federal tax purposes. Salesperson is under the control of Broker as to the result of Salesperson's work only and not as to the means by which such result is accomplished. This agreement shall not be construed as a partnership and Broker shall not be liable for any obligation incurred by Salesperson.

11. In accordance with law, Salesperson agrees that any and all listings of property, and all employment in connection with the real estate business shall be taken in the name of Broker. Such listings shall be filed with Broker within twenty-four hours after receipt of same by Salesperson.

Salesperson shall receive a commission in accordance with the current commission schedule set forth in the Broker's written policy based upon commissions actually collected from each firm listing solicited and obtained by Salesperson. In consideration therefore Salesperson agrees to and does hereby contribute all right and title to such listings to the Broker for the benefit and use of Broker. Salesperson and all other Salespeople associated with Broker to whom Broker may give the listing. Salesperson shall have the rights provided in paragraph 13 hereof with respect to listings procured by Salesperson prior to terminations.

12. On completion of work in process, this agreement may be terminated by Salesperson at any time. Except for cause, this agreement may not be terminated by Broker except on 30 days' notice to Salesperson. On the occurrence of any of the following causes, Broker may terminate this agreement:

(a) Election of Broker to sell its entire business, or to cease doing business at the office specified in paragraph 2;
(b) Any breach of this agreement by Salesperson;
(c) Cessation of Salesperson to be licensed;
(d) Failure of Salesperson to comply with any applicable law, or regulation of the Real Estate Commissioner;
(e) The filing by or against Salesperson of any petition under any law for the relief of debtors; and
(f) Conviction of Salesperson of any crime, other than minor traffic offenses.

13. When this agreement has been terminated, Salesperson's regular proportionate share of commission on any sales Salesperson has made that are not closed, shall, upon the closing of such sales, be paid to Salesperson, if collected by Broker, and except in cases of termination for cause Salesperson shall also be entitled to receive the portion of the commissions, received by Broker after termination, allocable to the listing (but not the sale) as set forth in Broker's current commissions schedule, on any listings procured by Salesperson during Salesperson's association with Broker, subject, however, to deductions as provided in paragraph 14.

14. In the event Salesperson leaves and has transactions pending that require further work normally rendered by Salesperson, Broker shall make arrangements with another Salesperson in the organization to perform the required work, and the Salesperson assigned shall be compensated for completing the details of pending transactions and such compensation shall be deducted from the terminated Salesperson's share of the commission.

15. Arbitration—In the event of disagreement or dispute between Salespersons in the office or between Broker and Salesperson arising out of or connected with this agreement which cannot be adjusted by and between the parties involved, the disputed disagreement shall be submitted to the Board of Realtors® of which Broker is a member for arbitration pursuant to the provisions of its Bylaws, said provisions being hereby incorporated by reference, and if the Bylaws of such Board include no provision for arbitration, then arbitration shall be pursuant to the rules of the American Arbitration Association, which rules are by this reference incorporated herein.

16. Salesperson shall not after the termination of this contract use to Salesperson's own advantage, or the advantage of any other person or corporation, any information gained for or from the files or business of Broker.

17. Salesperson agrees to indemnify Broker and hold Broker harmless from all claims, demands and liabilities, including costs and attorney's fees to which Broker is subjected by reason of any action by Salesperson taken or omitted pursuant to this agreement.

18. All notices hereunder shall be in writing. Notices may be delivered personally, or by mail, postage prepaid, to the respective addresses noted below. Either party may designate a new address for purposes of this agreement by notice to the other party. Notices mailed shall be deemed received as of 5:00 P.M. of the second business day following the date of mailing.

19. All prior agreements between the parties are incorporated in this agreement which constitutes the entire contract. Its terms are intended by the parties as a final expression of their agreement with respect to such terms as are included herein and may not be contradicted by evidence of any prior agreement or contemporaneous oral agreement. The parties further intend that this agreement constitutes the complete and exclusive statement of its terms and that no extrinsic evidence whatsoever may be introduced in any judicial or arbitration proceeding, if any, involving this agreement.

This agreement may not be amended, modified, altered or changed in any respect whatsoever except by a further agreement in writing duly executed by the parties hereto.

WITNESS the signature of the parties hereto the day and year first above written. In duplicate.

WITNESS _____

BROKER _____

ADDRESS _____

WITNESS _____

SALESPERSON as INDEPENDENT CONTRACTOR _____

ADDRESS _____

Attach Commission Schedules "Exhibits A and B."

To order, contact—California Association of Realtors®
525 S. Virgil Ave., Los Angeles, California 90020
Copyright© 1966, 1978, 1983, 1984, California Association of Realtors® (Revised 1984)

FORM I-14

Exhibit 1.2

Chapter 2 Quiz

1. A corporation is owned by its:

    (A) Partners
    (B) Creditors
    ✓(C) Stockholders
    (D) Attorneys

2. One of the most important requisites for a successful real estate office is:

    (A) A large advertising budget
    ✓(B) Accessibility and proximity to potential clients and customers
    (C) Hiring an unlimited number of licensees
    (D) Being open seven days a week

3. The simplest type of business entity to form is:

    ✓(A) Rent-a-desk
    (B) Individual proprietorship
    (C) Corporation
    (D) Syndicate

4. Selection of a sales manager may be considered necessary when there are ____ or more sales associates in an office.

    (A) 2
    ✓(B) 8
    (C) 25
    (D) 100

5. The corporate form of business operation:

    (A) Is artificial, invisible, intangible, and exists in the eyes of the law
    (B) Is an entity separate and apart from its stockholders, officers, or directors
    (C) Has the capacity to deal with property independently of its members
    ✓(D) All of the above

6. The profits of a single proprietorship belong to its:

    (A) Partners
    (B) Customers
    ✓(C) Owner
    (D) Shareholders

7. An entity which pays for the right to engage in a specific business and use its trademark and operating plan is a:

    (A) Corporation
    (B) Joint venture
    ✓(C) Franchise
    (D) Rent-a-desk

8. The basic functions of a manager are:

    (A) Identifying, selecting, planning, evaluating
    ✓(B) Planning, organizing, directing, controlling
    (C) Organizing, selecting, establishing, evaluating
    (D) Selecting, preparing, establishing, directing

9. A corporation which has relatively few stockholders and is often closely held is a:

    (A) Partnership
    ✓(B) Thin corporation
    (C) General corporation
    (D) Tax-option corporation

10. Commissioner's Regulation 2726 requires a signed written agreement between the salesperson and the broker if the salesperson is a(n):

    (A) Independent contractor
    (B) Broker associate
    (C) Employee
    ✓(D) Any of the above

Chapter 3
Agency Legislation Compliance, Residential Property

PREVIEW

Agency Legislation Compliance Manual

Sample Office Policies

Practical Analysis of Office Policies—Questions and Answers

How to Comply With Agency Legislation—Summary

New Agency Disclosure Law—Questions and Answers

AGENCY LEGISLATION COMPLIANCE MANUAL

This chapter reproduces major portions of the "Agency Legislation Compliance Manual—An Office Policy Guide for Realtors®," published by California Association of Realtors® Legal Department. Copies of the full text of the manual may be obtained from the California Association of Realtors®, 525 South Virgil Avenue, Los Angeles, CA, 90020, or from any local board of Realtors®.

A thorough understanding of agency is critical to success in the real estate industry. Therefore, it is important to be knowledgeable about the practical as well as the legal implications of the agency disclosure legislation.

This law, effective January 1, 1988, enacted Civil Code §§ 2373-2382 and regulates the disclosure of agency relationships in certain real estate transactions. The purpose of this manual is to provide assistance to Realtors® in implementing the agency disclosure legislation within the letter and spirit of the law. This manual is in three sections:

Section I, Sample Office Policies, contains suggested language for office policies from the perspective of both a listing and selling office. These sample office policies represent four approaches that appear to be the most common and practical. They do not, of course, include every possible office policy. Brokerage companies finding that none of the sample office policies on agency fits its needs should work with its own attorney to draft a suitable policy. The C.A.R. Legal Department does not recommend or endorse one policy or another. Each has its own pros and cons, which have been highlighted in Section II, Practical Analysis of Office Policies. (See Questions and Answers 8-10)

Section II, Practical Analysis of Office Policies, has questions and answers concerning the practical implementation of the agency disclosure law, such as use of the statutorily prescribed disclosure and confirmation forms.

Section III, Appendix, contains supplementary information on the agency disclosure law.

A comprehensive explanation of the details of the agency disclosure law from a legal perspective is contained in a Question and Answer memorandum titled "New Agency Disclosure Law." Where appropriate, reference is made in this manual to the "New Agency Disclosure Law" Questions and Answers.

By way of brief overview, the agency disclosure legislation is basically a series of laws requiring real estate licensees involved in certain real property transactions to take the following three steps with principals:

Step One DISCLOSE on a statutorily prescribed "Disclosure Regarding Real Estate Agency Relationships" form the types of agency relationships that can exist in a given transaction. (See also "New Agency Disclosure Law" Questions and Answers 20-31);

Step Two ELECT an agency relationship (i.e. single agency, representing buyers exclusively or sellers exclusively, or dual agency, representing both buyers and sellers in the same transaction). (See also "New Agency Disclosure Law" Questions and Answers 32-40); and

Step Three CONFIRM in writing the agency relationship elected using the statutorily prescribed language. (See also "New Agency Disclosure Law" Questions and Answers 32-40)

Under the agency disclosure law, an agent can participate in a given real estate transaction as a single agent or a dual agent. A single agent represents either a buyer exclusively or a seller exclusively, but not both; a dual agent represents both a buyer and seller in the same transaction. (See also "New Agency Disclosure Law," Question and Answer 4.)

There are some definitions of other key terms in the agency disclosure legislation which differ from the meaning of the same words in other contexts. For purposes of the agency disclosure law and this manual, the following definitions apply:

Agent—employing broker. See also "New Agency Disclosure Law" Question and answer 14.)

Associate Licensee—a salesperson or broker who has "hung his/her license" under an employing broker. (See also "New Agency Disclosure Law" Question and Answer 15.)

Buyer—a transferee in a real property transaction who seeks the services of an agent in more than a casual, transitory, or preliminary manner, with the object of entering into a real property transaction, including a vendee or lessee.

Real Property—property improved with one to four dwelling units, any leasehold in this type of property exceeding one year's duration, and mobilehomes, when offered for sale or sold through an agent. (See also "New Agency Disclosure Law" Questions and Answers 8-11.)

Sale—a transaction for the transfer of real property from a seller to a buyer, including a sale, exchange, real property sales contract and leasehold exceeding one year's duration. (See also "New Agency Disclosure Law" Question and Answer 12.)

For purposes of this manual, an "in-house" sale includes a sale in which one brokerage company is both the listing and selling agent. This is true even if different associate licensees in the agent's brokerage company work with the buyer and seller, and even if the different associate licensees work out of different branch offices of the agent's brokerage company. (See also "New Agency Disclosure Law" Question and Answer 45.)

OFFICE POLICY A

Seller's Agency Exclusively Whether Listing or Selling

Listing

Policy

1. (Agent's Company Name) represents the seller exclusively when we are the listing agent but not the selling agent.

2. (Agent's Company Name) represents the seller exclusively and not the buyer when we are both the listing and selling agent.

3. (Agent's Company Name) will cooperate and split commissions with a selling agent from any other brokerage company that either (a) accepts the subagency offered through the MLS and represents the seller exclusively, or (b) rejects the subagency offered through the MLS and represents the buyer exclusively. Offers from any other brokerage company requesting dual agency must be referred to the office manager.

Implementation

1. Give the agency disclosure from (C.A.R. Standard Form AD-11) to the seller at an appropriate time prior to the seller's signing of a listing. Get a signed acknowledgement of receipt for the form. [STEP ONE: DISCLOSE]

2. Inform the seller of our policy to represent the seller exclusively on the sale of an in-house listing. [STEP TWO: ELECT]

3. Point out to the seller that other brokerage companies may represent the buyer or seller. Any such relationship will be confirmed in writing no later than the signing of a deposit receipt.

4. If an offer properly confirms that we represent the seller exclusively as the listing agent, then nothing further is required. If the agency confirmation clause does not appear in an offer, or if it does appear but has been left blank, then confirm that we represent the seller exclusively in an agency confirmation form (C.A.R. Standard Form AC-6) no later than the signing of the deposit receipt. [STEP THREE: CONFIRM]

5. Make sure the agency relationship elected by the selling brokerage company is confirmed in the deposit receipt or agency confirmation form (C.A.R. Standard Form AC-6) no later than the signing of the deposit receipt.

Selling

Policy

1. (Agent's Company Name) represents the seller exclusively and not the buyer when we are both the listing and selling agent.

2. (Agent's Company Name) will cooperate with any other brokerage company by accepting the sub-agency offered through the MLS and therefore represents the seller exclusively and not the buyer.

Implementation

1. Give the agency disclosure form (C.A.R. Standard Form AD-11) to the buyer at an appropriate time prior to the buyer's signing of an offer. Get a signed acknowledgement of receipt for the form. [STEP ONE: DISCLOSE]

2. Inform the buyer of our policy to represent the seller exclusively on the sale of property we have listed. This policy avoids confusion since the seller has listed with and is already represented by us, and is paying the commission. Mention that although both agents represent the seller exclusively, all agents still have the duties described in the agency disclosure form. [STEP TWO: ELECT]

3. Point out to the buyer that we can show them properties filed with the MLS that are listed with any other brokerage company by becoming an agent of the seller. This means that on MLS properties, we would not have to make separate arrangements for payment of the commission from the listing brokerage company, seller or buyer. Mention that although both agents represent the seller exclusively, all agents still have the duties described in the agency disclosure form.

4. When calling the listing brokerage company prior to preparing an offer, verify that the listing brokerage company represents the seller exclusively and fill in the agency confirmation clause in the offer accordingly. [STEP THREE: CONFIRM]

5. Provide the agency disclosure form (C.A.R. Standard Form AD-11) to the seller prior to presentation of an offer or earlier, if practical. Get a signed acknowledgement of receipt for the form. This step does not need to be repeated for in-house sales. [STEP ONE: DISCLOSE]

6. Confirm in the deposit receipt that we represent the seller exclusively as the selling agent on the sale of property listed by any other brokerage company. [STEP THREE: CONFIRM]

OFFICE POLICY B

Dual Agency for In-House Sales and Single Agency Otherwise

Listing

Policy

1. (Agent's Company Name) represents the seller exclusively when we are the listing agent but not the selling agent.

2. (Agent's Company Name) represents both the buyer and the seller as a dual agent when we are both the listing and selling agent.

3. (Agent's Company Name) will cooperate and split commissions with a selling agent from any other brokerage company that either (a) accepts the subagency offered through the MLS and represents the seller exclusively, or (b) rejects the subagency offered through the MLS and represents the buyer exclusively. Offers from any other brokerage company requesting dual agency must be referred to the office manager.

Implementation

1. Give the agency disclosure form (C.A.R. Standard Form AD-11) to the seller at an appropriate time prior to the seller's signing of a listing. Get a signed acknowledgement of receipt for the form. [STEP ONE: DISCLOSE]

2. Inform the seller of our policy to represent both the buyer and seller as a dual agent on the sale of an in-house listing. [STEP TWO: ELECT]

3. Point out to the seller that other brokerage companies may represent the buyer or seller. Any such relationship will be confirmed in writing no later than the signing of a deposit receipt.

4. If an offer properly confirms our agency relationship as the listing agent, then nothing further is required. If the agency confirmation clause does not appear in an offer, or if it does appear but has been left blank, then confirm our agency relationship exclusively as the listing agent in an agency confirmation form (C.A.R. Standard Form AC-6) no later than the signing of the deposit receipt. [STEP THREE: CONFIRM]

5. Make sure the agency relationship elected by the selling brokerage company is confirmed in the deposit receipt or agency confirmation form (C.A.R. Standard Form AC-6) no later than the signing of the deposit receipt.

Selling

Policy

1. (Agent's Company Name) represents the buyer exclusively when we are the selling agent and not the listing agent.

2. (Agent's Company Name) represents both the buyer and seller as a dual agent when we are both the listing and selling agent.

Implementation

1. Give the agency disclosure form (C.A.R. Standard Form AD-11) to the buyer at an appropriate time prior to the buyer's signing of an offer. Get a signed acknowledgement of receipt for the form. [STEP ONE: DISCLOSE]

2. Inform the buyer of our policy to represent both the buyer and seller as a dual agent on the sale of an in-house listing. [STEP TWO: ELECT]

3. Inform the buyer of our policy to represent the buyer exclusively on the sale of property listed with any other brokerage company. [STEP TWO: ELECT]

4. When showing any other brokerage company's listings, reject the subagency offered through the MLS by informing the listing brokerage company of the rejection at the earliest practical time, preferably before showing the property. Check the MLS to determine whether the listing brokerage company is splitting the commission on the same terms offered to subagents. If not, either make separate arrangements with the buyer by entering into a written commission agreement with him/her (C.A.R. Standard Form CA-11) or make a separate arrangement with the listing broker, preferably in writing, and preferably prior to revealing the identity of the buyer.

5. When calling the listing brokerage company prior to preparing an offer, verify that the listing brokerage company represents the seller exclusively and fill in the agency confirmation clause in the offer accordingly. [STEP THREE: CONFIRM]

6. Provide the agency disclosure form (C.A.R. Standard form AD-11) to the seller prior to presentation of the offer or earlier, if practical. Get a signed acknowledgement of receipt for the form. This step does not need to be repeated for in-house sales. [STEP ONE: DISCLOSE]

7. Confirm in the deposit receipt that we represent the buyer exclusively as the selling agent on the sale of property listed by any other brokerage company. [STEP THREE: CONFIRM]

8. Confirm in the deposit receipt that we represent both the buyer and seller as a dual agent on the sale of an in-house listing. [STEP THREE: CONFIRM]

OFFICE POLICY C

Dual Agency for In-House Sales or as the Selling Agent and Seller's Agency Exclusively When Listing Only

Listing

Policy

1. (Agent's Company Name) represents the seller exclusively when we are the listing agent but not the selling agent.

2. (Agent's Company Name) represents both the buyer and the seller as a dual agent when we are both the listing and selling agent.

3. (Agent's Company Name) will cooperate and split commissions with a selling agent from any other brokerage company that either (a) accepts the subagency offered through the MLS and represents the seller exclusively, or (b) rejects the subagency offered through the MLS and represents the buyer exclusively or (c) accepts the subagency offered through the MLS and also represents the buyer (dual agency).

Implementation

1. Give the agency disclosure form (C.A.R. Standard Form AD-11) to the seller at an appropriate time prior to the seller's signing of a listing. Get a signed acknowledgement of receipt for the form. [STEP ONE: DISCLOSE]

2. Inform the seller of our policy to represent both the buyer and seller as a dual agent on the sale of an in-house listing. [STEP TWO: ELECT]

3. Point out to the seller that other brokerage companies may represent the buyer, seller or both. Any such relationship will be confirmed no later than the signing of a deposit receipt.

4. If an offer properly confirms our agency relationship as the listing agent, then nothing further is required. If the agency confirmation clause does not appear in an offer, or if it does appear but has been left blank, then confirm our agency relationship as the listing agent in an agency confirmation form (C.A.R. Standard Form AC-6) no later than the signing of the deposit receipt. [STEP THREE: CONFIRM]

5. Make sure the agency relationship elected by the selling brokerage company is confirmed in the deposit receipt or agency confirmation form (C.A.R. Standard Form AC-6) no later than the signing of the deposit receipt.

Selling

Policy

1. (Agent's Company Name) represents both the buyer and seller as a dual agent when we are the selling agent on properties listed with any other brokerage company because we accept the offer of subagency offered through the MLS.

2. (Agent's Company Name) represents both the buyer and seller as a dual agent when we are both the listing and selling agent.

Implementation

1. Give the agency disclosure form (C.A.R. Standard Form AD-11) to the buyer at an appropriate time prior to the buyer's signing of an offer. Get a signed acknowledgement of receipt for the form. [STEP ONE: DISCLOSE]

2. Inform the buyer of our policy to represent both the buyer and seller as a dual agent on the sale of property listed by us or any other brokerage company. [STEP TWO: ELECT]

3. Point out to the buyer that we can show them property in the MLS by becoming an agent of the seller. This means that on MLS properties, we would not have to make separate arrangements for payment of the commission from the listing brokerage company, seller or buyer. Inform the buyer that although both brokerage companies represent the seller, we would also represent them as a buyer and would therefore be a dual agent. Mention that all agents still have the duties described in the agency disclosure form. [STEP TWO: ELECT]

4. When calling the listing brokerage company prior to preparing an offer, verify that the listing brokerage company represents the seller exclusively and fill in the agency confirmation clause in the offer accordingly. [STEP THREE: CONFIRM]

5. Provide the agency disclosure form (C.A.R. Standard Form AD-11) to the seller prior to presentation of the offer or earlier, if practical. Get signed acknowledgement of receipt for the form. [STEP ONE: DISCLOSE]

6. Confirm in the deposit receipt that we represent both the buyer and seller as the selling agent. [STEP THREE: CONFIRM]

OFFICE POLICY D

Single Agency Whether Listing or Selling

Listing

Policy

1. (Agent's Company Name) represents the seller exclusively when we are the listing agent but not the selling agent.

2. On the sale of an in-house listing, we will refer a buyer to other brokerage companies if requested by the buyer. If the buyer does not wish to be represented by another brokerage company on the sale of an in-house listing, we represent the seller exclusively and not the buyer.

3. (Agent's Company Name) will cooperate and split commissions with a selling agent from any other brokerage company that either (a) accepts the subagency offered through the MLS and represents the seller exclusively, or (b) rejects the subagency offered through the MLS and represents the buyer exclusively. Offers from any other brokerage company requesting dual agency must be referred to the office manager.

Implementation

1. Give the agency disclosure form (C.A.R. Standard Form AD-11) to the seller at an appropriate time prior to the seller's signing of a listing. Get a signed acknowledgement of receipt for the form. [STEP ONE: DISCLOSE]

2. Inform the seller of our policy to represent the seller exclusively on the sale of an in-house listing. We will refer a buyer to other brokerage companies if requested by the buyer. [STEP TWO: ELECT]

3. Point out to the seller that other brokerage companies may represent the buyer or seller. Any such relationship will be confirmed in writing no later than the signing of a deposit receipt.

4. If an offer properly confirms that we represent the seller exclusively as the listing agent, then nothing further is required. If the agency confirmation clause does not appear in an offer, or if it does appear but has been left blank, then confirm that we represent the seller exclusively as the listing agent in an agency confirmation form (C.A.R. Standard Form AC-6) no later than the signing of the deposit receipt. [STEP THREE: CONFIRM]

5. Make sure the agency relationship elected by the selling office is confirmed in the deposit receipt or agency confirmation form (C.A.R. Standard Form AC-6) no later than the signing of the deposit receipt.

Selling

Policy

1. (Agent's Company Name) represents the buyer exclusively when we are the selling agent but not the listing agent.

2. (Agent's Company Name) will not represent a buyer in a sale of property we have listed.

3. On the sale of an in-house listing, we will refer a buyer to other brokerage companies if requested by the buyer. If the buyer does not wish to be represented by another brokerage company on the sale of an in-house listing, we represent the seller exclusively and not the buyer.

Implementation

1. Give the agency disclosure form (C.A.R. Standard Form AD-11) to the buyer at an appropriate time prior to the buyer's signing of an offer. Get a signed acknowledgement of receipt for the form. [STEP ONE: DISCLOSE]

2. Inform the buyer of our policy to represent the seller exclusively on the sale of an in-house listing. We will refer the buyer to other brokerage companies if requested by the buyer. If the buyer decides not to work with another brokerage company in order to purchase one of our listings, mention to the buyer that we will still represent the seller only. [STEP TWO: ELECT]

3. Inform the buyer of our policy to represent the buyer exclusively on the sale of property listed with any other brokerage company.

4. When showing any other brokerage company's listings, reject the subagency offered through the MLS by informing the listing brokerage company of the rejection at the earliest practical time, preferably before showing the property. Check the MLS to determine whether the listing brokerage company is splitting the commission on the same terms offered to subagents. If not, either make separate arrangements with the buyer by entering into a written commission agreement with him/her (C.A.R. Standard Form CA-11) or make a separate arrangement with the listing broker, preferably in writing, and preferably prior to revealing the identity of the buyer.

5. When calling the listing brokerage company prior to preparing an offer, verify that the listing brokerage company represents the seller exclusively and fill in the agency confirmation clause in the offer accordingly. [STEP THREE: CONFIRM]

Selling (Cont.)

6. Provide the agency disclosure form (C.A.R. Standard Form AD-11) to the seller no later than the presentation of the buyer's offer or earlier, if practical. Get a signed acknowledgement of receipt for the form. [STEP ONE: DISCLOSE]

7. Confirm in the deposit receipt that we represent the buyer exclusively as the selling agent on the sale of property listed with any other brokerage company. [STEP THREE: CONFIRM]

8. If a buyer decides to work with another brokerage company in order to purchase one of our listings, we will not represent the buyer as an agent in that transaction.

9. Confirm in the deposit receipt that we represent the seller as the selling agent on the sale of an in-house listing. [STEP THREE: CONFIRM]

SECTION II—PRACTICAL ANALYSIS OF OFFICE POLICIES

Establishing and Implementing an Office Policy on Agency

Question 1:
Is it important for an agent to develop an office policy on agency?

Answer:
Yes. An office policy on agency will assist the agent and associate licensees in a brokerage company to consistently comply with the agency disclosure law.

Since an agency relationship can only be created between an agent, defined in the agency disclosure law as the employing broker, and principal, the agent (employing broker) should determine as a matter of office policy which type of agency relationship to create with a principal. Although an associate licensee has direct contact with a prospective buyer or seller, it is *only* through the employing broker that an agency relationship is created.

In addition, an associate licensee's work with an actual or prospective buyer or seller is ultimately the responsibility of the agent, including disclosure, election and confirmation of the agency relationship between the agent and principal. Therefore, it is appropriate for the agent to establish an office policy on agency to guide associate licensees on how and when to disclose, elect and confirm an agency relationship.

Question 2:
How should an office policy on agency be communicated to the associate licensees of an agent?

Answer:
It is highly recommended that communication of all office policies, including the choice of which type of agency relationship to create with a principal, be communicated with associate licensees through an office policy manual. Associate licensees should be encouraged to discuss questions about any office policies, including agency, with the office manager.

Question 3:
How should an agent's office policy on agency be drafted?

Answer:
There are no guidelines in the agency disclosure law on the language to use in an office policy on agency. The sample office policies on agency in Section I of this manual were drafted to help guide agents in the development of a comprehensive approach to implementing the agency disclosure legislation. These sample policies do not, of course, cover every possible policy but merely those most commonly selected.

Question 4:
What choices of office agency policies does an agent have?

Answer:
A *selling agent* can choose to be a single agent, representing a buyer exclusively or seller exclusively, or a dual agent, representing both a buyer and seller in a specific transaction. A *listing agent* can choose to be a single agent, representing a seller exclusively, or a dual agent, representing both a buyer and seller in a specific transaction.

The *only choice an agent can never make is to be a buyer's agent exclusively when the agent is also the listing agent.* This is because a listing creates an agency relationship with a seller, eliminating the possibility of representing a buyer exclusively on the sale of that listing.

Question 5:
Can an office policy allow different agency elections depending on whether the agent is listing or selling property?

Answer:
Yes. For example, an agent can elect dual agency on an in-house sale and buyer's agency exclusively when selling property listed by any other real estate brokerage company. (See sample "Office Policy B") An agent can also choose to enter into only one type of

agency relationship for all transactions. For example, an agent can elect to always be a seller's agent exclusively, whether participating in a transaction as a listing or selling agent. (See sample "Office Policy A")

Once an office policy on agency is adopted, it should be followed consistently.

Question 6:
Under the agency disclosure law, who does a selling agent represent when selling a FSBO (For Sale by Owner)?

Answer:
The selling agent can represent the buyer, seller or both. The selling agent can become the buyer's agent by an express agreement between them, verbal or written. In addition, the agent's words or actions can reasonably lead the buyer to believe that he/she is being represented by the agent, thus creating an implied agency with the buyer. (See "New Agency Disclosure Law" Question and Answer 2.)

The selling agent can become the seller's agent if the seller gives the selling agent a listing. Even without a listing, a selling agent can still become the seller's agent unintentionally by the agent's words or actions. Of course, an agent can be informed by the seller that he/she does not wish to have representation by an agent, and the agent would have to honor the seller's position.

The selling agent can represent both the buyer and seller, thus becoming a dual agent, provided each principal consents to the dual agency.

It should be noted that the payment of compensation, whether by the buyer or seller, is not determinative of an agency relationship, but is merely one factor. (See "New Agency Disclosure Law" Question and Answer 41.)

Question 7:
What type of agency relationship is best?

Answer:
Agents differ on which agency relationships they prefer. One of the most important benefits of the agency disclosure legislation is that it preserves the agent's right to choose the agency relationship that best suits the agent's business. It should be noted, however, that the agency relationship with the most risk of liability is dual agency. (See Questions and Answers 8-10; see also "New Agency Disclosure Law" Question and Answer 42.)

It is highly recommended that agents take a preventive law approach to the agency disclosure law by *deciding* how to do business and *disclosing* that choice to buyers and sellers in all real estate transactions. This can be done by adopting an office policy on agency. (See Section I, Sample Office Policies)

Question 8:
What are some of the pros and cons of electing seller's agency exclusively?

Answer:

Seller's Agency Exclusively	
Pros	**Cons**
+ The seller may prefer to work only with an agent who will represent him/her exclusively. + The listing agent will have fiduciary duties to only one principal, the seller, rather than two principals, the buyer and the seller, who may have conflicting interests. + The selling agent cooperating on a listing through the MLS can collect the selling commission as the subagent of the listing agent through the MLS.	− If the buyer is found by an associate licensee of the listing agent, the buyer may choose to go to another real estate brokerage company that will represent him/her exclusively. − The listing or selling agent may inadvertently, through his/her words or actions, create an agency relationship with the buyer, thus becoming an undisclosed dual agent.

Question 9:
What are some of the pros and cons of electing buyer's agency exclusively?

Answer:

Buyer's Agency Exclusively	
Pros	**Cons**
+ The buyer may prefer to work only with an agent who will represent him/her exclusively. + The selling agent will have fiduciary duties to only one principal, the buyer, rather than two principals, the buyer and seller, who may have conflicting interests. + The listing agent may prefer to work with a buyer's agent exclusively, rather than subagents or dual agents, thereby avoiding possible liability for the acts or representations of subagents.	− An agent representing a buyer exclusively cannot sell his/her own listing to the buyer since, by definition, a listing creates an agency relationship with the seller. − The listing agent may be unwilling to split commissions with an agent representing a buyer exclusively. − The selling agent may inadvertently, through his/her words or actions, create an agency relationship with the seller or improperly reject a listing agent's offer of subagency, thereby becoming an undisclosed dual agent.

Question 10:
What are the pros and cons of electing dual agency?

Answer:

Dual Agency	
Pros	**Cons**
+ On the sale of an in-house listing, the "chilling effect" on a buyer of a listing agent representing the seller exclusively may be prevented. + The selling agent may still be able to collect commissions as the subagent of the listing agent through the MLS.	− There is a greater risk of agent liability when fiduciary duties are owed to different principals who may have conflicting interests. − The buyer may choose to go to an agent to represent him/her exclusively. − The seller may choose to go to an agent to represent him/her exclusively. − The seller may refuse to allow agents cooperating through the MLS to participate in a transaction other than as a seller's agent exclusively. − Consent from all parties to act as a dual agent may be cumbersome and difficult to obtain, especially for property not sold in-house.

Question 11:
Is it possible to create an office policy on agency that reduces the "cons" on Questions and Answers 8-10?

Answer:
Yes. Although no office will be risk free or perfect for all agents, the sample "Office Policies" in Section I of this manual were designed to meet the requirements of the agency disclosure law without disrupting the usual course of business.

Question 12:
Should a listing agent act as a dual agent on the sale of its listing by another brokerage company?

Answer:
Although this election is not prohibited in the agency disclosure legislation, it is unwise. The main reason a listing agent would generally consider acting as a dual agent on the sale of its listing by another brokerage company would be to "get the confirmation out of the way" so that it is taken care of whether the property is sold in-house or by another brokerage company. A number of legal and practical problems result from this situation.

First, it is a violation of the real estate law for an agent to act for both the buyer and seller without the knowledge or consent of all parties, and it may be cumbersome and difficult for a listing agent to obtain consent from both the buyer and seller to act as a dual agent on other than in-house sales. A buyer working with another brokerage company may not want to be represented by the listing agent who is also representing the seller.

Second, the agency disclosure legislation does not contemplate this situation at all and thus is silent on how and when a listing agent would disclose, elect and confirm its dual agency relationship with a buyer brought in by another brokerage company.

Third, other brokerage companies will probably assume that the listing agent represents the seller exclusively and complete the agency confirmation clause in the buyer's offer accordingly. This may unnecessarily require the seller to counter an otherwise acceptable offer.

Fourth, by acting as a dual agent, a listing agent is exposed to increased liability by virtue of owing fiduciary duties to different principals who may have conflicting interests.

In short, it is recommended that a listing agent *not* act as a dual agent on the sale of its listing by another brokerage company.

Question 13:
Why do the sample office policies specify that the listing agent will split the commission with other brokerage companies representing either buyers or sellers?

Answer:
This approach helps avoid conflicts with other brokerage companies with different agency policies. Not only will the listing agent's flexibility reduce unnecessary counter offers based solely on agency, but it will eliminate the need for cumbersome separate commission arrangements.

Question 14:
Once established, can an office policy on agency be changed?

Answer:
Yes. An agent is free to change his/her office policy on agency.

Question 15:
When can an associate licensee deviate from his/her agent's office policy on agency?

Answer:
Any time an associate licensee wants to deviate from an established office policy on agency, it is strongly recommended that prior permission be obtained from the office manager.

Question 16:
Can an agent representing a seller exclusively assist a buyer in a transaction without becoming the buyer's agent?

Answer:
Yes. An agent acting as a seller's agent exclusively can provide valuable assistance to a buyer without becoming the buyer's agent. As stated on the Disclosure Regarding Real Estate Agency Relationships form (C.A.R. Standard Form AD-11), an agent representing only the seller has the following affirmative obligations to *both* the buyer and seller:

(a) Diligent exercise of reasonable skill and care in performance of the agent's duties.

(b) A duty of honest and fair dealing and good faith.

(c) A duty to disclose all facts known to the agent materially affecting the value or desirability of property that are not known to, or within the diligent attention and observation of, the parties.

It is important that the agent's words or actions do not reasonably lead the buyer to believe that he/she is being represented by the seller's agent, thereby creating an agency relationship with the buyer by implication. This situation could commonly arise when a property is sold in-house by the listing office or when a cooperating broker through an MLS elects to be a seller's agent exclusively. (See also "New Agency Disclosure Law" Questions and Answers 2-3.)

Agency Disclosure and Confirmation Forms

Question: 17
Are all preprinted forms for disclosure and confirmation of agency relationships alike?

Answer
Yes. The agency disclosure legislation specifies the precise language for both the "Disclosure Regarding Real Estate Agency Relationships" (C.A.R. Standard form AD-11) and Agency Confirmation (C.A.R.'s "Confirmation of Agency Relationships" Standard Form AC-6). Therefore, the forms used should always look exactly like the C.A.R. Standard Forms. (See also "New Agency Disclosure Law" Questions and Answers 20 and 39.)

Question 18:
Can the disclosure or confirmation forms be modified?

Answer:
No. The agency disclosure legislation requires that all forms use only the statutory language, word for word. Forms which have been modified, even slightly, do not technically comply with the requirements of the agency disclosure law. (See also "New Agency Disclosure Law" Question and Answer 20.)

Question 19:
How should the blanks on the Disclosure Regarding Real Estate Agency Relationships for be filled in?

Answer:
The Disclosure Regarding Real Estate Agency Relationships form requests that the name of the recipient (Buyer/Seller) be filled in along with the date and time (including identification of AM/PM) of receipt. It also requests the name of the agent (employing broker) and the associate licensee's signature (broker or salesperson hanging his/her license under the employing broker). The buyer/seller should acknowledge receipt of the form by signing it.

Question 20:
How should the blanks on the agency confirmation form be filled in?

Answer:
The agency confirmation form requests the name of the listing agent (employing broker with the listing) and the selling agent (employing broker who finds a buyer). Additionally, the appropriate space should be marked to indicate whether the agent is representing the buyer exclusively, seller exclusively or both the buyer and seller. The buyer/seller should acknowledge receipt of the form by signing it. If the deposit receipt includes a completed agency confirmation clause, that clause need not be separately signed.

Question 21:
Does the agency disclosure law require that an agency relationship be confirmed on a separate agency confirmation form?

Answer:
No. An agency relationship can be confirmed *either* in an agency confirmation form (C.A.R. Standard Form AC-6) or in a deposit receipt which includes the statutorily prescribed agency confirmation language, such as the C.A.R. Real Estate Purchase Contract and Receipt for Deposit (C.A.R. Standard Form DLF-14)

The back of the form for Disclosure Regarding Real Estate Agency Relationships (C.A.R. Standard Form AD-11) should *not* be used to confirm an agency relationship. Although the back of the disclosure form reprints the agency disclosure law, including the mandatory confirmation language, there is no space provided for the required acknowledgements.

Question 22:
Can a buyer and seller sign separate copies of the agency confirmation form?

Answer:
Yes. The law does not require that one agency confirmation form be used by all agents in a single transaction. However, all agents can confirm their agency relationships in one place by using a deposit receipt with the required agency confirmation language.

Question 23:

Which agent prepares an agency confirmation form for the buyer?

Answer:
The selling agent should prepare the agency confirmation form for the buyer. This can be done by the selling agent (employing broker) or an associate licensee of the selling agent by completion of the agency confirmation clause in the body of a deposit receipt or in an agency confirmation form (C.A.R. Standard Form AC-6), which both the buyer and seller must sign.

Question 24:

Which agent prepares an agency confirmation form for the seller?

Answer:
It depends. It is highly recommended that a selling agent (employing broker) prepare an agency confirmation by calling the listing office prior to preparing an offer to verify the listing agent's relationship with the seller. In most cases, the listing agent will represent the seller exclusively.

If the agency confirmation language does not appear in the offer, or if it does appear but has been left blank, the listing agent (employing broker) or an associate licensee of the listing agent must confirm the agency relationship with the seller in an agency confirmation form (C.A.R. Standard Form AC-6) no later than the signing of the deposit receipt. If the listing agent represents the seller exclusively, this form needs to be signed only by the listing agent or associate licensee preparing the form and the seller; and a copy of it need *not* be given to the selling agent or buyer.

Question 25:

What should be done if a selling agent *incorrectly* completes the listing agent's portion of the agency confirmation clause?

Answer:
If the agency confirmation in *incorrect*, the listing agent can assist the seller in making the necessary changes as part of a counter offer to the buyer.

Question 26:

Does a change or correction in only the agency confirmation clause on an offer constitute a counteroffer?

Answer:
Yes. Since the agency confirmation clause in the body of an offer is a term of the agreement, just like price or length of escrow, modification of the clause will generally result in a counteroffer.

Question 27:

What should be done if a seller refuses to accept an offer solely because the agency confirmation provides that the selling agent will be a buyer's agent exclusively or a dual agent?

Answer:
A seller can refuse to accept an offer based on the agency selected by the selling agent. If this occurs, the seller may wish to counter the buyer's offer, specifying the agency relationship the seller would find acceptable, and the buyer and the selling agent can modify their agency relationship accordingly. (See "New Agency Disclosure Law" Question and Answer 40.) Otherwise, this is a term of an offer which must be negotiated.

Even though the seller can specify which agency relationship he/she would find acceptable between the buyer and selling agent, the seller *cannot create* that relationship between the buyer and selling agent.

Question 28:

Should an agent obtain multiple agency confirmation forms from a buyer or seller, one of which confirms single agency, representing a buyer exclusively or seller exclusively, and one confirming dual agency?

Answer:
No. The purpose of the agency disclosure law is to be sure that buyers and sellers clearly understand whether or not a particular agent is representing him/her in a specific transaction. Obtaining multiple agency confirmation forms, each of which confirms a different agency relationship with a principal, does not help a principal understand who, if anyone, represents him or her in a given transaction.

Subagency

Question 29:

How is the subagency relationship created?

Answer:
When a listing is filed with a Board of Realtors® Multiple Listing Service (MLS), the listing agent is extending an offer of subagency to all other members of that MLS to find a ready, willing and able buyer on the terms of the listing or other terms acceptable to the seller. When a selling agent accepts the listing agent's offer of subagency, the selling agent becomes an agent of the seller and owes the seller the same fiduciary duties as the listing agent.

Question 30:

Can a selling agent reject a listing agent's offer of subagency through an MLS?

Answer:
Yes. However, California law is unclear on exactly how or when a selling agent has accepted an offer of subagency. Therefore, the earlier subagency is rejected, the more likely the rejection will be successful.

The selling agent should call the listing agent as soon as practical to reject subagency. The selling agent should also check the MLS to determine whether the listing agent is splitting the commission on the same terms offered to subagents. If not, the selling agent should *either* make separate arrangements with the buyer by entering into a written commission agreement with him/her (C.A.R. Standard Form CA-11) *or* make a separate arrangement with the listing broker, preferably in writing, and preferably prior to revealing the identity of the buyer to the listing agent.

Question 31:
How should a selling agent protect his/her commission if payment is to be made directly by a buyer or seller on the sale of unlisted property?

Answer:
A selling agent seeking to collect a commission directly from a buyer or seller on the sale of unlisted property should enter into a commission agreement with that principal (C.A.R. "Commission Agreement" Standard Form CA-11). The "Commission Agreement," when properly filled in, creates a binding commission agreement which can be reconfirmed in the "acceptance" portion of a deposit receipt.

Question 32:
Since the agency disclosure legislation did not become effective until January 1, 1988, how [were] pre-1988 pending listings treated in 1988?

Answer:
. . . it was not required that listing agents give a disclosure form to a seller if the listing was signed before January 1, 1988. The selling agent must still give the disclosure form to a *buyer* prior to his/her signing of an offer *on* or *after* January 1, 1988. The selling agent must also give the disclosure form to the seller . . . prior to the presentation of any offer on or after January 1, 1988. (See "New Agency Disclosure Law" Questions and Answers 20-31.)

In addition, on all covered transactions entered into on or after January 1, 1988, agency confirmations must be completed no later than the signing of the deposit receipt.

Question 33:
Are mortgage brokers covered by the agency disclosure legislation?

Answer:
It depends. The agency disclosure law applies only to *sales* of residential one to four unit property, which are defined as including not only sales, but also exchanges, real property sales contracts (sometimes referred to as installment or land contracts) and leases for longer than one year. Mortgage brokers participating in covered transactions as agents performing services other than brokering loans are required to comply with the agency disclosure legislation just like any other agent.

SECTION III APPENDIX—HOW TO COMPLY WITH AGENCY LEGISLATION

Listing Agents

What?	Who?	When?	How?
Disclose	Provide disclosure to seller*.	Prior to entering into the listing agreement.	Retain signed copy of disclosure form for your file.
Elect	Tell seller whether you are seller's agent or dual agent.	As soon as practicable (ASAP).	Orally or in writing.
Confirm	Confirm with seller whether you are seller's agent or dual agent.	Prior to or coincident with seller's execution of deposit receipt.	In the deposit receipt or another writing by seller and listing agent.

* Listing agent's relationship with the buyer is discussed below.

Agents Selling Their Own Listings

(For an office selling their own listing, *In addition* to the above, the office **must** do the following:)

What?	Who?	When?	How?
Disclose	Provide disclosure form to buyer.	ASAP before buyer executes offer.	Retain signed copy of disclosure form for your file.
Elect	Tell buyer and seller whether you are seller's agent or dual agent.	ASAP.	Orally or in writing.
Confirm	Confirm with buyer and seller whether you are seller's agent or dual agent.	Prior to or coincident with buyer's and seller's execution of the deposit receipt.	In the deposit receipt or another writing by buyer, seller, and listing agent.

Selling Agents

What?	Who?	When?	How?
Disclose	Provide disclosure form to buyer.	ASAP before buyer executes offer (i.e., after more than a casual, transitory, or preliminary inquiry).	Retain signed copy of disclosure form for your file.
	Provide disclosure form to seller.	ASAP before presenting seller with offer.	(1) Obtain signed copy directly from seller or through listing agent. or (2) Provide by certified mail to seller.
Elect	Tell buyer and seller whether you are seller's agent, buyer's agent, or dual agent.	ASAP.	Orally or in writing.
Confirm	Confirm with buyer and seller whether you are seller's agent, buyer's agent, or dual agent.	Prior to or coincident with buyer's and seller's execution of the deposit receipt.	In the deposit receipt or another writing by buyer, seller, and selling agent.

A Quick Refresher on Basic Agency Law

Question 1:

Under existing California law, what is an agent?

Answer:

Since 1872, California Civil Code § 2295 has provided that: "An agent is one who represents another, called the principal, in dealings with third persons. Such representation is called agency." Therefore, a real estate licensee, who acts on behalf of others in selling, buying, exchanging, or leasing real estate, becomes an agent in the legal sense.

Question 2:

How is an agency relationship created?

Answer:

Whether an agency relationship exists is a question of fact. An agency relationship may be created by an express contract or may be implied by the actions of the parties. Thus, formalities are not necessarily required to create an agency relationship.

Question 3:

In general, what duties are owed by agents to their principals?

Answer:

Once an agency relationship is created, it becomes a *fiduciary* relationship. A fiduciary relationship creates the highest duties known under the law owed by the agent to his/her principal. This obligation of diligent and faithful service is the same as that of a trustee. Specific fiduciary duties include loyalty, obedience, disclosure, confidentiality, reasonable care and diligence, and accounting.

Question 4:

What is a dual agent?

Answer:

It has long been established that a real estate licensee may act for *both* buyer and seller in a real estate transaction provided full disclosure has been made to all parties and their consent has been obtained. If the real estate licensee has *not* given full disclosure and obtained consent of the principals involved to act as a dual agent, serious liability and risks occur. Specifically, in this situation the real estate licensee becomes an "undisclosed" dual agent and thus breaches the agent's duty of loyalty to the principal. California law specifically forbids real estate licensees from acting as undisclosed dual agents (Business and Professions Code § 10176(d)) and subjects offenders to disciplinary action. In addition, the principals of an undisclosed dual agent may rescind the purchase and sale agreement even without a showing of actual fraud and injury. The principals may thus legally avoid any obligation under the contract including the payment of commission. Principals also have recourse for any damages suffered as a result of the undisclosed dual agency. One of the main purposes of the new agency legislation is to help consumers and licensees avoid undisclosed dual agency problems. (See Question 5.)

Overview of California's Agency Legislation

Question 5:

What is the need for and purpose of the new agency legislation?

Answer:

The California Legislature enacted the new agency legislation in order to:

- Further the education of consumers on the existence of various types of agency relationships which may occur in residential real property transactions.

- Require disclosure to principals by their agents of the various types of agency relationships which may occur.

- Provide the disclosure in simple, comprehensive and non-technical terms.

- Require uniformity of the disclosure to help consumers understand the various agency relationship options available.

In addition, uniform written disclosures will help real estate licensees avoid undisclosed dual agent status and other unintended or accidental agency relationships. Because written records will be maintained in the real estate licensee's file, potential problems and liabilities should be reduced significantly.

Question 6:

What is the agency legislation?

Answer:

In general, the agency legislation (AB 1034-California Civil Code §§ 2372-2382) is a new law requiring real estate licensees involved in certain real property transactions to provide written disclosures to both the seller and the buyer of the agency relationship options which are available, to secure their agreement to a particular form of agency, and to confirm that agreement in writing.

Question 7:

When did the new agency legislation become effective?

Answer:

The effective date [was] January 1, 1988 . . . .

Question 8:

Does the agency legislation apply to all real property?

Answer:
No. The agency legislation specifically applies to real property improved with one to four dwelling units (including mobilehomes) whether owner occupied or not. However, the methods and forms of disclosure may be used on a voluntary basis in all real property transactions. (See Question 10, 11, 12.)

Question 9:
Would raw land zoned for residential development be subject to the mandatory disclosures?

Answer:
No. The new law applies to "improved" real property.

Question 10:
What is the position of the Commissioner of Real Estate with respect to "mixed use" commercial–industrial properties?

Answer:
In a recent letter to the President of the California Association of Realtors®, the Commissioner of Real Estate stated:

1. "Existing law requiring disclosure of a 'dual agency' relationship remains unchanged.

2. The Department of Real Estate will work with organized real estate and the major real estate licensee firms in an attempt to obtain their support and cooperation in requiring that the disclosure requirements of AB 1034 for one to four family residential dwellings would also be utilized by their respective real estate salespersons when listing and selling those 'mixed use' commercial and industrial properties, which I refer to as 'mom and pop' investment properties, which are not covered by the provisions of AB 1034. It is my understanding that the disclosure requirements of this bill will be applicable to 'mixed use' properties containing one to four residential units. I believe the 'mixed use' area can create the most difficulty with respect to lack of disclosure of agency relationships to the unsophisticated sellers/buyers oftentimes involved in these transactions."

Question 11:
Does this mean that commercial/industrial transactions and business opportunities are exempt?

Answer:
In some respects, yes. However, this only means that licensees involved in transactions of property other than one to four dwelling units do not need to use the specific method of disclosure required by the new law. All of the other statutes and case law regarding disclosure of agency and dual agency are still in effect and would apply to commercial/industrial transactions as well. The Commissioner of Real Estate, in his letter referenced in Question 10 above, also stated that "The Department of Real Estate does intend to enforce the existing law requiring disclosure of a dual agency

representation. The Department's enforcement efforts will apply to all sophisticated commercial and industrial transactions, as well as the so-called 'mixed use'." It is good preventive practice for those licensees dealing with properties other than one to four dwelling units to use either the type of disclosure mandated by the new law or comparable disclosures to avoid problems under the other existing laws governing disclosure of agency relationships.

Question 12:
Does the agency legislation apply to all types of real property transactions?

Answer:
No. The agency legislation specifically applies to "sales" transactions when the property (1-4 dwelling units) is offered or sold through a real estate licensee. In addition to typical deposit receipt transactions, this would also include transactions using a real property sales contract (installment land sale contract) as well as *leasing* of such property for *more than one year.*

Question 13:
Must both the buyer and seller have their own agent in every real property transaction?

Answer:
No, not necessarily. It is not uncommon in a real property transaction for the agent, or even more than one agent in the transaction, to represent only one party to the transaction (most commonly, the seller). The new law does not compel any particular agency relationship, nor compel agency at all.

Definitions Under the Agency Legislation
Question 14:
How is an "agent" defined in the new law?

Answer:
For purposes of the new law, an "agent" includes one with a real estate broker's license *and* ". . . under whose license a listing is executed or an offer to purchase is obtained." (Civil Code § 2373(a)) So "agent" is synonymous with the employing broker.

Question 15:
Are salespersons covered by the new agency legislation?

Answer:
Yes. The new law uses the term "associate licensee" to refer to ". . . a person who is licensed as a real estate broker or salesperson . . . *and* who is either licensed under a broker or has entered into a written contract with the broker to act as the broker's agent . . . and to function under the broker's supervision in the capacity of an associated licensee." (Civil Code § 2373(b)) This means that the term "associate licensee" is synonymous with all salespersons and any broker associates who have "hung their license" under an employing broker.

Question 16:

Under the new agency legislation, is there any difference between the duties owed by "agents" and "associate licensees" to principals or third parties?

Answer:

No. The employing broker is ultimately responsible for the actions of his or her salespersons and broker associates who act on his/her behalf. ". . . When an associate licensee owes a duty to a principal, or to any buyer or seller who is not a principal, in a real property transaction, that duty is equivalent to the duty owed to that party by the broker for whom the associate licensee functions." (Civil Code § 2373 (b))

Question 17:

How is a "listing agent" defined in the new law?

Answer:

The listing agent is a person who has obtained a listing of real property to act as an agent for compensation to sell the property or find or obtain a buyer.

Question 18:

How is a "selling agent" defined in the new law?

Answer:

The "selling agent" means either: (1) a listing agent who acts alone (i.e., a listing agent selling his or her own listing); or (2) an agent who acts in cooperation with a listing agent, and who sells or finds and obtains a buyer for the real property; or (3) an agent who locates property for a buyer for which no listing exists and presents an offer to purchase to the seller. Basically, the selling agent is the person who works with the buyer.

Question 19:

What are the steps necessary for compliance with the new agency legislation?

Answer:

The new law requires three steps. The first step (DISCLOSURE) is a mandatory disclosure form given to every buyer and seller which explains the agent's responsibilities to buyers and sellers. The second step (ELECTION) is the selection of the agency relationship in the particular transaction. The third step (CONFIRMATION) is the mandatory confirmation of this selection in writing.

Mandatory Disclosure Form: Step One

Question 20:

How do I comply with the first step of giving the mandatory disclosure form to buyers and seller?

Answer:

The disclosure form, mandated by law, must be given to every buyer and seller in applicable transactions by real estate licensees. This form basically describes the agency relationship alternatives available and the agent's duties to the respective parties under each alternative. The licensee must obtain a signed acknowledgement from the buyer and seller that they have received a copy of this disclosure. NOTE: The new law requires the entire text of the statute be printed on the backside of the disclosure form. C.A.R. form AD-11 complies with this "step one" requirement.

Question 21:

What if the seller or buyer refuses to sign an acknowledgement for receipt of the form?

Answer:

The statute provides that "In any circumstances in which the seller or buyer refuses to sign an acknowledgement of receipt . . . the agent, or an associate licensee acting for an agent, shall set forth, sign, and date a written declaration of the facts of the refusal." (civil code § 2374.5)

Question 22:

When is this "step one" disclosure form given?

Answer:

It depends on whether the licensee is a listing or selling agent and whether it is being given to the buyer or the seller. Detailed answers are set forth in Questions 23 through 31.

Question 23:

When does the listing agent provide this "step one" disclosure form to the seller?

Answer:

The listing agent must provide the disclosure to the seller *prior* to entering into a listing agreement.

Question 24:

When does the selling agent provide the "step one" disclosure form to the seller?

Answer:

The selling agent must give the disclosure form to the seller as soon as practicable *prior* to presenting the seller with an offer. In other words, *both* the listing agent *and* selling agent must provide the seller with separate disclosure forms. See Question 23.

Question 25:

Must two "step one" disclosure forms be given to the seller if the selling agent is also the listing agent?

Answer:

No. If the selling agent is also the listing agent ("in-house" sale), then only one disclosure form for the seller is necessary even though more than one associate licensee from the same office is involved (i.e., the one provided to the seller prior to the listing being signed). See Questions 23 and 28.

Question 26:
How does the selling agent go about providing the seller with the "step one" disclosure form?

Answer:
Depending on the given circumstances, there are several methods to satisfy this requirement:

1) If the selling agent is able to deal on a face-to-face basis with the seller, then the selling agent should hand the disclosure form to the seller, and obtain the acknowledgement of receipt ". . . *prior* to presenting the seller with an offer to purchase . . ."

2) If the selling agent is *not* able to " . . . deal on a face-to-face basis with the seller, the disclosure form prepared by the selling agent may be furnished to the seller . . ." through:

   a) the listing agent who is then required to deliver it to the seller and obtain the acknowledgement of receipt for the selling agent from the seller; *or,*

   b) ". . . by certified mail addressed to the seller at his or her last known address, in which case no *signed acknowledgment of receipt is required.*" (Civil Code § 2374(b)&(c)).

Question 27:
Is a listing agent required to furnish a "step one" disclosure form to a buyer?

Answer:
No, *UNLESS* the listing agent is also the selling agent in an "in-house" sale situation. In that event, the combined listing agent/selling agent is required to provide the buyer with the disclosure form. See Question 28 and Questions 43 through 46.

Question 28:
When does the selling agent give the "step one" disclosure form to prospective buyers?

Answer:
"The selling agent shall provide the disclosure form to the buyer as soon as practicable prior to execution of the buyer's offer to purchase . . ." (Civil Code § 2374(d)). See Questions 29 and 30.

Question 29:
What if the selling agent does not prepare ("write") the buyer's offer, such as when the buyer or the buyer's attorney prepares the offer?

Answer:
". . . If the offer to purchase is not prepared by the selling agent, the selling agent shall present the disclosure form to the buyer not later than the next business day after the selling agent receives the offer to purchase from the buyer." (Civil Code § 2374(d)).

Question 30:
What does the statute mean about providing the "step one" disclosure form . . . "as soon as practicable prior to execution of the buyer's offer to purchase . . ."?

Answer:
The statute specifically tells you the *latest* time at which the "step one" disclosure form *must* be provided, but does not specifically state *how soon* it must be provided to the buyer. The statute gives some general guidance in its definition of a "buyer" as one " . . . who seeks the services of an agent in more than a casual, transitory, or preliminary manner, with the object of entering into a real property transaction . . ." (Civil Code § 2373(c)). Therefore, it would appear that casual visitors to an open house, for example, would not be "buyers" within the meaning of the statute. It is recommended that the "step one" disclosure form be provided by selling agents at the point in time when the selling agent determines he or she is working with a serious buyer.

Question 31:
What must the licensee do with the acknowledged copy of the disclosure forms or with the declaration discussed in Question 21?

Answer:
The Real Estate License Law (Business and Professions Code § 10148) requires the broker to keep for three years copies of all ". . . documents executed by him or obtained by him in connection with any transaction for which a real estate broker license is required."

Election and Written Confirmation of Agency Relationship: Steps Two and Three

Question 32:
After the "step one" mandatory disclosure form is given, how do I proceed to steps two and three?

Answer:
The "step one" mandatory disclosure form is designed to give an explanation of the agency relationship options which are available and a list of the respective duties of licensees to both buyers and sellers. Licensees *still need* to discuss with their clients and customers *which* agency will be used in their particular relationship. The new law requires licensees to make an election ("step two") and written confirmation ("step three") of the agency relationship selected. In other words, buyers and sellers need to know which licensees are seller's agents, which are buyer's agents and which are acting as dual agents for both parties.

Question 33:
When should the election and written confirmation of an agency relationship take place?

Answer:
This depends on whether a licensee is a listing or selling agent and whether or not they are dealing with a seller or a buyer. For detailed answers see Questions 34 through 38.

The Selling Agent's Election and Written Confirmation

Question 34:
When does the selling agent make an election and written confirmation to be the seller's agent, buyer's agent or a dual agent of both parties?

Answer:
The selling agent must *disclose the election* of agency representation *as soon as practicable.* The election *may be oral* but the parties must *confirm* it in writing in either the contract to purchase or a separate writing signed by the seller, buyer and the selling agent prior to or at the time the purchase contract is signed by the buyer and seller. It is recommended that selling agents disclose the election of agency representation to buyers and sellers as soon as possible *after* the "step one" mandatory disclosure form has been presented to the buyer and seller. The earlier the election is made the better. This will help avoid allegations by the buyer or seller that the selling agent *acted* one way but later disclosed, and attempted to confirm, an inconsistent agency status. Employing brokers are advised to adopt an *office policy* of agency representation that can only be varied with the employing broker's written approval. See Question 40.

Question 35:
What are the agency relationship options available for election by the selling agent?

Answer:
The selling agent may elect to act ". . . exclusively as the buyer's agent, exclusively as the seller's agent, or as a dual agent representing both the buyer and the seller . . ." (Civil Code § 2375.5(a)).

Question 36:
How can the selling agent act "exclusively as the seller's agent"?

Answer:
The selling agent may be a subagent of the seller and thus, an agent of the listing agent if the selling agent accepts an offer of that subagency through the Multiple Listing Service or otherwise and confirms it in writing as discussed under Question 34. In addition, if the selling agent and the listing agent are the same (an "in-house" sale), the licensee and the parties may elect that the licensee represent the seller only, instead of acting as a dual agent (the only other available option).

In these situations, the buyer, who is *not* a principal of the selling agent, receives various services from the selling agent which are offered on behalf of, and for the benefit of, the seller, who is *the principal of the selling agent.*

The Listing Agent's Election and Written Confirmation

Question 37:
When does the listing agent make an election and written confirmation of the agency relationship to the seller?

Answer:
The listing agent shall disclose the agency election to the seller "As soon as practicable . . ." and this election ". . . shall be confirmed in the contract to purchase and sell real property or in a separate writing executed or acknowledged by the seller and the listing agent prior to or coincident with execution of the contract by the seller." (Civil Code § 2375.5(b)). It is recommended that as soon as possible *after* the listing agent provides the "step one" mandatory disclosure form to the seller (which must be provided *prior* to entering into the listing agreement) that the listing agent then proceed to disclose the election of agency representation to the seller. Employing brokers are advised to adopt an *office policy* of agency representation for the office's listings that can only be varied with the employing broker's approval and documentation.

Question 38:
What are the agency relationship options available for election by the listing agent?

Answer:
Unlike the selling agent who has three options (See Question 35), the listing agent only has two options. The listing agent may act either ". . . exclusively as the seller's agent or as a dual agent representing both the buyer and the seller . . ." (Civil Code § 2375.5(b)). Since the definition of a listing agent is one who already has an agency relationship with the seller, it is impossible for the listing broker to act exclusively as the buyer's agent. In addition, the new law specifically prohibits a listing agent from acting exclusively as a buyer's agent.

It is crucial to understand that different associate licensees (salespersons) of the *same real estate firm* (whether in different branch offices or the same office) are considered *one entity.* It is not possible for one licensee to act exclusively as the seller's agent and another licensee in the same firm to act exclusively as the buyer's agent. In this situation there are only two agency relationship options legally available—either both associate licensees are acting (through the listing agent) exclusively as the seller's agent or both associate licensees are acting (through the listing agent) as the dual agent of both the buyer and the seller.

Mandatory Confirmation Form For Listing and Selling Agents

Question 39:
Under the new agency law, is there a specific way in which the agency relationship election must be confirmed?

Answer:
Yes. The new law sets forth a mandatory check box format that must be used to confirm in writing the agency relationship selected. This mandatory confirmation language may be ". . . in the contract to purchase and sell real property or in a separate writing . . ." (C.A.R. form AC-6 may be used to comply.) The mandatory format is as follows:

_____ is the agent of (check one):
   (Name of Listing Agent)
[ ] the seller exclusively; or
[ ] both the buyer and seller.

_____ is the agent of (check one):
(Name of Selling Agent if not
the same as the Listing Agent)
[ ] the buyer exclusively; or
[ ] the seller exclusively; or
[ ] both the buyer and seller.
(Civil Code § 2375.5(c)).

(Remember: The name of an associate licensee is not filled in in either of the blanks on the form. See Questions 14 through 18.)

Question 40:
After an agency relationship election has been confirmed, may the agency relationship be changed?

Answer:
Yes. "A contract between the principal and agent may be modified or altered to change the agency relationship at any time *before* the performance of the act which is the object of agency relationship." (Civil Code § 2381).

For example, consider the following typical fact situation:

You are working with a prospective buyer (to whom you have given the "step one" mandatory disclosure form). The buyer decides that he/she wants to make an offer on an MLS property listed with another office. You elect to exclusively represent the buyer and this election is confirmed in writing with your buyer and the prospective seller. After an offer and several counters, negotiations break down and your buyer decides he/she wants to make an offer on one of your "in-house" listings. Since you are already a seller's listing agent, it is *not* possible for you to continue to exclusively represent the buyer regarding that particular property. So you elect to become a dual agent of both the buyer and the seller with their consent. You confirm this *changed* agency relationship in writing with both the buyer and seller.

Other Provisions

Question 41:
If the seller pays the commission, does that mean the licensee represents the seller?

Answer:
Not necessarily. Existing case law is confirmed in the new agency law which states that the ". . . payment of compensation or the obligation to pay compensation to an agent by the seller or buyer is not necessarily determinative of a particular agency relationship between an agent and the seller or buyer. A listing agent and a selling agent may agree to share any compensation or commission paid . . . and the terms of any such agreement shall not necessarily be determinative of a particular relationship." (Civil Code § 2377).

Question 42:
What if I prefer a particular type of agency relationship; does this new law limit my abilities to select the one I prefer?

Answer:
No. The statute specifically provides that an agent may select ". . . as a condition of the agent's employment, a specific form of agency relationship . . ." as long as the proper disclosures are given and it is not specifically prohibited by law. (Civil Code § 2378).

Question 43:
May a licensee sell his/her own listing (an "in-house" listing)?

Answer:
Yes. The law specifically allows an agent to sell his/her own listing ("in-house" listing). However, the agency relationship selected must be disclosed and confirmed in writing; i.e., exclusively representing the seller or a dual agent of both the buyer and the seller. See Questions 37 and 38.

Question 44:
Do I have to be a dual agent if I sell my own listing?

Answer:
No. An agent selling his/her own listing *may* represent the seller only. In this case, it is very important to disclose this election to the buyer as early as possible since the buyer may assume you are his/her agent as well. When agents sell their own listing exclusively as the seller's agent, the buyer is unrepresented. However, the seller's agent still has affirmative obligations to the buyer to diligently exercise reasonable skill and care, provide full disclosure of material facts, and deal honestly, fairly and in good faith. (These obligations are spelled out in the "step one" disclosure form.) See Questions 36, 37, 38, and 43.

Question 45:
Can I change agency relationships by assigning a different salesperson in the same office or a branch office to assist the buyer?

Answer:
No. The "Agent" in a transaction is the *broker* under whose license the salespeople are operating. If an office has a listing, the broker will always be the seller's agent. If different associate licensees work with the seller and buyer, *both* associate licensees still will be the agent of the seller. However, if the broker *also* elects to be the agent of the buyer by becoming a dual agent, then the different associate licensees also will be dual agents of both the buyer and the seller. In either case, it is important to discuss the agency representation arrangement selected with both the buyer and the seller as soon as possible. See Questions 36, 37, 38, 43 and 44.

Question 46:
As a dual agent, am I obligated to tell a buyer that the seller will sell for less than the listing price? Or, conversely, to tell the seller that a buyer will buy for more than the offering price?

Answer:
No. "A dual agent shall not disclose to a buyer that the seller is willing to sell the property at price less than the listing price, without the express written consent of the seller. A dual agent shall not disclose to the seller that a buyer is willing to pay a price greater than the offering price without the express written consent of the buyer.

"This section does not alter in any way the duty or responsibility of a dual agent to any principal with respect to confidential information other than price." (Civil Code § 2379).

Liabilities and Remedies

Question 47:
What are the penalties if I fail to comply with the new agency law?

Answer:
The new agency law does not provide for specific penalties for failing to comply with its provisions. However, the new agency law reminds all licensees that this new law shall not ". . . be construed to either diminish the duty of disclosure owed buyers and sellers by agents and their associate licensees, subagents, and employees or to relieve agents and their associate licensees, subagents, and employees from liability for their conduct in connection with acts governed by this article or for any breach of a fiduciary duty or a duty of disclosure." (Civil Code § 2382). See Question 4.

Question 48:
Could I lose my license for failing to comply with the new agency law?

Answer:
The new agency law does not specifically provide for revocation of a license. However, Business and Professions Code § 10176(d) does provide that the Commissioner may revoke a real estate license if a licensee is guilty of ". . . Acting for more than one party in a transaction without the knowledge or consent of all parties thereto." See Questions 4, 10 and 11.

Agency Education

Question 49:
What are the new educational requirements?

Answer:
Although AB 1034 (the new agency law) does not require a specific type of education for licensees, another law (SB 491 (Montoya)) has been enacted that requires a mandatory three hour educational course as a part of the ongoing required 45 hours of continuing education in order to renew a real estate license. The course must cover ". . . agency relationships and duties in a real estate brokerage practice, including instruction in the disclosures to be made and the confidences to be kept in the various agency relationships between licensees and the parties to real estate transactions." (Business and Professions Code § 10170.5(b)).

DISCLOSURE REGARDING
REAL ESTATE AGENCY RELATIONSHIPS

(As required by the Civil Code)

CALIFORNIA ASSOCIATION OF REALTORS® (CAR) STANDARD FORM

When you enter into a discussion with a real estate agent regarding a real estate transaction, you should from the outset understand what type of agency relationship or representation you wish to have with the agent in the transaction.

SELLER'S AGENT

A Seller's agent under a listing agreement with Seller acts as the agent for the Seller only. A Seller's agent or a subagent of that agent has the following affirmative obligations:

To the Seller:
(a) A Fiduciary duty of utmost care, integrity, honesty, and loyalty in dealings with the Seller.

To the Buyer & the Seller:
(a) Diligent exercise of reasonable skill and care in performance of the agent's duties.
(b) A duty of honest and fair dealing and good faith.
(c) A duty to disclose all facts known to the agent materially affecting the value or desirability of property that are not known to, or within the diligent attention and observation of, the parties.

An agent is not obligated to reveal to either party any confidential information obtained from the other party which does not involve the affirmative duties set forth above.

BUYER'S AGENT

A selling agent can, with a Buyer's consent, agree to act as agent for the Buyer only. In these situations, the agent is not the Seller's agent, even if by agreement the agent may receive compensation for services rendered, either in full or in part from the Seller. An agent acting only for a Buyer has the following affirmative obligations:

To the Buyer:
(a) A fiduciary duty of utmost care, integrity, honesty, and loyalty in dealings with the Buyer.

To the Buyer & Seller:
(a) Diligent exercise of reasonable skill and care in performance of the agent's duties.
(b) A duty of honest and fair dealing and good faith.
(c) A duty to disclose all facts known to the agent materially affecting the value or desirability of the property that are not known to, or within the diligent attention and observation of, the parties.

An agent is not obligated to reveal to either party any confidential information obtained from the other party which does not involve the affirmative duties set forth above.

AGENT REPRESENTING BOTH SELLER & BUYER

A real estate agent, either acting directly or through one or more associate licensees, can legally be the agent of both the Seller and the Buyer in a transaction, but only with the knowledge and consent of both the Seller and the Buyer.

In a dual agency situation, the agent has the following affirmative obligations to both the Seller and the Buyer:
(a) A fiduciary duty of utmost care, integrity, honesty and loyalty in the dealings with either Seller or the Buyer.
(b) Other duties to the Seller and the Buyer as stated above in their respective sections.

In representing both Seller and Buyer, the agent may not, without the express permission of the respective party, disclose to the other party that the Seller will accept a price less than the listing price or that the Buyer will pay a price greater than the price offered.

The above duties of the agent in a real estate transaction do not relieve a Seller or a Buyer from the responsibility to protect their own interests. You should carefully read all agreements to assure that they adequately express your understanding of the transaction. A real estate agent is a person qualified to advise about real estate. If legal or tax advice is desired, consult a competent professional.

Throughout your real property transaction you may receive more than one disclosure form, depending upon the number of agents assisting in the transaction. The law requires each agent with whom you have more than a casual relationship to present you with this disclosure form. You should read its contents each time it is presented to you, considering the relationship between you and the real estate agent in your specific transaction.

This disclosure form includes the provisions of article 2.5 (commencing with Section 2373) of Chapter 2 of Title 9 of Part 4 of Division 3 of the Civil Code set forth on the reverse hereof. Read it carefully.

I/WE ACKNOWLEDGE RECEIPT OF A COPY OF THIS DISCLOSURE.

BUYER/SELLER_____ Date_____ TIME_____ AM/PM

BUYER/SELLER_____ Date_____ TIME_____ AM/PM

AGENT _____ By _____ Date_____
(Please Print)   (Associate Licensee or Broker-Signature)

CONFIRMATION
REAL ESTATE AGENCY RELATIONSHIPS

Subject Property Address_____

The following agency relationship(s) is/are hereby confirmed for this transaction:

LISTING AGENT: _____

is the agent of (check one):
☐ the Seller exclusively; or
☐ both the Buyer and Seller

SELLING AGENT: _____

(if not the same as Listing Agent)
is the agent of (check one):
☐ the Buyer exclusively; or
☐ the Seller exclusively; or
☐ both the Buyer and Seller

I/WE ACKNOWLEDGE RECEIPT OF A COPY OF THIS CONFIRMATION.

Seller_____ Date_____   Buyer_____ Date_____

Seller_____ Date_____   Buyer_____ Date_____

Listing Agent_____ By_____ Date_____
(Please Print)   (Associate Licensee or Broker-Signature)

Selling Agent_____ By_____ Date_____
(Please Print)   (Associate Licensee or Broker-Signature)

A REAL ESTATE BROKER IS QUALIFIED TO ADVISE ON REAL ESTATE. IF YOU DESIRE LEGAL ADVICE, CONSULT YOUR ATTORNEY.

This form is available for use by the entire real estate industry. The use of this form is not intended to identify the user as a REALTOR®. REALTOR® is a registered collective membership mark which may be used only by real estate licensees who are members of the NATIONAL ASSOCIATION OF REALTORS® and who subscribe to its Code of Ethics.

Copyright© 1987, CALIFORNIA ASSOCIATION OF REALTORS®
525 South Virgil Avenue, Los Angeles, California 90020

FORM AD-11/AC-6
(combined)

OFFICE USE ONLY
Reviewed by Broker or Designee _____
Date _____

EQUAL HOUSING
OPPORTUNITY
SF-Nov-88

Exhibit 2

1. An agent is defined by California Civil Code as one who represents another, called the principal, in dealings with:

   (A) Lawyers
   (B) Institutions
   (C) Lenders
   √(D) Third persons

2. An agent owes a *fiduciary* duty to:

   √ (A) The principal only
   (B) The third person only
   √(C) Both the principal and the third person
   (D) All persons he or she deals with

3. The new agency disclosure law requires that an agent in certain real property transactions:

   (A) Disclose the type of agency
   (B) Elect an agency relationship
   (C) Confirm in writing the agency relationship elected
   √(D) All of the above

4. To assist the agent (broker) and associate licensees in consistently complying with the agency disclosure law, a broker should:

   (A) Avoid having an office policy because it would be too limiting
   √(B) Adopt an office policy about agency relationships for that office
   (C) Adopt the state mandated standard office policy
   (D) Require each independent contractor to adopt his/her own agency policy

5. A "listing agent" can choose to be:

   (A) Agent for the seller only
   (B) Dual agent for seller and buyer
   (C) Agent for the buyer only
   √(D) Either (A) or (B)

6. A "selling agent" can choose to be:

   (A) Agent for the seller only
   (B) Agent for the buyer only
   (C) Dual agent for seller and buyer
   √(D) Any of the above

7. Once an office policy on agency has been established:

   √ (A) A broker is free to change his/her policy
   (B) An office policy can be changed only with DRE approval
   √(C) An office policy cannot be changed
   (D) An associate licensee can change the policy to make closing a deal easier

8. A seller's agent owes to a buyer who is not his/her principal:

   (A) Diligent exercise of reasonable care and skill
   (B) A duty of honest and fair dealing
   (C) A duty to disclose all material facts about the property
   √(D) All of the above

9. Placing a listing with a multiple listing service (MLS) is an offer of subagency to all other members of the MLS. A cooperating broker (selling agent) can:

   (A) Accept the offer of subagency
   (B) Reject the offer of subagency
   (C) Ignore the offer of subagency
   √(D) Either (A) or (B)

10. If the seller pays the commission:

    (A) The broker is the seller's agent
    (B) The broker cannot be the buyer's agent
    (C) The broker cannot be a dual agent
    √(D) The payment of commission is not necessarily determinative of the agency relationship

Chapter 4
The Listing Process

LISTING CONTRACTS

A listing agreement is an employment contract by which a principal employs a broker as a "listing agent" to do certain things for the principal for the purpose of attempting to negotiate the sale or purchase of real property. An agent holding a listing is bound by the law of agency to certain obligations to the principal (generally the seller) that do not exist between buyer and seller.

Types of Listings   Listings vary in who is the principal (seller or buyer), who is authorized to find a buyer (open or exclusive), basis for payment of commission, etc.

Open Listing. An open listing (Non-Exclusive Authorization and Right to Sell, Exhibit 3)is a written agreement in which a broker (possibly more than one) is authorized on a nonexclusive basis to attempt to bring about the sale of a property. The owner or some other person may bring about a sale of the property without being liable to the open listing broker for the commission. In essence, the seller maintains maximum flexibility without a commitment to pay a commission. An open listing may or may not contain a termination date.

☐ *Disadvantage to Owner*. There may be a lack of concentrated sales effort by any one licensee or office. A broker holding only an open listing cannot be expected to devote time, effort, and money in marketing the property when the broker has so little chance of even recovering costs. An owner who will give only an open listing cannot expect a good marketing effort.

□ *Disadvantage to Broker*. Money, time, and effort may be wasted if another broker is the procuring cause, or if the owner sells the property himself.

Exclusive Agency Listing. This is a written agreement in which the owner reserves the right to sell the property himself without payment of a commission, but one broker is designated the "listing agent" and will be paid a commission if he *or another broker* brings about a sale. The split of commission between listing and selling broker is determined by the listing broker. A definite termination date is required. (Exhibit 4)

□ *Disadvantage to Owner*. The listing office may expend limited effort because of the uncertainty of commission.

□ *Disadvantage to Broker*. Money, time, and effort may be wasted if the owner makes the sale himself.

Exclusive Authorization and Right to Sell. This is a written agreement in which the listing broker has sole and exclusive right to sell during the stipulated term (Exhibit 5). Regardless of who makes the sale (the owner or any other person, licensed or not) the listing broker is entitled to the commission. A definite termination date is required. This type of listing is most desirable for the broker. "Exclusive right to sell" and "exclusive listing" are other names for this type of listing.

□ *Advantage to Owner*. The listing office can afford to concentrate its efforts on making the sale exclusively or in cooperation with other offices; they know a commission will be paid if the property is sold. These definite terms avoid misunderstandings regarding payment of the commission.

□ *Advantage to Broker*. The broker has the assurance of a commission regardless of who is the procuring cause, with complete protection while sharing the listing with other brokers.

Multiple Listing **A Marketing Technique.** This is a listing affiliated with a Multiple Listing Service (MLS) in which all of the member brokers cooperate and pool their efforts to process and distribute listings to the other members of the MLS. A definite termination date is required for all "exclusive" listings. (Exhibit 6)

□ *Advantage to Owner*. The owner has wide exposure of the listed property with assurance of concentrated effort and avoidance of commission misunderstandings.

□ *Advantage to Broker*. The listing office retains control of the shared listing. Broad exposure of the listing provides assistance for all properties including the "hard-to-sell" types.

Net Listing **A Special Commission Agreement.** The commission is not predetermined. A clause in a net listing contract usually permits the agent to retain as compensation all money received in excess of an amount set by the seller. A definite termination date is required if exclusive.

Dangers. A net listing is perfectly legitimate, but it may lead to a charge of fraud, misrepresentation, or other abuse. Therefore, the Real Estate Law requires that the agent reveal to both buyer and seller, in writing, within 30 days of closing, the exact selling price involved.

Disclosure. Disclosure must be made prior to or at the time the principal is bound to the transaction. The law allows this disclosure by the escrowholder's closing statement. Failure to disclose the amount of the agent's compensation in a net listing sale, as required by law, is cause for revocation or suspension of the license.

Option vs. Listing **Option.** An option is a contract between principals. It is a written agreement whereby the owner of real property agrees to sell the property to an optionee at a fixed price within a certain time. The terms of financing, payments, etc., should also be specified in the agreement.

Combination Listing-Option. Occasionally a broker will use a combination listing-option form. However, caution must be exercised as the broker will then occupy a dual status as an agent and a principal, a direct and absolute conflict of interest. Full disclosure of the broker's expected profit as well as all offers and information regarding the property must be made to the principal (property owner). The Real Estate Law further requires the principal's written approval of the amount of the broker's profit before the option is exercised. The effect of the law is to minimize the use of the combination listing-option.

Buyer's Listing **Exclusive Authorization to Locate Property.** In this type of written agreement, often called the *buyer's listing,* the buyer contracts the broker to locate property. When the broker locates the property and the buyer purchases it, a commission is paid by the buyer. Due diligence must be exercised in this arrangement, and full disclosure must be made to the seller that the broker is representing the buyer. Other commission arrangements may be made between buyer and seller provided the broker has made full disclosure and obtains written approval from the buyer and seller.

Listing Form The listing should be in writing, and standard forms are available. As a general rule, an oral contract (oral listing) is not enforceable in court and is considered poor business practice.

Accurate and Complete Information. Full information regarding the subject property is essential to preparing a listing form and multiple listing service information form. Several CAR standard forms are included as Exhibits 3 through 6.

SOURCES OF LISTINGS

Salable listings are the lifeblood of every profitable, productive real estate office. The sources of listings include but are not limited to the following.

Daily Contact Talk to everyone you meet. Tell them you are in real estate.

Friends. Frequently call on friends, relatives, and acquaintances to inform them you are ready to serve their real estate needs.

"Bird Dogs." People who will refer business to you are valuable assets. They can supply you with leads. Get to know your mechanic, banker, hairdresser, doctor, etc.

Social Groups, Church, Country Club. Whatever organization you belong to, communicate your involvement in real estate.

Business Cards. Leave your card at every appointment or opportunity, e.g., with your tip at a restaurant. It pays to advertise.

Be a Good Neighbor. Get involved in your neighborhood, give a helping hand whenever needed.

Farming The term "farming" is used to describe the systematic prospecting (cultivation) of listings in a specific area of around 300 to 500 homes, following careful selection and thought.

Letters. Send out letters of introduction expressing your desire to serve the real estate needs of the community, and follow up with a personal visit.

Canvassing. Regular and consistent house to house canvassing will develop a rapport with the homeowners and reemphasize your desire to serve their real estate needs.

Reminders. Leave a reminder every time you call on a home, regardless of whether you talk to the homeowner: your business card, pamphlet, announcement, open house invitation, memo pad, newsletter, etc.

Telephone Prospecting The telephone can be a successful tool for obtaining appointments with the homeowner. Appointments can lead to listings.

Practice. Rehearse the main points of your presentation. Use effective phrases. Practice and polish your delivery.

Communicate. Share your enthusiasm.

Persevere. Be persistent. Make a contract with yourself to call a certain number of homeowners per day or week.

Customer Referrals   Your past customers and clients can be a great source of new business and can help in building a clientele.

Keep a File. Maintain a current and ready file of all former buyers and sellers.

Keep in Touch. Periodically contact former clients and customers by phone calls or greeting cards to let them know you're still actively in the real estate business.

Keep Them Happy. A satisfied client or customer is the best advertisement.

For Sale by Owner   "By Owner" ads or signs are the perfect clue to who has a house for sale.
(FSBO)   These ads are an open invitation and challenge to your desire to be of service.

Non-Threatening Approach. Call on the owners. Put them at ease; tell them you are not asking for their listing at this time. Ask to see their home and their asking price because you want to be completely informed about available housing; besides, you may have a customer for their home. Don't antagonize them; they want to do it on their own.

Tentative Inquiry. Ask if they would cooperate if you produced a buyer.

Persist. Try to make friends. Offer to help. Above all be sincere. Make call-backs to check on their success or lack of success.

Floor Time   Learn to respond creatively to any ad call. Remember each incoming call has probably cost your office $10 or more for advertising.

Responding to Calls. Before beginning your floor time, study the current ads, the properties being advertised, and your current listings. Know your products. Be able to respond informatively and politely without "giving away the store." Avoid hesitant, uncertain responses to questions. You must give the callers the favorable impression that you are in business to serve them in an efficient, businesslike manner.

Buyers Are Also Sellers. Many ad callers will probably have to sell their homes before being able to buy others. Offer to pick up the callers at their homes, to save their coming to your office. Ask to visit their home. You can learn a great deal about them and their lifestyle. And you may be able to list their home for sale.

Expired Listings   Listings should be updated periodically because of the rapid general rise in California property values. The overpriced listing of yesterday may be most salable today. Sellers of expired listings may want to update prices, and if their motivation to sell is still strong, they will be receptive to your new marketing ideas.

Local Newspaper   The local newspaper can keep you abreast of what is happening in your area. For example:

Weddings frequently translate into the need for a place to live.

Garage Sale Ads may mean pending house sales.

Births may lead to families looking for larger homes.

For Rent Ads may be the perfect time for owners to sell their investment, or change their investment needs.

Divorces may lead to listings and/or buyers seeking other homes.

Death Notices. Probate sales indicate available property.

Promotions may mean moving up in housing needs.

Business Transfer Notices are an excellent source of salable listings where the seller motivation is high. Relocation services can be a profitable specialization.

Open House   The majority of shoppers are potential buyers and/or sellers. "This house may not be the one for you, but we have others. Will you need to sell your present home?" Every visitor to an open house is a prospect—a potential future customer or client.

RECOGNIZING MARKETABLE LISTINGS

Listings are necessary to the success of your office. They are the lifeblood, the inventory, and the key element in your business. You must keep a steady flow of marketable listings through your office if you are to continue to be successful. They must be in sufficient quantity to assure the realization of sales and income goals.

Marketable Listings   Not every listing is a marketable one. The following standards can help in deciding if a listing is worth your effort.

Seller's Expectations. Is the listing priced realistically, and does the seller have a strong motive for selling?

Buyers' Abilities. Is the property in the price range of your prospects? The listing inventory must fit your market.

Good Image. The quality, terms, and conditions must reflect the desired image and reputation of your professional service.

Rejected Listings Remember to seek marketable listings realistically priced and efficiently serviceable, otherwise reject them. Let other brokers gain the seller's disfavor. Listings which should be rejected include:

White Elephants. These are properties which cannot be sold in a reasonable period of time with a reasonable effort expended.

Unlawful Discrimination. Listings in which the seller wants to discriminate because of race, creed, country of origin, color, sex, age, or marital status must be rejected. Unlawful discrimination is prohibited by federal and state fair housing laws, the Commissioner's Regulations (Article 10, Section 2780-2782), and Article 10 of the NAR Code of Ethics.

PINNING DOWN THE LISTING CONTRACT

You are most likely to be successful if you develop a systematic approach to your listing procedure. You are selling yourself, your company and your service.

"AIDA" The old AIDA approach may help you on both listing and selling appointments. AIDA is a mnemonic for:

Attention. Calling your prospect's attention to who you are so you can help them get desired results.

Interest. Arousing your prospect's interest in the services you offer.

Desire. Creating desire by showing specifically how you can help.

Action. Getting your client to sign the listing.

Preparation for the Listing Appointment Getting a listing involves educating the seller.

Do Your Homework. Research your market to suggest a salable listing price for the seller's decision. Have the supporting facts and figures on paper for documentation purposes.

Utilize the Competitive Market Analysis. The CMA provides the sellers with facts about the market value of their properties, i.e., what buyers are willing and not willing to pay for a comparable home in the same area. (See Exhibit 11, Chapter 5.)

The CMA consists of information regarding recent sales, comparable homes currently on the market, expired listings of comparable homes, area market conditions, drawbacks and assets, recommended terms, and other critical marketing conditions. It gives the listing presentation factual support and allows the seller to respond to facts, not personal opinion. It also provides a basis for future adjustment of price or financial terms.

Financing. Research the area's availability of financing by consulting with local loan brokers, lenders, and escrow officers.

Forecast Profits. The Estimated Seller's Proceeds form (Exhibit 4) provides the seller with a forecast of net proceeds from the sale. Different methods of financing produce different net proceeds.

The Listing Appointment The appointment with the prospective client should be planned and structured to achieve its purpose. Proceed with the business at hand—get the listing!

Scheduling. Set your appointment for a time when both husband and wife, or co-owners, can be there. Visit briefly and obtain additional pertinent information. Do not disclose all material information in advance. Do not leave an unsigned contract.

Logistics. Reinspect the home from a prospective buyer's viewpoint. Discuss negative factors and what might be done to overcome possible buyer's objections. Try to arrange the seating where you will be facing them both to observe their nonverbal, facial expressions. Avoid or minimize all distractions, such as TV or stereo.

Selling. Sell your office, its fine reputation, and your broker's integrity.

☐ Sell yourself, but be a good listener.

☐ Sell your marketing plan; show them in writing, point by point, what you propose to do for them. Include your office's Homeowner's Warranty Plan in your marketing presentation.

☐ Present the documented suggested selling price (Competitive Market Analysis), but leave the precise decision to them.

☐ Try to ascertain the motivation to sell (relocation, speculation, investment).

☐ Inquire about the sellers' financing capabilities: can they offer an all-inclusive trust deed, carry first, second, third notes, etc.

Closing Strategy. Close with confidence. Complete the listing contract but ask their decision on the selling price. Use trial closes:

☐ Do you have an extra key?

☐ May we put a sign on the property?

☐ Do you have a bowl to hold visiting brokers' cards?

Check your progress by watching the sellers' reactions to trial closes. Write with confidence. Write methodically.

- ☐ Ask questions and engage in small talk while writing.
- ☐ Avoid discussing potential problem subjects.
- ☐ Ask for the sellers' "approval in writing," not their signatures.

Complete all forms that should be completed at this time, primarily to obtain information that you will need later. (See Exhibits 7-10 and 16)

- ☐ Estimated Seller's Proceeds
- ☐ Seller's Affidavit of Nonforeign Status
- ☐ Real Estate Transfer Disclosure Statement
- ☐ Lock Box Authorization Addendum
- ☐ Seller Financing Disclosure Statement (if seller financing is a possibility).

Leave with confidence. Once the listing is signed and all information obtained, leave promptly. Reinforce the sellers' decision to list and thank them for their confidence in you and your office. Gather your paperwork and leave immediately.

SERVICING THE LISTING

Obtaining the listing is only the beginning.

Due Diligence Under the listing contract, the seller has the right to expect "due diligence" from you and your office to find the buyer who is ready, willing, and able to buy the property. Due diligence may require:

Marketing. A complete marketing strategy utilizes such services as: sign on the property; classified advertising, special ads, promotional activity; open house; office/MLS caravan; showing to qualified prospects; other broker cooperation if not in MLS; personal contact with prior potential buyers; property activity report; reevaluation of listing price, terms, or conditions as appropriate, using competitive market analysis; and renegotiation of listing extension or renewal.

Additional Servicing Activities. Consideration should be given to obtaining loan commitments. Assist the owner in arranging to fix up or make ready for sale with services like painting, landscaping, etc.

Constant Communication Contact with the seller is extremely important. The seller should be kept informed in the following ways:

Showings. Telephone (whenever possible) reports of all showings of the property by yourself, your office, and other brokers, preferably on a weekly basis.

Other Exposure. Telephone the results of advertising, open house, MLS caravan.

Literature. Give the seller copies of ads, promotional literature, MLS camera card.

Comparable Sales. Notify seller of any sales of like property that occur in the same area.

Good Will. Visit the seller in person (if possible) often. Establishing good rapport is helpful, especially when price adjustments or listing renewals need to be discussed.

THE SALES COMMISSION

Commission Earned   Ordinarily the broker is entitled to a commission when the broker produces a buyer, ready, willing and able to purchase the property for the price and on the terms specified by the principal, regardless of whether the sale is ever consummated. Contracts may expressly provide that no commissions are payable except upon a completed sale or on an installment of the purchase price when paid by the buyer, and such a provision controls in the absence of fraud or prevention of performance by the principal. The broker must be the procuring cause of the sale; it is not sufficient that the broker merely introduces the seller and buyer, if they are unable to agree upon the terms of the sale within the time period of the agency.

The broker may, however, have a cause of action for the payment of commission under the listing contract if the property is sold after the listing has expired to the buyer introduced by the broker during the term of the listing. A broker who holds an Exclusive Right to Sell Listing will have earned a commission if the property is sold by anyone, including the owner. In probate sales, the court must approve all commissions.

Legal Requirements   There are two additional requirements before the broker can recover a commission for selling real property.

A Written Contract. The Statute of Frauds (Civil Code Section 1624) specifies that an agreement authorizing or employing an agent to purchase or sell real estate, or lease for more than a year, must be in writing in order for the agent to claim compensation or a commission.

Licensing. The broker must be able to prove he or she was licensed at the time of the transaction.

Commission Amount Real estate commissions are negotiable. They are not fixed by law or trade association.

Private Contract. The commission agreement is a contractual matter agreed upon in writing between the broker and the principal.

Consumer Protection. The Real Estate Law (B & P Code § 10147.5) requires that any commission agreement form (usually the listing) must contain the statement: "Notice: The amount or rate of real estate commission is not fixed by law. They are set by each broker individually and may be negotiable between the seller and broker." This section also decrees that "The amount or rate of compensation shall not be printed in any such agreement."

TERMINATION OF THE LISTING

A listing is a contract. As such it may be terminated in various ways, including but by no means limited to consummation of the sale.

Mutual Agreement of the Parties **Sale.** Sale of the property, brought about by the parties as planned, terminates the listing.

Termination Date. Expiration of a specified term, as agreed at the time of the listing, also terminates the contract.

Other Agreement. Mutual agreement to terminate the contract is possible at any time.

Unilateral Revocation or Nonperformance With one exception, both the principal and the agent have the *power* to terminate an agency relationship even if neither has the contractual *right* to do so. The one who does unilaterally terminate the agency may be held to be in breach of contract. An owner who decides to withdraw the property from the market may be held liable for a commission. The one exception is that a principal does not have the power unilaterally to terminate an agency coupled with an interest.

Nonperformance by Broker. Unless there is prior written agreement, the broker will not be reimbursed for sales expenses if the broker fails to find the ready, willing, and able buyer for the property.

Outside Occurrences **Extinction of the Subject.** Destruction of the property, for example, terminates the agency (listing).

Death or Incapacity of either the principal or the agent terminates the agency.

NON EXCLUSIVE AUTHORIZATION AND RIGHT TO SELL

THIS IS INTENDED TO BE A LEGALLY BINDING AGREEMENT — READ IT CAREFULLY.
CALIFORNIA ASSOCIATION OF REALTORS® (CAR) STANDARD FORM

1. RIGHT TO SELL. I hereby employ and grant _____ hereinafter called "Agent," the non exclusive and revocable right commencing on _____ , 19_____ , and expiring at midnight on _____ , 19_____ , unless terminated prior thereto by written notice of prior sale or exchange, to sell or exchange the real property situated in _____ , County of_____ , California described as follows:

_____

_____

_____

2. TERMS OF SALE. The purchase price shall be $_____ , to be paid on the following terms:

_____

_____

    (a) The following items of personal property are to be included in the above-stated price:

_____

_____

_____

    (b) Agent is hereby authorized to accept and hold on my behalf a deposit upon the purchase price.

    (c) Evidence of title to the property shall be in the form of a California Land Title Association Standard Coverage Policy of Title Insurance in the amount of the selling price to be paid for by_____ .

    (d) I warrant that I am the owner of the property or have the authority to execute this agreement. I hereby authorize a FOR SALE sign to be placed on my property by Agent. I authorize the Agent named herein to cooperate with sub-agents.

    3. Notice: The amount or rate of real estate commissions is not fixed by law. They are set by each broker individually and may be negotiable between the seller and broker.

    COMPENSATION TO AGENT. I hereby agree to compensate Agent as follows:

    (a) $_____ **or**_____ % of the selling price if the property is sold during the term hereof, or any extension hereof, by Agent, on the terms herein set forth or any other price and terms I may accept.

    (b) the compensation provided for in subparagraph (a) above if property is sold, conveyed or otherwise transferred within_____ days after the termination of this authority or any extension thereof to anyone with whom Agent has had negotiations prior to final termination, provided I have received notice in writing, including the names of the prospective purchasers, before or upon termination of this agreement or any extension thereof.

    4. In any action or proceeding to enforce this agreement, the prevailing party shall receive reasonable attorney's fees and costs.

    5. In the event of an exchange, permission is hereby given Agent to represent all parties and collect compensation or commissions from them, provided there is full disclosure to all principals of such agency. Agent is authorized to divide with other agents such compensation or commissions in any manner acceptable to them.

    6. I agree to save and hold agent harmless from all claims, disputes, litigation, and/or judgments arising from any incorrect information supplied by me or from any material fact concerning the property which I fail to disclose.

    7. This property is offered in compliance with state and federal anti-discrimination laws.

    8. Other provisions: _____

_____

    9. I acknowledge that I have read and understand this Agreement, and that I have received a copy hereof.

Dated _____ , 19____ _____ , California

Owner _____ Owner _____

Address _____ City-State-Phone _____

Agent _____ Address-City _____

THIS STANDARDIZED DOCUMENT FOR USE IN SIMPLE TRANSACTIONS HAS BEEN APPROVED BY THE CALIFORNIA ASSOCIATION OF REALTORS® IN FORM ONLY. NO REPRESENTATION IS MADE AS TO THE APPROVAL OF THE FORM OF ANY SUPPLEMENTS NOT CURRENTLY PUBLISHED BY THE CALIFORNIA ASSOCIATION OF REALTORS® OR THE LEGAL VALIDITY OR ADEQUACY OF ANY PROVISION IN ANY SPECIFIC TRANSACTION. IT SHOULD NOT BE USED IN COMPLEX TRANSACTIONS OR WITH EXTENSIVE RIDERS OR ADDITIONS.
A REAL ESTATE BROKER IS THE PERSON QUALIFIED TO ADVISE ON REAL ESTATE TRANSACTIONS. IF YOU DESIRE LEGAL OR TAX ADVICE, CONSULT AN APPROPRIATE PROFESSIONAL.

This form is available for use by the entire real estate industry. The use of this form is not intended to identify the user as a REALTOR®. REALTOR® is a registered collective membership mark which may be used only by real estate licensees who are members of the NATIONAL ASSOCIATION OF REALTORS® and who subscribe to its Code of Ethics.

┌─── OFFICE USE ONLY ───┐
Reviewed by Broker or Designee_____
Date _____

Copyright© 1983, CALIFORNIA ASSOCIATION OF REALTORS®
525 South Virgil Avenue, Los Angeles, California 90020   FORM NEA-11   SF-Nov-87

REPRINTED BY PERMISSION CALIFORNIA ASSOCIATION OF REALTORS®. ENDORSEMENT NOT IMPLIED

Exhibit 3

EXCLUSIVE AGENCY AUTHORIZATION AND RIGHT TO SELL

THIS IS INTENDED TO BE A LEGALLY BINDING AGREEMENT - READ IT CAREFULLY.

CALIFORNIA ASSOCIATION OF REALTORS® (CAR) STANDARD FORM

1. **RIGHT TO SELL.** I hereby employ and grant _____ hereinafter called "Agent," the exclusive and irrevocable Agency right commencing on _____ , 19_____ , and expiring at midnight on_____ , 19_____ , to sell or exchange the real property situated in_____ . County of _____ , California described as follows:
_____
_____

2. **TERMS OF SALE.** The purchase price shall be $_____ , to be paid on the following terms:
_____
_____
_____

    (a) The following items of personal property are to be included in the above-stated price:_____
_____
_____

    (b) Agent is hereby authorized to accept and hold on my behalf a deposit upon the purchase price.

    (c) Evidence of title to the property shall be in the form of a California Land Title Association Standard Coverage Policy of Title Insurance in the amount of the selling price to be paid for by _____ .

    (d) I warrant that I am the owner of the property or have the authority to execute this agreement. I hereby authorize a FOR SALE sign to be placed on my property by Agent. I authorize the Agent named herein to cooperate with sub-agents.

3. **Notice: The amount or rate of real estate commissions is not fixed by law. They are set by each broker individually and may be negotiable between the seller and broker.**

    COMPENSATION TO AGENT. I hereby agree to compensate Agent as follows:

    (a) $_____ or_____% of the selling price if the property is sold during the term hereof, or any extension thereof, by Agent, on the terms herein set forth or any other price and terms I may accept, or through any other agent. $_____ or_____% of the price shown in 2, if said property is withdrawn from sale, without the consent of Agent, or made unmarketable by my voluntary act during the term hereof or any extension thereof.

    (b) The compensation provided for in subparagraph (a) above if property is sold, conveyed or otherwise transferred within _____ days after the termination of this authority or any extension thereof to anyone with whom Agent has had negotiations prior to final termination, provided I have received notice in writing, including the names of the prospective purchasers, before or upon termination of this agreement or any extension thereof. However, I shall not be obligated to pay the compensation provided for in subparagraph (a) if a valid listing agreement is entered into during the term of said protection period with another licensed real estate broker and a sale, lease or exchange of the property is made during the term of said valid listing agreement.

    (c) It is expressly understood that this is an Exclusive Agency listing and except as to a sale to any prospective purchaser who has initially been introduced to or shown the property and been informed of the price by Agent, during the above term or any extension hereof, I reserve the right to sell the property to any purchaser without any obligation for commission to Agent except as above provided.

    (d) I agree to notify Agent in writing within 24 hours of my acceptance of any offer of sale, lease or exchange including identity of parties, price and terms.

4. I agree not to offer the property for sale or exchange at a lower price than stated above.

5. In any action or proceeding to enforce this agreement, the prevailing party shall receive reasonable attorney's fee and costs.

6. In the event of an exchange, permission is hereby given Agent to represent all parties and collect compensation or commissions from them, provided there is full disclosure to all principals of such agency. Agent is authorized to divide with other agent such compensation or commissions in any manner acceptable to them.

7. I agree to save and hold agent harmless from all claims, disputes, litigation, and/or judgments arising from any incorrect information supplied by me or from any material fact known to me concerning the property which I fail to disclose.

8. This property is offered in compliance with state and federal anti-discrimination laws.

9. Other provisions:_____
_____

10. I acknowledge that I have read and understand this Agreement, and that I have received a copy hereof.

Dated _____ , 19_____   _____ , California

Owner _____   Owner _____

Address _____   City - State - Phone _____

11. In consideration of the above, Agent agrees to use diligence in procuring a purchaser.

Agent _____   Address - City _____

By_____   Phone _____ Date _____

NO REPRESENTATION IS MADE AS TO THE LEGAL VALIDITY OF ANY PROVISION OR THE ADEQUACY OF ANY PROVISION IN ANY SPECIFIC TRANSACTION. IF YOU DESIRE LEGAL ADVICE, CONSULT YOUR ATTORNEY.

To order, contact — California Association of Realtors®
525 S. Virgil Avenue, Los Angeles, California 90020
Copyright© 1983, California Association of Realtors®   FORM EA-11

OFFICE USE ONLY
Reviewed by Broker or Designee _____
Date _____

EQUAL HOUSING OPPORTUNITY

SF-June-87

REPRINTED BY PERMISSION CALIFORNIA ASSOCIATION OF REALTORS®. ENDORSEMENT NOT IMPLIED

Exhibit 4

EXCLUSIVE AUTHORIZATION AND RIGHT TO SELL

THIS IS INTENDED TO BE A LEGALLY BINDING AGREEMENT — READ IT CAREFULLY.
CALIFORNIA ASSOCIATION OF REALTORS® (CAR) STANDARD FORM

1. **EXCLUSIVE RIGHT TO SELL:** I hereby employ and grant _____ hereinafter called "Broker," the exclusive and irrevocable right commencing on _____, 19____, and expiring at midnight on _____, 19____, to sell or exchange the real property situated in the City of _____, County of _____, California described as follows: _____
_____

2. **TERMS OF SALE:** The purchase price shall be _____
_____ ($_____), to be paid as follows _____

The following items of personal property are included in the above stated price: _____
_____

3. **TITLE INSURANCE:** Evidence of title shall be a California Land Title Association policy of title insurance in the amount of the selling price.
Notice: The amount or rate of real estate commissions is not fixed by law. They are set by each Broker individually and may be negotiable between the Seller and Broker.

4. **COMPENSATION TO BROKER:** I hereby agree to compensate Broker, irrespective of agency relationship(s), as follows:
   (a) ____ percent of the selling price, or $_____, if the property is sold during the term hereof, or any extension thereof, by Broker or through any other person, or by me on the terms herein set forth, or any other price and terms I may accept, or ____ percent of the price shown in 2, or $_____, if said property is withdrawn from sale, transferred, conveyed, leased, or rented without the consent of Broker, or made unmarketable by my voluntary act during the term hereof or any extension thereof.
   (b) The compensation provided for in subparagraph (a) above if property is sold, conveyed or otherwise transferred within ____ calendar days after the termination of this authority or any extension thereof to anyone with whom Broker has had negotiations prior to final termination, provided I have received notice in writing, including the names of the prospective purchasers, before or upon termination of this agreement or any extension hereof. However, I shall not be obligated to pay the compensation provided for in subparagraph (a) if a valid listing agreement is entered into during the term of said protection period with another licensed real estate broker and a sale, lease or exchange of the property is made during the term of said valid listing agreement.
   (c) I authorize Broker to cooperate with other brokers, to appoint subagents, and to divide with other brokers such compensation in any manner acceptable to brokers.
   (d) In the event of an exchange, permission is hereby given Broker to represent all parties and collect compensation or commissions from them, provided there is full disclosure to all principals of such agency. Broker is authorized to divide with other brokers such compensation or commissions in any manner acceptable to brokers.
   (e) Seller shall execute and deliver an escrow instruction irrevocably assigning Broker's compensation in an amount equal to the compensation provided in subparagraph (a) (above) from the Seller's proceeds.

5. **DEPOSIT:** Broker is authorized to accept and hold on Seller's behalf a deposit to be applied toward purchase price.

6. **HOME PROTECTION PLAN:** Seller is informed that home protection plans are available. Such plans may provide additional protection and benefit to a Seller and Buyer. Cost and coverage may vary.

* 7. **KEYBOX:** I authorize Broker to install a KEYBOX:
   Refer to reverse side for important keybox information.   (Initial) YES (____/____) NO (____/____)

8. **SIGN:** Authorization to install a FOR SALE/SOLD sign on the property: (Initial) YES (____/____) NO (____/____)

9. **PEST CONTROL:** Seller shall furnish a current Structural Pest Control Report of the main building and all structures of the property, except _____   (Initial) YES (____/____) NO (____/____)

10. **DISCLOSURE:** Unless exempt, Seller shall provide a Real Estate Transfer Disclosure Statement concerning the condition of the property. I agree to save and hold Broker harmless from all claims, disputes, litigation, and/or judgments arising from any incorrect information supplied by me, or from any material fact known by me which I fail to disclose.   (Initial) _____

* 11. **TAX WITHHOLDING:** Seller agrees to perform any act reasonably necessary to carry out the provisions of FIRPTA (Internal Revenue Code §1445) and California Revenue and Taxation Code §§18805 and 26131, and regulations promulgated thereunder. Refer to the reverse side for withholding provisions and exemptions.

12. **EQUAL HOUSING OPPORTUNITY:** This property is offered in compliance with federal, state, and local anti-discrimination laws.

* 13. **ARBITRATION OF DISPUTES:** Any dispute or claim in law or equity arising out of this contract or any resulting transaction shall be decided by neutral binding arbitration in accordance with the rules of the American Arbitration Association, and not by court action except as provided by California law for judicial review of arbitration proceedings. Judgment upon the award rendered by the arbitrator(s) may be entered in any court having jurisdiction thereof. The parties shall have the right to discovery in accordance with Code of Civil Procedure §1283.05. The following matters are excluded from arbitration hereunder: (a) a judicial or non-judicial foreclosure or other action or proceeding to enforce a deed of trust, mortgage, or real property sales contract as defined in Civil Code §2985, (b) an unlawful detainer action, (c) the filing or enforcement of a mechanic's lien, (d) any matter which is within the jurisdiction of a probate court, or (e) an action for bodily injury or wrongful death, or for latent or patent defects to which Code of Civil Procedure §337.1 or §337.15 applies. The filing of a judicial action to enable the recording of a notice of pending action, for order of attachment, receivership, injunction, or other provisional remedies, shall not constitute a waiver of the right to arbitrate under this provision.
"NOTICE: BY INITIALLING IN THE SPACE BELOW YOU ARE AGREEING TO HAVE ANY DISPUTE ARISING OUT OF THE MATTERS INCLUDED IN THE 'ARBITRATION OF DISPUTES' PROVISION DECIDED BY NEUTRAL ARBITRATION AS PROVIDED BY CALIFORNIA LAW AND YOU ARE GIVING UP ANY RIGHTS YOU MIGHT POSSESS TO HAVE THE DISPUTE LITIGATED IN A COURT OR JURY TRIAL. BY INITIALLING IN THE SPACE BELOW YOU ARE GIVING UP YOUR JUDICIAL RIGHTS TO DISCOVERY AND APPEAL, UNLESS THOSE RIGHTS ARE SPECIFICALLY INCLUDED IN THE 'ARBITRATION OF DISPUTES' PROVISION. IF YOU REFUSE TO SUBMIT TO ARBITRATION AFTER AGREEING TO THIS PROVISION, YOU MAY BE COMPELLED TO ARBITRATE UNDER THE AUTHORITY OF THE CALIFORNIA CODE OF CIVIL PROCEDURE. YOUR AGREEMENT TO THIS ARBITRATION PROVISION IS VOLUNTARY."
"WE HAVE READ AND UNDERSTAND THE FOREGOING AND AGREE TO SUBMIT DISPUTES ARISING OUT OF THE MATTERS INCLUDED IN THE 'ARBITRATION OF DISPUTES' PROVISION TO NEUTRAL ARBITRATION."
(Initial) BROKER (_____) SELLER (_____)

14. **ATTORNEY'S FEES:** In any action, proceeding or arbitration arising out of this agreement, the prevailing party shall be entitled to reasonable attorney's fees and costs.

15. **ADDITIONAL TERMS:**

16. **ENTIRE AGREEMENT:** I, the Seller, warrant that I am the owner of the property or have the authority to execute this agreement. The Seller and Broker further intend that this agreement constitutes the complete and exclusive statement of its terms and that no extrinsic evidence whatsoever may be introduced in any judicial or arbitration proceeding, if any, involving this agreement.
I acknowledge that I have read and understand this agreement, including the information on the reverse side, and have received a copy.

17. **CAPTIONS:** The Captions in this agreement are for convenience of reference only and are not intended as part of this agreement.

Date _____, 19____   _____, California
Seller _____   Address _____
Seller _____   City _____ State _____ Phone _____
In consideration of the above, Broker agrees to use diligence in procuring a purchaser.
Real Estate Broker _____   By _____
Address _____   City _____ Date _____

Exhibit 5.1

7. **KEYBOX:** A keybox designed as a repository of a key to the above premises, will permit access to the interior of the premises by Participants of the Multiple Listing Service (MLS), their authorized licensees and prospective buyers. If property is not seller occupied, seller shall be responsible for obtaining occupants' written permission for use of the keybox. Neither listing nor selling broker, MLS or Board of REALTORS® is an insurer against theft, loss, vandalism or damage attributed to the use of keybox. SELLER is advised to verify the existence of, or obtain appropriate insurance through their own insurance broker.

11. **TAX WITHHOLDING:** Under the Foreign Investment in Real Property Tax Act (FIRPTA), IRC 1445, *every* Buyer of U.S. real property *must,* unless an exemption applies, deduct and withhold from Seller's proceeds 10% of the gross sales price. Under California Revenue and Taxation Code §§18805 and 26131, the Buyer must deduct and withhold an additional one-third of the amount required to be withheld under federal law. The primary FIRPTA exemptions are: No withholding is required if (a) Seller provides Buyer with an affidavit under penalty of perjury, that Seller is not a "foreign person," or (b) Seller provides Buyer with a "qualifying statement" issued by the Internal Revenue Service, or (c) Buyer purchases real property for use as a residence and the purchase price is $300,000 or less and if Buyer or a member of Buyer's family has definite plans to reside at the property for at least 50% of the number of days it is in use during each of the first two twelve-month periods after transfer. Seller agrees to execute and deliver as directed any instrument, affidavit or statement, reasonably necessary to carry out those statutes and regulations promulgated thereunder.

13. **ARBITRATION:** Arbitration is the referral of a dispute to one or more impartial persons for final and binding determination. It is private and informal, designed for quick, practical, and inexpensive settlements. Arbitration is an orderly proceeding, governed by rules of procedure and standards of conduct prescribed by law.

ENFORCEMENT OF ARBITRATION AGREEMENTS
UNDER CALIFORNIA CODE OF CIVIL PROCEDURE SECTIONS 1281, 1282.4, 1283.1, 1283.05, 1287.4 & 1287.6

§ 1281. A written agreement to submit to arbitration an existing controversy or a controversy thereafter arising is valid, enforceable and irreversible, save upon such grounds as exist for the revocation of any contract.

§ 1282.4. A party to the arbitration has the right to be represented by an attorney at any proceeding or hearing in arbitration under this title. A waiver of this right may be revoked; but if a party revokes such waiver, the other party is entitled to a reasonable continuance for the purpose of procuring an attorney.

§ 1283.1. (a) All of the provisions of Section 1283.05 shall be conclusively deemed to be incorporated into, made a part of, and shall be applicable to, every agreement to arbitrate any dispute, controversy, or issue arising out of or resulting from any injury to, or death of, a person caused by the wrongful act or neglect of another.
(b) Only if the parties by their agreement so provide, may the provisions of Section 1283.05 be incorporated into, made a part of, or made applicable to, any other arbitration agreement.

§ 1283.05. To the extent provided in Section 1283.1 depositions may be taken and discovery obtained in arbitration proceedings as follows:
(a) After the appointment of the arbitrator or arbitrators, the parties to the arbitration shall have the right to take depositions and to obtain discovery regarding the subject matter of the arbitration, and, to that end, to use and exercise all of the same rights, remedies, and procedures, and be subject to all of the same duties, liabilities, and obligations in the arbitration with respect to the subject matter thereof, as provided in Chapter 2 (commencing with Section 1985) of, and Article 3 (commencing with Section 2016) of Chapter 3 of, Title 3 of Part 4 of this code, as if the subject matter of the arbitration were pending in a civil action before a superior court of this state, subject to the limitations as to depositions set forth in subdivision (e) of this section.
(b) The arbitrator or arbitrators themselves shall have power, in addition to the power of determining the merits of the arbitration, to enforce the rights, remedies, procedures, duties, liabilities, and obligations of discovery by the imposition of the same terms, conditions, consequences, liabilities, sanctions, and penalties as can be or may be imposed in like circumstances in a civil action by a superior court of this state under the provisions of this code, except the power to order the arrest or imprisonment of a person.
(c) The arbitrator or arbitrators may consider, determine, and make such orders imposing such terms, conditions, consequences, liabilities, sanctions, and penalties, whenever necessary or appropriate at any time or stage in the course of the arbitration, and such orders shall be as conclusive, final, and enforceable as an arbitration award on the merits, if the making of any such order that is equivalent to an award or correction of an award is subject to the same conditions, if any, as are applicable to the making of an award or correction of an award.
(d) For the purpose of enforcing the duty to make discovery, to produce evidence or information, including books and records, and to produce persons to testify at a deposition or at a hearing, and to impose terms, conditions, consequences, liabilities, sanctions, and penalties upon a party for violation of any such duty, such party shall be deemed to include every affiliate of such party as defined in this section. For such purpose:
(1) The personnel of every such affiliate shall be deemed to be the officers, directors, managing agents, agents, and employees of such party to the same degree as each of them, respectively, bears such status to such affiliate; and
(2) The files, books, and records of every such affiliate shall be deemed to be in the possession and control of, and capable of production by, such party. As used in this section, "affiliate" of the party to the arbitration means and includes any party or person for whose immediate benefit the action or proceeding is prosecuted or defended, or an officer, director, superintendent, member, agent, employee, or managing agent of such party or persons.
(e) Depositions for discovery shall not be taken unless leave to do so is first granted by the arbitrator or arbitrators.

§ 1287.4. If an award is confirmed, judgment shall be entered in conformity therewith. The judgment so entered has the same force and effect as, and is subject to all the provisions of law relating to, a judgment in a civil action; and it may be enforced like any other judgment of the court in which it is entered.

§ 1287.6. An award that has not been confirmed or vacated has the same force and effect as a contract in writing between the parties to the arbitration.

Exhibit 5.2

CALIFORNIA ASSOCIATION OF REALTORS

EXCLUSIVE AUTHORIZATION AND RIGHT TO SELL
MULTIPLE LISTING AUTHORIZATION
THIS IS INTENDED TO BE A LEGALLY BINDING AGREEMENT — READ IT CAREFULLY.
CALIFORNIA ASSOCIATION OF REALTORS® (CAR) STANDARD FORM

1. **EXCLUSIVE RIGHT TO SELL:** I hereby employ and grant _____ hereinafter called "Broker," the exclusive and irrevocable right commencing on _____ , 19_____ , and expiring at midnight on _____ , 19_____ , to sell or exchange the real property situated in the City of _____ , County of _____ , California described as follows: _____

2. **TERMS OF SALE:** The purchase price shall be _____ _____ ($_____), to be paid as follows _____

   The following items of personal property are included in the above stated price: _____

3. **MULTIPLE LISTING SERVICE (MLS):** Broker is a Participant of _____ ASSOCIATION/BOARD OF REALTORS® Multiple Listing Service (MLS) and this listing information will be provided to the MLS to be published and disseminated to its Participants in accordance with its Rules and Regulations. Broker is authorized to cooperate with other real estate brokers, to appoint subagents and to report the sale, its price, terms and financing for the publication, dissemination, information and use by authorized Association/Board members, MLS Participants and Subscribers.

4. **TITLE INSURANCE:** Evidence of title shall be a California Land Title Association policy of title insurance in the amount of the selling price.

   Notice: The amount or rate of real estate commissions is not fixed by law. They are set by each Broker individually and may be negotiable between the Seller and Broker.

5. **COMPENSATION TO BROKER:** I hereby agree to compensate Broker, irrespective of agency relationship(s), as follows:
   - (a) _____ percent of the selling price, or $_____ , if the property is sold during the term hereof, or any extension thereof, by Broker or through any other person, or by me on the terms herein set forth, or any other price and terms I may accept, or _____ percent of the price shown in 2, or $_____ , if said property is withdrawn from sale, transferred, conveyed, leased, or rented without the consent of Broker, or made unmarketable by my voluntary act during the term hereof or any extension thereof.
   - (b) The compensation provided for in subparagraph (a) above if property is sold, conveyed or otherwise transferred within _____ calendar days after the termination of this authority or any extension thereof to anyone with whom Broker has had negotiations prior to final termination, provided I have received notice in writing, including the names of the prospective purchasers, before or upon termination of this agreement or any extension hereof. However, I shall not be obligated to pay the compensation provided for in subparagraph (a) if a valid listing agreement is entered into during the term of said protection period with another licensed real estate broker and a sale, lease or exchange of the property is made during the term of said valid listing agreement.
   - (c) I authorize Broker to cooperate with other brokers, to appoint subagents, and to divide with other brokers such compensation in any manner acceptable to brokers.
   - (d) In the event of an exchange, permission is hereby given Broker to represent all parties and collect compensation or commissions from them, provided there is full disclosure to all principals of such agency. Broker is authorized to divide with other brokers such compensation or commissions in any manner acceptable to brokers.
   - (e) Seller shall execute and deliver an escrow instruction irrevocably assigning Broker's compensation in an amount equal to the compensation provided in subparagraph (a) (above) from the Seller's proceeds.

6. **DEPOSIT:** Broker is authorized to accept and hold on Seller's behalf a deposit to be applied toward purchase price.

7. **HOME PROTECTION PLAN:** Seller is informed that home protection plans are available. Such plans may provide additional protection and benefit to a Seller and Buyer. Cost and coverage may vary.

* 8. **KEYBOX:** I authorize Broker to install a KEYBOX: (Initial) YES (____/____) NO (____/____)
   Refer to reverse side for important keybox information.

9. **SIGN:** Authorization to install a FOR SALE/SOLD sign on the property: (Initial) YES (____/____) NO (____/____)

10. **PEST CONTROL:** Seller shall furnish a current Structural Pest Control Report of the main building and all structures of the property, except _____ (Initial) YES (____/____) NO (____/____)

11. **DISCLOSURE:** Unless exempt, Seller shall provide a Real Estate Transfer Disclosure Statement concerning the condition of the property. I agree to save and hold Broker harmless from all claims, disputes, litigation, and/or judgments arising from any incorrect information supplied by me, or from any material fact known by me which I fail to disclose. (Initial) (____/____)

* 12. **TAX WITHHOLDING:** Seller agrees to perform any act reasonably necessary to carry out the provisions of FIRPTA (Internal Revenue Code §1445) and California Revenue and Taxation Code §§18805 and 26131, and regulations promulgated thereunder. Refer to the reverse side for withholding provisions and exemptions.

13. **EQUAL HOUSING OPPORTUNITY:** This property is offered in compliance with federal, state, and local anti-discrimination laws.

* 14. **ARBITRATION OF DISPUTES:** Any dispute or claim in law or equity arising out of this contract or any resulting transaction shall be decided by neutral binding arbitration in accordance with the rules of the American Arbitration Association, and not by court action except as provided by California law for judicial review of arbitration proceedings. Judgment upon the award rendered by the arbitrator(s) may be entered in any court having jurisdiction thereof. The parties shall have the right to discovery in accordance with Code of Civil Procedure §1283.05. The following matters are excluded from arbitration hereunder: (a) a judicial or non-judicial foreclosure or other action or proceeding to enforce a deed of trust, mortgage, or real property sales contract as defined in Civil Code §2985, (b) an unlawful detainer action, (c) the filing or enforcement of a mechanic's lien, (d) any matter which is within the jurisdiction of a probate court, or (e) an action for bodily injury or wrongful death, or for latent or patent defects to which Code of Civil Procedure §337.1 or §337.15 applies. The filing of a judicial action to enable the recording of a notice of pending action, for order of attachment, receivership, injunction, or other provisional remedies, shall not constitute a waiver of the right to arbitrate under this provision.**

   "NOTICE: BY INITIALLING IN THE SPACE BELOW YOU ARE AGREEING TO HAVE ANY DISPUTE ARISING OUT OF THE MATTERS INCLUDED IN THE 'ARBITRATION OF DISPUTES' PROVISION DECIDED BY NEUTRAL ARBITRATION AS PROVIDED BY CALIFORNIA LAW AND YOU ARE GIVING UP ANY RIGHTS YOU MIGHT POSSESS TO HAVE THE DISPUTE LITIGATED IN A COURT OR JURY TRIAL. BY INITIALLING IN THE SPACE BELOW YOU ARE GIVING UP YOUR JUDICIAL RIGHTS TO DISCOVERY AND APPEAL, UNLESS THOSE RIGHTS ARE SPECIFICALLY INCLUDED IN THE 'ARBITRATION OF DISPUTES' PROVISION. IF YOU REFUSE TO SUBMIT TO ARBITRATION AFTER AGREEING TO THIS PROVISION, YOU MAY BE COMPELLED TO ARBITRATE UNDER THE AUTHORITY OF THE CALIFORNIA CODE OF CIVIL PROCEDURE. YOUR AGREEMENT TO THIS ARBITRATION PROVISION IS VOLUNTARY."
   "WE HAVE READ AND UNDERSTAND THE FOREGOING AND AGREE TO SUBMIT DISPUTES ARISING OUT OF THE MATTERS INCLUDED IN THE 'ARBITRATION OF DISPUTES' PROVISION TO NEUTRAL ARBITRATION."
   (Initial) BROKER (_____) SELLER (____/____)

15. **ATTORNEY'S FEES:** In any action, proceeding or arbitration arising out of this agreement, the prevailing party shall be entitled to reasonable attorney's fees and costs.

16. **ADDITIONAL TERMS:** _____

17. **ENTIRE AGREEMENT:** I, the Seller, warrant that I am the owner of the property or have the authority to execute this agreement. The Seller and Broker further intend that this agreement constitutes the complete and exclusive statement of its terms and that no extrinsic evidence whatsoever may be introduced in any judicial or arbitration proceeding, if any, involving this agreement.

I acknowledge that I have read and understand this agreement, including the information on the reverse side, and have received a copy.

Date _____ , 19_____ _____ , California
Seller _____ Address _____
Seller _____ City _____ State _____ Zip _____
In consideration of the above, Broker agrees to use diligence in procuring a purchaser. Phone _____
Real Estate Broker _____ By _____
Address _____ City _____ Date _____

OFFICE USE ONLY
Reviewed by Broker or Designee _____
Date _____

EQUAL HOUSING OPPORTUNITY

* REFER TO REVERSE SIDE FOR ADDITIONAL INFORMATION.
Copyright© 1988, CALIFORNIA ASSOCIATION OF REALTORS®
525 South Virgil Avenue, Los Angeles, California 90020
Revised 3/89

FORM A-14

REPRINTED BY PERMISSION CALIFORNIA ASSOCIATION OF REALTORS® . ENDORSEMENT NOT IMPLIED

Exhibit 6

ESTIMATED SELLER'S PROCEEDS
CALIFORNIA ASSOCIATION OF REALTORS® STANDARD FORM

SELLER _____

PROPERTY ADDRESS _____

BROKER _____

This estimate is based on costs associated with _____ financing.   ESTIMATED CLOSING DATE _____

PROJECTED SELLING PRICE $ _____

ENCUMBRANCES

First Trust Deed	$ _____
Second Trust Deed	_____
Other Encumbrances	_____
TOTAL	$ _____

PROJECTED GROSS EQUITY $ _____

ESTIMATED COSTS

ESTIMATED CREDITS

ESTIMATED COSTS		ESTIMATED CREDITS	
Escrow	$ _____	Prorated Taxes	$ _____
Sub Escrow	_____	Prorated Insurance	_____
Recording	_____	Prorated Rents	_____
Drawing Deed	_____	Impound Accounts	_____
Title Insurance	_____	Other	_____
Transfer Tax	_____	Other	_____
Notary	_____		
Pre-Payment Penalty	_____		
Forwarding or Transfer	_____		
Reconveyance	_____		
Interest	_____		
Discount @ %	_____	TOTAL ESTIMATED COSTS	$ _____
Preparation of Documents	_____	LESS ESTIMATED CREDITS	$ _____
Taxes	_____		
Appraisal	_____	NET SELLER'S COSTS	$ _____
Structural Pest Control Inspection	_____	PURCHASE MONEY NOTE	
Structural Pest Control Repairs	_____	(if any)	_____
FHA-VA or Lender	_____	ESTIMATED SELLER'S	
Home Warrantee	_____	CASH PROCEEDS	$ _____
Brokerage	_____		
Buyer's Fees	_____		
Miscellaneous Fees	_____		
TOTAL	$ _____		

This estimate based upon the above projected selling price, type of financing, and estimated closing dates, has been prepared to assist the seller in computing his costs. Lenders and escrow companies will vary in their charges; therefore, these figures cannot be guaranteed by the broker or his representatives.

I have read the above figures and acknowledge receipt of a copy of this form.

Presented by: _____

Seller _____ Date _____   Address: _____

_____ Date _____   Phone No.: _____

The estimated seller's proceeds calculated above will vary according to any difference in unpaid loan balances, bonds assessments, other liens, impound account, if any, and any expenses for required repairs. All estimates and information are from sources believed reliable but not guaranteed.

Exhibit 7

SELLER'S AFFIDAVIT
OF NONFOREIGN STATUS
CALIFORNIA ASSOCIATION OF REALTORS® STANDARD FORM

(FOREIGN INVESTMENT IN REAL PROPERTY TAX ACT)

Section 1445 of the Internal Revenue Code provides that a transferee of a U.S. real property interest must withhold tax if the transferor is a foreign person. To inform the transferee that withholding of tax is not required upon the disposition of a U.S. real property interest located at _____

by_____ [name of transferor],
I hereby certify the following (if an entity transferor, on behalf of the transferor):

THIS SECTION FOR INDIVIDUAL TRANSFEROR(S):

1. I am not a nonresident alien for purposes of U.S. income taxation;

2. My U.S. taxpayer identifying number (Social Security number) is _____ ; and

3. My home address is _____

_____.

THIS SECTION FOR CORPORATION, PARTNERSHIP, TRUST, OR ESTATE TRANSFEROR(S):

1. _____ [name of transferor]
   is not a foreign corporation, foreign partnership, foreign trust, or foreign estate (as those terms are defined in the Internal Revenue Code and Income Tax Regulations);

2. _____ [name of transferor]'s U.S. employer
   identification number is _____ ;

3. _____ [name of transferor]'s office address
   is _____ ; and

4. I, the undersigned individual, declare that I have authority to sign this document on behalf of
   _____ [name of transferor].

THIS SECTION FOR ALL TRANSFEROR(S):

_____ [name of transferor]
understands that this certification may be disclosed to the Internal Revenue Service by transferee and that any false statement I have made here (or, for entity transferor, contained herein) could be punished by fine, imprisonment, or both.

Under penalties of perjury I declare that I have examined this certification and to the best of my knowledge and belief it is true, correct and complete.

Date _____ Signature _____

Typed or Printed Name _____

Title [if signed on behalf
of an entity transferor] _____

IMPORTANT NOTICE:

An affidavit should be signed by each individual or entity transferor to whom or to which it applies. Before you sign, any questions relating to the legal sufficiency of this form, or to whether it applies to a particular transaction, or to the definition of any of the terms used, should be referred to an attorney, a certified public accountant, or other professional tax advisor, or to the Internal Revenue Service.

Exhibit 8.1

FOREIGN PERSON DEFINED

THE FOLLOWING GENERAL INFORMATION is provided to assist sellers in determining whether they are "foreign persons" for purposes of the Foreign Investment in Real Property Tax Act (FIRPTA), IRC Section 1445.

FIRPTA requires a buyer to withhold and send to the Internal Revenue Service 10 percent of the gross sales price of a U.S. real property interest if the seller is a *foreign person*. No withholding is required for a seller who is a U.S. person (that is, not a foreign person). In order for an individual to be a U.S. person, he/she must be either a U.S. *citizen*, or a U.S. *resident alien*. The test must be applied separately to *each* seller in transactions involving more than one seller.

Even if the seller is a foreign person, withholding will not be required in every circumstance. The reader should consult more comprehensive material for a discussion of the exceptions and other rules. See, for example, CALIFORNIA ASSOCIATION OF REALTORS® standard form AB-11, *Buyer's Affidavit that Buyer is Acquiring Property for Use as a Residence and that Sales Price Does Not Exceed $300,000*, and the publications referred to under "For More Information," below.

The facts in a particular case may yield a result different from the general rule. Accordingly, parties to a transaction desiring advice should consult their own attorney, certified public accountant, or other professional tax advisor, or the Internal Revenue Service.

NONRESIDENT ALIEN INDIVIDUAL. An individual, whose residence is not within the United States **and** who is not a U.S. citizen, is a nonresident alien. The term includes a nonresident alien fiduciary.

An alien actually present in the United States, who is not just staying temporarily (a mere transient or sojourner), is a U.S. resident for income tax purposes. An alien is considered a U.S. resident and **not** subject to withholding under FIRPTA if the alien meets either the **green card test** or the **substantial presence test** for the calendar year.

Green card test. An alien is a U.S. resident if the individual was a lawful permanent resident of the United States at any time during the calendar year. This is known as the "green card" test.

Substantial presence test. Alternatively, an alien is considered a U.S. resident if the individual meets the substantial presence test for the calendar year. Under this test, the individual must by physically present in the United States on at least:

1) 31 days during the current calendar year, and
2) 183 days during the current year and the 2 preceding years, counting all the days of physical presence in the current year but only 1/3 the number of days of presence in the first preceding year and only 1/6 the number of days in the second preceding year.

Days of presence in the United States. Generally, a person is treated as physically present in the United States on any day he/she is physically present in the country at any time during the day. However, if a person regularly commutes to work in the United States from a residence in Canada or Mexico, he/she is not treated as present in the United States on any day during which he/she so commutes. Also, if an individual is in transit between two points outside the United States and is physically present in the country for less than 24 hours, he/she is not treated as present in the United States on any day during the transit. In addition, the individual is not treated as present in the United States on any day during which he/she is unable to leave the country because of a medical condition which arose while here.

Exempt Individual. For the substantial presence test, do not count days for which a person is an exempt individual. An exempt individual is anyone in the following categories:

1) An individual temporarily present in the United States because of (a) full-time diplomatic or consular status, (b) full-time employment with an international organization, or (c) membership in the immediate family of a person described in (a) or (b).
2) A teacher or trainee, temporarily present in the United States under a "J" visa (other than as a student), who substantially complies with the requirements of the visa. An individual will not be exempt under this category for a calendar year if he/she was exempt as a teacher or trainee or as a student for any 2 calendar years during the preceding 6 calendar years.
3) A student, temporarily present in the United States under an "F" of "J" visa, who substantially complies with the requirements of the visa. Generally, a person will not be exempt as a student for any calendar year after the fifth calendar year for which he/she was exempt as a student or as a teacher or trainee. However, the individual may continue to be exempt as a student beyond the fifth year if he/she is in compliance with the terms of the student visa and does not intend to permanently reside in the United States.

Closer connection to foreign country. Even if an individual would otherwise meet the substantial presence test, that person is nevertheless not treated as meeting the test for the current calendar year if he/she:

1) Is present in the United States on fewer than 183 days during the current year, and
2) Has a tax home in a foreign country and has a closer connection to that country than to the United States.

However, this exception to the substantial presence test will not apply for any year during which an individual has an application for adjustment of status pending or takes other steps to apply for status as a lawful permanent resident of the United States.

Dual status. Is is possible to be both a nonresident alien and a resident alien during the same tax year. Usually this occurs for the year a person arrives in or departs from the United States. Special rules apply.

Other special provisions apply to individuals who were U.S. residents for at least three years, cease to be U.S. residents, and then become U.S. residents again.

Nonresident alien individuals married to U.S. citizens or resident aliens may choose to be treated as resident aliens for most income tax purposes. However, these individuals are **considered nonresidents** for purposes of withholding taxes on nonresident aliens.

A FOREIGN PERSON OR PARTNERSHIP is one that does not fit the definition of a domestic corporation or partnership. A **domestic corporation or partnership** is one that was created or organized in the United States, or under the laws of the United States or of any U.S. state or territory.

Guam and Virgin Islands Corporations. A corporation created or organized in, or under the law of, Guam or the Virgin Islands is not considered a foreign corporation for the purpose of withholding tax for the tax year if:

1) At all times during the tax year less than 25% in value of the corporation's stock is owned, directly or indirectly, by foreign persons, and
2) At least 20% of the corporation's gross income is derived from sources within Guam or the Virgin Islands (as the case may be) for the 3-year period ending with the close of the preceding tax year of the corporation (or the period the corporation has been in existence, if less).

A NONRESIDENT ALIEN TRUSTEE, ADMINISTRATOR, OR EXECUTOR of a trust or an estate is treated as a nonresident alien, even though all the beneficiaries of the trust or estate are citizens or residents of the United States.

EFFECT OF TAX TREATIES. The rules for determining U.S. residency status do not override tax treaty definitions of residency. For example, if a person is a U.S. resident under these rules but is a resident of a treaty country (and not a U.S. resident) under an income tax treaty, he/she is still eligible for the treaty benefits extended to residents of that country.

OTHER INDIVIDUALS AND ENTITIES. Still other rules cover alien seamen, aliens who are citizens of a U.S. possession, and aliens who are residents of the Virgin Islands, Puerto Rico, Guam, the Northern Mariana Islands, or Cuba, and to foreign private foundations, associations, charitable institutions, and other organizations.

FOR MORE INFORMATION. More detailed information can be found in IRS Publications 515, *Withholding Tax on Nonresident Aliens and Foreign Corporations*, and 519, *U.S. Tax Guide for Aliens*, available from the Internal Revenue Service. The definition above is derived from those two publications.

Exhibit 8.2

LOCK BOX AUTHORIZATION ADDENDUM
CALIFORNIA ASSOCIATION OF REALTORS® STANDARD FORM

The undersigned (SELLER) having entered into a listing agreement with _____(BROKER)

dated _____pertaining to the sale of _____(PREMISES)

hereby authorizes BROKER to use a lock box. SELLER acknowledges that:

1. A lock box is designed as a repository of a key to the above premises, permitting access to the interior of the premises by Participants of the Multiple Listing Services (MLS), their authorized licensees, and prospective buyers.

2. BROKER advises and suggests that SELLER/TENANT safeguard or remove valuables now located within the premises.

3. It is not a requirement of the MLS or BROKER that a SELLER allow use of a lock box.

4. Where a TENANT occupies the property, the TENANT'S consent is required.

Neither listing nor selling BROKER, MLS, or BOARD OF REALTORS® is an insurer against the loss of personal property. SELLER/TENANT

is advised to verify the existence of, or obtain appropriate insurance through their own insurance agent.

Receipt of a copy is hereby acknowledged.

Dated _____   Dated _____

Broker _____   SELLER _____

By _____   SELLER _____

TENANT: I have read the above and consent to the placement of a lock box on the premises.
Receipt of a copy is hereby acknowledged.

Dated _____   TENANT_____

                                          TENANT_____

NO REPRESENTATION IS MADE AS TO THE LEGAL VALIDITY OF ANY PROVISION OR THE ADEQUACY OF ANY PROVISION IN ANY SPECIFIC TRANSACTION. A REAL ESTATE BROKER IS THE PERSON QUALIFIED TO ADVISE ON REAL ESTATE TRANSACTIONS. IF YOU DESIRE LEGAL ADVICE CONSULT YOUR ATTORNEY.

To order, contact—California Association of Realtors®
525 S. Virgil Avenue, Los Angeles, California 90020
Copyright© 1984, California Association of Realtors®   FORM LBA-11

Exhibit 9

SELLER FINANCING DISCLOSURE STATEMENT
(California Civil Code 2956-2967)
CALIFORNIA ASSOCIATION OF REALTORS® STANDARD FORM

This three page disclosure statement from the purchaser (buyer) and vendor (seller) is prepared by an arranger of credit [defined in Civil Code 2957 (a)] and provided to **both** the purchaser (buyer) and vendor (seller) in a residential real estate sales transaction involving four or fewer units whenever the seller has agreed to extend credit to the buyer as part of the purchase price.

Buyer: _____

Seller: _____

Arranger of Credit: _____

Real Property: _____

A. Credit documents: This extension of credit by the seller is evidenced by note and deed of trust ☐, all-inclusive note and deed of trust ☐, installment land sale contract ☐, lease/option (when parties intend transfer of equitable title) ☐, other ☐, (specify) _____
_____

B. Credit terms:

1. ☐ See attached copy of credit documents referred to in Section A above for description of credit terms; **or**

2. ☐ The terms of the credit documents referred to in Section A above are: Principal amount $_____ interest at
_____% per annum payable at $_____ per _____ (month/year/etc.) with the entire unpaid principal and accrued
interest of approximately $_____ due _____ 19 _____ (maturity date).

Late Charge: If any payment is not made within _____ days after it is due, a late charge of $_____ or _____% of the installment due may be charged to the buyer.

Prepayment: If all or part of this loan is paid early, the buyer will ☐, will **not** ☐, have to pay a prepayment penalty as follows: _____
_____
_____

Due On Sale: If any interest in the property securing this obligation is sold or otherwise transferred, the seller has ☐, does **not** have ☐, the option to require immediate payment of the entire unpaid balance and accrued interest.

Other Terms: _____
_____
_____

C. Available information on loans/encumbrances * that will be **senior** to the seller's extension of credit:

	1st	2nd	3rd
1. Original Balance	$_____	$_____	$_____
2. Current Balance	$_____	$_____	$_____
3. Periodic Payment (e.g. $100/month)	$_____/_____	$_____/_____	$_____/_____
4. Amt. of Balloon Payment	$_____	$_____	$_____
5. Date of Balloon Payment	_____	_____	_____
6. Maturity Date	_____	_____	_____
7. Due On Sale ('Yes' or 'No')	_____	_____	_____
8. Interest Rate (per annum)	_____%	_____%	_____%
9. Fixed or Variable Rate: If Variable Rate:	☐ a copy of note attached ☐ variable provisions are explained on attached separate sheet	☐ a copy of note attached ☐ variable provisions are explained on attached separate sheet	☐ a copy of note attached ☐ variable provisions are explained on attached separate sheet
10. Is Payment Current?	_____	_____	_____

☐ SEPARATE SHEET WITH INFORMATION REGARDING OTHER SENIOR LOANS/ENCUMBRANCES IS ATTACHED.

 * IMPORTANT NOTE: Asterisk (*) denotes an estimate.

D. Caution: If any of the obligations secured by the property calls for a balloon payment, then seller and buyer are aware that refinancing of the balloon payment at maturity may be difficult or impossible depending on the conditions in the mortgage marketplace at that time. There are no assurances that new financing or a loan extension will be available when the balloon payment is due.

> REPRINTED BY PERMISSION CALIFORNIA ASSOCIATION OF REALTORS® . ENDORSEMENT NOT IMPLIED

TT-L5-FG

Exhibit 10.1

SELLER FINANCING DISCLOSURE STATEMENT
(California Civil Code 2956-2967)
CALIFORNIA ASSOCIATION OF REALTORS® STANDARD FORM

E. Deferred interest:

"Deferred interest" results when the buyer's periodic payments are less than the amount of interest earned on the obligation, or when the obligation does not require periodic payments. This accrued interest will have to be paid by the buyer at a later time and may result in the buyer owing more on the obligation than at origination.

☐ The credit being extended to the buyer by the seller does **not** provide for "deferred interest."; **or**

☐ The credit being extended to the buyer by the seller does provide for "deferred interest."

    The credit documents provide the following regarding deferred interest:

    ☐ All deferred interest shall be due and payable along with the principal at maturity (simple interest); **or**

    ☐ The deferred interest shall be added to the principal _____ (e.g., annually, monthly, etc.) and thereafter shall bear interest at the rate specified in the credit documents (compound interest); **or**

    ☐ Other (specify) _____

F. All-Inclusive Deed of Trust or Installment Land Sale Contract:

☐ This transaction does **not** involve the use of an all-inclusive (or wraparound) deed of trust or an installment land sale contract; **or**

☐ This transaction **does** involve the use of either an all-inclusive (or wraparound) deed of trust or an installment land sale contract which provides as follows:

    1) In the event of an acceleration of any senior encumbrance, the responsibility for payment or for legal defense is:

    ☐ **Not** specified in the credit or security documents; **or**

    ☐ Specified in the credit or security documents as follows:

    _____

    _____

    2) In the event of the prepayment of a senior encumbrance, the responsibilities and rights of seller and buyer regarding refinancing, prepayment penalties, and any prepayment discounts are:

    ☐ **Not** specified in the credit or security documents; **or**

    ☐ Specified in the credit or security documents as follows:

    _____

    _____

    3) The financing provides that the buyer will make periodic payments to _____

    [e.g., a collection agent (such as a bank or savings and loan); seller; etc.] and that _____

    will be responsible for disbursing payments to the payee(s) on the senior encumbrance(s) and to the seller.

CAUTION: The parties are advised to consider designating a neutral third party as the collection agent for receiving buyer's payments and disbursing them to the payee(s) on the senior encumbrance(s) and to the seller.

G. Buyer's creditworthiness: Section 580(b) of the California Code of Civil Procedure generally limits a seller's rights in the event of a default by the buyer in the financing extended by the seller, to a foreclosure of the property.

☐ No disclosure concerning the buyer's creditworthiness has been made to the seller; **or**

☐ The following representations concerning the buyer's creditworthiness have been made by the buyer(s) to the seller:

1. Occupation: _____	1. Occupation: _____
2. Employer: _____	2. Employer: _____
3. Length of Employment: _____	3. Length of Employment: _____
4. Monthly Gross Income: _____	4. Monthly Gross Income: _____
5. Buyer has ☐, has **not** ☐, provided seller a current credit report issued by: _____	5. Buyer has ☐, has **not** ☐, provided seller a current credit report issued by: _____
6. Buyer has ☐, has **not** ☐, provided seller a completed loan application.	6. Buyer has ☐, has **not** ☐, provided seller a completed loan application.
7. Other (specify): _____	7. Other (specify): _____
_____	_____
_____	_____

H. Insurance:

☐ The parties' escrow holder or insurance carrier has been or will be directed to add a loss payee clause to the property insurance protecting the seller; **or**

☐ No provision has been made for adding a loss payee clause to the property insurance protecting the seller. Seller is advised to secure such clauses or acquire a separate insurance policy.

To order, contact—California Association of Realtors®
525 S. Virgil Avenue, Los Angeles, California 90020
Copyright © 1983, California Association of Realtors®

FORM SFD-11-2

TT-L5-FG

Exhibit 10.2

SELLER FINANCING DISCLOSURE STATEMENT
(California Civil Code 2956-2967)
CALIFORNIA ASSOCIATION OF REALTORS® STANDARD FORM

I. Request for notice:

☐ A Request for Notice of Default under Section 2924(b) of the California Civil Code has been or will be recorded; **or**

☐ No provision for recording a Request for Notice of Default has been made. Seller is advised to consider recording a Request for Notice of Default.

J. Title Insurance:

☐ Title insurance coverage will be provided to **both** seller and buyer insuring their respective interests in the property; **or**

☐ No provision for title insurance coverage of **both** seller and buyer has been made. Seller and buyer are advised to consider securing such title insurance coverage.

K. Tax service:

☐ A tax service has been arranged to report to seller whether property taxes have been paid on the property. _____ [e.g., seller, buyer, etc.] will be responsible for the continued retention and payment of such tax service; **or**

☐ No provision has been made for a tax service. Seller should consider retaining a tax service or otherwise determine that the property taxes are paid.

L. Recording:

☐ The security documents (e.g., deed of trust, installment land contract, etc.) will be recorded with the county recorder where the property is located; **or**

☐ The security documents will **not** be recorded with the county recorder. Seller and buyer are advised that their respective interests in the property may be jeopardized by intervening liens, judgments or subsequent transfers which **are** recorded.

M. Proceeds to buyer:

☐ Buyer will **NOT** receive any cash proceeds at the close of the sale transaction; **or**

☐ Buyer will receive approximately $ _____ from _____ [indicate source from the sale transaction proceeds of such funds]. Buyer represents that the purpose of such disbursement is as follows: _____

_____

N. Notice of Delinquency:

☐ A Request for Notice of Delinquency under Section 2924(e) of the California Civil Code has been or will be made to the Senior lienholder(s); **or**

☐ No provision for making a Request for Notice of Delinquency has been made. Seller should consider making a Request for Notice of Delinquency.

The above information has been provided to: (a) the buyer, by the arranger of credit and the seller (with respect to information within the knowledge of the seller); (b) the seller, by the arranger of credit and the buyer (with respect to information within the knowledge of the buyer).

Arranger of Credit _____

Dated _____ , 19____.   By _____

Buyer and seller acknowledge that the information each has provided to the arranger of credit for inclusion in this disclosure form is accurate to the best of their knowledge.

Buyer and seller hereby acknowledge receipt of a completed copy of this disclosure form.

Dated _____ , 19____.   Dated _____ , 19____.

Buyer _____   Seller _____

Buyer _____   Seller _____

A REAL ESTATE BROKER IS THE PERSON QUALIFIED TO ADVISE ON REAL ESTATE. IF YOU DESIRE LEGAL ADVICE, CONSULT YOUR ATTORNEY.

To order, contact—California Association of Realtors®
525 S. Virgil Avenue, Los Angeles, California 90020
Copyright© 1983, Revised 1985, California Association of Realtors®   FORM SFD-11-3

EQUAL HOUSING OPPORTUNITY
TT-L5-FG

Exhibit 10.3

Chapter 4 Quiz

1. The "AIDA" approach to listing procedure refers to:

   (A) Arrange, involve, direct, adjust
   (B) Ask, involve, decide, authorize
   (C) Acquaintance, inquiry, decision, action
   ✓(D) Attention, interest, desire, action

2. In which type of listing is the percentage of commission not predetermined?

   (A) Multiple listing
   (B) Option
   ✓(C) Net listing
   (D) Combination listing-option

3. Under an exclusive right to sell listing, the listing broker is entitled to a commission:

   (A) If the broker negotiates the sale
   (B) If any other broker negotiates the sale
   (C) If the owner negotiates the sale
   ✓(D) Any of the above

4. Under the listing contract, the seller has the right to expect _____ from the broker and his office to find the ready, willing, and able buyer.

   ✓(A) Due diligence
   (B) An advertisement
   (C) A telephone call
   (D) An open house

5. The contract which entitles the listing broker to a commission regardless of who makes the sale is a(n):

   (A) Open listing
   ✓(B) Exclusive authorization and right to sell listing
   (C) Deposit receipt
   (D) Exclusive agency listing

6. A listing may be terminated by any of the following except:

   (A) Agreement of the parties
   (B) Expiration of the specified term
   ✓(C) Tenant of property owner
   (D) Death of either principal or agent

7. Professional real estate licensees consider which type of listing the most desirable one to obtain?

   (A) Net listing
   ✓(B) Exclusive listing
   (C) Exclusive agency listing
   (D) Open listing

8. The contract by which a principal employs a broker to represent the principal in procuring a buyer for property is called a(n):

   (A) Contract for the sale of real estate
   ✓(B) Listing agreement
   (C) Deposit receipt
   (D) Option to buy

9. A written agreement in which the owner reserves the right to sell his own property without paying a commission, but agrees to pay a commission to the listing agent if any other licensee brings about a sale is a(n):

   ✓(A) Open listing
   ✓(B) Exclusive agency listing
   (C) Exclusive right to sell listing
   (D) Net listing

10. A written agreement authorizing a broker or brokers on a nonexclusive basis to bring about the sale of the property, and allowing the principal himself to sell without paying a commission, is a(n):

    (A) Net listing
    (B) Exclusive agency listing
    (C) Exclusive right to sell listing
    ✓(D) Open listing

Chapter 5
Property Valuation of Listings

PREVIEW

Value

Appraisal and Its Uses

Competitive Market Analysis

Appraisal Report Form

Three Approaches to Value Estimation

Overpriced Listing Problems

VALUE

Value has been defined as the relationship between desirous persons and things desired. It relates to the ability of one good to command other commodities in exchange. It may also be defined as the present worth of future rights, benefits, net income, or amenities. Value is a mental concept dependent upon utility; it is not inherent in any object and must be related to persons.

Value, Price, and Cost   Value, price, and cost can be the same amount, or they can be different amounts.

Value. Value relates to the *purchasing power* of the money the property will command; it is what a property is worth.

Price. Price is the *amount* of money that is given or paid for a property. It is an indication of value in terms of money.

Cost. Cost refers to the total *past* expenditures.

Examples

☐ The home you sold yesterday was *priced* at $160,000. It may have been *valued* at $160,000 by the buyer and seller, and $160,000 might also have been the total amount of expenditures or *cost*.

☐ The home you sold last month may have been *valued* at $140,000, but the buyer may have paid $145,000 (*price*) for the home and then spent another $15,000 for landscaping and new carpeting bringing the total *cost* to $160,000.

Value Concepts

Because value depends on people's desires, there are infinite types and definitions of value. They can be roughly categorized as:

Objective Value. Value may be considered as the power to command other commodities in exchange (excludes sentiment).

Subjective Value. Value in use refers to the value to a specific owner-user. It is also referred to as utility value and is based on sentiment.

Market Value. A widely accepted definition of market value is the highest price estimated in terms of money which a property will bring if exposed for sale in the open market, given reasonable time to find a knowledgeable buyer, i.e., one who is cognizant of all the property's existing and potential uses and purposes.

Relation to Price. In most cases, market value means market price. The essence of the market value concept lies in the exchangeability of the property as the test of value.

Essential Elements of Value

In order to have market value, four elements must be present.

Utility. The value of an object depends on its power to render a service or satisfaction.

Scarcity. A limited supply of the object relative to the demand for it, i.e., a lack of relative abundance, creates value.

Demand. Desire for the object gives it value, if it is supported by the ability to purchase the object. In other words, an *effective* demand is one with individual(s) who are ready, willing, and able to buy.

Transferability. It must be feasible to convey control and possession of the rights of ownership; a seller must be able to provide marketable title.

Forces Influencing Value

Real estate licensees often say that the three most important factors which influence property value are location, location, and location. However, a location's value is affected over time by forces in the world around it. The four major forces interacting upon and influencing property values are:

Social. This includes changing life styles and priorities regarding crime, law and order, education, family structure, social and cultural activities; rate of growth or decline in population and household formation; divorce rate, birth rate, death rate and other demographic factors.

Political or Governmental. Property value is affected by growth/no-growth decisions; policies regarding air, noise, and aesthetic pollution; zoning, building, health and safety ordinances; governmental fiscal and monetary policies; governmental attitudes toward business development and energy programs.

Economic. This includes employment and unemployment levels, incomes and interest rates, community economic base structure, governmental attitudes toward availability and prices of energy supplies.

Physical. Value varies with quality of construction and materials, size and shape of the parcel, influence of weather elements on the property, degree of maintenance or lack of it on the property and site.

Basic Principles of Real Property Values

The value and the price of real estate are governed by many basic economic principles, including the principles of:

Change. Nothing remains static; real property values are constantly changing. Social, political, economic, and physical forces are continually at work causing property values to increase or decrease in value. The real estate licensee who values properties for listing purposes must be sensitive to change. Every change in the social, political, economic, and physical forces will affect the property value in one way or another.

Highest and Best Use. This means the use which is most likely to produce the highest net return to the land over a given period of time. Net return refers to the yield left after all costs. Highest net return can include amenities as well as monetary yields. A highest and best use analysis may lead to the decision that a physically sound single-family residence on a downtown lot, zoned commercial, be torn down and the unpaved lot be used for a revenue-producing parking lot, or for a public park.

Supply and Demand. Market value is determined by the interaction of supply and demand as of the date of the appraisal. Value increases as supply decreases and demand increases. Conversely, value decreases as supply increases and demand decreases. If demand is constant, value increases as supply decreases, and decreases as supply increases. If supply is constant, value increases as demand increases, and decreases as demand decreases.

Example

A choice oceanfront view, a scarce and desirable commodity in California, continuously commands an increase in market value as population (demand) increases.

Substitution. Property value generally tends to be determined by the cost of acquiring an equally desirable substitute property. That cost tends to set the upper limit of value.

Conformity. Value tends to be maximized by a reasonable degree of conformity, but tends to decrease with monotonous uniformity. When surrounded by properties of greater value, property generally increases in value. Conversely, when surrounded by properties of lesser value, property value tends to decrease.

The appraisal process is a systematic and orderly approach to an estimate or opinion of value. There are several types of appraisal, having different roles in real estate practice.

Appraisal in General A general definition of appraisal is a supportable estimate or opinion of value as of a specific date. The accuracy of the appraisal depends upon the appraiser's skill in obtaining the necessary pertinent data, ability to organize and analyze the data, and good judgment in the evaluation of that data. Generally, the more skill and experience the appraiser has, the better will be the judgment.

"Certified Appraisal" This is defined by California Civil Code §1922, effective January 1, 1988, as an act or process, for or in expectation of compensation, to produce an analysis, opinion, or conclusion relating to the value of specified interests in identified real property, when that act or process or the communication of its results is termed or designated as a "certified appraisal" or by any other term or identification which is likely to be confused with a certified appraisal, including, but not limited to, "registered appraisal" or "licensed appraisal," or is knowingly performed or prepared in response to a requirement or provision in law for the performance or furnishing of a certified appraisal.

"Certified Appraisal Report." Under the same law, this means any communication, written or oral, of an analysis, opinion, or conclusion relating to the value of real property which is termed a certified appraisal report or is in any way described as a communication of the results of a certified appraisal.

Regulations. On and after January 1, 1988, any person performing a "certified appraisal" or issuing a "certified appraisal report" must comply with extensive requirements of Civil Code Section 1922 et seq.

Uses of Appraisal Most often clients seek appraisal advice for setting a listing price on property they have for sale, but there are other uses as well, such as estimating property values for buyers, loan purposes, insurance purposes, condemnation (eminent domain) proceedings, inheritance tax and capital gains tax, divorce proceedings, property tax assessment, dissolution of a partnership, justification of casualty losses, depreciable basis for investment properties, and tax basis for charitable deductions.

Rule 41C The Office of Thrift Supervision, formerly known as the Federal Home Loan Bank Board, issues regulations for the appraisal policies of "insured associations and service corporations," since the soundness of their mortgage loans and real estate investments depends to a great extent on the adequacy of the appraisals used to support those transactions. Requirements include:

Appraisers' Qualifications. Appraisers must demonstrate "experience, education, and facilities" appropriate to the standards of the FHLBB and the fiscal management needs of the institution.

Content. Written appraisals must be fully documented, descriptive, current, unbiased, self-contained, and understandable by a third party.

FNMA/FHLMC Standards. Compliance with Fannie Mae and Freddie Mac appraisal guidelines and use of FNMA/FHLMC form reports is sufficient for appraisals on existing one to four family dwellings and multi family properties.

Valuation by Licensee
Appraisal is not an exact science. It is an art based upon the experience and judgment of the appraiser. The real estate licensee can learn the basic method used in estimating real estate values, obtain pertinent data, and with full knowledge of the forces that affect value, approach the listing process in a professional manner. With sound data and good judgment, the licensee will be able to recommend reasonable listing prices to clients.

COMPETITIVE MARKET ANALYSIS

A competitive market analysis is not a true appraisal, but is a form commonly used by real estate licensees to assist owners to arrive at realistic understandings about probable market values and appropriate, realistic listing prices. A typical market analysis (Exhibit 11) will identify three kinds of comparable or similar properties:

☐ Properties on the market now

☐ Properties recently sold, suggesting acceptable to low market prices.

☐ Properties recently on the market but not sold, possibly because they were overpriced.

Properties for Sale
This section looks at what is currently on the market: the competition, what sellers are trying to get for their property. Prices here probably indicate the upper range of value, the ceiling, for the subject property.

Properties Sold
This section notes what has recently been sold: what buyers have been willing to pay. It suggests the lower range of value, the floor. This is probably the best indicator of current value, and may be the most important information on the form.

Properties Not Sold
These are listings which have been taken off the market or expired: what buyers are not willing to pay. These prices probably exceed the upper limit of value for the subject property and tell what happens if you price it higher, i.e., the property may not sell.

APPRAISAL REPORT FORM

Qualified, competent real property appraisers must be objective and disinterested when submitting their final estimate of value, in one of three forms of written reports.

Form Report   The form report usually consists of a standard one- to four-page checklist form used by many lending institutions when appraising for loan purposes. Most savings and loans use the Federal National Mortgage Association (FNMA or "Fannie Mae")-Federal Home Loan Mortgage Corporation (FHLMC or "Freddie Mac") *Uniform Residential Appraisal Report* forms containing check boxes and spaces for pertinent data and photographs of the subject property (Exhibit 12). This type of report is commonly used for single-family residential property.

Letter Report   The letter report is essentially a summary. It consists of a brief description of the property, the purpose of and type of value sought, the value estimate as of a specific date, and the appraiser's signature and professional designation. This type of appraisal report is used when the client is familiar with the property and the neighborhood. Supporting data is not necessary, unless the client specifically asks for it, and the fee is commensurate with the appraiser's time, knowledge, and expertise.

Narrative Report   This is the most complete, documented report, containing all pertinent information regarding the area, the property, and the rationale and calculations leading to the final estimate in value. Because it involves the most comprehensive analysis and documentation and is time consuming, it is the most expensive of all three appraisal report forms. This type of report is often requested by attorneys, governmental agencies, corporations, and institutional investors.

THREE APPROACHES TO VALUE ESTIMATION

In estimating value for listing and sales purposes, the appraiser will most likely use a variation of the form report and three approaches: market, cost, and income. The appraiser will utilize all three approaches in each appraisal; however, only one approach will be emphasized in the final estimation, the one which is determined most relevant to the type of the property, the purpose of the appraisal, and the availability and validity of the analyzed data. A competent appraiser will *not* average the value estimates of the three separate approaches.

Market Data Approach   This approach is often called comparable or sales analysis method and is also called the adjusted sales price comparison approach.

Data. This approach compares recent sales of similar properties in the subject property area. The market data approach must take into account the type of property being appraised, the number of sales of comparable properties ("comps"), including the price, terms, and conditions of the sales, and an adjustment for differences between the subject property and the "comps."

Principle. This approach is based upon the principle of substitution, which states that the cost of acquiring an equally desirable property without undue delay ordinarily sets the upper limits of value for the subject property.

Method. Adjustments are made for age, condition, size, location, date of sale, financing terms, features and amenities, and other relevant factors.

Use. This approach is often emphasized in the value estimation of single-family residences.

Market Data Approach Illustration

Data	Comp A	Comp B	Comp C	Subject Property
Price	$135,000	$120,200	$123,500	?
Date of Sale	1990	1989	1988	1990-appraisal
Lot	Equal	Equal	Better	–
Design/Floor Plan	Better	Equal	Equal	–
Bedrooms	3	3	3	3
Baths	1 3/4	1	1 3/4	1 3/4
Condition	Better	Equal	Equal	–

Assume market prices increased 5% per year (not compounded) and that the price difference for each plus or minus feature (better or poorer) averages $1,500. What should the recommended listing price be?

Solution	Comp A	Comp B	Comp C	Subject Property
Price	$135,000	$120,200	$123,500	–
Date of Sale	-0- *	+6,010*	+12,350*	–
Lot	-0- *	-0-*	–1,500 *	–
Design/Floor Plan	–1,500*	-0-*	-0-*	–
Bedrooms	-0- *	-0-*	-0-*	–
Baths	-0- *	+1,500*	-0-*	–
Condition	–1,500*	-0-*	-0-*	–
TOTAL	$132,000	$127,710	$134,350	–

* = Adjustments

Solution: Indicated value range for subject property is $127,710 to $134,350.

Recommended listing price: $130,000.

Rationale: Comparable sale "B" is most similar in terms of lot, design/floor plan and condition; however, subject property has an additional 3/4 bath. Subject property is not quite equal to the most recent sale "A." Therefore, a recommended listing price is $130,000.

Cost Approach This is also called the reproduction or replacement approach.

> **Principle.** This approach addresses the property in terms of what it would cost to replace (reproduce) the improvements with equal utility, including loss in value from depreciation. The appraiser relies on costs involved in replacing the improvements in today's economy.
>
> **Data.** The appraiser takes the following into account:
>
> □ *Land.* The estimated value of the land as though it were vacant.
>
> □ *Building Cost.* An estimate of the replacement cost of the improvements as of the date of the appraisal, including labor and material costs of replacing the improvements.
>
> □ *Depreciation.* An estimate of the accrued depreciation (any loss in value applicable to the property as of the appraisal date). Depreciation includes loss in value due to wear and tear or physical deterioration, functional obsolescence (outdated design, style, or equipment), and economic obsolescence (loss in value due to external forces).
>
> **Use.** This approach is often used to appraise new structures before occupancy, and those properties that do not have comparable sales or are difficult or impossible to appraise by the income approach, such as a church building.

Cost Approach Illustration

Three year old, three bedroom, 1-3/4 bath home, 1700 square feet, on quarter of an acre lot, landscaped and with swimming pool.

Step 1.	Land Value, as if vacant		$35,000
Step 2.	Estimated Replacement Cost, as if new		
	1700 sq. ft.@ $50 per sq. ft.		$85,000
	Landscaping, etc.		8,000
	Swimming Pool		12,000
	Total Replacement Cost		$105,000
Step 3.	Total Replacement Cost		$105,000
	Less: Estimated loss from Accrued Depreciation		– 10,000
	Replacement Cost less Depreciation		95,000
	Estimate of Value via the Cost Approach		$130,000

This estimate supports the listing price of $130,000 suggested by the Market Data Approach.

Income Approach This is also called the capitalization method, and as its name suggests, applies to income-producing properties.

Principles. This approach is used to estimate the present worth or value of future benefits, that is, the stream of future net income from the property. This method is in effect a prediction, based on stabilization of gross income, allowances for vacancy and collection losses, stabilization of expenses, net operating income, selection of an appropriate capitalization method and rate, and the assumption that the property is free and clear of loans.

Data and Method. The procedure for estimating value by the income approach is as follows:

☐ Estimation of *gross scheduled income*. This means income from all sources at 100 percent occupancy.

☐ Deduction of a reasonable amount for vacancy and collection losses to arrive at an *effective gross income*.

☐ Estimation of all *operating expenses*: management, wages, utilities, advertising, repairs, taxes, and insurance. Debt service is not considered.

☐ Deduction of operating expenses from effective gross income results in the *net operating income*.

☐ Selection of an appropriate *capitalization rate*. This is based on mortgage interest rates and/or the rate of return an investor would want as a reasonable return on an investment of this type.

Use. This approach is often emphasized in appraising rented commercial property and apartments.

Variations. There are more and less complex methods of appraisal using capitalization. Differences apply mainly to the way the capitalization rate is determined.

☐ *Band of Investment Method.* This complex technique uses weighted averages of the different rates applicable to the various components of the invested capital, i.e., one rate for mortgage payments and another, generally higher, for return on investors' equity.

☐ *Comparative Sales Method.* If enough comparable sales are available, a going market rate can be found by dividing the net incomes from those properties by their sales prices.

Income Approach Illustration

Assume the subject property is a new 10-unit apartment building with a potential gross income of $100,000. The vacancy and income loss allowance is estimated to be 5% of the scheduled gross income. Operating expenses are estimated at $45,000. The expected life of the building is 50 years.

The prevailing financing terms for this type of property are a 75% loan-to-value ratio at 9.5% interest for 25 years. Investors typically require a 12% return on comparable properties.

Computation of the indicated value of the property:

Potential Gross Income	**$100,000**
Less: Allowance for Vacancy and Income Loss (5%)	**– 5,000**
Effective Gross Income	**$ 95,000**
Less: Operating Expenses	**– 45,000**
Net Operating Income	**$ 50,000**

---

1. Band of Investment Method

First Mortgage   .75 x .1048*   =   .0786
(*where .1048 is the mortgage constant for the given loan terms.)

Equity   .25 x .12   =   +.03

Capitalization Rate   =   .1086

Value   = $\dfrac{I}{R}$ = $\dfrac{\$50,000}{.1086}$ = $460,405   rounded to $460,000

---

2. Comparative Sales Method

Assume the analysis of comparable sales indicates that 10% is the appropriate capitalization rate.

Value   = $\dfrac{I}{R}$ = $\dfrac{\$50,000}{.10}$ = $500,000

Gross Monthly Multipliers This is a variation on the market data approach based on gross income. Most homes are purchased for owner-user shelter and not income. Therefore, appraisers give greatest weight to the estimate of a house's value by the market approach, and relatively little to the income approach. However, it is possible to use *gross monthly multipliers* in place of the income approach when appraising single-family houses.

Definition. The gross monthly multiplier is a ratio that states the relationship between the monthly rental income and the value of the property.

Method. An appraiser may observe that houses of a certain type sell for a certain number of times their gross monthly rental. For example, an observed multiplier of 160 times a monthly rental of $810 indicates a sales price of $129,600. The appraiser arrives at the gross monthly multiplier of 160 by observing sales prices and rental values of similar houses and dividing the sales price by the gross monthly rent, e.g., $129,600 ÷ $810 = 160. For the method to work, there must be enough comparable homes rented and sold to provide data. This is often not the case.

Use. The gross monthly multiplier can be used for an estimate of value by the income method to support a suggested listing price, but this method produces only a rough estimate or ballpark figure. The licensee should rely more heavily on the market data estimate for listing houses for sale.

OVERPRICED LISTING PROBLEMS

Most sellers of real property will look upon the licensee as being the professional in home values and selling prices in the area. However, they will almost certainly have a price in mind based upon rumors, hearsay, hopes, and possibly facts. In your fiduciary relationship capacity you must be truthful and sincere with your clients. If the client insists upon an unrealistic listing price it might be better to turn down the opportunity to list at that price. Let some other licensee face the unhappy client when the property doesn't sell. You may get the listing later on at a more appropriate price and terms.

Dangers Licensees who take overpriced listings are likely to find reluctance to show the property by both the listing office and other usually cooperating offices, have difficulty justifying their advertising expense, have difficulty servicing the unrealistically priced listings, dread facing the unhappy seller, and lose the listing and the client.

Rewards A licensee who refuses to take overpriced listings will tend to develop good licensee-client relationships, build a professional practice on a sound business basis, minimize competition, have a better return on effort expended, and form a habit of success.

COMPETITIVE MARKET ANALYSIS

PROPERTY ADDRESS _____ DATE _____

PROPERTY DESCRIPTION:	Bd rms	Ba	FR/ Den	Reported Sq. Ft.	Other

ON MARKET NOW

EXISTING LOANS						NEW FINANCING	
FIRST			SECOND			SELLER MAY CARRY	
Reported Balance	Rate	Type	Reported Balance	Rate	Type	List Price	Days on Mkt

REPORTED SOLD PAST 12 MONTHS

	OTHER TERMS & COMMENTS
Sale Price	Financing	Date Sold	Other Terms & Comments

REPORTED EXPIRED PAST 12 MONTHS

Amount	Rate	Term	Other Terms & Comments

GENERAL COMMENTS:

PROBABLE MARKETING RANGE $ _____

Information reported herein is based upon published reports or matters of public record.
No representation is made or intended that this information is accurate or complete.
Financing information may not reflect specific loan terms.

The undersigned acknowledge receipt of a copy.

_____ Date _____

COMPANY _____
AGENT _____
PHONE _____

_____ Date _____

To order, contact CALIFORNIA ASSOCIATION OF REALTORS®
525 So. Virgil Avenue, Los Angeles, California 90020

REPRINTED BY PERMISSION CALIFORNIA ASSOCIATION OF REALTORS®. ENDORSEMENT NOT IMPLIED

CRC ℗ ™

Exhibit 11

Property Description & Analysis   **UNIFORM RESIDENTIAL APPRAISAL REPORT**   File No. ☐☐

SUBJECT

Property Address	Census Tract
City　　　　County　　　　State　　Zip Code	LENDER DISCRETIONARY USE
Legal Description	Sale Price $
Owner/Occupant　　　　　Map Reference	Date
Sale Price $　　　Date of Sale	Mortgage Amount $
Loan charges/concessions to be paid by seller $	Mortgage Type
R.E. Taxes $　　　Tax Year　　　HOA $/Mo.	Discount Points and Other Concessions
Lender/Client	Paid by Seller $

PROPERTY RIGHTS APPRAISED
☐ Fee Simple
☐ Leasehold
☐ Condominium (HUD/VA)
☐ De Minimis PUD

Source

NEIGHBORHOOD

LOCATION	☐ Urban	☐ Suburban	☐ Rural
BUILT UP	☐ Over 75%	☐ 25-75%	☐ Under 25%
GROWTH RATE	☐ Rapid	☐ Stable	☐ Slow
PROPERTY VALUES	☐ Increasing	☐ Stable	☐ Declining
DEMAND/SUPPLY	☐ Shortage	☐ In Balance	☐ Over Supply
MARKETING TIME	☐ Under 3 Mos.	☐ 3-6 Mos.	☐ Over 6 Mos.

PRESENT LAND USE %	LAND USE CHANGE	PREDOMINANT	SINGLE FAMILY HOUSING
Single Family	Not Likely ☐	OCCUPANCY	PRICE $(000)　AGE (yrs)
2-4 Family	Likely ☐	☐ Owner	
Multi-family	In process ☐	☐ Tenant	Low
Commercial	To:	☐ Vacant (0-5%)	High
Industrial		☐ Vacant (over 5%)	Predominant
Vacant			—

NEIGHBORHOOD ANALYSIS	Good	Avg.	Fair	Poor
Employment Stability	☐	☐	☐	☐
Convenience to Employment	☐	☐	☐	☐
Convenience to Shopping	☐	☐	☐	☐
Convenience to Schools	☐	☐	☐	☐
Adequacy of Public Transportation	☐	☐	☐	☐
Recreation Facilities	☐	☐	☐	☐
Adequacy of Utilities	☐	☐	☐	☐
Property Compatibility	☐	☐	☐	☐
Protection from Detrimental Cond.	☐	☐	☐	☐
Police & Fire Protection	☐	☐	☐	☐
General Appearance of Properties	☐	☐	☐	☐
Appeal to Market	☐	☐	☐	☐

Note: Race or the racial composition of the neighborhood are not considered reliable appraisal factors.
COMMENTS:

SITE

Dimensions	Topography
Site Area　　　　Corner Lot	Size
Zoning Classification　　　Zoning Compliance	Shape
HIGHEST & BEST USE: Present Use　　Other Use	Drainage

UTILITIES	Public	Other	SITE IMPROVEMENTS	Type	Public	Private
Electricity	☐		Street		☐	☐
Gas	☐		Curb/Gutter		☐	☐
Water	☐		Sidewalk		☐	☐
Sanitary Sewer	☐		Street Lights		☐	☐
Storm Sewer	☐		Alley		☐	☐

View	
Landscaping	
Driveway	
Apparent Easements	
FEMA Flood Hazard Yes* ___ No ___	
FEMA* Map/Zone	

COMMENTS (Apparent adverse easements, encroachments, special assessments, slide areas, etc.):

IMPROVEMENTS

GENERAL DESCRIPTION	EXTERIOR DESCRIPTION	FOUNDATION	BASEMENT	INSULATION
Units	Foundation	Slab	Area Sq. Ft.	Roof ☐
Stories	Exterior Walls	Crawl Space	% Finished	Ceiling ☐
Type (Det./Att.)	Roof Surface	Basement	Ceiling	Walls ☐
Design (Style)	Gutters & Dwnspts.	Sump Pump	Walls	Floor ☐
Existing	Window Type	Dampness	Floor	None ☐
Proposed	Storm Sash	Settlement	Outside Entry	Adequacy
Under Construction	Screens	Infestation		Energy Efficient Items:
Age (Yrs.)	Manufactured House			
Effective Age (Yrs.)				

ROOM LIST

ROOMS	Foyer	Living	Dining	Kitchen	Den	Family Rm.	Rec. Rm.	Bedrooms	# Baths	Laundry	Other	Area Sq. Ft.
Basement												
Level 1												
Level 2												

Finished area **above** grade contains:　Rooms;　Bedroom(s);　Bath(s);　Square Feet of Gross Living Area

INTERIOR

SURFACES	Materials/Condition	HEATING		KITCHEN EQUIP.		ATTIC	
Floors		Type		Refrigerator	☐	None	☐
Walls		Fuel		Range/Oven	☐	Stairs	☐
Trim/Finish		Condition		Disposal	☐	Drop Stair	☐
Bath Floor		Adequacy		Dishwasher	☐	Scuttle	☐
Bath Wainscot		COOLING		Fan/Hood	☐	Floor	☐
Doors		Central		Compactor	☐	Heated	☐
		Other		Washer/Dryer	☐	Finished	☐
		Condition		Microwave	☐		
Fireplace(s) #		Adequacy		Intercom	☐		

IMPROVEMENT ANALYSIS	Good	Avg.	Fair	Poor
Quality of Construction	☐	☐	☐	☐
Condition of Improvements	☐	☐	☐	☐
Room Sizes/Layout	☐	☐	☐	☐
Closets and Storage	☐	☐	☐	☐
Energy Efficiency	☐	☐	☐	☐
Plumbing-Adequacy & Condition	☐	☐	☐	☐
Electrical-Adequacy & Condition	☐	☐	☐	☐
Kitchen Cabinets-Adequacy & Cond.	☐	☐	☐	☐
Compatibility to Neighborhood	☐	☐	☐	☐
Appeal & Marketability	☐	☐	☐	☐

AUTOS

CAR STORAGE:		Attached ☐	Adequate ☐	House Entry ☐
No. Cars	Garage ☐ Carport ☐	Detached ☐	Inadequate ☐	Outside Entry ☐
Condition	None ☐	Built-In ☐	Electric Door ☐	Basement Entry ☐

Estimated Remaining Economic Life　　　Yrs.
Estimated Remaining Physical Life　　　Yrs.

Additional features:

COMMENTS

Depreciation (Physical, functional and external inadequacies, repairs needed, modernization, etc.):

General market conditions and prevalence and impact in subject/market area regarding loan discounts, interest buydowns and concessions:

Freddie Mac Form 70　10/86　　　　　　　　　　　　　　　　　　　Fannie Mae Form 1004　10/86

Exhibit 12.1

UNIFORM RESIDENTIAL APPRAISAL REPORT   File No.

Purpose of Appraisal is to estimate Market Value as defined in the Certification & Statement of Limiting Conditions.

COST APPROACH

BUILDING SKETCH (SHOW GROSS LIVING AREA ABOVE GRADE)
If for Freddie Mac or Fannie Mae, show only square foot calculations and cost approach comments in this space.

ESTIMATED REPRODUCTION COST - NEW - OF IMPROVEMENTS:

Dwelling	_____ Sq. Ft. @ $ _____	= $ _____
	_____ Sq. Ft. @ $ _____	= _____
Extras _____		= _____
		= _____
Special Energy Efficient Items _____		= _____
Porches, Patios, etc. _____		= _____
Garage/Carport _____ Sq. Ft. @ $ _____		= _____
Total Estimated Cost New		= $ _____

	Physical	Functional	External
Less			
Depreciation _____			= $ _____
Depreciated Value of Improvements			= $ _____
Site Imp. "as is" (driveway, landscaping, etc.)			= $ _____
ESTIMATED SITE VALUE			= $ _____
(If leasehold, show only leasehold value.)			
INDICATED VALUE BY COST APPROACH			= $ _____

(Not Required by Freddie Mac and Fannie Mae)
Does property conform to applicable HUD/VA property standards?   ☐ Yes   ☐ No
If No, explain:

Construction Warranty   ☐ Yes   ☐ No
Name of Warranty Program _____
Warranty Coverage Expires _____

The undersigned has recited three recent sales of properties most similar and proximate to subject and has considered these in the market analysis. The description includes a dollar adjustment, reflecting market reaction to those items of significant variation between the subject and comparable properties. If a significant item in the comparable property is superior to, or more favorable than, the subject property, a minus (−) adjustment is made, thus reducing the indicated value of subject; if a significant item in the comparable is inferior to, or less favorable than, the subject property, a plus (+) adjustment is made, thus increasing the indicated value of the subject.

SALES COMPARISON ANALYSIS

ITEM	SUBJECT	COMPARABLE NO. 1		COMPARABLE NO. 2		COMPARABLE NO. 3	
Address							
Proximity to Subject							
Sales Price	$		$		$		$
Price/Gross Liv. Area	$	$		$		$	
Data Source							
VALUE ADJUSTMENTS	DESCRIPTION	DESCRIPTION	+ (−) $ Adjustment	DESCRIPTION	+ (−) $ Adjustment	DESCRIPTION	+ (−) $ Adjustment
Sales or Financing Concessions							
Date of Sale/Time							
Location							
Site/View							
Design and Appeal							
Quality of Construction							
Age							
Condition							
Above Grade Room Count	Total ¦ Bdrms ¦ Baths	Total ¦ Bdrms ¦ Baths		Total ¦ Bdrms ¦ Baths		Total ¦ Bdrms ¦ Baths	
Gross Living Area	Sq. Ft.	Sq. Ft.		Sq. Ft.		Sq. Ft.	
Basement & Finished Rooms Below Grade							
Functional Utility							
Heating/Cooling							
Garage/Carport							
Porches, Patio, Pools, etc.							
Special Energy Efficient Items							
Fireplace(s)							
Other (e.g. kitchen equip., remodeling)							
Net Adj. (total)		☐ + ☐ − $		☐ + ☐ − $		☐ + ☐ − $	
Indicated Value of Subject			$		$		$

Comments on Sales Comparison:

INDICATED VALUE BY SALES COMPARISON APPROACH .... $ _____
INDICATED VALUE BY INCOME APPROACH (If Applicable) Estimated Market Rent $ _____ /Mo. x Gross Rent Multiplier _____ = $ _____
This appraisal is made ☐ "as is" ☐ subject to the repairs, alterations, inspections or conditions listed below ☐ completion per plans and specifications.
Comments and Conditions of Appraisal:

Final Reconciliation:

RECONCILIATION

This appraisal is based upon the above requirements, the certification, contingent and limiting conditions, and Market Value definition that are stated in
☐ FmHA, HUD &/or VA instructions.
☐ Freddie Mac Form 439 (Rev. 7/86)/Fannie Mae Form 1004B (Rev. 7/86) filed with client _____ 19 _____ ☐ attached.
I (WE) ESTIMATE THE MARKET VALUE, AS DEFINED, OF THE SUBJECT PROPERTY AS OF _____ 19 _____ to be $ _____

I (We) certify: that to the best of my (our) knowledge and belief the facts and data used herein are true and correct; that I (we) personally inspected the subject property, both inside and out, and have made an exterior inspection of all comparable sales cited in this report; and that I (we) have no undisclosed interest, present or prospective therein.

Appraiser(s) SIGNATURE _____   Review Appraiser SIGNATURE _____   ☐ Did ☐ Did Not
NAME _____   (if applicable) NAME _____   Inspect Property

Freddie Mac Form 70 10/86   Fannie Mae Form 1004 . 10/86

Exhibit 12.2

PHOTOGRAPH ADDENDUM: SUBJECT PROPERTY

Borrower/Client_____

Lender_____

Property Address_____

| | | Street | |
| City | County | State | Zip |

FRONT VIEW OF
SUBJECT PROPERTY

REAR VIEW OF
SUBJECT PROPERTY

STREET SCENE

ADDITIONAL PHOTOGRAPHS ON REVERSE SIDE

Exhibit 12.3

Chapter 5 Quiz

1. The "power of one good to command others in exchange" is a definition of:

    (A) Commodity
    (B) Price
    (C) Value
    (D) Demand

2. The four essential elements of value are:

    (A) Cost, location, demand, and financing
    (B) Utility, scarcity, demand, transferability
    (C) Time, title, interest, and possession
    (D) Consent, consideration, legality, and capacity

3. Generally, the most expensive type of appraisal report form is the:

    (A) Letter report
    (B) Freddie Mac form
    (C) Narrative report
    (D) Fannie Mae form

4. In the market data approach to value, it is necessary to:

    (A) Capitalize the net income
    (B) Estimate the replacement cost of the entire property
    (C) Compare sales of similar properties
    (D) Estimate the highest and best use

5. When comparing properties, which of the following factors would *not* be important in the market data approach?

    (A) Original cost
    (B) Dates of sales
    (C) Lot sizes
    (D) Appearance and condition

6. In the cost approach to value, it is necessary to:

    (A) Stabilize the gross income
    (B) Stabilize the operating expenses
    (C) Consider sales of similar properties
    (D) Estimate the replacement cost of the improvements

7. In appraisal terms, depreciation is defined as loss in value due to:

    (A) Any cause
    (B) Physical deterioration
    (C) Functional obsolescence
    (D) Economic obsolescence

8. In the cost approach, the appraiser deducts depreciation from the improvements. This depreciation represents:

    (A) Loss of value due to any cause
    (B) Cost to recycle the improvements
    (C) Capitalized value from rental losses
    (D) Recycle costs to increase rental rates

9. What is the estimate of value of a stream of annual net income of $10,000, if comparable sales indicate that a 10% capitalization rate is appropriate?

    (A) $1,000,000
    (B) $120,000
    (C) $100,000
    (D) $12,000

10. What would the gross rent multiplier (GRM) be on a duplex with a sales price of $100,000 and a monthly rental rate per unit of $500?

    (A) 200
    (B) 100
    (C) 110
    (D) 220

Chapter 6
Advertising

WHAT IS ADVERTISING?

Advertising is a paid form of communication with an identifiable sponsor used to disseminate information, usually in a persuasive manner, about a product or service available for purchase. To attract attention to the product or service, advertising uses various special techniques of preparing and distributing public announcements.

Reasons for Advertising Real estate businesses, and businesses in general, have four basic messages they seek to convey through advertising.

Attention and Interest. Advertisers seek to attract buyers and sellers, and influence them to act favorably.

Awareness of Services. Property owners who are potential sellers need to be made aware of your services through various forms of advertising.

Products. Salable listings are the specific products, the necessary ingredients for successful real estate practice. They are your inventory and, as such, need to be promoted.

Favorable Image. Buyers will be attracted to the office that creates a favorable image and generates confidence that it is capable of helping them satisfy their needs.

Types of Advertising Advertising can be classified according to whether it promotes a specific product or the advertiser in general.

Institutional Advertising. Image-oriented advertising is usually developed to benefit an entire company.

Product Advertising. Some advertising contains information about a product or service, information selected and designed to influence a buying decision. In the field of real estate, product advertising is the most common form of advertising, usually in the form of classified advertising. It is an important means of generating leads and initiating purchases. Such advertising commonly contains detailed information about an available property.

Real Estate. Real estate advertising is both institutional and product-oriented. Of particular importance to the real estate licensee are the advertisements which are used to attract attention to:

☐ *Your Product*. Real estate.

☐ *Your Services*. As licensed agents.

☐ *Your Business*. Your real estate office.

Advertising in Real Estate In the real estate profession, advertising embraces all forms of attracting attention: general and specific, classified and institutional, newspaper, radio, television, billboard, and show-card. In addition, there are less direct forms of advertising.

Office Design. The appearance of a real estate office tells the public much about the real estate company.

Public Relations. A broker's or salesperson's participation in community activities indirectly speaks to the community about the licensee's business.

Appearance. The licensee's professional attitudes and appearance reflect on the business and indirectly advertise the business.

ADVERTISING MEDIA

In our society, printed forms of advertisement dominate by sheer volume, though personal recommendation may still be the most powerful.

Newspapers There are three general classifications of newspapers:

Metropolitan Newspapers. Major papers serve a market area population of approximately 1,000,000 or more, e.g., *Los Angeles Times*, *New York Times*, *San Francisco Chronicle*, *The Wall Street Journal*.

Local Newspapers. These serve populated areas under 1,000,000 persons, e.g., San Luis Obispo's *Telegram Tribune*, *Contra Costa Times*.

Special Interest Publications. Of varying size, circulation, and frequency, these include professional journals and magazines (*California Real Estate* or local board newsletters), ethnic publications serving specific populations, military readership (active and retired), and publications of organized labor groups and other special-interest users of real estate—Chambers of Commerce, historic preservation, churches, schools, recreational, retirement, etc.

Signs   Signs are visible to everyone, working for you 24 hours a day.

Property Signs. "For Sale" and "For Lease" advertisements located on the property offer both specific and institutional advertising value. They invite inquiries about the specific property, as well as promoting general recognition of the firm. "Sale pending" and "Sold" signs advertise the office's success.

Automobile Signs. These display the real estate firm's name and logo.

Office Signs. Signs on the successful real estate office should be distinctive, in good taste, and highly visible to pedestrian and automobile traffic. As a sound investment, greater amounts should be spent on the office sign than on the "For Sale" or "For Lease" signs which are susceptible to theft or destruction.

Billboards. These offer visibility of message with little wasted circulation. They usually require services of an advertising agency for consultation and design. They are financially feasible for strong local firms as well as regional or national firms. Normally a firm does not buy a single billboard. Instead, it leases or buys a "showing" of a certain number of billboards at various locations for at least one month before the message is changed.

Other Signs. Opportunities will vary with the locality. Examples include bus stop bench advertising and taxi or bus cards.

Direct Mail   Advertising by direct mail can be effective, especially for a firm that concentrates on an identifiable geographic area or market sector.

Brochures. Attractively prepared pieces promote either the firm's services in general or specific properties.

Flyers and Letters. Mailings may use such themes as "Just Listed" or "Just Sold," "Meet Your Neighbor," or "Tell a Friend—Select your Neighbor." Calendars, maps, or other keepsakes are also a possibility.

Free Valuation or Competitive Market Analysis. Such an offer should contain a disclaimer that it is not intended to solicit other licensees' listings, in case a property is already listed with another broker, and should not be called an "appraisal" unless the evaluation process will involve a written estimate of value using recognized appraisal techniques.

Open-House Announcements. New office open-house announcements attract clients for listings, qualified buyers, and related business services (escrow officers, bankers, etc.).

Directories These are valuable because they are consulted when the prospects themselves realize they need a service. Their motivation is high. Examples of directories include the phone company white and yellow pages, business and professional directories which often carry advertisements, e.g., Chamber of Commerce Business and Industrial Directory, and a variety of both neighborhood and ethnic directories.

Broadcast Media Radio and television are less often used than the printed word, but for that very reason can sometimes be extremely effective. Local AM and FM stations may be practical for the small or medium size firm. Television is less commonly used, mainly because of the expense. National TV has been used for successful institutional advertising for national companies and franchise operations. Local TV advertising requires repetition with relatively high cost. It is usually more successful for institutional advertising and larger firms' image building. It is less practical for smaller firms operating in a large area, or for selling specific properties. There is also the possibility of publicity through press releases to local news programs.

ADVERTISING TECHNIQUES

Product advertising (specific) and institutional advertising (general) have different goals and therefore different techniques.

Institutional Advertising Building the firm's image and identity is the objective of institutional advertising. It is utilized to sell the real estate firm's services, not a specific property. Advertising should be attention-getting, memorable, and seen repeatedly. The goal of institutional advertising is long-term results.

Published Ads. "Tombstone" ads in local regional and national newspapers simply identify the firm's name and address, with considerable open space and possibly a brief announcement. Realty association publications such as California Association of Realtors® and National Association of Realtors® magazines run tombstone ads and possibly ads identifying specialized services offered.

Signs. Billboards, bus stop benches, and taxi and bus card ads with company name and phone number do not advertise a specific property; rather they are intended to promote name recognition.

Press Releases. Press releases to both print and broadcast media can be very effective. Technically the press release is a form of *publicity* as distinguished from paid advertising. The press release can tell about community involvement, recognition, awards, etc., or can report unique or outstanding accomplishments of the office, its executives or its associates. A press release should establish who, what, when, where, and why early in the text, and include a picture if possible.

Keepsakes. Promotional items should be used in good taste, and should be useful so that they will be seen often. These include calendars, key rings, match books, phone message pads, and imprinted pens. They should clearly display the real estate firm's name and logotype (logo), a distinctive design suitable for media use. It should give a positive impression, and be quickly readable for favorable image building. It is especially important to emphasize the firm's location.

Product Advertising   In contrast to institutional advertising, product advertising aims primarily at selling specific properties or services. It is designed for immediate or short-term results: generating incoming phone calls in response to specific advertisements, and attracting specific types of clients or customers, e.g., income property investors.

Classified Ads. Classifieds in newspapers, periodicals, and magazines are prepared quickly and are relatively inexpensive to run. Cost may be reduced by contracting to run a minimum number per period. The ads may be run in blocks or scattered.

Display Ads. These are large showy ads, often costly to prepare. They are useful in direct mail for securing listings. They can create the impression of a firm's being larger than it actually is and can have an impact beyond the real estate office market area.

"For Sale." Signs on property are most effective when the logo and color scheme are coordinated and a minimum of wording is used. A distinctive slogan may be incorporated.

Property Briefs. These are another form of brochure. To be effective they must be complete, contain accurate information, be readable, understandable, attractively packaged and used with discretion.

Stationery. Real estate office stationery and business cards should be distinctively designed, professional in appearance, and coordinated with the appropriate logo and color scheme.

ADVERTISING BUDGETS

A total annual advertising budget should be established in the firm's operating budget, and allocated monthly and by medium.

Budgeting Considerations

Budgeting must respond to the realities of business. Every budget is a working budget, constantly under review.

Seasonal Fluctuations. Budget planning should consider high and low listing and selling months. Heavy listing months should be preceded by ads designed to attract new listings. For peak sales months advertising programs should be designed to attract buyers.

Advertising Budget

a. Ad budget for month of _____: $1,800

b. Allocation:

(1)	Newspapers	Days	Classified	Display	
	No. 1	FSS	$700.00	-	
	No. 2	MT	$300.00	-	
	No. 3	WEEK		$250.00	
	Subtotal		$1,000.00	+ $250.00	= $1,250.00

(2)	Signs			
	On-site	3 @ $60.00	$180.00	
	Stakes	3 @ $25.00	$75.00	
	Installation and Removal		$355.00	= $610.00

(3)	Donations/Contributions	$50.00

(4)	Stationery, Business Cards, Flyers	$200.00

	TOTAL	$2,110.00
	Budget	1,800.00
	(Over)	($310.00)

Cost-Effectiveness. The program that costs least is not necessarily the least expensive. The cost per ad call is more important than the ad cost. For example, a $500 ad that attracts 100 calls is far better than a $200 ad that produces only 20 calls.

Budget Review. Budget should be reviewed periodically for possible revision to consider market conditions and the competitors' programs.

Cost-Cutting Ideas Practical experience shows a number of ways to control advertising costs without sacrificing effectiveness. An established advertising policy within the firm can prevent costly mistakes and hard feelings. Higher priced properties usually require more expensive advertising, such as brochures, display ads, and flyers. Lower priced properties generally are combined in less expensive classified ads.

Ad Writing. Listing associates are usually required to prepare rough drafts of ads. To accomplish this task they generally set aside specific weekly ad writing time. The associate must recognize that not all ads can be run as frequently as requested and that successful ads may be repeated without change if the property is still available.

Working With Newspapers. Use a contract when appropriate, and respect weekly deadlines.

Review Results. Periodic evaluation of effectiveness is required. Devise your own means for checking results. Codes or different phone numbers may be used to test effectiveness of various media.

AD WRITING IDEAS

Well thought out ads result in more telephone calls, and more telephone calls lead to more sales.

Four Basic Elements A classified ad should include the following elements. Omitting one or more of these elements may result in a customer merely calling for missing information—or no response at all.

Price. Including the price in the ad facilitates ad response. Buyers generally know what their particular price range is and tend not to respond to ads without a listed price. It saves time to discuss other important items.

Location. While general location should be given, a specific address should never be given. You want to *take* customers to a property, not send them.

Terms. If attractive terms are offered or will be considered, these facts should be disclosed.

Description. Indicate how many units, bedrooms, square feet, etc.

Visit the Property The optimum time to write the ad is right after the listing is signed, when the pertinent information is easily recallable and enthusiasm is high. Write the ad with a clear picture of the property and its features in mind.

Preparation   Allow adequate time for preparing a good advertising copy.

Brevity   Frequently, a brief ad is more effective than a lengthy one.

Description. Describe the property in a specific, simple, and believable manner.

Candor. Be informative and honest.

Style. Use complete short sentences that are pleasant, comfortable, and understandable. Avoid abbreviations and overuse of capital letters; they tend to detract from the message. Rather than piling up "ands", start a new sentence. Use original wording; avoid cliches. In short, try to make every word count; use "picture words" with strong connotative power to establish desired impressions.

Headlines   An effective headline is brief and to the point. Its primary purpose is to attract attention, arouse interest, and create desire. The language should be simple yet provocative, to encourage the reader to read the ad.

Effective Copy   The most effective advertising is most likely to be created when the writer:

Sets Goals. Identifies what is to be achieved.

Analyzes Audience. Identifies who the customers are and addresses them on their own terms.

Arouses Interest. Develops a distinctive advertising style for interesting messages and specific prospects.

Know Your Newspapers   Have a file of each newspaper's classified sections readily available for comparison.

MEASURING AD RESULTS

Advertising and the advertising budget should be constantly monitored for effectiveness.

Cost and Result   Cost of each listing ad should be analyzed and inquiry results should be tabulated to increase the effectiveness of the advertising program.

Informing Owners   Individual records of ads should be kept in the listing file and a copy of each ad should be sent to each property owner.

Logging Responses Devise a method to tabulate the number of calls and appointments for each ad. Provide a code which shows sources of listings and sales. Record-keeping by licensees should be simple, yet detailed enough to maximize listings and sales.

Answering Ad Calls When answering the telephone ad calls, licensees should have

Knowledge of Inventory. Knowledge should be based on personal inspection tours prior to running the ads. An ad call sheet and copies of the published ads plus a similar properties list must all be immediately at hand for the licensee taking the call.

Incoming Call Register. Records should be kept to facilitate follow-up procedures. The licensee must have immediately available a copy of the MLS sheet, and if appropriate, also the data sheet and income property statement.

LEGAL AND ETHICAL REGULATIONS

Advertising has great power to induce people to act, and it must be used with care. To this end, numerous laws and professional codes of ethics govern advertising practices.

Truth in Lending (Federal Reserve Regulation Z) The Truth in Lending Law, which is enforced primarily by the Federal Trade Commission (FTC), requires complete disclosure when specific credit terms are used in advertisements, including real estate ads.

Compliance. Anyone placing an advertisement for consumer credit must comply with the advertising requirements of Regulation Z. Real estate brokers and home builders who place ads must comply even if they are not "creditors" in the financing being advertised.

Disclosure of Credit Terms. If an advertisement contains any one of the following terms, the ad must also disclose other credit terms:

☐ Downpayment, including value of any "trade-in" when a developer extends credit

☐ Number of payments or period of repayment

☐ Amount of any payment

☐ Amount of any finance charge.

Other Disclosures. If any of the above terms is used, then the following three disclosures must be given: downpayment, terms of repayment, and "annual percentage rate" (or the abbreviation "APR").

Commercial Loans. Commercial loans to builders, developers, or on rental property are exempt from Regulation Z.

State Regulations Provisions relating to advertising are found in several parts of the California Business and Professions Code and the Real Estate Commissioner's Regulations in the California Code of Regulations.

False, Misleading, or Deceptive Advertising. Under B&P Code §10177(c), licensees are subject to disciplinary action when they are parties to false advertising. This section also applies to subdivision sales.

License Requirement. B&P Code §10140.6 provides that advertising of acts which require a license must contain a disclosure that a licensee is performing such acts, with minor exceptions for rental ads.

Broker Identification. B&P Code §10162 and Comm. Reg. Art. 9, §2770 require that every licensed real estate broker shall have and maintain a definite place of business in California and display his or her license there. Commissioner's Regulations, Article 9, §2770 specifies that ads shall not be under the name of a salesperson unless the name of the employing broker is also given.

Advertising Without Owner's Consent. Under B&P Code §10177, advertising without the owner's consent, or without the broker's consent, if another broker's listing, may lead to disciplinary action for false advertising.

Mortgage Loan Brokerage and Trust Deeds. B&P Code §10235 makes it unlawful to advertise, indicate, or otherwise imply a specific yield or return on any note other than the interest rate specified in the note unless the ad sets forth the actual interest rate and the discount.

Ethical Considerations Advertising is also subject to abuses which may not be technically illegal, but are contrary to accepted standards of ethical conduct.

Misrepresentation. National Association of Realtors® Code of Ethics cites advertising regulations for member Realtors®. Articles 3, 9, and 19 all warn against misrepresentation. (See Chapter 1)

Permission Required. Brokers should obtain permission prior to advertising unlisted property or other brokers' listings, and before quoting testimonials from customers, etc.

Wrongfully Claiming Credit. A broker should not claim credit for other brokers' sales of company listings.

Chapter 6 Quiz

1. Free valuations, or competitive market analyses, should contain disclaimers that they are:

   (A) Not fee appraisals
   (B) Not intended to solicit other licensees' listings
   ✓(C) Both (A) and (B)
   (D) Neither (A) nor (B)

2. Allocation of monthly advertising dollars should consider:

   (A) High and low listing and selling months
   (B) Ads designed to obtain listings prior to listing months
   (C) Attracting buyers prior to peak sales months
   (D) All of the above

3. Federal Reserve Regulation Z is also known as the:

   (A) Interstate Land Sales Disclosure Act
   (B) Truth in Lending Law
   (C) Anti-Discrimination Act
   (D) Fair Employment Act

4. Advertising can be defined as:

   (A) Communication about a product or service
   (B) The preparation and distribution of public announcements to attract attention
   (C) Both (A) and (B)
   (D) Neither (A) nor (B)

5. The basic reason for advertising in real estate is best stated as:

   (A) Attracting the attention of sellers
   (B) Attracting the attention of buyers
   (C) Obtaining the attention and interest of buyers and sellers and influencing them to act favorably
   (D) Making the company name well-known

6. The suggested basic elements in classified real estate ads do *not* include:

   (A) Price
   (B) Location
   (C) Terms
   (D) Personal property items

7. Federal Reserve Regulation Z exempts:

   (A) Number, amount, and due date of the payments
   (B) Amount of credit extended including finance charges
   (C) Commercial loans to builders, developers, or rental property on which the owner does not reside
   (D) Right to rescind

8. Which of the following statements regarding national television advertising is *not* true?

   (A) More successful in selling unique properties
   (B) More successful for national companies' institutional advertising
   (C) More successful for franchise company institutional advertising
   (D) None of the above

9. When answering telephone ad calls, licensees should have in their possession:

   (A) An ad call sheet
   (B) Copies of the actual ads
   (C) A similar properties list
   (D) All of the above

10. General institutional advertising is utilized for all of the following *except*:

    (A) For long-term results
    (B) To sell a specific property
    (C) To create attention and interest in the firm's non-institutional or direct advertising
    (D) To sell a real estate firm's services

THE PHILOSOPHY OF PROSPECTING

A prospect is a potential customer (purchaser or seller). Prospecting means to search for a potential purchaser or seller of real property. It may involve sifting through many leads to find a prospect.

Selling Yourself The basic step of successful prospecting is selling yourself. You are asking strangers to entrust you with one of the most important business transactions in their lives. Make certain the prospect knows your name, has your business card, and knows where and how to contact you. Project a good first impression: positive mental attitude, physical fitness, professional dress, and good grooming. Establish a warm, friendly rapport which inspires confidence that you are knowledgeable, trustworthy, and professional. Build upon your office's professional reputation and name recognition. Be accommodating and willing to show your prospects any property, including other offices' listings and try to generate attention, interest, and enthusiasm.

A Good Prospecting Plan Basic to successfully obtaining prospects is an individualized prospecting plan that has realistic goals and good time management. Important features include:

Specialization. Selection of and concentration on a specific area(s) of real estate give focus to prospecting efforts. These concentrations may include:

☐ Geographic location or preference (e.g., 15 mile radius, specific neighborhoods)

☐ Price of property (e.g., $100,000 to $200,000, over $1,000,000)

☐ Type of property (e.g., ranch, commercial, agricultural, residential)

☐ Type of transaction (e.g., exchanges, syndications, leases)

Knowledge and Identification. Take time to understand your prospects:

☐ Social, political, economic viewpoints

☐ Buyer motivations

☐ Buyer interests.

Self-Promotion. Instill in others a personal and professional confidence in you and your firm.

Association and Affiliation. Associate with an office that is compatible with your area of specialization, philosophy, and style of operation, and has a good, professional image.

Execution of Plan. Be persistent but flexible enough to modify the plan to suit individual prospects. Use a variety of prospecting techniques to meet each prospect's individual needs. Be consistent and diligent.

Evaluation of Progress. Your real estate practice should be a constant learning process. Continue techniques and methods which are successful. Modify those which do not work.

Persistence and Diligence
The key components of prospecting success are persistence and diligence. A positive outlook, a desire to succeed, and tenacity are important assets. "Each 'no' brings you that much closer to a 'yes'."

PROSPECTING METHODS AND PROCEDURES

Though personal factors are important in prospecting, the techniques can and must be learned.

Comprehensive Analysis
The successful search for buyers begins with knowing the inventory, through comprehensive analysis of the characteristics and qualities of each listing.

Location. The licensee should be familiar with the property's site and physical location in relation to places of employment, shopping, schools and other social and cultural facilities, transportation, and neighborhood attributes and features.

Zoning. The licensee must know current zoning of the property and probability of changes because of rezoning, variances, or changes in neighborhood characteristics. Zoning designations include but are not limited to: low-density residential, high-density residential, commercial, retail, wholesale, professional office, light or heavy industrial, agricultural, and recreational.

Property Features and Conditions. The informed licensee knows that a prospective buyer will be concerned with the intrinsic character of the property and the financial considerations which will shape the transaction. Important features and conditions include type, size, quality of construction, grounds and landscaping, architectural design and desirability of floor plan, condition, price, and financing terms and conditions.

Financial Aspects of Income Producing Property. In addition to the information above, investors in income property want to know volume, quality, and durability of income, volume and durability of expenses, and leases, including information about who pays what, inflation escalation clauses, and options to renew.

Prospecting Methods

There are many different ways of prospecting. The degree of success of each will vary with the individual salesperson, with different types of property, and with different prospects.

Direct Methods. The licensee directly approaches selected individuals, in person or by phone or by personal letter.

☐ Ask an owner of listed property for names of potential buyers.

☐ Circularize the neighborhood with "Choose Your Neighbor" flyers.

☐ Discuss the advantages of property ownership with tenants of listed properties.

☐ Check with business and professional contacts for names of potential buyers.

☐ Inquire whether commercial tenants may be considering expansion or reduction of facilities as their business grows or declines.

☐ Prospect by telephone. Potential buyers should be approached with the goal of obtaining an appointment. Provide adequate information to get their attention and interest.

☐ Use direct mail. Write personalized letters, which include well prepared property briefs, to a carefully screened and selected list of potential buyers. Follow up with a telephone call for an appointment.

☐ Make personal contacts. Potential buyers of specific properties may be sought in a professional, dignified manner from fellow members of civic, social, religious, and business organizations.

Indirect Methods. The market at large is presented with information or an invitation, and interested individuals take the initiative to approach the licensee.

☐ Write advertisements. This method requires careful selection of language, media, and timing.

☐ Post on-site "For Sale" signs. This method can result in inquiries leading to appointments.

☐ Mail promotional literature to a selected market area. Flyers, leaflets, brochures, pamphlets, and personalized newsletters are among the wide variety of mailing pieces, all of which should conclude, "Please call for an appointment."

SOURCES OF PROSPECTS

Prospects may be selected by the licensee on the basis of recommendations, demographics, etc., or they may self-select in response to an ad or an open house.

Phone Canvass The goal of telephone prospecting is to obtain the appointment. Effective telephone technique is a valuable tool in prospecting.

Phone Technique. Practice presentation, delivery, and tone. Project enthusiasm in your voice. Be prepared to overcome resistance or objections to your presentation.

Discipline. Commit yourself to making a specific number of calls per week. Be persistent and diligent.

Strategy. Studies show that buyers of homes in one area frequently come from a similar "move-out" area. It may be advantageous to use a reverse telephone directory of a "move-out" area in your market to canvass prospective buyers.

Incoming Calls Most often the incoming call is in response to an ad. The agent should be prepared for this type of caller.

Identify Yourself. Answer with your name and that of your office.

Ask Caller to Read Ad. This is a convenient ice-breaker which gives you time to organize your thoughts, allows you to review the subject property's data, and gives you an idea of the caller's personality.

Obtain Information from Caller. Get the caller's name, phone number, and any other pertinent details regarding his or her real estate needs. Record the information on an incoming ad call register.

Control Information that You Provide. Try not to give the specific street address of the property to the caller, as you want to show the property. Often the seller will give specific instructions not to give out the street address over the phone, preferring to show the property by appointment.

Be Flexible. Keep in mind that the property called about is usually not the property bought. Be prepared for both the uncertain, hesitant caller and the pushy, aggressive caller.

Offer Your Services. Discourage callers from calling other ads of other offices by offering to do the calling for them.

Personal Contact

There are many opportunities for telephone and face-to-face prospecting.

Former Customers. Those who are ready to buy or sell again may be ready to move up in price range, or may need to move to accommodate changes in family size, employment, etc.

Business and Professional Contacts. These may be a source of buyer prospect referrals to service their company's or their own real estate needs.

For Sale By Owner. Most sellers are also buyers. A FSBO may be ready to accept assistance in relocating to your market area.

Current Prospects. Listed in your office files will be former prospects whose desires or needs may have changed since their earlier contact.

Office "Drop-ins." These contacts give an excellent opportunity for you to convert them into prospective customers.

Business and Industry Personnel Offices. Cultivate contacts at the personnel offices of key local employers for productive buyer referrals. Transferees into your market area need housing almost immediately.

Community Clubs and Organizations. Obtain speaking engagements to talk about your area of expertise. Bring your business cards and other information to hand out to your audience. Join a fraternal organization; club members are an excellent source of buyer prospects.

Apartment Owners. Become acquainted with owners and property managers of multi-dwelling complexes to get exposure to the tenants who are another source of prospective buyers.

Others. Friends, acquaintances, and others can act as "bird dogs" to provide you with names of buyer prospects.

Open House

Each house that is shown will have only one buyer, but everyone who visits it will be exposed to your services and the idea of buying.

Getting Information. Open houses are most useful in developing prospects for other properties, since most "drop-ins" do not buy that specific open house but they are prospective buyers of some property.

☐ Interview and questioning techniques may reveal the prospect's name, degree of interest, and possibility of follow-up to show properties more consistent with their needs and ability to qualify.

☐ Be a good listener; visitors can give important information about their family needs and interests.

☐ Try to fill in a Home Buyer's Analysis (Exhibit 13) with prospective buyers. This will give you direction as to kind of property and price range the buyer is seeking.

☐ Ask the visitors to sign the guest register; this is your follow-up record of who attended your open house.

Giving Information. The open house gives you the opportunity to give out information about the house which is open, and about your other offerings and services. Be prepared with all pertinent information regarding the house; if you cannot answer a specific question, assure the visitor you will obtain the information the following day. Pass out your business card and other pertinent information, such as a flyer about the house.

☐ *Mechanics of Showing.* Arrange a predetermined path to show the house; try to end the tour in the most appealing room.

☐ *Financing Information.* Prepare Estimated Buyer's Cost sheets (Exhibit 17, Chapter 9) showing the various types of financing arrangements.

Mailing Lists Membership lists of professional, business, trade, union, social, and fraternal organizations may be available for purchase or use for the mailing of flyers, brochures, pamphlets, newsletter, etc.

Advertising and Signs "For Sale" signs may be the best means of indirect prospecting for buyers.

Locating Serious Buyers. Respondents to ads and signs are usually sincere buyers.

Qualifying Buyers. Ads and signs can help qualify the buyer as to type of property, desired area, and price range, if price was quoted in the ad.

Referrals Many people believe that the best form of advertising is a satisfied customer and that the best prospects are the referrals by these former customers. Consequently, it pays to:

Keep in Contact. Become reacquainted from time to time.

Show Appreciation. Send greeting cards, flowers, household gifts to former customers at appropriate times during the year.

QUALIFYING YOUR PROSPECTS

You must qualify your buyer as to *what* they will buy, *where* they will buy, *when* they will buy, *how* they will buy, and from *whom* they will buy.

Buyer Needs vs. Wants
The buyer's real desires and needs must be tactfully elicited during the early meetings with your prospect to avoid "spinning your wheels." Unless you learn how to interview tactfully, you may not learn how to distinguish between the prospective buyer's actual and stated needs and desires.

Buyer Motivation
To meet their needs more accurately, determine what is motivating them to buy at this time. Reasons may include marital status, family size, job transfer, layoff, or promotion, and the buyer's financial condition.

Financial Qualification
Lenders expect repayment of loans to proceed smoothly, without difficulties in collection or servicing.

Estimating Reliability. Clues to borrower's ability and willingness to pay include employment stability, income prospects, history of debt management, and net worth.

Rules of Thumb. Financial institutions have their own standards which real estate licensees should use as "rules of thumb" in estimating what financing a prospective buyer/borrower will qualify for. Lenders generally prefer that not more than 25% of an applicant's gross income be spent for housing. Housing costs plus other long-term monthly debt generally should not exceed 33% of monthly income. Some institutions use gross annual income multipliers which suggest that the maximum price of the home purchased should not exceed $2\frac{1}{2}$ or 3 or 4 times the borrower's income.

Practical Qualifying. Most professional real estate licensees now use financial calculators. One of the many practical uses of a financial calculator is for pre-qualifying prospective buyers and counseling them accordingly. The four quantities that go into an amortization table can be entered into a financial calculator. Given any three quantities, the calculator can compute the fourth quantity. The four quantities are:

- *Time or Term.* The number of payments to be made over the life of the loan.

- *Interest Rate.* The periodic interest rate, e.g., the monthly rate if payments are made monthly.

- *Payment.* The periodic payment amount.

- *Loan Amount.* Shown as "present value" on some calculators.

> **Example**
>
> The prospective buyers can afford monthly home mortgage payments of $1,000, plus taxes and insurance. If they could obtain a 30 year loan at 10% interest, how much could they borrow?
>
> Term—30 years
>
> Interest—10%
>
> Payment—$1,000
>
> Loan Amount—would be shown to be $113,950
>
> If this family has $20,000 for a downpayment, plus closing costs, they will be able to buy a home at a price of about $134,000. Don't disappoint them by first convincing them that your $200,000 listing is the perfect home for them, and then telling them they can't buy your listing because they "don't qualify."

Prohibited Discrimination. The federal Equal Credit Opportunity Act prohibits lenders from judging a borrower's creditworthiness on the basis of such factors as marital status, family planning intention, and part-time income. The licensee should avoid any appearance of using these criteria to qualify prospects.

Property Needs As you are interviewing your prospect, fill out a Home Buyer's Analysis form (Exhibit 13).

Residential Property Prospect. Take time to become acquainted with the prospect's "real" needs. Observe his or her tastes, life style, and if possible, present home and neighborhood. Make note of family size, educational level, and recreational activities. Be careful to avoid anything that could be construed as unlawful discrimination, such as allowing your analysis to be influenced by the prospect's race, sex, or physical disability, or the racial composition of the neighborhood.

Residential Income Property Prospect. Determine whether the prospect is a tenant or investor. If the prospect is a tenant in the market for a home, qualify according to personal needs and desires and financial ability.

Investor Prospect. Investors should be qualified as to management ability, financial standing, and track record. All of the following should be considered: knowledge of area and properties, property management practices, price range sought, downpayment available, leverage anticipation, investment returns sought, ability to carry negative cash flows, loan and lender's requirements, personal and/or business financial statement, and credit rating.

Commercial Property Prospect. For the investor, investor-occupant, and tenant, determine: location and accessibility requirements, physical features (e.g., size, layout, condition, amenities) required, financial qualification, including purchase price or rental range, downpayment or lease duration, lender's requirements or lease features, and investment returns sought.

HOME BUYER'S ANALYSIS

Personal Data:

Name: (husband) _____ Phone (office) _____
      (wife) _____ (home) _____
Address: (home) _____
    (work) (husband) _____
    (work) (wife) _____

Other Family Data: Boys _____   Cars _____
                     Girls _____   Boat _____
                     Relatives _____   Schools _____
                     Pets _____   Church _____

Needs:

Bedrooms _____   Baths _____   Separate Dining Room _____
Sq. Ft. _____   1 or 2 Story _____   Separate Fam. Rm. _____
Style _____   Fireplace _____   Din. Rm. / Fam. Combo _____
Lot Size _____   Garage Capacity _____   Fam. Rm. / Kitch. Combo _____
Location _____   Special Needs _____
Possession _____

Finances:

Capabilities: Down Payment Max. _____
              Now or From Sale of Own Home _____
              Monthly Payment _____
                (including Taxes, Insurance) _____
                (excluding Taxes, Insurance) _____
              Type Loan Needed _____
Other Equities: Amount, Details _____
Location _____
Trade-In Possibility _____
_____

Employment Notes:

Husband: Company _____   Address _____
           Position _____   How Long _____ Salary _____
Wife: Company _____   Address _____
      Position _____   How Long _____ Salary _____

Additional Items:

How Came in Contact _____
Other Data _____
_____
_____
_____

Exhibit 13

Chapter 7 Quiz

1. The goal of prospecting by telephone is to:

   (A) Provide adequate information
   (B) Gain attention
   (C) Obtain an appointment
   (D) Ask for referrals

2. The most significant aspect of successful prospecting involves:

   (A) Proper telephone usage
   (B) Selling yourself
   (C) Familiarity with available financing
   (D) Handling the incoming call

3. "Bird dogs" are individuals who:

   (A) Specialize in wilderness property
   (B) Provide names of prospects
   (C) Transfer into your market area
   (D) Drop in to your office

4. Most often the incoming call is in response to:

   (A) An ad
   (B) Your presentation
   (C) A referral
   (D) An open house

5. Selling yourself to prospects requires:

   (A) Projecting a good first impression
   (B) A good professional reputation
   (C) Establishing rapport
   (D) All of the above

6. Which of the following is *not* an essential part of a good prospecting plan?

   (A) Selection of and concentration on a specific area of real estate
   (B) Knowledge and identification of your prospects
   (C) Self-promotion
   (D) Ethnic grouping

7. A prospect is:

   (A) A potential customer
   (B) A potential buyer
   (C) A potential seller
   (D) Any of the above

8. Media prospecting is an example of _____ prospecting.

   (A) Direct
   (B) Indirect
   (C) Neither "A" nor "B"
   (D) Both "A" and "B"

9. You must qualify your buyers as to:

   (A) What, where, and when they will buy
   (B) How they will buy and from whom
   (C) Both "A" and "B"
   (D) Neither "A" nor "B" above

10. When phone canvassing it is most important to:

    (A) Practice your presentation, delivery, and tone
    (B) Project enthusiasm in your voice
    (C) Be persistent and diligent
    (D) All of the above

Chapter 8
Buyer Brokerage

DOES "YOUR" BROKER REPRESENT YOU?

The following is quoted from the FTC publication entitled "Does 'Your' Broker Represent You?"

If you are buying a home, you also may want to talk with several real estate brokers about your housing needs. This will help you determine which broker is best suited to assist you.

If you are buying a home, you may believe—as many consumers do—that the broker you have chosen legally represents your interests. While this may be the case, it is not necessarily so. Real estate brokers may represent the seller, the buyer, or both. However, according to most Multiple Listing Services, any broker assisting the buyer usually works under the seller's broker and owes primary allegiance to the seller rather than the buyer.

If you want to be sure that the broker represents your interests as a homebuyer, it is advisable that you obtain a written agreement or letter from your broker spelling out that relationship.

Whom the broker represents can be important to you. For example, if a broker showing you homes legally represents the seller, he or she is obligated to seek the highest possible price for the seller and thus may not be able to advise you, the homebuyer, what approximate lower price the seller may be willing to accept.

Or if, as a homebuyer, you tell a broker the true "top price" you are willing to pay for a home without having an agreement of confidentiality, such information might be passed on to the seller without your knowledge or approval. That could result in the seller's insisting upon that higher price and your paying more than you otherwise might have paid. As a homebuyer, therefore, you should carefully consider whether you want to disclose confidential information to a broker who has not agreed to represent you.

Any broker may agree to represent you, as the homebuyer, and some brokers are beginning to specialize in legally representing buyers. Having a "buyer's broker" may offer you some advantages. For example, a buyer's broker may be more motivated to spot problems with a home you are considering and may be able to obtain more favorable purchasing terms. Buyers' brokers may or may not charge you a fee. This is because a buyer's broker can legally share in the commission paid by the seller, as long as you (the homebuyer), the homeseller, and the seller's broker agree to this. You can try to locate buyers' brokers by asking friends and looking for advertisements in your newspaper and the Yellow Pages.

TRADITIONAL AGENCY RELATIONSHIPS

Since real estate brokers started using exclusive listing contracts to protect their rights to commissions several generations ago, the listing contract has been the fundamental way of establishing a formal agency relationship between a seller and a broker. The relationship *contractually* established the broker as the *agent of the owner*, hired by the owner to carry out the objectives of the agency, to market the property, exposing the property to the market to *find* the third party who might become a ready, willing and able buyer, and then to negotiate with that prospective buyer to sell the property. In negotiating with a prospective buyer (a customer) the agent does so on behalf of and in the name of the owner (the broker's client). It is as if the owner (the principal) were negotiating with that prospective buyer, because in fact the owner *is* negotiating with that prospective buyer through his or her agent.

Legal Definition An agent is one who represents another, called the principal, in dealing with third persons. (Civil Code Section 2295)

Fiduciary Duty The word "fiduciary" comes from the same Latin root from which we get the modern English word "fidelity," which means "faithful." The agent is a fiduciary, that is he or she owes a fiduciary obligation to his or her principal. The agent must be "on the side" of his or her principal. While the agent owes to the third party a duty of fairness, honesty, skill and disclosure of material facts about the property, the agent does not owe a *fiduciary* obligation to the third party. To expect a fiduciary duty to the third party would be to expect the impossible; one cannot be faithful to two different interests which are opposed. This concept is not new in real estate, in law, or in modern western civilization. It is found in the English language Bible, expressed as: "No servant can serve two masters." (Luke 16:13)

Question of Fact The agency relationship is a question of fact, not of contract. In litigation where agency is at issue, a court looks to the facts in the specific case. If the court finds that A in fact has, with B's authority, acted as B's agent in negotiating with C, then the agency relationship with the fiduciary obligation has existed, even if there was no contract between A and B and there was no consideration paid to B (a gratuitous agency).

The Problem   In the example in the previous paragraph, suppose B (the agent) has led C to believe that B is acting as C's agent in negotiating with A. A court might find that B was, in fact, C's agent. Clearly, an unauthorized dual agency has existed, a *divided* agency. B has been a "double agent," an unlawful practice.

DUAL AGENCY

An authorized dual agency, agreed to by all parties, is lawful.

Escrow   The most frequently encountered dual agency in the real estate industry is the escrow. A buyer and seller, adversaries (but not enemies) while negotiating at arm's length with each other, once they have a contract, in effect go together to the escrowholder, asking the escrow holder to be *their* agent in carrying out the terms of their contract. The escrowholder will never represent one in negotiating with the other to resolve differences. The escrowholder will never carry out the instructions of one in contradiction to the instructions of the other. The escrowholder owes a fiduciary obligation only to their *mutual* interests—a true and reasonable dual agency.

Difficult Task   The broker who undertakes the task of acting as a dual agent in negotiating the sale of real estate is not likely to represent either very well. The agent is really acting only as a "middle man" who is not on either side. The California legislature recognized this difficulty by enacting the agency relationship disclosure law (Civil Code Sections 2373 et seq.), which provides that a dual agent may not disclose to a seller that a buyer would be willing to pay a higher price than offered, and may not disclose to a buyer that a seller would be willing to sell at a lower price than listed.

Third Person   An agent is a person who represents another, the principal, in dealing with third persons. When a broker takes a listing, becoming the agent of the owner, and finds a prospective buyer (third person), and negotiates a sale of the client's property to that customer, the broker has done exactly what he or she was hired to do. This *does not* create a dual agency. Only if the broker unlawfully leads the third person to believe the broker is the buyer's agent is an undisclosed (unlawful) divided agency created. If the broker carries out the objective of the agency properly, who represents the buyer? Who is on the buyer's side? Generally, unless the buyer seeks the counsel of an attorney, no one is on the buyer's side.

Duties to the Third Person   The NAR Code of Ethics, Article 7, states: "In accepting employment as an agent, the Realtor® pledges himself to protect and promote the interests of the client. This obligation of absolute fidelity to the client's interests is primary, but it does not relieve the Realtor® of the obligation to treat fairly all parties to the transaction."

130   *Buyer Brokerage*

Buyer's Protection. When the customer (third person) comes to the real estate broker seeking information about properties that the broker may have available to sell, is that customer exposed to great risk and danger by dealing with the seller's agent who is not a fiduciary to this customer? Well, the customer is not totally without protection because the agent does owe significant duties to the third person, including the duty to negotiate fairly, honestly, with skill and diligence, and full disclosure of material facts about the property. Generally people in any business try to give outstanding service to their customers. On the other hand, if a buyer wants someone to be *on his side*, faithful to his interest, he may want the services of his own agent (fiduciary)—a real estate broker or an attorney.

BUYER'S BROKER

The practice of buyer brokerage is growing more common among real estate brokers who want to avoid the risks of undisclosed dual agency, and who want to represent the *buyer only* in negotiating a sale, providing the buyer with complete agency service and protection.

Counseling In most cases the services provided to the client (buyer) begin with counseling. Often buyers finally buy properties quite different from what they first say they want. Most experienced real estate licensees can remember prospects they have chauffeured for days, showing many properties, before learning that they bought other properties through other brokers. Generally, prospective buyers feel no sense of loyalty to any real estate licensee unless that licensee has "sold" his or her services to that prospect. The broker offering a buyer's brokerage is first a salesperson *selling* services to a prospective client. Once the broker has a contract to provide those brokerage services, the broker can then proceed in the task of a "buying agent" who truly represents that prospective buyer in locating and negotiating for the purchase of a suitable property. (Notice that the California agency disclosure law incorrectly defines this agent as the "selling agent.")

Sources of Properties **In-House Transactions.** The buyer's broker has no limitations in searching for suitable properties for clients. An obvious first source of properties for your *prospective* buyers would be properties listed by your office. If such a property seems to be what your prospect might need or want, you should *not* contract as the buyer's agent. Offer your services to that buyer as your customer. Remember that a customer (buyer) can receive excellent services and significant protection by buying through a licensed real estate broker. A listing agent can also be the selling agent without creating a dual agency.

Multiple Listing Service (MLS). The MLS of a Board of Realtors® is an extremely rich source of properties for sale. The placing of a listing with a multiple listing service is an invitation to the participants in the MLS for subagency.

☐ **Subagency of Seller**. If that invitation for subagency is accepted, the cooperating broker becomes the subagent of the seller, owing a fiduciary obligation to the seller, and making the owner liable for the acts of the subagent, just as any principal is liable for the actions of his or her agent within the scope of the agent's authority.

☐ **Agency for Buyer**. The buyer's broker can also reject the invitation to subagency and proceed under single agency to represent the buyer. Following proper counseling of the client, the buyer's broker can search out suitable properties to show. When the truly suitable property is found, the broker's task is not to sell the property to the buyer; it is to sell the client's (buyer's) offer to the owner, negotiating terms most suitable for the buyer. The owner is the "third person."

Unlisted Properties. There are many other sources where a suitable property may be found for the broker's client.

☐ **FSBOs**. Properties "for sale by owner" might include some property ideally suited for your client. An owner who wishes to avoid the payment of a commission would likely be very interested in showing the property to a buyer's broker.

☐ **Probate Sales**. Many properties are sold in probate. Some are listed with brokers but many are not. Listed or not, these properties are especially suitable for buyer's brokers.

☐ **Foreclosures**. Properties in foreclosure are also rich sources for brokers who have buyers.

☐ **REO**. "Real Estate Owned" by lenders as a result of foreclosure can be an outstanding source of properties for brokers with buyers. Lenders are often anxious to sell, and can make attractive financing available.

☐ **New Subdivisions and Condominium Conversions**. New developments which are being sold "in house" without offers of "cooperation" (commission splits) with other brokers are available for cooperation without commission splits. Buyer's brokers will be welcome.

☐ **Not on the Market**. Any property, on the market or not, might become available to a broker who has a buyer. Any broker who is not trying to sell a property to a buyer can concentrate on selling an offer to an owner.

HOW ARE COMMISSIONS PAID?

Seller May Pay California law specifies that the payment of the commission is not the determining factor in establishing the principal-agent relationship (Civil Code Section 2377). A commission paid by the seller can be shared between a listing agent and a selling agent whether the selling agent is a subagent of the seller, a dual agent, or the buyer's agent.

Buyer May Pay The buyer who wants someone to represent him or her is likely to be willing to pay a fee, especially if the buyer feels that an agent can really negotiate a "better deal" for him.

☐ *Flat Fee*. A certain fee can be agreed upon in the employment agreement. The broker would likely require an agreement for a certain minimum fee whether or not the buyer actually buys.

☐ *Hourly Fee*. Some brokers charge an hourly fee for time spent on the agency, similar to the way attorneys calculate their fees.

☐ *Percentage*. Percentage commissions are less attractive to both broker and buyer because a buyer's broker must strive to get the lowest possible price for the client (consistent with the terms of the purchase). The lower the price, the lower the fee. There may be a fear that the lower the fee, the less service available to the client.

BUYER'S BROKER CONTRACTS

Sample Forms The following two forms (Exhibits 14 and 15) are examples of those available in the market for use in buyer brokerage. These two forms are produced by and available from Professional Publishing Corporation, 122 Paul Drive, San Rafael, California 94903.

☐ Buyer's Broker Employment Agreement (Exhibit 14)

☐ Purchase Agreement and Deposit Receipt for Buyer Representation (Exhibit 15)

BUYER'S BROKER EMPLOYMENT AGREEMENT

The undersigned _____, hereinafter designated as CLIENT,
hereby employs _____, hereinafter designated as BROKER,
for the purpose of exclusively assisting Client to locate property of a nature outlined below or other property acceptable to Client, and to negotiate terms and
conditions acceptable to Client for purchase, exchange, lease, or option of or on such property. This agreement shall commence this date and terminate at
midnight of _____, 19_____.

GENERAL NATURE, LOCATION, AND REQUIREMENTS OF PROPERTY.

_____
_____
_____
_____
_____
_____
_____
_____
_____
_____
_____

PRICE RANGE, AND OTHER TERMS AND CONDITIONS.

_____
_____
_____
_____
_____
_____
_____
_____
_____

RETAINER FEE. Client agrees to pay, and Broker acknowledges receipt of a retainer fee of $_____, as compensation for initial
professional counseling, consultations and research. Said fee is non-refundable, but shall be credited against the Brokerage Fee.

In the event state law so requires, Broker shall deposit and account for said Retainer Fee in Broker's Trust Account.

COMPENSATION TO BROKER. Client agrees to pay Broker, as compensation:

a) For locating property acceptable to Client and for negotiating the purchase or exchange, a fee of $_____, or _____% of the acquisition
price, or $_____ per hour.

b) For obtaining an option on a property acceptable to Client, a fee of $_____, and to pay Broker the balance of a fee equal to _____% of the
purchase price in the event the option is exercised or assigned prior to expiration of the option.

c) For locating a property acceptable to Client and negotiating a lease thereon, a fee of _____.

IF:

1. Client or any other person acting for Client or in Client's behalf, purchases, exchanges, obtains an option for, or leases any real property of the nature
described herein, during the term hereof, through the services of Broker or otherwise.

2. Client or any other person acting for Client or in Client's behalf, purchases, exchanges, obtains an option for, or leases any real property of the nature
described herein, within one year after termination of this agreement, which property Broker, Broker's agent, or cooperating brokers presented or
submitted to Client during the term hereof and the description of which Broker shall have submitted in writing to Client, either in person or by mail, **within
ten (10) days after termination of this agreement.**

**NOTICE: The amount or rate of real estate commissions is not fixed by law. They are set by each broker individually
and may be negotiable between the buyer and the broker.**

AGENCY RELATIONSHIP. Broker agrees to act as agent for Client only in any resulting transaction, provided that Broker may cooperate with other
brokers and their agents in an effort to locate property or properties in accordance with this agreement, and may divide fees in any manner acceptable to them.
If Broker receives compensation from anyone other than Client, Broker shall make full disclosure, and such compensation shall be credited against Client's
obligation hereunder.

In addition, Broker will provide appropriate Agency Disclosure as required by law.

BROKER'S OBLIGATIONS. In consideration of Client's agreement set forth above, Broker agrees to use diligence to achieve the purpose of this
agreement.

CLIENT'S OBLIGATIONS. Client agrees to provide Broker, upon request, relevant personal and financial information to assure Client's ability to
acquire property outlined above. Client further agrees to view or consider property of the general nature set forth in this Agreement, and to negotiate in good
faith to acquire such property if acceptable to Client. In the event completion of any resulting transaction is prevented by Client's default, Client shall pay Broker
the compensation provided for herein upon such default.

ATTORNEY FEE. If any action is brought to enforce the terms of this agreement, or arising out of the execution of this agreement, or to collect fees, the
prevailing party shall be entitled to receive from the other party a reasonable attorney fee to be determined by the court in which such action is brought.

ENTIRE AGREEMENT. Time is of the essence. The terms hereof constitute the entire agreement and supersede all prior agreements, negotiations and
discussions between the parties. This Agreement may be modified only by a writing signed by each of the parties.

Receipt of a copy of this agreement is hereby acknowledged.   DATED: _____ TIME: _____

Buyer's Broker: _____   _____ Client

By: _____   _____ Client

Address: _____   Address: _____

Phone: _____   Phone: _____

FORM 100 (2-89)   COPYRIGHT © 1989, BY PROFESSIONAL PUBLISHING CORP, 122 PAUL DR, SAN RAFAEL, CA 94903 (415) 472-1964   **PROFESSIONAL PUBLISHING**

Exhibit 14

PURCHASE AGREEMENT AND DEPOSIT RECEIPT
FOR BUYER REPRESENTATION

RECEIVED from _____

_____, hereinafter designated as BUYER, the amount set forth below as **DEPOSIT** (Item 1-A) on account of the

PRICE TO SELLER of $_____ (_____

_____**DOLLARS**),

for the real property situated in the City of _____, County of _____, State of _____,

described as _____

_____

☐ Buyer does ☐ Buyer does not intend to occupy the property as his/her residence.

1. **FINANCING TERMS AND LOAN PROVISIONS.**

A. $_____ **DEPOSIT** evidenced by ☐ Check or ☐ Other: _____, payable to _____
held uncashed until acceptance and one day thereafter deposited with: _____

B. $_____ **ADDITIONAL CASH DEPOSIT** in escrow ☐ within_____days from acceptance, ☐ upon receipt of Loan
Commitment per Item 2, ☐ other: _____

C. $_____ **BALANCE OF CASH PAYMENT at close of escrow.**

FIRST LOAN

D. $_____ **PROCEEDS FROM NEW FIRST LOAN:** ☐ CONVENTIONAL, ☐ FHA, ☐ VA:
☐ FIXED RATE: For _____ years, Interest not to exceed _____%, payable at approximately $ _____ p/mo,
including Taxes and Insurance, with the balance due not less than _____ years.
☐ ARM: For _____ years, Initial Interest Rate not to exceed _____%, with Initial Monthly Payments of $_____ p/mo,
and Maximum Life Time Rate not to exceed _____%. ☐ including Taxes & Insurance.
☐ OTHER: _____
Loan fee not to exceed _____% plus $ _____, Discount points not to exceed _____% payable by _____.
In the event of FHA or VA financing, the **FHA AMENDMENT** (Item 9) or **VA AMENDMENT** (Item 10), respectively, printed on Page 2, is
made a part of this agreement.
MIP, if any, to be ☐ financed, ☐ paid in cash.

E. $_____ **EXISTING FIRST LOAN:** ☐ ASSUMPTION OF, ☐ SUBJECT TO existing first loan of record:
☐ FHA, ☐ VA, ☐ CONVENTIONAL, ☐ PRIVATE _____, ☐ FIXED RATE, ☐ ARM: _____
☐ OTHER: _____

payable at $_____ per month, with interest currently at _____%, ☐ including Taxes and Insurance,
with Interest Rate to be adjusted not to exceed _____%. Other terms: _____

Held by: _____. Assumption Fee, if any, not to exceed _____%.
All charges related to assumption shall be paid by Buyer.
☐ **ASSUMPTION OF LOAN WITH RELEASE OF LIABILITY:** Buyer shall assume Seller's Potential Indemnity
Liability to the U.S. Government for the repayment of the loan.
☐ **ASSUMPTION OF VA LOAN WITH SUBSTITUTION OF ENTITLEMENT.**
Paragraph 1-E is conditioned upon Buyer's approval of terms of said loan pursuant to Item 3, EXISTING LOANS.

F. $_____ **SELLER FINANCING:** First Loan secured by the property, payable at $_____ per month, or more, including
_____% interest, with the balance due _____ years from date of conveyance, ☐ due on sale.
A late charge of $_____ shall be due on monthly payments tendered more than _____ days late.
See Item 5, CREDIT APPROVAL.

JUNIOR LOANS

G. $_____ **PROCEEDS FROM NEW SECOND LOAN:** ☐ FIXED RATE, ☐ OTHER:_____

Amortization _____ years, with Interest not to exceed _____%, payable at approximately $_____ p/mo,
with the balance due not less than _____ years. ☐ Other terms: _____
_____. Loan fee not to exceed _____%.

H. $_____ **EXISTING SECOND LOAN** ☐ ASSUMPTION OF, ☐ SUBJECT TO existing second loan of record:
☐ FIXED RATE, ☐ OTHER: _____

payable at $_____ per month, with interest currently at _____%. Interest Rate to be adjusted
to: _____%. Other terms: _____

Held by: _____. Assumption Fee, if any, not to exceed _____%.
All charges related to assumption shall be paid by Buyer.
Conditioned upon Buyer's approval of terms of said loan pursuant to Item 3, EXISTING LOANS.

I. $_____ **SELLER FINANCING:** ☐ SECOND, ☐ THIRD LOAN secured by the property, payable at $_____ per
month, or more, including _____% interest, with the balance due _____ years from date of conveyance,
☐ due on sale.
A late charge of $_____ shall be due on monthly payments tendered more than _____ days late.
See Item 5, CREDIT APPROVAL.

J. $_____ **OTHER:** _____
_____

K. $_____ **TOTAL TO SELLER** Any net differences between the approximate balances of encumbrances shown above, which are
to be assumed or taken subject to, and the actual balances at close of escrow shall be adjusted in ☐ Cash,
☐ Other: _____

L. $_____ **BUYER'S BROKER FEE** payable at closing ☐ by Buyer, ☐ by sharing fee with Listing Broker.

M. $_____ **TOTAL PURCHASE PRICE PAID BY BUYER (not including closing costs).**

2. **LOAN APPROVAL.** Conditioned upon Buyers' ability to obtain a commitment for new financing for the herein property from a lender of Buyers'
choice, and/or consent to assumption of existing financing provided for in this agreement, **within** _____ **days of acceptance.** Buyer shall notify
Seller in writing whether or not such commitment was obtained within said time. Buyer shall use his best efforts to qualify for and obtain said financing
and shall complete and submit a loan application **within five (5) days of acceptance.**
In the event a loan commitment or consent is obtained but not honored without fault of Buyer, then Buyer may terminate this agreement and have
all deposits returned less expenses incurred to the date of cancellation of this transaction.

Buyer [_____] [_____] and Seller [_____] [_____] have read this page.

FORM 101-SA.1 (5-89) COPYRIGHT © 1989, BY PROFESSIONAL PUBLISHING CORP. 122 PAUL DR, SAN RAFAEL, CA 94903 (415) 472-1964

PROFESSIONAL PUBLISHING

Exhibit 15.1

3. **EXISTING LOANS.** Seller shall, **within three (3) days of acceptance**, provide Buyer with all Notes and Deeds of Trust to be assumed or taken subject to, and **within five (5) days of receipt thereof** Buyer shall in writing notify Seller of his approval or disapproval of the terms of said documents, which shall not be unreasonably withheld. **Within three (3) days of acceptance**, Seller shall submit written request for a current Statement of Condition on the above loan. Seller warrants that all loans in the transaction will be current at close of escrow.

4. **DUE ON SALE CLAUSE.** If the note and deed of trust or mortgage for any existing loan contains an acceleration or DUE ON SALE clause, the lender may demand full payment of the entire loan balance as a result of this transaction. Both parties acknowledge that they are not relying on any representation by the other party or the broker with respect to the enforceability of such a provision in existing notes and deeds of trust or mortgages, or deeds of trust or mortgages to be executed in accordance with this agreement. Both parties have been advised by the broker to seek independent legal advice with respect to these matters.

5. **CREDIT APPROVAL.** In the event of Seller Financing, Buyer shall furnish Seller **within three (3) days of acceptance**, a customary financial statement for the sole purpose of credit approval, which approval shall not be unreasonably withheld. Buyer authorizes Seller to engage the services of a reputable credit reporting agency for this purpose at Buyer's expense and Seller shall notify Buyer **within ten (10) days of receipt** of financial statement, of approval or disapproval of Buyer's credit.

6. **BALLOON PAYMENT.** **Both parties acknowledge they have not received or relied upon any statements or representations made to them by Broker regarding availability of funds, or rate of interest at which funds might be available, when Buyer becomes obligated to refinance or pay off the remaining balance of any loan pursuant to the terms of this agreement.**

7. **PRORATIONS.** Rents, taxes, interest, payments on Bonds and Assessments assumed by Buyer, Homeowner Association fees, and other expenses of the property to be prorated as of the date of recordation of the deed. Security deposits, advance rentals, or considerations involving future lease credits shall be credited to Buyer.

8. **REASSESSMENT OF PROPERTY TAX.** Buyer is advised that the property will be reassessed upon change of ownership which may result in a tax increase.

9. **FHA FINANCING.** In the event of FHA financing, it is expressly agreed that, notwithstanding any other provisions of this contract, the Buyer shall not be obligated to complete the purchase of the property described herein or to incur any penalty by forfeiture of earnest money deposits or otherwise unless the Seller has delivered to Buyer a written statement issued by the Federal Housing Commissioner, setting forth the appraised value of the property (excluding closing costs) for mortgage insurance purposes of not less than the amount specified as the purchase price, which statement the Seller hereby agrees to deliver to the Buyer promptly after such appraised value statement is made available to the Seller. The Buyer shall, however, have the privilege and option of proceeding with the consummation of the contract without regard to the amount of the appraised valuation made by the Federal Housing Commissioner.

THE APPRAISED VALUATION IS ARRIVED AT TO DETERMINE THE MAXIMUM MORTGAGE THE DEPARTMENT OF HOUSING AND URBAN DEVELOPMENT WILL INSURE. HUD DOES NOT WARRANT THE VALUE OR THE CONDITION OF THE PROPERTY. THE BUYER SHOULD SATISFY HIMSELF/HERSELF THAT THE PRICE AND CONDITION OF THE PROPERTY ARE ACCEPTABLE.

10. **VA FINANCING.** In the event of VA financing, it is expressly agreed that, notwithstanding any other provisions of this contract, the Buyer shall not incur any penalty by forfeiture of earnest money or otherwise be obligated to complete the purchase of the property described herein, if the contract purchase price or cost exceeds the Reasonable Value of the property established by the Veterans Administration. The Buyer shall, however, have the privilege and option of proceeding with the consummation of this contract without regard to the amount of the Reasonable Value established by the Veterans Administration. Escrow Fee to be paid by Seller.

11. **DEFINITIONS.** *BROKER* includes cooperating brokers and all sales persons. *DAYS* means calendar days unless otherwise specified. *DATE OF ACCEPTANCE* means the date the Seller accepts the offer or the Buyer accepts the counter offer. *DELIVERED* means personally delivered or transmitted by facsimile machine or mailed by certified mail; in the event of mailing, delivery shall be deemed to have been made on the day following the date of mailing, evidenced by the postmark on the envelope containing the delivered material. The *MASCULINE* includes the feminine and the *SINGULAR* includes the plural.

12. **TIME IS OF THE ESSENCE.** Time is of the essence of this agreement. All modifications and extensions shall be in writing and signed by all parties.

13. **CONDITIONS SATISFIED/WAIVED IN WRITING.** Each condition or contingency, approval and disapproval herein shall be satisfied according to its terms or waived in writing by the benefiting party **within the time limits specified** (or any extension thereof agreed to by the parties in writing), or this agreement shall terminate and all deposits returned to Buyer less expenses incurred by Buyer to the date of cancellation of this transaction. This paragraph contemplates that each party shall diligently pursue the completion of this transaction.

In this agreement **bold print** is used where such time limits are specified.

14. **INSURANCE.** In the event of Seller Financing, Buyer shall obtain hazard insurance prepaid for one year in an amount satisfactory to the loan holders and covering one hundred percent replacement cost of improvements, and to name holders of the secured loans as additional loss payees. Buyer agrees further to annually increase said insurance if necessary, to equal the current replacement cost of the property during the term of the loan holders' mortgages. Buyer shall instruct the insurance carrier to deliver to Seller before close of escrow a certificate providing for 30 days written notice in the event of cancellation.

15. **DESTRUCTION OF IMPROVEMENTS.** If the improvements of the property are destroyed, materially damaged, or found to be materially defective prior to close of escrow, Buyer may terminate the transaction by written notice delivered to Seller's broker or agent, and all deposits shall be returned to Buyer. In the event Buyer does not elect to terminate the agreement, Buyer shall be entitled to receive in addition to the property any insurance proceeds payable on account of the damage or destruction.

16. **NOTICE OF VIOLATIONS.** By acceptance hereof Seller warrants that he has no notice of violations relating to the property from City, County, or State agencies.

17. **EXAMINATION OF TITLE.** In addition to any encumbrances referred to herein, Buyer shall take title to the property subject to: [1] Real Estate Taxes not yet due, and [2] Covenants, Conditions, Restrictions, Rights of Way, and Easements of record, if any, which do not materially affect the value or intended use of the property.

Within three (3) days from acceptance Buyer shall order a preliminary Title Report and CC&R's if applicable. **Ten (10) days from receipt** thereof are allowed the Buyer to examine the title to the property and to report in writing any valid objections thereto. All exceptions to title contained in such report (other than monetary liens) shall be deemed approved unless written objection is delivered to Seller **within said ten (10) days.** If Buyer objects to any exceptions to the title, Seller shall use due diligence to remove such exceptions at his own expense **before close of escrow.** But if such exceptions cannot be removed **before close of escrow,** all rights and obligations hereunder may, at the election of the Buyer, terminate and the deposit shall be returned to Buyer less expenses incurred by Buyer to date of termination, unless he elects to purchase the property subject to such exceptions. If Seller concludes he is unwilling or unable to remove such objections, Seller shall so notify Buyer **within ten (10) days of receipt of said objections.** In that event Buyer may terminate this agreement and have all deposits returned less expenses incurred to date of termination.

Buyer [_____] [_____] and Seller [_____] [_____] have read this page.

FORM 101-SA.1(a) (5-89)   COPYRIGHT © 1989. BY PROFESSIONAL PUBLISHING CORP. 122 PAUL DR. SAN RAFAEL. CA 94903 (415) 472-1964

 PROFESSIONAL PUBLISHING

Exhibit 15.2

18. BONDS AND ASSESSMENTS. In the event there is a Bond or Assessment which has an outstanding principal balance and is a lien upon this property, such principal shall be ☐ paid by Seller, or ☐ assumed by Buyer. In the event of assumption, said obligation(s) ☐ shall, ☐ shall not be deducted from the Purchase Price at close of escrow. (This paragraph is not concerned with ongoing payments collected on the property tax bill for assessments which are not liens upon this property.)

19. CLOSING. On or before _____, or within _____ **days of acceptance**, whichever is later, both parties shall deposit with an authorized Escrow Holder, to be selected by ☐ Buyer, ☐ Seller, all funds and instruments necessary to complete the sale in accordance with the terms hereof. ☐ Where customary, signed Escrow Instructions to be delivered to Escrow Holder **within** _____ **days of acceptance.** Escrow Fee to be paid by_____. Transfer Tax(es), if any, to be paid by _____.

20. EVIDENCE OF TITLE, in the form of ☐ a policy of Title Insurance, ☐ Other: _____ paid by _____.

21. VESTED TITLE. Title shall vest as _____ unless otherwise designated in Escrow Instructions. *(The manner of taking title may have significant legal and tax consequences. If in doubt, Buyers should obtain advice from their legal or tax counsel.)*

22. SURVIVAL. The omission from escrow instructions of any provision herein shall not waive the right of any party. All representations or warranties shall survive the conveyance of the property.

23. PHYSICAL POSSESSION. Physical possession of the property, with keys to all property locks, alarms, and garage door openers, shall be delivered to Buyer (check the appropriate box):

☐ Upon recordation of the deed, **OR**

☐ After recordation of the deed, but not later than **midnight of** _____. Seller agrees to pay Buyer the sum of ☐ Buyer's PITI or ☐ $ _____ per day, as a day to day tenant, from recordation to the date hereinabove set forth (or any lesser sum in proportion to the actual date possession is delivered), to leave in escrow a sum equal to the above per diem amount multiplied by the number of days from date of closing to date allowed above for delivery of possession, and that all or so much of said sum as may be appropriate shall be delivered to the person(s) entitled thereto on the date possession is delivered or on the date set forth above, whichever is sooner.

Seller understands that continued occupancy beyond the date specified above constitutes a breach of this agreement in the absence of any written agreement between the parties to the contrary.

24. FIXTURES. All items permanently attached to the property, including attached floor coverings, draperies with hardware, shades, blinds, window and door screens, storm sash, combination doors, awnings, light fixtures, television antennas, electric garage door openers with controls, outdoor plants and trees, are included in the purchase price free of liens, EXCLUDING: _____

25. PERSONAL PROPERTY. The following personal property, on the premises when inspected by Buyer, is included in the purchase price and shall be transferred to Buyer free of liens by a Bill of Sale at close of escrow. No warranty is implied as to the condition of said property: _____

26. MAINTENANCE. Seller covenants that the heating, air-conditioning (if any), electrical, sewer, septic system, gutters and downspouts, sprinkler (if any), and plumbing systems including the water heater, as well as built-in appliances and other mechanical apparatus shall be in **working order** on the date possession is delivered. Seller shall replace any cracked or broken glass including windows, mirrors, shower and tub enclosures. Until possession is delivered Seller shall maintain landscaping, grounds and pool (if any). Seller agrees to deliver the property in a neat and clean condition with all debris removed. The following items are specifically excluded from the above: _____

Nothing disclosed by Seller in the SELLER DISCLOSURE STATEMENT (Item 27) shall require Seller to correct or improve the condition disclosed except as otherwise agreed to in writing.

Buyer and Seller understand and acknowledge that Broker shall not in any circumstances be liable for any breach in this clause.

27. SELLER DISCLOSURE STATEMENT. Seller ☐ shall, ☐ shall not provide Buyer as soon as practicable before transfer of title a completed Property Disclosure Statement. Such statement may be provided on PPC Form 109.1 and 109.2, or in California on Form 109.3-CAL and 109.4-CAL.

27-A. BUYER'S APPROVAL. If such Disclosure Statement is delivered to Buyer after the execution of this offer, Buyer is allowed to terminate this agreement by written notice delivered to Seller or Seller's agent **within three (3) days after delivery in person, or five (5) days after delivery by deposit in the mail** and have all deposits returned less expenses incurred to date by Buyer to date of termination.

27-B. DISCLAIMER. Buyer understands that the above Disclosure Statements are not substitutes for property inspections by professionals, including but not limited to engineers, architects, general contractors, and structural pest control operators, and Buyer has the opportunity to retain at Buyers' expense such professionals as he believes are appropriate. Buyer understands and acknowledges that the brokers and agents in the transaction cannot warrant the condition of the property or guarantee that all defects have been disclosed by Seller.

Buyer acknowledges that he has not received or relied upon any representations by either the **Broker or the Seller with respect to the condition of the property which are not contained in this agreement or in the disclosure statements.**

Seller agrees to hold all brokers and agents in the transaction harmless and to defend and indemnify them from any claim, demand, action or proceedings resulting from any omission or alleged omission by Seller in his Disclosure Statement.

28. ACCESS TO PROPERTY. Seller agrees to provide reasonable access to the property to Buyer and inspectors representing Buyer as provided in this agreement and to representatives of lending institutions for appraisal purposes.

29. HAZARDOUS MATERIALS. Hazardous Materials Statement (PPC Form 109.8) ☐ is, ☐ is not attached hereto.

30. PROVISIONS ON THE REVERSE SIDE. The provisions *initialed below* by Buyer, *printed in full on the reverse side (page 4)*, are included in this agreement.

[_____] A. Pest Control Inspection, paid by ☐ Buyer, ☐ Seller   [_____] I. Home Protect. Ctr.   ☐ Plan _____

[_____] B. Existing Pest Control Report Dated:_____,   ☐ paid by ☐ waived by _____

  By _____,   [_____] J. Contingent upon the sale of _____

[_____] C. Subject to Buyer's Approval of Pest Control Report   _____

[_____] D. Waiver of Pest Control Inspection   [_____] K. Owners Association Disclosure

[_____] E. Inspections of Physical Condition of Property, to be   [_____] L. Flood Hazard Zone Disclosure

  approved or disapproved within _____ days of acceptance   [_____] M. Rental Property

[_____] F. Roof Report to Seller within _____ days of acceptance   [_____] N. Rent Control Ordinance

[_____] G. City and County Report ordered within _____ days of acceptance   [_____] O. Smoke Detector(s) provided by _____

[_____] H. Maintenance Reserve in the amount of $ _____

Buyer [_____] [_____] and Seller [_____] [_____] have read this page.

FORM 101-SA.2 (5-89)   COPYRIGHT © 1989, BY PROFESSIONAL PUBLISHING CORP., 122 PAUL DR, SAN RAFAEL, CA 94903 (415) 472-1964   **PROFESSIONAL PUBLISHING**

Exhibit 15.3

PAGE 4 of 5 PAGES

______ **30-A. PEST CONTROL INSPECTION.** The main building and all structures on the property to be inspected by a licensed structural pest control operator. Seller to pay for: (1) Elimination of infestation and/or infection of wood-destroying pests or organisms, (2) For repair of damage caused by such infestation and/or infection, (3) For correction of conditions which caused said damage and (4) For repair of plumbing and other leaks affecting wood members, including repair of leaking stall showers, in accordance with said pest control operator's report. Seller shall not be responsible for preventive work where no damage is found, except where required for FHA or VA financing.

If the inspecting structural pest control operator recommends further inspection of inaccessible areas, Buyer may require that said areas be inspected. If any infestation or infection is discovered by such inspection, the additional cost of such inspection and additional required work shall be paid by Seller. If no such infestation or infection is discovered, the additional cost of inspecting such inaccessible areas and the work required to return the property to its original condition shall be paid by Buyer.

Funds for work specified in said report, to be done at Seller's expense, shall be held in escrow and disbursed by escrow holder upon receipt of Notice of Work Completed by a licensed structural pest control operator selected by Seller certifying that the property is free of evidence of active infestation or infection.

As soon as the same are available, copies of the report, and any certification or other proof of completion of the work shall be delivered to the agents of Buyer and Seller who are authorized to receive the same on behalf of their principals.

______ **30-B. EXISTING PEST CONTROL REPORT ACCEPTED BY BUYER.** Buyer accepts existing pest control report on the property by the licensed structural pest control operator listed under **Item 30-B.** Seller's obligations shall be as set forth in **Item 30-A** above.

______ **30-C. SUBJECT TO BUYER'S APPROVAL OF PEST CONTROL REPORT.** Property to be purchased in its present condition with no charge to Seller for any pest control work. However, Buyer shall have the right to have the property inspected and to obtain a report from a licensed structural pest control operator. Buyer shall be deemed to have approved said report unless written notice to the contrary is delivered to Seller or his agent **within fifteen (15) days of acceptance.** In the event Buyer does not approve the report, he may have his deposit returned and both parties shall be relieved of all obligations hereunder.

Buyer acknowledges that he has not received or relied upon any representations by either the Broker or the Seller, with respect to the condition of the property.

______ **30-D. WAIVER OF PEST CONTROL INSPECTION.** Buyer has satisfied himself about the condition of the property and agrees to purchase the property in its present condition without the benefit of a structural pest control inspection.

Buyer acknowledges that he has not received or relied upon any representations by either the Broker or the Seller, with respect to the condition of the property.

______ **30-E. INSPECTION OF PHYSICAL CONDITION OF PROPERTY.** Buyer shall have the right, at his expense, to select licensed contractors or other qualified professionals to inspect the subject property, including but not limited to matters structural, geological, plumbing, heating, air conditioning, electrical, built-in appliances, well, pool, septic tank, hazardous materials, and survey. Buyer shall, upon Seller's written request, furnish Seller at no cost copies of all inspection reports obtained. Buyer shall approve or disapprove all inspection reports obtained in writing, **within the number of days specified under item 30-E.** If Seller does not agree to correct any unacceptable conditions **within three (3) days from receipt of such notice,** Buyer may elect to terminate this agreement. In the event of such termination all deposits shall be returned less expenses incurred by Buyer to the date of cancellation.

______ **30-F. ROOF INSPECTION.** Buyer, at his expense, may order a roof report from a licensed general or roofing contractor. **Within the number of days specified under Item 30-F,** copies of the report shall be delivered to the agents of Buyer and Seller who are authorized to receive the same on behalf of their principals.

Within three (3) days following receipt of the report, Seller may [a]: elect to pay the cost of all work recommended by such report; or [b]: elect to pay none or only a portion of the cost of such work. Written notice of such election shall be delivered to Buyer or his agent.

In the event Seller does not agree to pay for all such work, Buyer may elect to pay the balance of the cost of such work or terminate all rights and obligations to the parties under this agreement. Written notice of such election shall be delivered to Seller or his agent **within seven (7) days following receipt** of Seller's notice. In the event of such termination, Buyer shall be entitled to a full refund of all deposits excluding the cost of the above roof inspection report. If no written election is made **within seven (7) days,** Buyer shall have no right to terminate this agreement, and Seller shall be responsible for the cost of that portion of the work which he elected to pay.

In the event Seller has elected to pay the cost of all such work, he shall have the right to have such work performed by a licensed general or roofing contractor of his choice.

______ **30-G. CITY AND COUNTY INSPECTION REPORT.** If local ordinance requires that the property be inspected **or a report issued** for compliance with local building and permit regulations, standards, and ordinances as a condition to sale or transfer, Seller shall, **within the number of days specified under item 30-G,** notify the appropriate local agency to cause the property to be inspected, **or to issue the required report** at the earliest practicable date. If Seller does not agree to pay for correction of any violations shown in the report, Buyer may pay the cost of the required corrections or terminate this agreement. In the event of termination all deposits shall be returned less expenses incurred by Buyer to date of termination.

______ **30-H. MAINTENANCE RESERVE.** Seller agrees to leave in escrow a maintenance reserve in the amount **specified under Item 30-H.** If in the reasonable opinion of a qualified technician any of the terms listed under Item 26, MAINTENANCE, are not in normal working order, Buyer shall furnish Seller a copy of said technician's inspection report and/or submit written notice to Seller of non-compliance of any of the conditions under MAINTENANCE **within seven (7) days from date occupancy is delivered.**

In the event Seller fails to make the repairs and or corrections **within five (5) days of receipt of said report or notice,** Seller herewith authorizes the escrow holder to disburse to Buyer against bills for such repairs or corrections the sum of such bills, not to exceed the amount reserved. Said reserve shall be disbursed to Buyer or returned to Seller **not later than fifteen (15) days from date occupancy is delivered.**

______ **30-I. HOME PROTECTION CONTRACT**, paid for by the party specified under **Item 30-I,** shall become effective upon close of escrow for not less than one year, unless both parties have waived such Home Protection Contract, as specified under **Item 30-I.** The brokers herein have informed both parties that such protection programs are available, but do not approve or endorse any particular program.

______ **30-J. CONTINGENCY RELEASE CLAUSE.** Subject to the sale and conveyance of "Buyer's Property," described in **Item 30-J,** within the time specified for closing of Seller's property. Seller shall have the right to continue to offer the herein property for sale and to accept written offers subject to the rights of Buyer. Should Seller accept such an offer, then Buyer shall be delivered written notice of such acceptance. In the event Buyer will not waive this condition in writing **within three (3) days of receipt of such notice,** then this agreement shall be terminated and all deposits be returned to Buyer and escrow cancelled.

______ **30-K. OWNERS ASSOCIATION DISCLOSURE.** Buyer shall take title subject to the governing documents of the development, including Declaration of Restrictions or C C & R's, By-Laws, Articles of Incorporation, Rules and Regulations currently in force, and Financial Statement of the Owners Association, as applicable to common interests including Condominiums, PUD's, Stock Cooperatives, or Time Shares, to be delivered to Buyer for his approval **within fifteen (15) days of acceptance.** Buyer shall be deemed to have approved said documents unless written notice to the contrary is delivered to Seller or his agent **within five (5) days of receipt** by Buyer, in which case Buyer may have his deposit returned and both parties shall be relieved of all obligations hereunder.

In addition, Seller delivers to Buyer before close of escrow a written statement from the owners association documenting the amount of any delinquent assessments including penalties, attorney's fees, and other charges provided for in the management documents. Such charges shall be credited to Buyer at close of escrow.

______ **30-L. FLOOD HAZARD ZONE.** Buyer has been advised that the property is located in an area which the Secretary of HUD has found to have special flood hazards and that, pursuant to the National Flood Insurance Program, it will be necessary to purchase flood insurance in order to obtain any loan secured by the property from any federally regulated financial institution or a loan insured or guaranteed by an agency of the U.S. Government. The purpose of the Program is to provide flood insurance at reasonable cost. For further information consult your lender or insurance carrier.

______ **30-M. RENTAL PROPERTY.** Buyer to take property subject to existing leases and rights of parties in possession on month-to-month tenancies. Within **seven (7) days of acceptance** Seller shall deliver to Buyer for his approval copies of existing leases and rental agreements as well as copies of any outstanding notices sent to tenants, and a written statement of all oral agreements with tenants, incured defaults by Seller or tenants, claims made by or to tenants, a statement of all tenants' deposits held by Seller, and a complete statement of rental income and expenses, all of which Seller warrants to be true and complete.

Conditioned upon Buyer's inspection and approval of all rental units **within five (5) days of acceptance.** Said documents shall be deemed to have been approved unless written notice to the contrary is delivered to Seller **within seven (7) days of receipt** of said documents. In case of disapproval Buyer may terminate this agreement and have his deposit returned less expenses incurred by Buyer to date of termination.

During the pendency of this transaction Seller agrees that no changes in the existing leases or rental agreements shall be made, nor new leases or rental agreements entered into, nor shall any substantial alterations or repairs be made or undertaken without the written consent of the Buyer.

Security deposits, advance rentals, or considerations involving future lease credits shall be credited to Buyer in escrow.

Seller shall furnish Buyer with copies of any service and/or equipment rental contracts with respect to the property which run beyond close of escrow.

______ **30-N. RENT CONTROL ORDINANCE.** Buyer is aware that a local ordinance is in effect which regulates the rights and obligations of property owners. It may also affect the manner in which future rents can be adjusted.

______ **30-O. SMOKE DETECTOR(S).** In accordance with local ordinance smoke detectors shall be installed at the expense of the party indicated under Item 30-O. If required, said smoke detectors shall be inspected by the appropriate City or County agency prior to close of escrow and a compliance report obtained.

Buyer [________] [________] and Seller [________] [________] have read this page.

FORM 101-SA.2(a) (5-89)

COPYRIGHT © 1989, BY PROFESSIONAL PUBLISHING CORP, 122 PAUL DR, SAN RAFAEL, CA 94903 (415) 472-1964

PROFESSIONAL PUBLISHING

Exhibit 15.4

31.   DEFAULT. In the event Buyer shall default in the performance of this agreement, Seller may, subject to any rights of the broker herein, retain Buyer's deposit on account of damages sustained and may take such actions as he deems appropriate to collect such additional damages as may have been actually sustained, and Buyer shall have the right to take such action as he deems appropriate to recover such portion of the deposit as may be allowed by law.

32.   ATTORNEY FEES. In any action or proceeding involving a dispute between Buyer, Seller and/or Broker, arising out of the execution of this agreement or the sale, or to collect commissions, the prevailing party shall be entitled to receive from the other party a reasonable attorney fee to be determined by the court or arbitrator(s).

33.   ADDITIONAL TERMS AND CONDITIONS.

_____
_____
_____
_____
_____
_____
_____
_____
_____
_____
_____
_____
_____
_____
_____
_____
_____
_____
_____
_____
_____
_____
_____
_____
_____
_____

34.   ADDENDA: The following addenda, signed and dated by both parties, are attached and made a part of this agreement _____

35.   EXPIRATION OF OFFER. This offer shall expire unless acceptance is delivered to Buyer or to _____ on or before _____ ☐ AM ☐ PM, _____, 19_____.

36.   ENTIRE AGREEMENT. This document contains the entire agreement of the parties and supersedes all prior agreements or representations with respect to the property which are not expressly set forth herein. This agreement may be modified only by a writing signed and dated by both parties. **Both parties acknowledge that they have not relied on any statements of the real estate agent or broker which are not herein expressed.**

A Real Estate Broker or Agent is qualified to advise on Real Estate. If you have any questions concerning the legal sufficiency, legal effect or tax consequences of this document or the transaction related thereto, consult with your Attorney or Accountant.

The undersigned Buyer acknowledges that he/she has thoroughly read and approved each of the provisions contained herein and agrees to purchase the herein described property for the price and on the terms and conditions specified. Buyer acknowledges receipt of a copy of this agreement.

DATED: _____   DATED: _____   TIME: _____
Buyer's Broker _____   Buyer _____
By _____   Buyer _____
Broker's Initials _____   Date _____   Buyer _____

ACCEPTANCE

37.   COMMISSION. Seller agrees to pay in cash the following real estate commission for services rendered, which commission Seller hereby irrevocably assigns from escrow: _____% of the accepted price or $ _____ to: _____, the Listing Broker. The fee of Buyer's Broker ☐ is paid by Buyer ☐ is paid by sharing commission with Listing Broker, irrespective of the agency relationship. Escrow instructions with respect to commissions may not be amended or revoked without the written consent of the broker(s) herein.

Commission shall also be payable upon any default by Seller, or the mutual recission by Buyer and Seller, which prevents completion of the sale. This agreement shall not limit the rights of Broker and Seller provided for in any existing listing agreement.

SELLER UNDERSTANDS THAT BUYER'S BROKER NAMED HEREIN IS THE AGENT OF THE BUYER, AND IS NOT THE AGENT OF THE SELLER OR A SUBAGENT OF SELLER'S BROKER, REGARDLESS OF AGREEMENTS WITH RESPECT TO PAYMENT OF COMMISSIONS OR RIGHTS GRANTED UNDER MULTIPLE LISTING AGREEMENTS.

38.   FOREIGN INVESTMENT AND REAL PROPERTY TAX ACT (IRC Section 1445). Unless the property is acquired for use by Buyer as a primary residence and is sold for no more than $300,000, Seller agrees to provide Buyer with (a) NON-FOREIGN SELLER AFFIDAVIT (PPC Form 101-V), **OR** (b) WITHHOLDING CERTIFICATION FORM from the Internal Revenue Service stating that withholding is not required.

Seller acknowledges that he/she has read and understands the provisions of this agreement and agrees to sell the herein described property for the price and on the terms and conditions specified.

Seller acknowledges receipt of a copy of this agreement. Authorization is hereby given the Broker(s) in this transaction to deliver a signed copy hereof to Buyer and to disclose the terms of sale to members of a Multiple Listing Service or Board of REALTORS at close of escrow.

Subject to: _____

DATED: _____   TIME: _____
Seller's Broker _____   Seller _____
By _____   Seller _____
Broker's Initials _____   Date _____   Seller _____

Buyer acknowledges receipt of a copy of the accepted agreement. DATE: _____ TIME: _____ Buyer _____

FORM   101-SA.3   (5-89)   COPYRIGHT © 1989, BY PROFESSIONAL PUBLISHING CORP., 122 PAUL DR., SAN RAFAEL, CA 94903 (415) 472-1964   **PROFESSIONAL PUBLISHING**

Exhibit 15.5

This CONTINGENCY LOG is NOT PART OF THE PURCHASE AGREEMENT. It is intended only for convenience of the brokers and the parties. It is a summary of deadlines within which the contingencies provided for in the agreement must be satisfied or waived.

NOTE: The number of days printed in bold in the agreement are the days shown below with *. The number of days which were filled in on the agreement, need to be inserted. The "Deadline" is arrived at by adding the number of days allowed for contingency removal to the Date of Acceptance.

Professional Publishing Computer Software for Residential Forms automatically prints out this summary with all contingency time limits and calculates final dates on a separate blank sheet.

Publisher or programmer cannot be responsible for accuracy of computer calculations.

	CONTINGENCY LOG				
	Date of Acceptance:		Date of Closing:		
		Party responsible for Removal	Days from Acceptance	Days from Receipt of Report	Dead line	Date Contingency removed in writing
Item	Contingency					
1-B	ADDITIONAL DEPOSIT	Buyer				
2	LOAN APPROVAL					
	Loan Commitment	Buyer				
	Submit Loan Application	Buyer	5*			
3	EXISTING LOANS					
	Copies Loan Doc's to Buyer	Seller	3*			
	Approval Loan Doc's by Buyer	Buyer		5*		
	Order Statement Condition	Seller	3*			
5	CREDIT APPROVAL					
	Financial Statement to Seller	Buyer	3*			
	Approval Financial Statement	Seller		10*		
17	EXAMINATION OF TITLE					
	Preliminary Title Report ordered	Buyer	3*			
	Report Objections to Title	Buyer		10*		
19	CLOSING					
	Days to Close	Buyer/Seller				
	Escrow Instructions (So.Cal)	Buyer/Seller				
27-A	PURCHASER'S APPROVAL					
	Approval of Form 109.1 or 109.3C	Buyer				
	Approval of Form 109.2 or 109.4C	Buyer				
30-A	Pest Control Inspection					
30-B	Existing Pest Ctr. Report					
30-C	Subj to Buyer's Approval	Buyer	15*			
30-E	PHYSICAL PROPERTY CONDITION					
	Approval Inspection Report	Buyer				
30-F	ROOF INSPECTION					
	Report to Seller	Buyer				
	Seller's Election to Pay	Seller		3*		
	Buyer's Election to Quit	Buyer		7*		
30-G	CITY/COUNTY INSPECTION					
	Order Report	Seller				
30-H	MAINTENANCE RESERVE					
	Notice of Non-Compliance	Buyer	7 days	from date	of	occupancy
30-J	CONTINGENT SALE PROPERTY					
	Contingency Removal by Buyer	Buyer				
30-K	OWNERS ASSOCIATION					
	Condo Doc's to Purchaser	Seller	15*			
	Approval of Doc's by Buyer	Buyer		5*		
30-M	RENTAL PROPERTY					
	Copies of Leases etc.	Seller	7*			
	Inspection of Rental Units	Buyer	5*			
	Approval of Loan Documents	Buyer		7*		

Exhibit 15.6

Chapter 8 Quiz

1. When a purchaser is buying a home through the services of a real estate broker, the broker always represents the buyer:

    (A) As the buyer's agent
    (B) As the seller's agent
    (C) As a dual agent
    ✓(D) None of the above

2. The broker who is the seller's agent is obligated to try to negotiate a sale:

    (A) At the highest possible price, consistent with the terms
    (B) At the lowest possible price, consistent with the terms
    (C) At a price easiest for the broker to sell
    (D) Any of the above

3. A traditional exclusive listing creates an agency relationship between:

    (A) The broker and the salesperson
    (B) The salesperson and the owner
    (C) The buyer and the salesperson
    (D) The broker and the owner

4. If the seller of real estate pays the brokerage commission:

    (A) That fact alone establishes the broker as the seller's agent
    (B) That fact prevents the broker from acting as the buyer's agent
    (C) That fact is not necessarily determinative of the agency relationships
    (D) None of the above

5. In case of litigation:

    (A) Agency is a question of contract, depending on consideration
    (B) A gratuitous agency is not recognizable
    (C) Agency is a question of fact, not of contract
    (D) Agency is a question of contract, not of fact

6. A dual agency is:

    (A) Never lawful
    (B) Lawful if agreed to by all parties
    (C) Lawful if at least one of the parties agrees
    (D) Lawful if the broker does not disclose the fact

7. A buyer's broker owes a fiduciary duty to:

    (A) Both buyer and seller
    (B) Seller only
    (C) Buyer only
    (D) The escrow company

8. The escrowholder usually acts as:

    (A) A dual agent
    (B) A single agent
    (C) An agent of the seller only
    (D) An agent of the buyer only

9. Sources of properties for a buyer's broker include:

    (A) A Multiple Listing Service
    (B) Unlisted properties
    (C) Probate sales
    (D) All of the above

10. Other sources of properties for a buyer's broker include:

    (A) "Real estate owned" by lenders
    (B) New subdivisions
    (C) Properties not on the market
    (D) All of the above

PREVIEW

The Sales Process

Six Sales Skills for Success

Effective Business Communication

The Sales Strategy

Showing the Property

Disclosure Upon Transfer of Residential Property

The Real Estate Sales Portfolio

THE SALES PROCESS

Sales is the process of assisting someone to make a decision about a product or service that will satisfy a need or desire. In this case, the "someone" is the "prospect" who has now become your "customer."

Assistance. You are responsible for supplying whatever information is needed to help your customer make a decision. Use non-technical terms or, if necessary, explain complicated terminologies.

Decision. Since decision making is a critical function involving success or failure, it can be a stressful event for your customer. The decision to buy a particular home will affect how your customer lives for a long time.

Psychology. People try to avoid stressful situations, such as decision making, as much as possible. Try to modify their behavior, supply them with valid information, and help them decide.

Goal of the Sales Process: A Decision The decision can be either positive or negative; what is important is that a decision is reached, and the sales process completed.

Positive Decision. The outcome may be that the customer decides to buy the product or service.

Negative Decision. The customer may also decide to reject the product or service in question. However, if the customer still has the need or desire, you have a responsibility and opportunity to help him select another product or service. The sales process is repeated until the customer's need is satisfied.

Example

A customer asks about a certain property advertised for sale. You give him the information and ask if there is any further interest in the property. The answer is no. This is one complete sales process; however, if the need or desire remains, it is your responsibility as a sales professional to repeat the process until the need or desire is satisfied.

Salesperson's Assets The selling process should begin with a formal or informal self-analysis by the salesperson to determine personal attributes that need to be strengthened and others that must be eliminated or overcome. In order to be successful, you need:

Concern. Have a sincere interest in your customer's needs.

Enthusiasm. Stimulate curiosity, generate enthusiasm, and retain your customer's interest.

Presence. Maintain good health, a professional attitude, and optimism.

Sensitivity. Observe and interpret your customer's reactions, especially nonverbal communication, and apply appropriate selling techniques at the right time.

Receptivity. Be an interested listener.

Business Expertise. Demonstrate your initiative, self-confidence, creativity, and organization.

Integrity. Be of unquestionable integrity.

SIX SALES SKILLS FOR SUCCESS

The ability to close a sale requires mastery of certain basic skills. They are:

Questioning Selling requires the ability to ask good questions. Questions determine which path in the sales process you should follow.

Shortening the Process. Guidance through skillful questioning may significantly reduce the time a customer takes to make a decision.

Open Questions. Questions like "How do you visualize your ideal home?" allow customers great freedom of response and require creative solutions on your part, since they have no predetermined answers.

Closed Questions. Other questions restrict answers to a few choices or perhaps only one choice. "Which do you prefer, a two-story or single-story home?" "Will the balance of the downpayment be available by the 25th of the month?"

Sequence. You may find the best procedure is to start with an open question, follow with a second open question, and then ask a closed question to determine the path toward the decision.

Example

(Open question) "What do you like about these two neighborhoods?" (second open question) "What don't you like about them?" (followed by the closed question) "In which of the two neighborhoods do you prefer to live?"

Handling Objections   In almost any transaction, there will be pros and cons. Sooner or later the customer will bring up objections and reservations. There is a definite skill to responding to these.

Reasons for Objections. Objections may be factual or emotional in origin. In either case, they are real to the customer.

☐ Some event may keep the customer from continuing.

☐ There may be a lack of communication. Try to avoid using technical real estate terminology. Use language that the average person can easily understand.

☐ Vital facts may have been overlooked. Ask leading questions to check the customer's comprehension.

☐ Fear or nervousness holds many customers back. This may be the most expensive purchase in the customer's life. There may be concern about qualifying for a loan or the time required to close the deal. Inspire customer confidence in yourself and your firm.

Objections as Selling Tools. "No objections" often means no interest. Discussing objections keeps the selling process going. Because the customers remain silent, do not assume you are doing an excellent job. Their silence could simply mean a lack of interest or that they are politely waiting for you to finish before closing the conversation. Draw them out; solicit objections; get them involved. Do not trivialize their objections, argue, or say or imply that the customers are wrong. Hear them out; be a good listener. An objection means they have some interest.

Start out by acknowledging their previous statements. "I see what you mean, but ...." "I can understand your point of view, but ...." Use your counter to reinforce selling points. Don't win an argument and lose the sale.

Real Objections. Objections based on fact are true barriers to reaching a goal. One way to overcome real objections is to weigh difficulties against benefits. If objections outweigh benefits, change the goal; however, if benefits outweigh difficulties, continue on your sales path.

Strategies for handling a real objection include:

☐ Rephrase the objection as a question

☐ Put the difficulties in perspective by noting the positive features and the total other benefits

☐ Review goals to assist in deciding whether to continue or change objectives. Remember, at worst you have learned some more about the customer's requirements.

Examples

☐ "Is that one feature enough to keep you from having and enjoying all the other things you want in a house? It does offer easy access."

☐ "Is being far from the freeway worth more to you than having a home you can enjoy and afford in the school district you want? Is its location more important than the low downpayment or low interest rates?"

☐ "If it is that important to you, then let's find another home," or "If it is not that important, let me show you the rest of this beautiful home."

Imaginary Objections. Objections based on confusion, misconception, or lack of information are imaginary objections. You can overcome them by presenting the facts. Strategies for handling an imaginary objection include:

☐ Rephrase the objection as a question.

☐ Answer it directly with facts.

☐ Offer proof if required.

Example

Imaginary Objection: "We can't afford this home."

☐ "Are you worried about the downpayment and the monthly payments?"

☐ "Well, the owner has agreed to help with the financing so you only need a small downpayment, and the assumable loan has a very low interest rate so the payments will be much lower than on most comparable homes."

☐ "This data sheet has all the information. Let me show you how it will work out."

Removing Doubt, Offering Proof

An unsure, hesitant customer needs to have proof to allow progress toward the desired goal. If you do not provide proof, the path to the goal is blocked and your customer's problem cannot be solved.

Doubt/Proof Response. Your customer's statements or questions expressing doubt or skepticism can be handled in the following manner:

☐ Rephrase the statement or question, putting it into a positive light.

☐ Offer proof of the positive aspects.

☐ Explain the benefits to your customer.

Example

Doubt/Proof Situation: "Do we really want to buy a home?"

☐ "If you're concerned that there are not enough benefits in home ownership, let me explain some of them to you."

☐ "This recent local newspaper article lists 23 ways that home ownership can benefit a young couple."

☐ "Home ownership means tax advantages, appreciation, and security."

Reinforcing the Customer's Positive Remarks

Positive remarks may just be politeness, but they should always be treated seriously as an indication that you are close to a decision point.

Positive Support Approach. Maximum advantage can be obtained by using a structured approach.

☐ Offer agreement.

☐ Paraphrase the remark in a positive manner.

☐ Refer to the appropriate benefits.

Example

Positive Support: "This home has everything we've been looking for, and the price is in the range we've wanted."

☐ "Yes, it certainly is."

☐ "It is as closely matched to your needs as any home on the market."

☐ "Now you can entertain at home, the children can walk to school, and your place of business is only five minutes away."

Introducing New Information In situations where customers fail to observe desirable features or overlook pertinent facts, new information may be needed.

Technique. Avoid making customers feel foolish for having overlooked the information themselves. Introduce a general statement about a subject and include new information. Derive specific information from the general statement.

Example

Providing New Information. The customer has indicated a desire for recreational facilities, but has not mentioned those nearby.

☐ "Many people move into this particular area because of the outstanding recreation facilities."

☐ "This home is within walking distance of two pools and a children's playground. And the tennis club is within one block."

Obtaining a Commitment When the customer is ready to make a decision, request a verbal commitment so that you can be sure the problem is solved.

Closing Commitment. Structure this strategy for maximum impact and minimum risk of your customer's changing his or her mind.

☐ Assume the positive decision.

☐ Summarize the appropriate benefits to your customer.

☐ Request a commitment from your customer.

Example

Closing Commitment: "This is the house we've been looking for."

☐ Observe the positive attitude - "You really like this house."

☐ "Yes, it is the most desirable home in this neighborhood."

☐ "What do you think you should do?" or stronger, "What do you think is the only sensible thing you should do?"

Strategy. Present only one choice with the request for your customer's commitment. Your question must be worded very carefully to assure the commitment. If this approach fails, repeat the steps to find the problem and continue along the sales path to the commitment again. Repeat the process until the desired decision has been reached.

EFFECTIVE BUSINESS COMMUNICATION

Effective communication in sales is a structured method of determining the customer's need or desire and then guiding him or her to a decision that satisfies the need or desire.

Identifying and Understanding the Goal

What are the buyer's (and seller's) motivations? Determine what problem the customer is trying to solve and the underlying reason for the problem, need, or desire.

Underlying Reasons. Knowing the goal is not sufficient; the underlying reasons must also be known.

Ask Questions. Ascertain the customer's goal and motivation. Generally, buyers' and sellers' motivations involve occupancy, change in lifestyle, investment, speculation, or a combination of these.

- □ *Occupancy Goals.* Residential property buyers and people seeking business locations have occupancy as their primary motivation or goal.

- □ *Change in Lifestyle.* Some buyers or sellers have needs resulting from job relocation or displacement, illness, death, change in marital status, change in family size, etc.

- □ *Investment Goals.* Buyers with investment goals are seeking real estate acquisitions that provide long-term capital gains, cash flow, appreciation, tax shelters, and positive returns (yield) on investment.

- □ *Speculation Goals.* Buyers willing to accept additional risks on the chance of quick (short-term) or considerable profit are known as speculators. Sellers who will sell only if they can get above the market price may also fit this category.

Empathize. Let customers know you understand their problem and will do everything you can to help solve it.

Guiding the Customer to the Goal

This step requires providing information necessary for your customer to make a decision as well as allowing her or him to "discover" the steps toward the goal.

Provide Information. Educate customers about the current market and financing situation. A competitive market analysis gives customers a picture of the market and an idea of what price to offer.

Use Questions to Guide. Allowing the customer to "discover" information independently is more convincing than providing it yourself.

Convince the Customer. Be sure the customer knows that you are a knowledgeable professional who can give expert opinion, especially at the critical moment when a decision is apparent.

Don't Waste Time. When a prime, qualified customer is seriously looking for a solution to a housing problem, give 100% of your efforts to this customer. Act quickly and press for a decision.

Requesting a Decision The final and most important step is to request a decision. It requires your customer to make a decision.

Preparation. If the first steps have been accomplished effectively, the last step will be simple. You will sense when the costumer is ready to decide.

An Express Commitment. The process is complete only when your customer has made an explicit decision, orally or in writing. Remember, an implied decision is not a decision.

THE SALES STRATEGY

The salesperson is always planning. General planning and organizing before and between sales means you are ready for detailed planning of specific transactions as they arise.

Presale Planning Planning before you have a customer is one of the most important requisites for success in selling. Successful preplanned sales strategy requires effective organization of your time.

Time for Research. Set aside adequate time so that you will be able to gather all the facts about your buyer, your seller, and appropriate properties and develop and implement your sales strategy.

Activity Reports. Compile records to help accomplish your goals and objectives.

Good Work Habits. Consistent sales effort is promoted by good work habits. "Plan your work and work your plan" is sound advice to follow during your entire career.

Organizing the Sales Process When you have a customer, the sales process is tailored to the specific property, buyer, and seller.

Know the Property The customer looks to you for expertise. Visit each property before showing it, observing its amenities and learning its positive and negative aspects in order to discuss them intelligently with your customer. Review all of the listing data, including the financing information. Be prepared to show comparable properties.

Know the Customer What are the customer's needs and desires: shelter, security, pride of ownership, safety, investment, etc.?

Qualifications. Ascertain the buyer's personal and financial qualifications. This information enables you to concentrate on a realistic price range and specific preferences, saving time for both customer and agent. Prepare and fill out a Home Buyer's Analysis (Exhibit 13, Chapter 7) to ascertain qualifications in more detail, including the amount of cash available for the downpayment, the amount of monthly payments the customer can afford (including taxes and insurance), and personal preferences such as bedrooms and baths or special features needed.

Degree of Motivation. To find out how motivated your customers are, ask leading questions like:

- ☐ "Do you own your own home?"

- ☐ "Do you intend to sell it before purchasing another?"

- ☐ "Do you presently have it listed with another broker or do you intend to sell it yourself?"

If your customers are not motivated, they will usually not want to answer your probing questions or demand your full time effort. Weed out the "spectators."

Type of Motivation. Is the customer primarily inspired by reason or emotion? Emotion makes people buy what they want, not what they need. Logic makes people think, emotion makes them act. If emotion is the motivator, sell the ideas and benefits, not the property. People usually know what they don't want before they know what they want, so try to learn the *negative motivators* of your customer. This will save save time and enable you to anticipate objections.

Agency Relationship. If your customers are highly motivated they will want you to serve them full time and to be informed of your activities on their behalf. Be careful, however, not to mislead a customer into thinking you are his or her agent.

Service Needs. Successful selling means maximum satisfaction of your customer's needs for confidence, information, and advice, as well as the actual product (the property and financing).

- ☐ *Confidence.* Reinforce to your customer:

  - That the property is right for him or her.
  - That the offering price and financing are within negotiating range.
  - That you are morally and legally above reproach.

☐ *Information*. Offer complete knowledge accurately.

- Be informed on current market conditions.
- Be current with the available financing alternatives.
- Be prepared to explain the pros and cons of each type of financing.

☐ *Advice*. Be a trusted counselor.

- Honor the confidentiality of your customer's personal information, but be aware of your fiduciary obligation to your principal (the seller) when a listing has engaged you as agent.
- Recommend seeking counsel from an attorney or tax advisor when appropriate.

Know the Seller **Motivation to Sell**. If the sale involves a single-family residence, can you convert the seller into a prospect for another home in your market area, or a relocation referral prospect? What are the seller's plans for the proceeds from the sale: will the seller be reinvesting all or part in a similar property, or looking for another investment medium?

Seller's Financing Capabilities. Residential financing in tight money situations has rapidly moved into a practice already common in commercial property, where the seller extends credit to help finance the sale.

SHOWING THE PROPERTY

In many ways, this is the central event in the sales process. As with any introduction, a good first impression is all-important.

Know the Property Prior to the showing, tour the homes you are going to show. A good test of your familiarity is whether you can show the home without the listing information in your hands.

How Many to Show. Plan on showing at least three but not more than six homes at any one time.

Anticipate Questions. Be able to anticipate and answer your customer's questions and objections regarding each property.

Don't Pretend to Know All Answers. If you don't have an answer to a question, say that you will find the answer and get back to them. This gives you an opportunity to contact the customer again.

Prepare the Property for Showing

The customers will be trying to visualize themselves living in the home. Make the picture as attractive and uncomplicated as possible.

Seller's Presence. Make the appointment at an approximate time. Suggest that the sellers leave upon your arrival, or encourage them to stay out of the way.

Visual and Aural Atmosphere. Have the house looking neat, with a minimum of clutter or highly personal items which could keep the buyers from seeing it as their home. The drapes should be open and lights turned on, to project a cheerful, warm, and bright atmosphere. Soft music may be played.

Olfactory Atmosphere. Suggest the sellers bake something in the oven; the aroma of freshly baked apple pie or cinnamon rolls will produce a friendly and inviting feeling.

Taking the Customers to the Property

Take Customers in Your Car. The trip to the property can be an important adjunct to the showing itself. You will gain the valuable opportunity to chat, obtain pertinent information, and observe reactions between showings. If customers follow in their car they may never follow you back to the office. Maintain a clean and comfortable car.

Plan Your Route. Choose your approach to project the best impression. Why go through an industrial area or an area of less desirable homes, when you can take the "scenic" route?

Point Out Community Facilities. Go by schools, churches, libraries, shopping centers, etc. Sell the neighborhood and community.

Point Out Comparable Homes. Also point out homes which are priced higher than the one being shown, and recently sold homes and their selling prices.

Don't Tell All About the Property. Let customers discover its features on their own. However, if the property has an obvious negative feature, it is best to prepare customers for it.

Presenting the Property

Property Features. Use your knowledge of the property to focus the buyers' observation. Set the stage by pointing out the outstanding features before you enter the house. Point out specific qualities and amenities of particular rooms, rather than saying, "This is a bathroom" or "This is the kitchen." Discuss the finer points of the house intelligently. Be sure to point out any unusual features.

Put Buyers at Ease. Reinforce and build upon positive reactions, and give them confidence in their skill as buyers. Encourage the buyers to reinspect the house alone while you are still on the premises; allow them to discuss the house privately. Suggest that the customers take notes on the homes as they see them, after they return to the car, to aid their memory.

Observing and Questioning. Be alert for any "negative motivators." Pay particular attention to things which excite the potential buyers. Encourage them to start "living in the home." For example, "Which bedroom will the boys have? Where will you put the TV?"

Action. Determine your next step based upon customers' reaction. If the customers react favorably to a particular house, suggest that they take a second look. You should provide the transportation, but allow them to make this inspection on their own to confirm their reactions and to strengthen their impressions. Proceed to obtain the offer and close. If you sense the house is not right for your customers, cut the inspection short and move on to other properties.

DISCLOSURE UPON TRANSFER OF RESIDENTIAL PROPERTY

Selling concentrates on positive features of the property, but licensees have ever-increasing responsibilities to disclose all aspects of financing and property conditions. To all practical purposes, the principle of "caveat emptor" no longer applies to real estate sales.

Applicability Under Civil Code §§1102 et seq., operative January 1, 1987, the transferor of any real property improved with one to four dwelling units must deliver to the buyer a detailed disclosure statement about the property. (Exhibit 16)

Time of Delivery. Disclosure must be delivered as soon as practicable before transfer of title or prior to the execution of any real property sales contract, lease/option, or ground lease coupled with improvements.

Statement of Compliance. The transferor must indicate on the face of the deposit receipt, or on a separate document, that the disclosure requirement has been complied with.

Right of Rescission. If the disclosure is delivered after execution of the purchase offer, the transferee may cancel in writing up to 3 days after personal delivery, or 5 days after mailing of the disclosure statement.

Broker's Duty to Inspect Under Civil Code §2079, it is the duty of a real estate broker, to a prospective purchaser of residential real property comprising one to four dwelling units, to inspect the property and disclose relevant findings.

Extent of Inspection. The law requires the broker to conduct a reasonably competent and diligent visual inspection of the property offered.

Material Facts. The broker must disclose all facts materially affecting the value or desirability that such an investigation would reveal.

Exclusions. This inspection does not include areas that are reasonably and normally inaccessible, and if common areas are included, does not include an inspection of more than the unit.

Home Inspection Services. As disclosure requirements expand, so does the possibility of exposure to liability for undisclosed defects in a property, even if unknown to the seller or licensee. This has resulted in a new and growing specialization of inspection services.

THE REAL ESTATE SALES PORTFOLIO

Your professional attitude and appearance will be enhanced if you develop a well organized package of current pertinent information on each property to use for your presentation. Depending on the property and the customers, typical contents may include:

- ☐ Complete listing information
- ☐ Deposit receipt form
- ☐ Competitive market analysis
- ☐ Finance data (existing loans, available loans, seller-backed loans taxes and assessments)
- ☐ Estimated buyer's cost statement (Exhibit 17), spelling out down-payments and financing options
- ☐ City and neighborhood data indicating schools, shopping areas, churches, demographics
- ☐ Pictures of the property and the neighborhood.

REAL ESTATE TRANSFER DISCLOSURE STATEMENT
(CALIFORNIA CIVIL CODE 1102, ET SEQ.)
CALIFORNIA ASSOCIATION OF REALTORS® (CAR) STANDARD FORM

THIS DISCLOSURE STATEMENT CONCERNS THE REAL PROPERTY SITUATED IN THE CITY OF_____
_____, COUNTY OF_____, STATE OF CALIFORNIA,
DESCRIBED AS_____
THIS STATEMENT IS A DISCLOSURE OF THE CONDITION OF THE ABOVE DESCRIBED PROPERTY IN COMPLIANCE
WITH SECTION 1102 OF THE CIVIL CODE AS OF _____, 19_____. IT IS NOT A WARRANTY
OF ANY KIND BY THE SELLER(S) OR ANY AGENT(S) REPRESENTING ANY PRINCIPAL(S) IN THIS TRANSACTION,
AND IS NOT A SUBSTITUTE FOR ANY INSPECTIONS OR WARRANTIES THE PRINCIPAL(S) MAY WISH TO OBTAIN.

I
COORDINATION WITH OTHER DISCLOSURE FORMS
This Real Estate Transfer Disclosure Statement is made pursuant to Section 1102 of the Civil Code. Other statutes require disclosures, depending upon the details of the particular real estate transaction (for example: special study zone and purchase-money liens on residential property).

Substituted Disclosures: The following disclosures have or will be in connection with this real estate transfer, and are intended to satisfy the disclosure obligations on this form, where the subject matter is the same:_____
_____
_____
_____
(LIST ALL SUBSTITUTED DISCLOSURE FORMS TO BE USED IN CONNECTION WITH THIS TRANSACTION)

II
SELLER'S INFORMATION
The Seller discloses the following information with the knowledge that even though this is not a warranty, prospective Buyers may rely on this information in deciding whether and on what terms to purchase the subject property. Seller hereby authorizes any agent(s) representing any principal(s) in this transaction to provide a copy of this statement to any person or entity in connection with any actual or anticipated sale of the property.

THE FOLLOWING ARE REPRESENTATIONS MADE BY THE SELLER(S) AND ARE NOT THE REPRESENTATIONS OF THE AGENT(S), IF ANY. THIS INFORMATION IS A DISCLOSURE AND IS NOT INTENDED TO BE PART OF ANY CONTRACT BETWEEN THE BUYER AND SELLER.

Seller ☐ is ☐ is not occupying the property.

A. The subject property has the items checked below (read across):

☐ Range   ☐ Oven   ☐ Microwave
☐ Dishwasher   ☐ Trash Compactor   ☐ Garbage Disposal
☐ Washer/Dryer Hookups   ☐ Window Screens   ☐ Rain Gutters
☐ Burglar Alarms   ☐ Smoke Detector(s)   ☐ Fire Alarm
☐ T.V. Antenna   ☐ Satellite Dish   ☐ Intercom
☐ Central Heating   ☐ Central Air Conditioning   ☐ Evaporator Cooler(s)
☐ Wall/Window Air Conditioning ☐ Sprinklers   ☐ Public Sewer System
☐ Septic Tank   ☐ Sump Pump   ☐ Water Softener
☐ Patio/Decking   ☐ Built-in Barbeque   ☐ Gazebo
☐ Sauna   ☐ Pool   ☐ Spa ☐ Hot Tub
☐ Security Gate(s)   ☐ Garage Door Opener(s)   ☐ Number of Remote Controls_____
Garage: ☐ Attached   ☐ Not Attached   ☐ Carport
Pool/Spa Heater: ☐ Gas   ☐ Solar   ☐ Electric
Water Heater: ☐ Gas   ☐ Solar   ☐ Electric
Water Supply: ☐ City   ☐ Well   ☐ Private Utility   ☐ Other_____
Gas Supply: ☐ Utility   ☐ Bottled
Exhaust Fan(s) in_____ 220 Volt Wiring in_____
Fireplace(s) in_____ ☐ Gas Starter
☐ Roof(s): Type:_____
☐ Other:_____ Age:_____ (approx.)

Are there, to the best of your (Seller's) knowledge, any of the above that are not in operating condition? ☐ Yes ☐ No If yes, then
describe. (Attach additional sheets if necessary.):_____
_____
_____

B. Are you (Seller) aware of any significant defects/malfunctions in any of the following? ☐ Yes ☐ No If yes, check appropriate space(s) below.
☐ Interior Walls ☐ Ceilings ☐ Floors ☐ Exterior Walls ☐ Insulation ☐ Roof(s) ☐ Windows ☐ Doors ☐ Foundation ☐ Slab(s)
☐ Driveways ☐ Sidewalks ☐ Walls/Fences ☐ Electrical Systems ☐ Plumbing/Sewers/Septics ☐ Other Structural Components
(Describe:_____
_____

If any of the above is checked, explain. (Attach additional sheets if necessary):_____)
_____
_____

Buyer and Seller acknowledge receipt of copy of this page, which constitutes Page 1 of 2 Pages.
Buyer's Initials (_____) (_____)   Seller's Initials (_____) (_____)

Copyright© 1989, CALIFORNIA ASSOCIATION OF REALTORS®
525 South Virgil Avenue, Los Angeles, California 90020
IN COMPLIANCE WITH CIVIL CODE SECTION 1102.6 / EFFECTIVE JANUARY 1, 1990.

┌─── OFFICE USE ONLY ───
│ Reviewed by Broker or Designee _____
│ Date _____

REAL ESTATE TRANSFER DISCLOSURE STATEMENT (TDS-14 PAGE 1 OF 2)

Exhibit 16.1

C. **Are you (Seller) aware of any of the following:**

1. Substances, materials, or products which may be an environmental hazard such as, but not limited to, asbestos, formaldehyde, radon gas, lead-based paint, fuel or chemical storage tanks, and contaminated soil or water on the subject property. .... ☐ Yes ☐ No
2. Features of the property shared in common with adjoining landowners, such as walls, fences, and driveways, whose use or responsibility for maintenance may have an effect on the subject property. .... ☐ Yes ☐ No
3. Any encroachments, easements or similar matters that may affect your interest in the subject property. .... ☐ Yes ☐ No
4. Room additions, structural modifications, or other alterations or repairs made without necessary permits. .... ☐ Yes ☐ No
5. Room additions, structural modifications, or other alterations or repairs not in compliance with building codes. ... ☐ Yes ☐ No
6. Landfill (compacted or otherwise) on the property or any portion thereof. .... ☐ Yes ☐ No
7. Any settling from any cause, or slippage, sliding, or other soil problems. .... ☐ Yes ☐ No
8. Flooding, drainage or grading problems. .... ☐ Yes ☐ No
9. Major damage to the property or any of the structures from fire, earthquake, floods, or landslides. .... ☐ Yes ☐ No
10. Any zoning violations, nonconforming uses, violations of "setback" requirements. .... ☐ Yes ☐ No
11. Neighborhood noise problems or other nuisances. .... ☐ Yes ☐ No
12. CC&R's or other deed restrictions or obligations. .... ☐ Yes ☐ No
13. Homeowners' Association which has any authority over the subject property. .... ☐ Yes ☐ No
14. Any "common area" (facilities such as pools, tennis courts, walkways, or other areas co-owned in undivided interest with others). .... ☐ Yes ☐ No
15. Any notices of abatement or citations against the property. .... ☐ Yes ☐ No
16. Any lawsuits against the seller threatening to or affecting this real property. .... ☐ **Yes** ☐ No

If the answer to any of these is yes, explain. (Attach additional sheets if necessary.): _____
_____
_____

Seller certifies that the information herein is true and correct to the best of the Seller's knowledge as of the date signed by the Seller.

Seller_____ Date_____

Seller_____ Date_____

III
AGENT'S INSPECTION DISCLOSURE
(To be completed only if the seller is represented by an agent in this transaction.)
THE UNDERSIGNED, BASED ON THE ABOVE INQUIRY OF THE SELLER(S) AS TO THE CONDITION OF THE PROPERTY AND BASED ON A REASONABLY COMPETENT AND DILIGENT VISUAL INSPECTION OF THE ACCESSIBLE AREAS OF THE PROPERTY IN CONJUNCTION WITH THAT INQUIRY, STATES THE FOLLOWING:

_____
_____

Agent (Broker
Representing Seller)_____ By_____ Date_____
        (PLEASE PRINT)   (ASSOCIATE LICENSEE OR BROKER-SIGNATURE)

IV
AGENT'S INSPECTION DISCLOSURE
(To be completed only if the agent who has obtained the offer is other than the agent above.)
THE UNDERSIGNED, BASED ON A REASONABLY COMPETENT AND DILIGENT VISUAL INSPECTION OF THE ACCESSIBLE AREAS OF THE PROPERTY, STATES THE FOLLOWING:

_____
_____

Agent (Broker
obtaining the Offer)_____ By_____ Date_____
        (PLEASE PRINT)   (ASSOCIATE LICENSEE OR BROKER-SIGNATURE)

V
BUYER(S) AND SELLER(S) MAY WISH TO OBTAIN PROFESSIONAL ADVICE AND/OR INSPECTIONS OF THE PROPERTY AND TO PROVIDE FOR APPROPRIATE PROVISIONS IN A CONTRACT BETWEEN BUYER AND SELLER(S) WITH RESPECT TO ANY ADVICE/INSPECTIONS/DEFECTS.

I/WE ACKNOWLEDGE RECEIPT OF A COPY OF THIS STATEMENT.

Seller_____ Date_____ Buyer_____ Date_____

Seller_____ Date_____ Buyer_____ Date_____

Agent (Broker
Representing Seller)_____ By_____ Date_____
        (PLEASE PRINT)   (ASSOCIATE LICENSEE OR BROKER-SIGNATURE)

Agent (Broker
obtaining the Offer)_____ By_____ Date_____
        (PLEASE PRINT)   (ASSOCIATE LICENSEE OR BROKER-SIGNATURE)

A REAL ESTATE BROKER IS QUALIFIED TO ADVISE ON REAL ESTATE. IF YOU DESIRE LEGAL ADVICE, CONSULT YOUR ATTORNEY.

This form is available for use by the entire real estate industry. The use of this form is not intended to identify the user as a REALTOR. REALTOR is a registered collective membership mark which may be used only by real estate licensees who are members of the NATIONAL ASSOCIATION OF REALTORS and who subscribe to its Code of Ethics.

Copyright© 1989, CALIFORNIA ASSOCIATION OF REALTORS®
525 South Virgil Avenue, Los Angeles, California 90020

Page 2 of _____ Pages.

OFFICE USE ONLY

Reviewed by Broker or Designee _____

Date _____

EQUAL HOUSING OPPORTUNITY

REAL ESTATE TRANSFER DISCLOSURE STATEMENT (TDS-14 PAGE 2 OF 2)

Exhibit 16.2

DISCLOSURE

Sellers of real property should be aware of their disclosure obligations under the California Court Cases, Statutes and Real Estate Law commentaries excerpted or paraphrased below:

SELLER DISCLOSURE OBLIGATIONS
UNDER CIVIL CODE SECTION 1102, ET SEQ.

Effective January 1, 1987, a transferor (seller) of real property including a residential stock cooperative containing 1 to 4 residential units (unless exempted under §1102.1) must supply a transferee (buyer) with a completed Real Estate Transfer Disclosure Statement in the form prescribed in Civid Code §1102.6.

EXEMPTED TRANSFERS: Summary of exempted transfers (Civil Code Section 1102.1) where Real Estate Transfer Disclosure Statement is **not** required:

a. Transfers requiring "a public report pursuant to §11018.1 of the Business & Professions Code" and transfers pursuant to §11010.4 of Business & Professions Code where no public report is required;
b. "Transfers pursuant to court order" (such as probate sales, sales by a bankruptcy trustee, etc.);
c. Transfers by foreclosure (including a deed in lieu of foreclosure and a transfer by a beneficiary who has acquired the property by foreclosure or deed in lieu of foreclosure);
d. "Transfers by a fiduciary in the course of the administration of a decedent's estate, guardianship, conservatorship, or trust."
e. "Transfers from one co-owner to one or more co-owners."
f. "Transfer made to a spouse" or to a direct blood relative;
g. "Transfers between spouses" in connection with a dissolution of marriage or similar proceeding;
h. Transfers by the State Controller pursuant to the Unclaimed Property Law;
i. Transfers as a result of failure to pay property taxes;
j. "Transfers or exchanges to or from any government entity."

TIMING OF DISCLOSURE AND RIGHT TO CANCEL (CIVIL CODE SECTION 1102.2):

a. In the case of a sale, the disclosures to the buyer shall be made "as soon as practicable before transfer of title."
b. "In the case of transfer by a Real Property Sales Contract, (Installment Land Sales Contract). . .or, by a lease together with an option to purchase, or ground lease coupled with improvements, as soon as practical before. . .the making or acceptance of an offer."

"If any disclosure, or any material amendment of any disclosure, required to be made by this article, is delivered after the execution of an offer to purchase, the transferee shall have three days after delivery in person or five days after delivery by deposit in the mail, to terminate his or her offer by delivery of a written notice of termination to the transferor or the transferor's agent."

SUBSTITUTED DISCLOSURES: (CIVIL CODE SECTION 1102.4)

a. Neither the transferor nor any listing or selling agent shall be liable for any error, inaccuracy, or omission of any information delivered pursuant to this article if the error, inaccuracy, or omission was not within the personal knowledge of the transferor or that listing or selling agent, was based on information timely provided by public agencies or by other persons providing information as specified in subdivision (c) that is required to be disclosed pursuant to this article, and ordinary care was exercised in obtaining and transmitting it.
b. The delivery of any information required to be disclosed by this article to a prospective transferee by a public agency or other person providing information required to be disclosed pursuant to this article shall be deemed to comply with the requirements of this article and shall relieve the transferor or any listing or selling agent of any further duty under this article with respect to that item of information.
c. The delivery of a report or opinion prepared by a licensed engineer, land surveyor, geologist, structural pest control operator, contractor, or other expert, dealing with matters within the scope of the professional's license or expertise, shall be sufficient compliance for application of the exemption provided by subdivision (a) if information is provided to the prospective transferee pursuant to a request therefor, whether written or oral. In responding to such a request, an expert may indicate, in writing, an understanding that the information provided will be used in fulfilling the requirements of Section 1102.6 and, if so, shall indicate the required disclosures, or parts thereof, to which the information being furnished is applicable. Where such a statement is furnished, the expert shall not be responsible for any items of information, or parts thereof, other than those expressly set forth in the statement.

OTHER DISCLOSURE REQUIREMENTS

I ". . .Where the seller knows of facts materially affecting the value or desirability of the property which are known or accessible only to him and also knows that such facts are not known to, or within the reach of the diligent attention and observation of the buyer, the seller is under a duty to disclose them to the buyer." Lingsch v. Savage, 213 Cal. App. 2d 729.
II "Concealment may constitute actionable fraud where seller knows of facts which materially affect desirability of property and seller knows such facts are unknown to buyer." Koch v. Williams, 193 Cal. App. 2d 537, 541.
III "Deceit may arise from mere nondisclosure." Massei v. Lettunich, 248 Cal. App. 2d 68, 72.
IV Failure of the seller to fulfill such duty of disclosure constitutes actual fraud. [Civil Code Section 1572(3)]
V **California Civil Code: §1709. Deceit—Damages** One who willfully deceives another with intent to induce him to alter his position to his injury or risk is liable for any damages which he thereby suffers. **§1710. Elements of Actionable Fraud** A deceit, within the meaning of the last section, is either: (1) The suggestion, as a fact, of that which is not true, by one who does not believe it to be true; (2) The assertion, as a fact, of that which is not true, by one who has no reasonable ground for believing it to be true; (3) The suppression of a fact, by one who is bound to disclose it, or who give information of other facts which are likely to mislead for want of communication of that fact; or (4) A promise, made without any intention of performing it.
VI "The maker of a fraudulent misrepresentation (seller) is subject to liability. . .to another (buyer) who acts in justifiable reliance upon it if the misrepresentation, although not made directly to the other (buyer), and that it will influence his conduct . . ." [parenthetical material added]. Restatement (2d) or Torts §533.
VII "The Seller may have an affirmative duty to disclose certain significant facts regarding the condition of his property. It is not enough for the seller to say nothing because he is not asked." California Real Estate Sales Transactions, §12.2, p.463 (Cal. C.E.B. 1967).
VIII "A buyer who has been defrauded by the seller has the choice of either: (A) Using the seller's fraud as a defense when and if the buyer refuses to follow through with his obligation under the contract; or (B) Using the seller's fraud as a basis for an action for affirmative relief in the form of an action for damages or for recission of the contract."
IX Exculpatory Clauses: "It is better for the seller to disclose the specific condition than to attempt to exculpate himself against its nondisclosure. In general, the exculpatory (e.g., "as is") clause provides little, if any, protection." California Real Estate Sales Transactions p.483 (Cal. C.E.B. 1967).

[The Above is a general statement of the seller disclosure obligations. Other disclosure may be required].

REPRINTED BY PERMISSION CALIFORNIA ASSOCIATION OF REALTORS® . ENDORSEMENT NOT IMPLIED

Exhibit 16.3

ESTIMATED BUYER'S COST

CALIFORNIA ASSOCIATION OF REALTORS® STANDARD FORM

BUYER _____

PROPERTY ADDRESS _____

BROKER _____

This estimate is based on costs associated with _____ financing.

Loan Amount $ _____ Interest _____ % Term _____ years.

ESTIMATED BUYER'S EXPENSES

Loan Origination Fee	$ _____	
Appraisal Fee	_____	
Credit Report	_____	
Tax Impounds	_____	
Insurance Impounds	_____	
Lenders Prepaid Interest	_____	
Other Lender Fees	_____	
Tax Service	_____	
Title Insurance Policy	_____	
ALTA Policy	_____	
Escrow Fee	_____	
Recording Fees	_____	
Notary Fees	_____	
Preparation of Documents	_____	
Fire Insurance	_____	
Structural Pest Control Inspection	_____	
Structural Pest Control Repairs	_____	
Home Warranty	_____	
Prorate Taxes	_____	
Other	_____	
TOTAL ESTIMATED EXPENSES	$ _____	

Estimated Expenses _____
Less Buyer's Credits _____
Net Estimated Expenses _____
Down Payment _____
TOTAL CASH REQUIRED $ _____

Projected Closing Date _____
Proposed Purchase Price $ _____

ESTIMATED CREDITS:

Prorated Taxes	_____
Rents	_____
Security Deposits	_____
Other	_____
Other	_____
TOTAL CREDITS	$ _____

PROJECTED MONTHLY PAYMENTS:

Principal & Interest	_____
Taxes	_____
Insurance	_____
Other	_____
Other	_____
TOTAL	$ _____

This estimate based upon the above proposed purchase price, type of financing, and projected closing date has been prepared to assist Buyer in computing his costs. Lenders and escrow companies will vary in their charges; therefore, these figures cannot be guaranteed by the broker or his representatives. All estimates and information are from sources believed reliable but not guaranteed.

I have read the above figures and acknowledge receipt of a copy of this form.

Buyer _____ Date _____ Presented by: _____

_____ Date _____ Address: _____

Phone No. _____

Exhibit 17

Chapter 9 Quiz

1. Because people tend to avoid stressful situations as much as possible:

   (A) They do not normally like to make decisions
   (B) The licensee must supply information and modify their behavior
   (C) They need assistance to make a decision to buy a home
   (D) A, B, and C are all correct

2. "How do you visualize your ideal home?" is an example of a(n):

   (A) Open question
   (B) Closed question
   (C) Positive support
   (D) None of the above

3. Some objections are _____ and can be eliminated, while some are _____ and can result in a change of goals.

   (A) Real, imaginary
   (B) Negative, positive
   (C) Imaginary, real
   (D) Positive, negative

4. In order to be successful, you should:

   (A) Have a sincere interest in your customer's needs
   (B) Generate enthusiasm and stimulate curiosity
   (C) Be an interested listener with initiative
   (D) All of the above

5. One major reason for driving the customer to the property in your car is:

   (A) It saves gas
   (B) They may not follow you back to your office or other designated meeting place
   (C) It lets them discover the property features on their own
   (D) You may deduct travel expense for IRS purposes

6. The ability to ask good questions is important primarily because it:

   (A) Demonstrates your knowledgeability
   (B) Determines which sales process path you should follow
   (C) Demonstrates you are an interested listener
   (D) Tests the customer's knowledge

7. The sales process is:

   (A) Getting a prospect to make a positive decision only
   (B) Getting a prospect to make a negative decision only
   (C) Making a decision for someone to avoid a stressful situation
   (D) Assisting someone to make a decision about a product or service that will satisfy a need or desire

8. Presale planning involves all of the following *except*:

   (A) Time management
   (B) Knowing the customer
   (C) Compiling activity reports
   (D) Developing good work habits

9. In order to be sure the problem is really solved, request your customer to make a verbal commitment when:

   (A) You have shown the customer all the way through the property
   (B) The customer has not expressed any objection
   (C) The customer is ready to make a decision
   (D) You know the customer

10. Which of the following is *not* a productive response to a real objection:

   (A) Offer agreement
   (B) Rephrase the objection as a question
   (C) Compare objection to the positive features and total other benefits
   (D) Review goals to continue or change

Chapter 10
Closing the Sale and Escrow Procedure

CUSTOMER BECOMES BUYER

When the "customer" is emotionally ready and reaches the critical moment to make a positive decision, his or her status changes to "buyer." If the buyer has no objections, proceed directly to the writing of the offer. However, if the interested customer needs further assistance or more time to decide, utilize closing techniques.

Obtaining the Offer Start "closing" from the very first contact with your customer; it is much better to close too early and too often than too late or not at all.

Trial Closes. Do not be afraid to ask customers to buy. Propose a closing after each showing. Consider only one property at a time and always have a deposit receipt form with you. Write vital information on the deposit receipt, not on a scratch pad.

Price and Sale Conditions. These must be presented attractively but realistically. Do not offer what you cannot perform, or you will lose the sale. If you are the seller's agent, you are obligated to get the highest price possible for the seller. Do not suggest that buyers cut the price; assuming sellers always come down a little may backfire. Unless buyers specify otherwise, assume that they will buy exactly as listed.

Persistence. Never lose sight of the goal you and your customer are pursuing. Do not get sidetracked while in the process of closing. Avoid interruptions. Have your phone calls put on hold during the closing session. Do not be discouraged if your first attempt to close fails. Resell the property, its fine location, its special features, the excellent financing. A top salesperson never takes "no" for an answer. Keep reselling and closing until you are convinced you are wasting your time.

The "No Objection" Buyer   If buyers are prepared to proceed without further persuasion, move confidently to the next step.

Prepare the Deposit Receipt. Engage in small talk while filling out the deposit receipt. Direct conversation to the exciting and positive qualities of the house. Avoid long periods of silence. Review the completed deposit receipt by reading it aloud and explaining the real estate terminology to your buyer(s). Get approval of each individual in a couple or group. Be sure they get their deposit receipt copy.

Confirm and Conclude. Offer to answer any immediate questions to avoid the possibility of "buyers' remorse." Finish the interview by congratulating them for deciding to buy a new home. Emphasize that time is of the essence. Start at once to get the offer accepted.

CLOSING TECHNIQUES

A variety of techniques allow the customers to be involved in the selling process as they make their final decision. When used properly by the skillful licensee, there is a technique which can lead almost every customer to a favorable decision.

Assumption Close   To assume simply means to take for granted that the buyer is going to buy.

Your Attitude. Be positive, absolute, and confident in everything you do and say. Don't ask if the buyer will buy; assume he or she will. However, be sure that the customer can qualify for the home.

Advantages. This close can be used in every selling situation. No offense is caused by assuming the buyer will buy. It utilizes gentle persuasion. No pressure is applied; the buyer is gently led to a decision.

The "Yes" Response   This technique promotes positive thinking. It involves asking plenty of questions that will bring about "yes" responses.

Objective. You want to elicit as many "yes" responses from the customer as possible. When it comes to the final decision, he or she will then be in a positive frame of mind and less apt to say "no."

Technique. Make positive selling statements ending in "isn't it," "don't you agree," "didn't you," "isn't that so," and similar endings.

- ☐ *"This is a lovely dining room, isn't it?"*
- ☐ *"Your children would love this spacious yard, wouldn't they?"*
- ☐ *"You wanted a separate family room like this, didn't you?"*

Reinforcement. Follow up each "yes" response with positive reinforcement.

Advantages. This technique can be used in every selling situation. It may be used often, as people generally like to agree, and allows the customer to be actively involved.

The "Order Blank" Close The licensee writes up the deposit receipt without direct confirmation from the customer that he or she will buy.

Questions. Begin by asking questions, the answers to which will be filled in on the deposit receipt.

- ☐ *"What is your full name, sir?"*
- ☐ *"What is your address?"*
- ☐ *"You know the drapes stay with the house, Mrs. George?"*

If there are no objections, assume you have sold the house.

The Alternate Choice Give the customer a choice between two items. This technique can be used for all closing situations.

Technique. Provide a series of choices between alternatives which are both desirable.

- ☐ *"I can meet you at 3 p.m. today, or would 6 p.m. be better?"*
- ☐ *"Would you like a home with 3 or 4 bedrooms?"*
- ☐ *"Would you prefer FHA insured financing with lower downpayment and higher monthly payments, or conventional financing with higher downpayment and lower monthly payments?"*

Avoid "No's." Do not ask the customer questions which can be answered negatively.

Reinforcement. Each time the customer gives a positive response to your alternate choice, reinforce his or her decision with a positive statement.

Steps to Decision. Each positive choice the customer makes brings him or her a step closer to making the final decision.

The "Balance Sheet" Close The "balance sheet" involves the actual writing, on paper, of the pros and cons of buying the property.

When to Use. This technique is often successful when customers have difficulty making up their minds.

Advantages. This reinforces positive reasons but allows customers to evaluate the negatives on their own.

Decision Point. When the "pros" outweigh the "cons," the customer will most likely buy.

The Testimonial Close This close emphasizes a particular feature of the property which has testimonial proof. For example, some customers can be convinced to buy if you impress them with famous personalities who live in the neighborhood, or with a feature which flatters them as smart consumers.

"Your Homeowner's Warranty, which will be in effect for a year on this house when you buy, is the same as your neighbor's. He told me his policy paid for replacing his hot water heater, garbage disposal, and dishwasher during his first seven months of ownership. His only cost each time was the $25.00 deductible. Don't you think this seller-paid policy makes this home a great buy?"

Fear of Loss This technique shows the customers that they will suffer a loss if they do not buy. In order to be powerful the loss must be based on facts, and relevant to the customers' personal and immediate situation.

"This home is the last one available in this particular subdivision. All the others have been sold. When the new tract is completed, this same style home will sell for $5,000 more. Wouldn't you rather buy now and save?"

Inducement The sale can sometimes be secured by promising a conditional request. But be sure the conditional request is feasible and possible.

"If the seller agrees to replace the drapes, what color would you like?" "If we close this transaction in 30 days, you can be moved in by the end of August. Won't it be nice to be settled by the time your children start school?"

This technique can often be incorporated when responding to a customer's question.

"Is the chandelier included in the sales price?" "Do you want the chandelier included in the sales price?"

Narrative Close This closing technique employs a third party to establish points. Salespersons often refer to former customers' experiences to promote credibility. Customers are apt to listen to and consider what you say if you produce verification of facts.

"I can understand your hesitation to make an offer. A former customer was very interested in that contemporary redwood home on the lake, but decided to postpone making an offer until his family could see it the following weekend. Well, the next day the home was sold and as it turned out, the family was very disappointed. Sometimes, it is best to trust your judgment and make the offer while you can, because it may not be there the next day."

Close on a "Buying Signal" A buying signal may be the customers' positive response to a minor matter, e.g., liking the carpet color, or a favorable tone, gesture, or facial expression. Frequently, these are signals that the customer has "bought the property." Be alert to these signals and proceed to close the sale.

Ask for the Deposit When you have studied your customers' qualifications, needs, wants, and motivations, and feel all or most are satisfied, ask for the deposit. Prospective buyers rarely volunteer to make an offer; they need to be encouraged to do so.

"We have been looking at several homes for the past six weeks and this one appears to be the best suited to your needs. How about making an offer on it today?"

WRITING THE OFFER

Writing an offer is a key step in negotiating a mutually acceptable agreement between buyer(s) and sellers(s). There may be one or more counter-offers before final agreement is reached.

The Deposit Receipt The offer is normally submitted to the seller in the form of a deposit receipt. This form has multiple purposes.

Receipt. This document first serves as a receipt for earnest money received as a deposit toward the purchase of real property.

Contract. When properly executed and signed by the buyers and sellers with complete copies delivered to both parties, the offer becomes a legal and binding contract. Any error, regardless of size, may completely invalidate the sale and your commission.

Consumer Information. The contract also contains information about property condition, financing, tax reporting, etc.

Filling in the Form   Although some offices prefer to print their own deposit receipt form with their company name and logo, a form widely used is the CAR Real Estate Purchase Contract and Receipt for Deposit (Exhibits 18 and 19). It is useful to write practice transactions under an experienced broker's supervision until a satisfactory proficiency has been reached.

Offer in Writing. Putting details of the transaction in writing minimizes the chance of dispute or challenge during negotiation and escrow and after closing.

Accurate Information. Use precise, clear language to discuss necessary contract provisions, and obtain exact and complete information.

☐ Date of agreement

☐ Names and addresses of the parties to the contract

☐ Description of the subject property

☐ Consideration (downpayment, total purchase price, method and time, new mortgage or trust deed, and existing mortgage or trust deed)

☐ Other provisions requested by either party, including structural pest control inspection, personal property included in sales price, contingencies, title vesting, repairs, and liquidated damages

☐ Date and place of closing.

Legal Advice. Licensees are discouraged from changing standard forms without legal advice; a standard form should not be used in complex transactions requiring riders or additions.

Interpretation. The law governs the priority status of various documents and parts of documents in case of conflict.

☐ The written or typed word supersedes the printed word on the form.

☐ In the event of inconsistencies between the general and specific provisions, the specific normally takes precedence over the general.

☐ When there is a discrepancy between the deposit receipt and the escrow instructions, the escrow instructions supersede the deposit receipt.

Fill In All Blanks. Or write "not applicable," as needed.

Copies. Be sure to give copies of the contract each time either party signs them.

Professional Environment. Real estate contracts should be completed when possible in a professional environment, such as your company's office, with a minimum of distraction and interruption.

Standard Forms   Two standard forms in common use, made available by California Association of Realtors®, are included here as Exhibits 18 and 19.

Long Form. Exhibit 18, the long form with financing clauses, includes detailed optional sections relating to the various disclosures and consumer protections likely to be involved, e.g., pest control, flood and geological hazards, energy and smoke detector retrofits, home protection plans.

Short Form. Exhibit 19, "for use in simple transactions," is less structured in regard to both financing and disclosure.

DISPOSITION OF THE DEPOSIT

The deposit of earnest money can be in the form of cash, check, promissory note, or other item of value. The expectation is that it will apply to the purchase price. However, provision must be made for other possibilities.

Disposition
When a licensee accepts an earnest money deposit with an offer on property, the deposit receipt that is written should contain complete instructions as to the disposition of the funds in the following events:

Offer Not Accepted. If the offer is not accepted, the offeror must get the deposit money back.

Buyer Fails to Complete Purchase. If the buyer defaults, does the seller get to keep the earnest money deposit?

Nonperformance By Seller. If the seller defaults, does the broker get paid a commission?

Handling of Buyer's Funds
The California Department of Real Estate and the Real Estate Law (B&P Code §10145) require licensees who receive a buyer's funds to deliver them to one of the following not later than the next business day, unless the licensee has written instructions to the contrary and that fact is disclosed to the principal.

- ☐ The seller
- ☐ The broker's trust fund account
- ☐ A neutral escrow depository.

Violations of the Real Estate Law
Improper handling of deposits can subject a licensee to disciplinary action by the Department of Real Estate and other authorities.

Commingling. The broker has committed an illegal act when a licensee mixes a principal's funds with his or her personal funds, such as placing the customer's money in the licensee's personal checking account. (Section 10176(e))

Conversion. An even worse offense is the illegal act of *conversion*, which involves the unlawful appropriation and use of a principal's funds.

Other Violations. Sections 10176 and 10177 of the Real Estate Law identify additional types of violations related to the deposit receipt.

PRESENTING THE OFFER

The licensee must next present the buyer's offer to the seller (or seller's agent), for the acceptance which will turn the deposit receipt into a *purchase contract*.

Successful Presentation

Presentation of the offer to the seller is a skill just as closing with the buyer is. It depends on:

Cooperation. In a cooperating sale, when you are the selling agent and not the listing agent, there must be cooperation between the two agents. The listing agent is the selling agent's best source of information regarding the seller's motivations. Exception: With an in-house sale, the presentation process becomes much simpler.

Speed. Time is of the essence. A selling agent may deliver an offer to the listing agent, or the two agents may go together to present the offer. The listing agent may make the appointment with the seller to present the offer. At times the listing agent may authorize the selling agent to present the offer to the seller.

Protocol. Following the local Board of Realtors'® regulations and customs is essential.

Strategy. Whether the listing agent makes the presentation alone or with the selling agent, knowing the ground rules will ensure a smooth, professional delivery.

Making the Appointment

Whenever possible, the offers should be presented in person. Rely on the telephone presentation only in special circumstances, such as with an out-of-town seller. Arrange the appointment for a time when all sellers can be present.

Don't Disclose Offer in Advance. Do not tell the seller the offering price over the telephone. Have someone in the office who knows nothing of the offer make the appointment. This will prevent accidental disclosure of the offering price or terms.

Out-of-Town Seller. An out-of-town seller should be requested to authorize you (by fax or telegram) to act in his or her behalf to accept, counter, or reject an offer. Mail the contract immediately for the seller's signature.

Preparing for the Presentation

Knowledge of the offer, the property, and the seller's position will provide a solid basis for an effective presentation.

Know the Offer. Essential details include price and terms, new mortgages and existing mortgages, date of possession and closing, and contingencies.

Seller's Proceeds. Prepare an estimated seller's proceeds sheet (Exhibit 7, Chapter 4), showing what this offer means in dollars and cents.

Price. Prepare a competitive market analysis. (Exhibit 11, Chapter 5). Is the offering price consistent with the market? How did the seller react to the competitive market analysis previously?

Seller's Attitude. Knowing the seller's motivations will help you present the offer in terms he or she can best understand and evaluate.

Property History. The offer must be considered in light of the property's activity record, including prior offers, price adjustment, and length of time on the market.

Persuasion. Be prepared to sell the offer if accepting the offer is in the seller's best interest.

Answering Objections. Be prepared. Devise a logical answer for all possible seller objections, keeping in mind the seller's best interest.

The Presentation Like showing and closing, this is a process which the licensee can control and direct.

Setting. Find a quiet, well-lighted room in which to make the presentation. Sit across from the seller(s) to observe body language and expressions.

Psychological Preparation. Before presenting the offer find out which one of the sellers makes the decisions. A leading question like, "What do you intend to do when the house is sold?" will usually be answered by the dominant seller. Determine the sellers' motives for selling. Give the sellers a brief descriptive introduction to the buyers.

Present the Written Offer. Wait until the sellers have finished reading the entire offer before discussing its contents.

Stay in Control. Remain confident, sincere, and objective throughout the presentation, and maintain open communication at all times.

Be Positive. State your ideas in positive terms. Discuss favorable aspects of the offer before discussing unfavorable aspects or the transaction as a whole.

Sell the Offer. Use your prepared competitive market analysis (CMA) and estimated seller's proceeds (ESP) documents to sell the offer.

☐ Explain each entry thoroughly.

☐ Emphasize that the CMA is based on facts established by the market.

Use Closing Techniques. Balance advantages of accepting the offer against disadvantages of not accepting it.

Example

Advantages of accepting:

☐ The offer is bona fide and backed by earnest money.

☐ Acceptance will give the sellers "peace of mind."

Disadvantages of not accepting:

☐ No other offer as good as the current one may be made.

☐ Delay may force the buyers out, terminating chances for negotiation.

☐ The longer the property remains unsold, the more it costs the seller.

Present All Offers. Even when an offer is pending, the licensee should continue to present all bona fide offers to the seller, up to the close of escrow, unless instructed otherwise.

Seller's Decision   The seller's reaction to the offer may be "yes," "no," or "maybe"–acceptance, rejection, or a counter offer.

Acceptance. If the sellers accept the offer as presented, the deposit receipt begins its transformation into a legally binding purchase contract.

☐ Enter the time and date of acceptance, the broker's name, and the commission amount before the seller signs the form.

☐ Give the seller a copy of the signed form.

☐ Notify the buyer (or buyer's agent, if appropriate) of the seller's acceptance by delivering a copy of the accepted contract.

☐ Obtain signed acknowledgment from the buyer; the contract then becomes legal and binding.

☐ Give the buyer a copy of the contract.

Rejection. An unqualified "no" means the seller refuses to accept the offer and all efforts to continue negotiation are terminated. Notify the offeror of the rejection of the offer.

Counter Offer. If the sellers cannot accept the offer as written, they may be prepared to negotiate their differences through a counter offer.

THE COUNTER OFFER

The counter offer form (Exhibit 20), when properly executed and signed by both parties, is a legal and binding contract which supersedes the original offer.

Prepare the Buyer Whenever an offer looks as if it may be unacceptable to the sellers, prepare the buyers for a possible compromise (counter offer). The goal is to keep the negotiating process alive.

Filling in the Form Follow a procedure similar to that used in completing the deposit receipt form. Use clear, precise language, and fill in all blank spaces correctly.

Amends Deposit Receipt. Prior to filling in the counter offer form, instruct the seller to sign the original deposit receipt form. Add "as amended by the attached addendum (counter offer)" in the acceptance clause.

Time Limits. Enter the time and date the seller signs the counter offer, and enter the length of time the seller will give the buyer to respond.

Presentation of Counter Offer Contact buyers (or selling agent, if appropriate) for an appointment to present the counter offer in person.

Be Positive. Emphasize items sellers agreed to in the original offer.

Be Objective and Sincere. Refer back to the competitive market analysis for supporting facts, if appropriate.

Buyer's Decision When a counter offer is made, the buyer in turn may accept, reject, or counter.

Acceptance. If buyers agree to the provisions of the counter offer:

- ☐ Enter time and date of buyers' signatures.
- ☐ Give them their copy of the signed form.
- ☐ Notify sellers (or listing agent, if appropriate) of buyers' acceptance by delivering a copy of the accepted contract to the sellers.
- ☐ Enter time and date of acceptance and amount of commission, and then obtain signed acknowledgment from the sellers. The contract then becomes legal and binding.
- ☐ Give the sellers their copy of the signed contract.

Rejection. The offer is rejected when the buyers refuse to accept the counter offer and all efforts to continue negotiation are terminated. Notify the owners of the rejection of their counter offer.

Counter the Counter Offer. If the buyers cannot agree to the provisions of the counter offer but are still interested in negotiating, complete a new deposit receipt form. Repeat the negotiation process until an agreement is reached.

NONPERFORMANCE

After the deposit receipt and/or escrow instructions have been signed by the principals, a legally enforceable contract to buy and sell exists, and breach of that contract is subject to legal remedies.

By Seller If the seller fails to complete the transaction, the buyer has several remedies. The buyer may seek:

Monetary Damages. The buyer may sue for compensation for damages suffered. In the absence of bad faith on the seller's part, the court may feel that the buyer is entitled to receive his money back plus certain normal expenses. If bad faith on the part of the seller is found, the court may order additional monetary penalties paid to the buyer to compensate for damages suffered.

Specific Performance. The buyer may sue for specific performance. Since no two parcels of property are exactly alike in their physical and economic characteristics, the court may take the position that money damages alone are not an adequate remedy for the buyer. In that case, the court could compel the seller to perform according to the agreement, i.e., sell the property.

Rescission and Refund. The parties may cancel the contract by mutual agreement, and the buyer takes the deposit back and looks for another property. (Exhibit 21)

By Buyer If the buyer fails to complete the transaction, the seller has several options available.

Damages. The seller may sue for monetary damages in a court action.

Specific Performance. The seller may sue to force the buyer to complete the transaction. This remedy is rare, since the seller would have received money if the sale had closed, and one dollar is the same as any other dollar. Therefore, money should in most cases compensate the seller.

Liquidated Damages. The seller may declare the contract forfeit and keep the buyer's deposit as stated in the liquidated damages clause of the deposit receipt.

Cancellation. The contract may be canceled by mutual consent and the deposit money returned. (Exhibit 21)

ESCROW

Escrow is a step in the transfer of real property, wherein the buyer and the seller deposit documents and/or money with a neutral third party (the escrowholder), with instructions to hold and deliver the documents and/or money subject to performance of specific conditions.

Reasons for an Escrow Although not required by law, except for court ordered transactions and business opportunities, escrow is almost universally used because it provides:

Safekeeping. Documents and money are entrusted to a neutral third party who is responsible for carrying out the terms of the contract.

Coordination. An agency is established to carry out the many details required for closing, as specified in the escrow instructions.

Receiving and Disbursing Funds. The escrow provides an orderly system for obtaining and recording documents (e.g., deeds), drawing up documents (e.g., notes), and computing the proration of taxes, insurance, interest, rents, etc.

Peace of Mind. Escrow provides a system that assures that all of the conditions of the sale will be met. The buyer is assured of receiving appropriate documents. The seller is assured of receiving appropriate funds. Both are assured that title will not be transferred until the moment when all conditions of the transaction have been met.

Essential Elements of an Escrow Escrow is a highly formalized process, governed by contract law and industry custom. There must be:

Valid Sales Contract. The contract between the buyer and seller must be in writing and involve competent parties, a subject property, and mutual agreement as to terms and conditions.

Escrow Instructions. The buyer's and seller's escrow instructions constitute a binding contract between the escrowholder, the buyer, and the seller, setting forth specific instructions from the buyer and seller to the escrowholder regarding the transfer of real property.

Conditional Delivery. Transfer instruments (deed and supporting documents) and money are delivered to the escrowholder, to be delivered to the parties when conditions are met.

Neutral Escrowholder. The escrowholder must be a neutral party, licensed by the Corporations Commissioner of California, and incorporated, with certain exceptions. Exempt from licensing are title companies, banks, savings and loan associations, trust companies, insurance companies, attorneys acting for clients, and real estate brokers for their own agency transactions.

Brokers as Escrowholders Licensed brokers may act as escrowholders without additional licensing under certain conditions.

Own Transactions Only. Brokers are exempt from the Corporations Commissioner's licensing requirement if they are holding escrow in connection with representing the buyer, seller, or both. A broker may not hold escrow for compensation in transactions of other brokers or individuals.

Handling of Funds. The broker must maintain and document all escrow funds in a trust account subject to the Real Estate Commissioner's inspection.

Termination of an Escrow The anticipated conclusion is through complete performance and subsequent closing of the escrow, i.e., consummation of the sale. However, other events may occur which end the escrow.

Voluntary Cancellation. The parties to the escrow (usually the principals) may cancel by mutual consent (Exhibit 21). If the seller has assigned the proceeds or a portion of the proceeds to a third party on the close of escrow, the assignee's consent may also be required. If the assignment is *contingent* on the close of escrow, the assignee's consent is not required.

Revocation. If one of the parties to the escrow fails to perform, remedies may apply for breach of contract.

Death or Incapacity. If one party dies or becomes incompetent leaving a legal escrow (an instrument of transfer has been deposited for delivery under a valid contract), the escrow is not revoked, and the party entitled to the benefits of the instrument is entitled to receive delivery of the instrument.

☐ If the seller dies not having deposited the deed into escrow, the buyer cannot receive title through the escrow, but may seek an action for specific performance against the representatives of the seller's estate.

☐ If the seller dies after depositing the deed into escrow but before closing, the buyer may still deposit the purchase price and be entitled to receive the deed.

Opening the Escrow After a legal and binding contract (purchase agreement) is established between the buyer and seller and the major contingencies (e.g., approval for a building permit, qualifying for a new loan, etc.) have been removed, the listing and/or selling agent may proceed to formally open the escrow.

Information. The responsible real estate agent(s) should get all necessary information involved in the transaction while preparing to open escrow. Using a checklist (Exhibit 22) may be helpful. Information needed includes:

- ☐ Names, addresses, phone numbers of the buyer, seller, broker(s) and salesperson(s)
- ☐ Copy of deed and title insurance policy
- ☐ Loan payment book
- ☐ Copy of fire insurance policy
- ☐ For rental property, list of tenants, rentals, payment dates, and deposits.

Transmission to Escrowholder. The agent transmits all pertinent information, documents, and deposit to the escrowholder, making sure to obtain the identification number of the escrow transaction and a receipt for the deposit check.

Instructions to Escrowholder. The agent instructs the escrowholder to prepare escrow instructions according to the terms of the purchase agreement contract. The terms and intent of the escrow instructions should be identical to those of the purchase agreement. Changes to the instructions (amendments) can be made only by mutual agreement between the parties.

Inconsistencies or Disagreements. If there is a serious difference of opinion between the parties or between the escrow instructions and the purchase agreement, the escrow instructions usually prevail. If the parties cannot agree, a court of law makes the determination, if necessary.

Escrow Procedure While procedures differ according to customs and location, the basic escrow procedure includes:

Preparation of the Escrow Instructions. At least four copies are needed, to distribute to the buyer, the seller, the listing agent, and the selling agent.

Title Report. The broker or escrowholder orders a title search and a preliminary title report.

Lender's Demands. The broker or escrowholder requests demand for payoff and/or beneficiary statement from the lender.

- ☐ Demand for payoff is requested if the seller intends to pay off existing loans through escrow.

- ☐ Beneficiary statements are requested when the buyer intends to assume or take the property subject to the existing loan.

New Loan Documents. If a new loan is being obtained, the escrowholder receives the new loan documents, unless processed through a separate loan escrow.

Inspection Reports. Escrowholder accepts structural pest control reports and other special reports as applicable.

Fire Insurance Policies. Escrowholder receives and accepts required insurance documents.

Closing Costs. Escrowholder computes closing costs, reflecting all of the above.

Closing Funds. After computing the amount, escrowholder requests closing funds from the buyer.

Audit. Transaction is checked for accuracy and completeness, in preparation to close.

Ordering the Close. The title company is instructed to record the new documents, such as deeds of reconveyance, grant deed, and new trust deeds.

Closing the Escrow Closing means distribution of the funds and documents which were held in escrow, accounting for the same, and seeing that all expenses are paid.

Disbursement of Funds and Documents. Closing is the time to distribute those items the escrow was created to hold:

- ☐ Proceeds of the sale to the seller
- ☐ Deed to the buyer
- ☐ Commission to the broker
- ☐ Any other demands or obligations

Closing or Settlement Statement. A separate written accounting is issued to buyer and seller detailing the distribution of all funds involved in the real estate transaction (Exhibit 23). The statement itemizes total receipts and disbursements of the buyer's and seller's funds, written in the form of cash demands, proceeds, charges, and prorations.

- ☐ Prorations are proportional divisions of obligations calculated according to closing date or other agreed time. Items prorated include taxes, insurance, rent, and in some cases interest.

- ☐ The total sales price and commission are clearly spelled out.

- ☐ The closing statements must comply with government regulations, notably the Real Estate Settlement Procedures Act (RESPA), as to form, content, and time of delivery.

Division of Charges. Local or regional customary practices usually establish the apportionment of various charges and fees; however, any party to the transaction may negotiate the division.

DIVISION OF CLOSING COSTS

CHARGES TO SELLERS

The Seller Commonly Pays

Appraisal charge*

Assessments

Beneficiary statement (report from the lender on the balance of an existing loan)

Broker commission

Discount points (VA)

Documentary transfer tax

Drawing grant deed

Drawing reconveyance deed(s)

Escrow services (commonly paid by seller in Southern California, by buyer in Northern California, or half and half in many counties)*

Interest on existing loan(s) from last monthly payment to closing date

Loan payoff(s)

Mortgagor discounts (points, paid by a seller for a buyer's purchase-money loan)*

Notary fees

Owner's title policy*

Payment of any tax arrears in full

Payment of other liens or judgments

Prepayment penalty

Recording reconveyance

Reimbursing buyer for prepaid rents and deposits

Tax service (FHA, VA)

Termite report and structural repair (if any)*

Other charges agreed upon by both buyer and seller

CHARGES TO BUYERS

The Buyer Commonly Pays

ALTA policy and inspection fee (if ordered)

Appraisal fee*

Assumption fee

Credit report fee

Discount points (except on VA)

Drawing of note(s) and trust deed(s)

Escrow services (commonly paid by seller in Southern California, by buyer in Northern California, or half and half in many counties)*

Fees for recording deed(s)

Fire insurance policy

If buyer assumes loan, adjustment on current loan payment interest, and impound, if any

Impounds

Interest on new loan from date of closing to the starting date of the first monthly payment period

Loan origination fee

Mortgage insurance premium (MIP) (FHA insured loans)

Notary fee

Prepaid insurance

Prepaid taxes

Private mortgage insurance

Recording of grant deed

Recording of trust deed

Reserves to lender for impounds (if impound account maintained)

Standard policy of title insurance*

Tax service (conventional)

VA service fee

Other charges or adjustments agreed upon by both buyer and seller

*Negotiable

Real Estate Agent's Responsibilities

Successful escrows result from constant delicate nurturing. Different geographic areas have different escrow customs and practices. Suggested responsibilities of real estate agents (buyer's and seller's) include:

Contact with Escrowholder. It is advisable for the agent to take charge of giving the escrowholder instructions, documents, and funds required to transfer the property.

Contact with Principals. The agent should personally deliver escrow instructions, deeds, and other documents requiring signatures to the buyer and seller, explain each document thoroughly, obtain the required notarization (acknowledgments), and give each party a copy of the signed document.

Review of Documents. The agent should check the escrow instructions for accuracy before delivery to the buyer and seller; check the preliminary title report for any possible complications to the closing, e.g., outstanding liens, assessments, delinquent taxes (selling agent); check the structural pest control report for any possible defects or infestation (selling agent); and verify other required compliances (Exhibit 24).

Collecting Commission. The escrow instructions should provide for the payment of the broker's commission. If the escrow does not close because of buyer's default or nonperformance, the broker(s) usually cannot receive a commission unless the seller succeeds in collecting damages from the buyer. If the parties mutually agree to cancel the escrow, the broker is usually entitled to a commission. If the seller defaults, the broker is usually entitled to recover a commission.

Monitoring Closing. The agent should check the closing or settlement statements for accuracy, and deliver them to the buyer and seller and explain charges and credits.

Responsibilities of the Escrowholder

Observing strict neutrality and loyalty to all parties, the escrowholder coordinates the numerous details of a real property transfer:

Receive all instructions, documents, and funds required to transfer property, according to the wishes of the buyer and seller.

Compare the escrow instructions upon receipt to insure that all parties are in mutual agreement.

Order preliminary title report, and title insurance policy after transfer has been completed.

Receive all necessary documents and approvals, such as: structural pest control report; fire insurance policy; demand for payoff statement; beneficiary statement; and new loan documents.

Compute closing costs.

Request closing funds from the buyer.

Audit file in preparation for closing.

Record documents (e.g., deed and trust deed) with county recorder.

Disburse funds and documents to the appropriate parties according to instructions.

Avoid, as a neutral fiduciary (dual agent),

Disclosing escrow information except to the parties concerned

Negotiating with the parties or offering advice

Amending the escrow instructions, unless written authorization is given by the parties.

TITLE INSURANCE

Title insurance is an insured statement of conditions of the title or ownership of a particular parcel of real property. Insurance protection is provided if the title turns out to be defective in some way. The policy shows who owns the property, according to the public records; tax or mortgage liens against the property, if any; and any other liens, assessments, or encumbrances of record.

Standard Coverage   The California Land Title Association (CLTA) standard coverage policy is an example of basic title insurance. Standard coverage insures against:

- ☐ Risks of record
- ☐ Forgery
- ☐ Impersonation
- ☐ Lack of capacity of the parties to the transaction.

Exceptions. The standard policy does not protect against:

- ☐ Defects in the title known to the policy holder
- ☐ Liens and/or easements not recorded
- ☐ Nonrecorded claims which could be ascertained by survey or physical inspection
- ☐ Mining claims, patents, water rights, zoning ordinances.

Extended Coverage Policy   Extended coverage insures against most of the general exceptions from the standard coverage policy, and requires an additional fee. The American Land Title Association (ALTA) policy is a common form of extended coverage policy, available to lender and owner.

FIRE AND CASUALTY INSURANCE

Hazard insurance policies may be assumed, or new policies may be purchased by the buyer. Lenders normally require insurance to the extent of their beneficial interest in the property (outstanding balance of the loan).

Standard Form Fire Insurance   Fire insurance may be a minimum coverage policy which covers all direct loss by fire or lightning, and the effects of the same, e.g., smoke damage, water damage caused by water used to put out the fire, and debris removal.

Endorsements   For an additional premium, endorsements may be added to the basic policy to cover other hazards such as windstorm, hail, earthquake, flood, vandalism, explosion, riot, or civil commotion.

Homeowner's Insurance   The most desirable policy for most homeowners is a package policy which offers comprehensive protection against the numerous hazards associated with home ownership.

Coverage. A homeowner's package normally combines standard fire insurance protection with coverage against theft, burglary, bodily injury, property damage, glass breakage, and personal liability.

Economy. The homeowner's policy was developed as an economical way to meet common needs at a lower premium rate.

Amount of Insurance   The law now limits the maximum amount of hazard insurance a homebuyer must purchase to qualify for a mortgage loan. In the past, some lenders required buyers to purchase coverage equal to the amount of their loan balance. The new law effectively states that lenders must accept *replacement cost* coverage. Since the home itself typically represents only 60% of the total property value, borrowers with high loan balances relative to the purchase price could realize substantial savings in premium costs. An insurance agent can advise.

REAL ESTATE PURCHASE CONTRACT AND RECEIPT FOR DEPOSIT
THIS IS MORE THAN A RECEIPT FOR MONEY. IT IS INTENDED TO BE A LEGALLY BINDING CONTRACT. READ IT CAREFULLY.
CALIFORNIA ASSOCIATION OF REALTORS® (CAR) STANDARD FORM

_____, California, _____, 19_____

Received from _____

herein called Buyer, the sum of _____ Dollars $ _____

evidenced by ☐ cash, ☐ cashier's check, ☐ personal check or ☐ _____, payable to _____

_____, to be held uncashed until acceptance of this offer as deposit on account of purchase price of

_____ Dollars $ _____

for the purchase of property, situated in _____, County of _____ California,

described as follows: _____ .

1. FINANCING: The obtaining of Buyer's financing is a contingency of this agreement.

  A. DEPOSIT upon acceptance, to be deposited into _____ $ _____

  B. INCREASED DEPOSIT within _____ days of acceptance to be deposited into _____ $ _____

  C. BALANCE OF DOWN PAYMENT to be deposited into _____ on or before _____ $ _____

  D. Buyer to apply, qualify for and obtain a NEW FIRST LOAN in the amount of . . . . $ _____
    payable monthly at approximately $ _____ including interest at origination not to exceed _____%,
    ☐ fixed rate, ☐ other _____ all due _____ years from date of origination. Loan fee not to
    exceed _____. Seller agrees to pay a maximum of _____ FHA/VA discount points.
    Additional terms _____

  E. Buyer ☐ to assume, ☐ to take title subject to an EXISTING FIRST LOAN with an approximate balance of . . . . $ _____
    in favor of _____ payable monthly at $ _____ including interest at _____% ☐ fixed rate,
    ☐ other _____. Fees not to exceed _____
    Disposition of impound account _____
    Additional terms _____

  F. Buyer to execute a NOTE SECURED BY a ☐ first, ☐ second, ☐ third DEED OF TRUST in the amount of . . . . $ _____
    IN FAVOR OF SELLER payable monthly at $ _____ ☐ or more, including interest at _____% all due
    _____ years from date of origination, ☐ or upon sale or transfer of subject property. A late charge of _____
    _____ shall be due on any installment not paid within _____ days of the due date.
    ☐ Deed of Trust to contain a request for notice of default or sale for the benefit of Seller. Buyer ☐ will, ☐ will not execute a request
    for notice of delinquency. Additional terms _____

  G. Buyer ☐ to assume, ☐ to take title subject to an EXISTING SECOND LOAN with an approximate balance of . . . . $ _____
    in favor of _____ payable monthly at $ _____ including interest at _____%
    ☐ fixed rate, ☐ other _____. Buyer fees not to exceed _____
    Additional terms _____

  H. Buyer to apply, qualify for and obtain a NEW SECOND LOAN in the amount of . . . . $ _____
    payable monthly at approximately $ _____ including interest at origination not to exceed _____% ☐ fixed rate,
    ☐ other _____, all due _____ years from date of origination.
    Buyer's loan fee not to exceed _____ Additional terms _____

  I. In the event Buyer assumes or takes title subject to an existing loan, Seller shall provide Buyer with copies of applicable notes and Deeds
    of Trust. A loan may contain a number of features which affect the loan, such as interest rate changes, monthly payment changes, balloon
    payments, etc. Buyer shall be allowed _____ calendar days after receipt of such copies to notify Seller in writing of disapproval.
    FAILURE TO NOTIFY SELLER IN WRITING SHALL CONCLUSIVELY BE CONSIDERED APPROVAL. Buyer's approval shall not be
    unreasonably withheld. Difference in existing loan balances shall be adjusted in ☐ Cash, ☐ Other _____

  J. Buyer agrees to act diligently and in good faith to obtain all applicable financing. _____

  K. ADDITIONAL FINANCING TERMS: _____

  L. TOTAL PURCHASE PRICE . . . . $ _____

2. OCCUPANCY: Buyer ☐ does, ☐ does not intend to occupy subject property as Buyer's primary residence.

3. SUPPLEMENTS: The ATTACHED supplements are incorporated herein:
    ☐ Interim Occupancy Agreement (CAR FORM IOA-11)   ☐ _____
    ☐ Residential Lease Agreement after Sale (CAR FORM RLAS-11)   ☐ _____
    ☐ VA and FHA Amendments (CAR FORM VA/FHA-11)   ☐ _____

4. ESCROW: Buyer and Seller shall deliver signed instructions to _____ the escrow holder, within _____ calendar days
of acceptance of the offer which shall provide for closing within _____ calendar days of acceptance. Escrow fees to be paid as follows: _____

_____

Buyer and Seller acknowledge receipt of copy of this page, which constitutes Page 1 of _____ Pages.

Buyer's Initials (_____) (_____)   Seller's Initials (_____) (_____)

THIS STANDARDIZED DOCUMENT FOR USE IN SIMPLE TRANSACTIONS HAS BEEN APPROVED BY THE CALIFORNIA ASSOCIATION OF REALTORS® IN FORM ONLY. NO REPRESENTATION IS MADE AS TO THE APPROVAL OF THE FORM OF ANY SUPPLEMENTS NOT CURRENTLY PUBLISHED BY THE CALIFORNIA ASSOCIATION OF REALTORS® OR THE LEGAL VALIDITY OR ADEQUACY OF ANY PROVISION IN ANY SPECIFIC TRANSACTION. IT SHOULD NOT BE USED IN COMPLEX TRANSACTIONS OR WITH EXTENSIVE RIDERS OR ADDITIONS.

A REAL ESTATE BROKER IS THE PERSON QUALIFIED TO ADVISE ON REAL ESTATE TRANSACTIONS. IF YOU DESIRE LEGAL OR TAX ADVICE, CONSULT AN APPROPRIATE PROFESSIONAL.

REPRINTED BY PERMISSION CALIFORNIA ASSOCIATION OF REALTORS®. ENDORSEMENT NOT IMPLIED

Copyright © 1989, CALIFORNIA ASSOCIATION OF REALTORS®
525 South Virgil Avenue, Los Angeles, California 90020
REVISED 2/89

OFFICE USE ONLY

Reviewed by Broker or Designee _____

Date _____

REAL ESTATE PURCHASE CONTRACT AND RECEIPT FOR DEPOSIT (DLF-14 PAGE 1 OF 4)

Exhibit 18.1

Subject Property Address: _____

5. **TITLE:** Title is to be free of liens, encumbrances, easements, restrictions, rights and conditions of record or known to Seller, other than the following: (a) Current property taxes, (b) covenants, conditions, restrictions, and public utility easements of record, if any, provided the same do not adversely affect the continued use of the property for the purposes for which it is presently being used, unless reasonably disapproved by Buyer in writing within _____ calendar days of receipt of a current preliminary report furnished at _____ expense, and (c) _____

Seller shall furnish Buyer at _____ expense a California Land Title Association policy issued by _____
_____ Company, showing title vested in Buyer subject only to the above. If Seller is unwilling or unable to eliminate any title matter disapproved by Buyer as above, Buyer may terminate this agreement. If Seller fails to deliver title as above, Buyer may terminate this agreement; in either case, the deposit shall be returned to Buyer.

6. **VESTING:** Unless otherwise designated in the escrow instructions of Buyer, title shall vest as follows: _____
_____

(The manner of taking title may have significant legal and tax consequences. Therefore, give this matter serious consideration.)

7. **PRORATIONS:** Property taxes, payments on bonds and assessments assumed by Buyer, interest, rents, association dues, premiums on insurance acceptable to Buyer, and _____ shall be paid current and prorated as of ☐ the day of recordation of the deed; or ☐ _____. Bonds or assessments now a lien shall be ☐ paid current by Seller, payments not yet due to be assumed by Buyer; or ☐ paid in full by Seller, including payments not yet due; or ☐ _____. County Transfer tax shall be paid by _____. The _____ transfer tax or transfer fee shall be paid by _____. **PROPERTY WILL BE REASSESSED UPON CHANGE OF OWNERSHIP. THIS WILL AFFECT THE TAXES TO BE PAID.** A Supplemental tax bill will be issued, which shall be paid as follows: (a) for periods after close of escrow, by Buyer (or by final acquiring party if part of an exchange), and (b) for periods prior to close of escrow, by Seller. TAX BILLS ISSUED AFTER CLOSE OF ESCROW SHALL BE HANDLED DIRECTLY BETWEEN BUYER AND SELLER.

8. **POSSESSION:** Possession and occupancy shall be delivered to Buyer, ☐ on close of escrow, or ☐ not later than _____ days after close of escrow, or ☐ _____

9. **KEYS:** Seller shall, when possession is available to Buyer, provide keys and/or means to operate all property locks, and alarms, if any.

10. **PERSONAL PROPERTY:** The following items of personal property, free of liens and without warranty of condition, are included: _____
_____
_____

11. **FIXTURES:** All permanently installed fixtures and fittings that are attached to the property or for which special openings have been made are included in the purchase price, including electrical, light, plumbing and heating fixtures, built-in appliances, screens, awnings, shutters, all window coverings, attached floor coverings, TV antennas, air cooler or conditioner, garage door openers and controls, attached fireplace equipment, mailbox, trees and shrubs, and _____ except _____

12. **SMOKE DETECTOR(S):** State law requires that residences be equipped with an operable smoke detector(s). Local law may have additional requirements. Seller shall deliver to Buyer a written statement of compliance in accordance with applicable state and local law prior to close of escrow.

13. **TRANSFER DISCLOSURE:** Unless exempt, Transferor (Seller), shall comply with Civil Code §§1102 et seq., by providing Transferee (Buyer) with a Real Estate Transfer Disclosure Statement: (a) ☐ Buyer has received and read a Real Estate Transfer Disclosure Statement; or (b) ☐ Seller shall provide Buyer with a Real Estate Transfer Disclosure Statement within _____ calendar days of acceptance of the offer after which Buyer shall have three (3) days after delivery to Buyer, in person, or five (5) days after delivery by deposit in the mail, to terminate this agreement by delivery of a written notice of termination to Seller or Seller's Agent.

14. **TAX WITHHOLDING:** Under the Foreign Investment in Real Property Tax Act (FIRPTA), IRC §1445, *every* Buyer of U.S. real property *must*, unless an exemption applies, deduct and withhold from Seller's proceeds 10% of the gross sales price. Under California Revenue and Taxation Code §§18805 and 26131, the Buyer must deduct and withhold an additional one-third of the amount required to be withheld under federal law. The primary FIRPTA exemptions are: No withholding is required if (a) Seller provides Buyer with an affidavit under penalty of perjury, that Seller is not a "foreign person," or (b) Seller provides Buyer with a "qualifying statement" issued by the Internal Revenue Service, or (c) Buyer purchases real property for use as a residence and the purchase price is $300,000 or less and Buyer or a member of Buyer's family has definite plans to reside at the property for at least 50% of the number of days it is in use during each of the first two twelve-month periods after transfer. Seller and Buyer agree to execute and deliver as directed any instrument, affidavit, or statement reasonably necessary to carry out those statutes and regulations promulgated thereunder.

15. **MULTIPLE LISTING SERVICE:** If Broker is a Participant of an Association/Board multiple listing service ("MLS"), the Broker is authorized to report the sale, its price, terms, and financing for the publication, dissemination, information, and use of the authorized Board members, MLS Participants and Subscribers.

16. **ADDITIONAL TERMS AND CONDITIONS:**

ONLY THE FOLLOWING PARAGRAPHS 'A' THROUGH 'K' *WHEN INITIALLED BY BOTH BUYER AND SELLER* ARE INCORPORATED IN THIS AGREEMENT.

Buyer's Initials   Seller's Initials
_____ / _____   _____ / _____   **A. PHYSICAL AND GEOLOGICAL INSPECTION:** Buyer shall have the right, at Buyer's expense, to select a licensed contractor and/or other qualified professional(s), to make "Inspections" (including tests, surveys, other studies, inspections, and investigations) of the subject property, including but not limited to structural, plumbing, sewer/septic system, well, heating, electrical, built-in appliances, roof, soils, foundation, mechanical systems, pool, pool heater, pool filter, air conditioner, if any, possible environmental hazards such as asbestos, formaldehyde, radon gas and other substances/products, and geologic conditions. Buyer shall keep the subject property free and clear of any liens, indemnify and hold Seller harmless from all liability, claims, demands, damages, or costs, and repair all damages to the property arising from the "Inspections." All claimed defects concerning the condition of the property that adversely affect the continued use of the property for the purposes for which it is presently being used (☐ or as _____) shall be in writing, supported by written reports, if any, and delivered to Seller within _____ calendar days FOR "INSPECTIONS" OTHER THAN GEOLOGICAL, and/or within _____ calendar days FOR GEOLOGICAL "INSPECTIONS," **of acceptance of the offer.** Buyer shall furnish Seller copies, at no cost, of all reports concerning the property obtained by Buyer. When such reports disclose conditions or information unsatisfactory to the Buyer, which the Seller is unwilling or unable to correct, Buyer may cancel this agreement. Seller shall make the premises available for all Inspections. BUYER'S FAILURE TO NOTIFY SELLER IN WRITING SHALL CONCLUSIVELY BE CONSIDERED APPROVAL.

Buyer's Initials   Seller's Initials
_____ / _____   _____ / _____   **B. CONDITION OF PROPERTY:** Seller warrants, through the date possession is made available to Buyer: (1) property and improvements, including landscaping, grounds and pool/spa, if any, will be maintained in the same condition as upon the date of acceptance of the offer, and (2) the roof is free of all known leaks, and (3) built-in appliances, and water, sewer/septic, plumbing, heating, electrical, air conditioning, pool/spa systems, if any, are operative, and (4) Seller shall replace all broken and/or cracked glass; (5) _____
_____

Buyer's Initials   Seller's Initials
_____ / _____   _____ / _____   **C. SELLER REPRESENTATION:** Seller warrants that Seller has no knowledge of any notice of violations of City, County, State, Federal, Building, Zoning, Fire, Health Codes or ordinances, or other governmental regulation filed or issued against the property. This warranty shall be effective until the date of close of escrow.

Buyer and Seller acknowledge receipt of copy of this page, which constitutes Page 2 of _____ Pages.
Buyer's Initials (_____) (_____)   Seller's Initials (_____) (_____)

REPRINTED BY PERMISSION CALIFORNIA ASSOCIATION OF REALTORS®. ENDORSEMENT NOT IMPLIED

OFFICE USE ONLY
Reviewed by Broker or Designee _____
Date _____

REAL ESTATE PURCHASE CONTRACT AND RECEIPT FOR DEPOSIT (DLF-14 PAGE 2 OF 4)

Exhibit 18.2

Subject Property Address _____

Buyer's Initials   Seller's Initials

_____ / _____   _____ / _____   **D. PEST CONTROL:** (1) Within _____ calendar days of acceptance of the offer, Seller shall furnish Buyer at the expense of ☐ Buyer, ☐ Seller, a current written report of an inspection by _____ , a licensed Structural Pest Control Operator, of the main building, ☐ detached garage(s) or carport(s), if any, and ☐ the following other structures on the property:

(2) If requested by either Buyer or Seller, the report shall separately identify each recommendation for corrective measures as follows:

"Section 1": Infestation or infection which is evident.

"Section 2": Conditions that are present which are deemed likely to lead to infestation or infection.

(3) If no infestation or infection by wood destroying pests or organisms is found, the report shall include a written Certification as provided in Business and Professions Code § 8519(a) that on the date of inspection "no evidence of active infestation or infection was found."

(4) All work recommended to correct conditions described in "Section 1" shall be at the expense of ☐ Buyer, ☐ Seller.

(5) All work recommended to correct conditions described in "Section 2," if requested by Buyer, shall be at the expense of ☐ Buyer, ☐ Seller.

(6) The repairs shall be performed with good workmanship and materials of comparable quality and shall include repairs of leaking showers, replacement of tiles and other materials removed for repairs. It is understood that exact restoration of appearance or cosmetic items following all such repairs is not included.

(7) Funds for work agreed to be performed after close of escrow, shall be held in escrow and disbursed upon receipt of a written Certification as provided in Business and Professions Code § 8519(b) that the inspected property "is now free of evidence of active infestation or infection."

(8) Work to be performed at Seller's expense may be performed by Seller or through others, provided that (a) all required permits and final inspections are obtained, and (b) upon completion of repairs a written Certification is issued by a licensed Structural Pest Control Operator showing that the inspected property "is now free of evidence of active infestation or infection."

(9) If inspection of inaccessible areas is recommended by the report, Buyer has the option to accept and approve the report, or within _____ calendar days from receipt of the report to request in writing further inspection be made. BUYER'S FAILURE TO NOTIFY SELLER IN WRITING OF SUCH REQUEST SHALL CONCLUSIVELY BE CONSIDERED APPROVAL OF THE REPORT. If further inspection recommends "Section 1" and/or "Section 2" corrective measures, such work shall be at the expense of the party designated in subparagraph (4) and/or (5), respectively. If no infestation or infection is found, the cost of inspection, entry and closing of the inaccessible areas shall be at the expense of the Buyer.

(10) Other _____

_____

Buyer's Initials   Seller's Initials

_____ / _____   _____ / _____   **E. FLOOD HAZARD AREA DISCLOSURE:** Buyer is informed that subject property is situated in a "Special Flood Hazard Area" as set forth on a Federal Emergency Management Agency (FEMA) "Flood Insurance Rate Map" (FIRM), or "Flood Hazard Boundary Map" (FHBM). The law provides that, as a condition of obtaining financing on most structures located in a "Special Flood Hazard Area," lenders require flood insurance where the property or its attachments are security for a loan.

The extent of coverage and the cost may vary. For further information consult the lender or insurance carrier. No representation or recommendation is made by the Seller and the Broker(s) in this transaction as to the legal effect or economic consequences of the National Flood Insurance Program and related legislation.

Buyer's Initials   Seller's Initials

_____ / _____   _____ / _____   **F. SPECIAL STUDIES ZONE DISCLOSURE:** Buyer is informed that subject property is situated in a Special Studies Zone as designated under §§ 2621-2625, inclusive, of the California Public Resources Code; and, as such, the construction or development on this property of any structure for human occupancy may be subject to the findings of a geologic report prepared by a geologist registered in the State of California, unless such a report is waived by the City or County under the terms of that act.

Buyer is allowed _____ calendar days from acceptance of the offer to make further inquiries at appropriate governmental agencies concerning the use of the subject property under the terms of the Special Studies Zone Act and local building, zoning, fire, health, and safety codes. When such inquiries disclose conditions or information unsatisfactory to the Buyer, which the Seller is unwilling or unable to correct, Buyer may cancel this agreement. BUYER'S FAILURE TO NOTIFY SELLER IN WRITING SHALL CONCLUSIVELY BE CONSIDERED APPROVAL.

Buyer's Initials   Seller's Initials

_____ / _____   _____ / _____   **G. ENERGY CONSERVATION RETROFIT:** If local ordinance requires that the property be brought in compliance with minimum energy Conservation Standards as a condition of sale or transfer, ☐ Buyer, ☐ Seller shall comply with and pay for these requirements. Where permitted by law, Seller may, if obligated hereunder, satisfy the obligation by authorizing escrow to credit Buyer with sufficient funds to cover the cost of such retrofit.

Buyer's Initials   Seller's Initials

_____ / _____   _____ / _____   **H. HOME PROTECTION PLAN:** Buyer and Seller have been informed that Home Protection Plans are available. Such plans may provide additional protection and benefit to a Seller or Buyer. The CALIFORNIA ASSOCIATION OF REALTORS® and the Broker(s) in this transaction do not endorse or approve any particular company or program:

a) ☐ A Buyer's coverage Home Protection Plan to be issued by _____

Company, at a cost not to exceed $_____ , to be paid by ☐ Buyer, ☐ Seller; or

b) ☐ Buyer and Seller elect not to purchase a Home Protection Plan.

Buyer's Initials   Seller's Initials

_____ / _____   _____ / _____   **I. CONDOMINIUM/P.U.D.:** The subject of this transaction is a condominium/planned unit development (P.U.D.) designated as unit _____ and _____ parking space(s) and an undivided interest in community areas, and _____ . The current monthly assessment charge by the homeowner's association or other governing body(s) is $_____ . As soon as practicable, Seller shall provide Buyer with copies of covenants, conditions and restrictions, articles of incorporation, by-laws, current rules and regulations, most current financial statements, and any other documents as required by law. Seller shall disclose in writing any known pending special assessment, claims, or litigation to Buyer. Buyer shall be allowed _____ calendar days from receipt to review these documents. If such documents disclose conditions or information unsatisfactory to Buyer, Buyer may cancel this agreement. BUYER'S FAILURE TO NOTIFY SELLER IN WRITING SHALL CONCLUSIVELY BE CONSIDERED APPROVAL.

Buyer's Initials   Seller's Initials

_____ / _____   _____ / _____   **J. LIQUIDATED DAMAGES:** If Buyer fails to complete said purchase as herein provided by reason of any default of Buyer, Seller shall be released from obligation to sell the property to Buyer and may proceed against Buyer upon any claim or remedy which he/she may have in law or equity; provided, however, that by initialling this paragraph Buyer and Seller agree that Seller shall retain the deposit as liquidated damages. If the described property is a dwelling with no more than four units, one of which the Buyer intends to occupy as his/her residence, Seller shall retain as liquidated damages the deposit actually paid, or an amount therefrom, not more than 3% of the purchase price and promptly return any excess to Buyer. Buyer and Seller agree to execute a similar liquidated damages provision, such as CALIFORNIA ASSOCIATION OF REALTORS® Receipt for Increased Deposit (RID-11), for any increased deposits. (Funds deposited in trust accounts or in escrow are not released automatically in the event of a dispute. Release of funds requires written agreement of the parties, judicial decision or arbitration.)

Buyer and Seller acknowledge receipt of copy of this page, which constitutes Page 3 of _____ Pages.

Buyer's Initials (_____) (_____)   Seller's Initials (_____) (_____)

OFFICE USE ONLY

Reviewed by Broker or Designee _____

Date _____

REAL ESTATE PURCHASE CONTRACT AND RECEIPT FOR DEPOSIT (DLF-14 PAGE 3 OF 4)

Exhibit 18.3

Subject Property Address _____

K. ARBITRATION OF DISPUTES: Any dispute or claim in law or equity arising out of this contract or any resulting transaction shall be decided by neutral binding arbitration in accordance with the rules of the American Arbitration Association, and not by court action except as provided by California law for judicial review of arbitration proceedings. Judgment upon the award rendered by the arbitrator(s) may be entered in any court having jurisdiction thereof. The parties shall have the right to discovery in accordance with Code of Civil Procedure § 1283.05. The following matters are excluded from arbitration hereunder: (a) a judicial or non-judicial foreclosure or other action or proceeding to enforce a deed of trust, mortgage, or real property sales contract as defined in Civil Code § 2985, (b) an unlawful detainer action, (c) the filing or enforcement of a mechanic's lien, (d) any matter which is within the jurisdiction of a probate court, or (e) an action for bodily injury or wrongful death, or for latent or patent defects to which Code of Civil Procedure § 337.1 or § 337.15 applies. The filing of a judicial action to enable the recording of a notice of pending action, for order of attachment, receivership, injunction, or other provisional remedies, shall not constitute a waiver of the right to arbitrate under this provision.

Any dispute or claim by or against broker(s) and/or associate licensee(s) participating in this transaction shall be submitted to arbitration consistent with the provision above only if the broker(s) and/or associate licensee(s) making the claim or against whom the claim is made shall have agreed to submit it to arbitration consistent with this provision.

"NOTICE: BY INITIALLING IN THE SPACE BELOW YOU ARE AGREEING TO HAVE ANY DISPUTE ARISING OUT OF THE MATTERS INCLUDED IN THE 'ARBITRATION OF DISPUTES' PROVISION DECIDED BY NEUTRAL ARBITRATION AS PROVIDED BY CALIFORNIA LAW AND YOU ARE GIVING UP ANY RIGHTS YOU MIGHT POSSESS TO HAVE THE DISPUTE LITIGATED IN A COURT OR JURY TRIAL. BY INITIALLING IN THE SPACE BELOW YOU ARE GIVING UP YOUR JUDICIAL RIGHTS TO DISCOVERY AND APPEAL, UNLESS THOSE RIGHTS ARE SPECIFICALLY INCLUDED IN THE 'ARBITRATION OF DISPUTES' PROVISION. IF YOU REFUSE TO SUBMIT TO ARBITRATION AFTER AGREEING TO THIS PROVISION, YOU MAY BE COMPELLED TO ARBITRATE UNDER THE AUTHORITY OF THE CALIFORNIA CODE OF CIVIL PROCEDURE. YOUR AGREEMENT TO THIS ARBITRATION PROVISION IS VOLUNTARY."

"WE HAVE READ AND UNDERSTAND THE FOREGOING AND AGREE TO SUBMIT DISPUTES ARISING OUT OF THE MATTERS INCLUDED IN THE 'ARBITRATION OF DISPUTES' PROVISION TO NEUTRAL ARBITRATION."

Buyer's Initials   Seller's Initials
___ / ___   ___ / ___

17. OTHER TERMS AND CONDITIONS: _____
_____
_____
_____
_____

18. ATTORNEY'S FEES: In any action, proceeding or arbitration arising out of this agreement, the prevailing party shall be entitled to reasonable attorney's fees and costs.

19. ENTIRE CONTRACT: Time is of the essence. All prior agreements between the parties are incorporated in this agreement which constitutes the entire contract. Its terms are intended by the parties as a final expression of their agreement with respect to such terms as are included herein and may not be contradicted by evidence of any prior agreement or contemporaneous oral agreement. The parties further intend that this agreement constitutes the complete and exclusive statement of its terms and that no extrinsic evidence whatsoever may be introduced in any judicial or arbitration proceeding, if any, involving this agreement.

20. CAPTIONS: The captions in this agreement are for convenience of reference only and are not intended as part of this agreement.

21. AGENCY CONFIRMATION: The following agency relationship(s) are hereby confirmed for this transaction:

LISTING AGENT: _____ is the agent of (check one):
(Print Firm Name)
☐ the Seller exclusively; or ☐ both the Buyer and Seller

SELLING AGENT: _____ (if not the same as Listing Agent) is the agent of (check one):
(Print Firm Name)
☐ the Buyer exclusively; or ☐ the Seller exclusively; or ☐ both the Buyer and Seller.

22. AMENDMENTS: This agreement may not be amended, modified, altered or changed in any respect whatsoever except by a further agreement in writing executed by Buyer and Seller.

23. OFFER: This constitutes an offer to purchase the described property. Unless acceptance is signed by Seller and a signed copy delivered in person, by mail, or facsimile, and received by Buyer at the address below, or by _____ who is authorized to receive it, on behalf of Buyer, within _____ calendar days of the date hereof, this offer shall be deemed revoked and the deposit shall be returned. Buyer has read and acknowledges receipt of a copy of this offer. This agreement and any supplement, addendum or modification relating hereto, including any photocopy or facsimile thereof, may be executed in two or more counterparts, all of which shall constitute one and the same writing.

REAL ESTATE BROKER _____   BUYER _____
By _____   BUYER _____
Address _____   Address _____
_____   _____
Telephone _____   Telephone _____

ACCEPTANCE

The undersigned Seller accepts and agrees to sell the property on the above terms and conditions and agrees to the above confirmation of agency relationships (☐ subject to attached counter offer).

Seller agrees to pay to Broker(s) _____
compensation for services as follows: _____ .
Payable: (a) On recordation of the deed or other evidence of title, or (b) if completion of sale is prevented by default of Seller, upon Seller's default, or (c) if completion of sale is prevented by default of Buyer, only if and when Seller collects damages from Buyer, by suit or otherwise, and then in an amount not less than one-half of the damages recovered, but not to exceed the above fee, after first deducting title and escrow expenses and the expenses of collection, if any. Seller shall execute and deliver an escrow instruction irrevocably assigning the compensation for service in an amount equal to the compensation agreed to above. In any action, proceeding, or arbitration between Broker(s) and Seller arising out of this agreement, the prevailing party shall be entitled to reasonable attorney's fees and costs. The undersigned has read and acknowledges receipt of a copy of this agreement and authorizes Broker(s) to deliver a signed copy to Buyer.

Date _____ Telephone _____   SELLER _____
Address _____   SELLER _____

Real Estate Broker(s) agree to the foregoing.
Broker _____ By _____ Date _____
Broker _____ By _____ Date _____

This form is available for use by the entire real estate industry. The use of this form is not intended to identify the user as a REALTOR®. REALTOR® is a registered collective membership mark which may be used only by real estate licensees who are members of the NATIONAL ASSOCIATION OF REALTORS® and who subscribe to its Code of Ethics.

OFFICE USE ONLY
Reviewed by Broker or Designee _____
Date _____

Page 4 of _____ Pages.

REPRINTED BY PERMISSION CALIFORNIA ASSOCIATION OF REALTORS®. ENDORSEMENT NOT IMPLIED

REAL ESTATE PURCHASE CONTRACT AND RECEIPT FOR DEPOSIT (DLF-14 PAGE 4 OF 4)

Exhibit 18.4

REAL ESTATE PURCHASE CONTRACT AND RECEIPT FOR DEPOSIT

THIS IS MORE THAN A RECEIPT FOR MONEY. IT IS INTENDED TO BE A LEGALLY BINDING CONTRACT. READ IT CAREFULLY.

CALIFORNIA ASSOCIATION OF REALTORS® STANDARD FORM

_____, California. _____, 19____

Received from _____

herein called Buyer, the sum of _____ Dollars $_____

evidenced by cash ☐, cashier's check ☐, or _____ ☐, personal check ☐ payable to _____

_____, to be held uncashed until acceptance of this offer, as deposit on account of purchase price of

_____ Dollars $_____

for the purchase of property, situated in _____, County of _____, California,

described as follows:

1. Buyer will deposit in escrow with _____ the balance of purchase price as follows:

_____

_____

_____

_____

_____

_____

_____

_____

_____

_____

_____

_____

_____

_____

_____

_____

_____

_____

_____

_____

Set forth above any terms and conditions of a factual nature applicable to this sale, such as financing, prior sale of other property, the matter of structural pest control inspection, repairs and personal property to be included in the sale.

2. Deposit will ☐ will not ☐ be increased by $_____ to $_____ within _____ days of acceptance of this offer.

3. Buyer does ☐ does not ☐ intend to occupy subject property as his residence.

4. The following supplements are incorporated as part of this agreement:

Other

☐ Structural Pest Control Certification Agreement   ☐ Occupancy Agreement   ☐ _____

☐ Special Studies Zone Disclosure   ☐ VA Amendment   ☐ _____

☐ Flood Insurance Disclosure   ☐ FHA Amendment   ☐ _____

5. Buyer and Seller shall deliver signed instructions to the escrow holder within _____ days from Seller's acceptance which shall provide for closing within _____ days from Seller's acceptance. Escrow fees to be paid as follows:

_____

6. Buyer and Seller acknowledge receipt of a copy of this page, which constitutes Page 1 of _____ Pages.

Buyer _____   Seller _____

Buyer _____   Seller _____

A REAL ESTATE BROKER IS THE PERSON QUALIFIED TO ADVISE ON REAL ESTATE. IF YOU DESIRE LEGAL ADVICE CONSULT YOUR ATTORNEY.

THIS STANDARDIZED DOCUMENT FOR USE IN SIMPLE TRANSACTIONS HAS BEEN APPROVED BY THE CALIFORNIA ASSOCIATION OF REALTORS® IN FORM ONLY. NO REPRESENTATION IS MADE AS TO APPROVAL OF SUPPLEMENTS NOT PUBLISHED BY CAR, THE LEGAL VALIDITY OF ANY PROVISION, OR THE ADEQUACY OF ANY PROVISION IN ANY SPECIFIC TRANSACTION. IT SHOULD NOT BE USED IN COMPLEX TRANSACTIONS OR WITH EXTENSIVE RIDERS OR ADDITIONS.

REPRINTED BY PERMISSION CALIFORNIA ASSOCIATION OF REALTORS®. ENDORSEMENT NOT IMPLIED

Copyright© California Association of Realtors® (Revised 1978), 1984)   FORM D-11-1

Exhibit 19.1

REAL ESTATE PURCHASE CONTRACT AND RECEIPT FOR DEPOSIT

The following terms and conditions are hereby incorporated in and made a part of Buyer's Offer

7.   Title is to be free of liens, encumbrances, easements, restrictions, rights and conditions of record or known to Seller, other than the following: (a) Current property taxes, (b) covenants, conditions, restrictions, and public utility easements of record, if any, provided the same do not adversely affect the continued use of the property for the purposes for which it is presently being used, unless reasonably disapproved by Buyer in writing within _____days of receipt of a current preliminary title report furnished at _____expense, and (c) _____

Seller shall furnish Buyer at _____expense a standard California Land Title Association policy issued by _____Company, showing title vested in Buyer subject only to the above. If Seller is unwilling or unable to eliminate any title matter disapproved by Buyer as above, Seller may terminate this agreement. If Seller fails to deliver title as above, Buyer may terminate this agreement; in either case, the deposit shall be returned to Buyer.

8.   Property taxes, premiums on insurance acceptable to Buyer, rents, interest, and _____ shall be pro-rated as of (a) the date of recordation of deed; or (b) _____. Any bond or assessment which is a lien shall be ____paid____ by _____. Transfer taxes, if any, shall be paid by _____.
                                                    assumed

9.   Possession shall be delivered to Buyer (a) on close of escrow, or (b) not later than _____days after close of escrow or (c) _____

10.   Unless otherwise designated in the escrow instructions of Buyer, title shall vest as follows: _____
_____

(The manner of taking title may have significant legal and tax consequences. Therefore, give this matter serious consideration.)

11.   If Broker is a participant of a Board multiple listing service ("MLS"), the Broker is authorized to report the sale, its price, terms, and financing for the information, publication, dissemination, and use of the authorized Board members.

12.   If Buyer fails to complete said purchase as herein provided by reason of any default of Buyer, Seller shall be released from his obligation to sell the property to Buyer and may proceed against Buyer upon any claim or remedy which he may have in law or equity; provided, however, that by placing their initials here Buyer: (   ) Seller: (   ) agree that Seller shall retain the deposit as his liquidated damages. If the described property is a dwelling with no more than four units, one of which the Buyer intends to occupy as his residence, Seller shall retain as liquidated damages the deposit actually paid, or an amount therefrom, not more than 3% of the purchase price and promptly return any excess to Buyer.

13.   If the only controversy or claim between the parties arises out of or relates to the disposition of the Buyer's deposit, such controversy or claim shall at the election of the parties be decided by arbitration. Such arbitration shall be determined in accordance with the Rules of the American Arbitration Association, and judgment upon the award rendered by the Arbitrator(s) may be entered in any court having jurisdiction thereof. The provisions of Code of Civil Procedure Section 1283.05 shall be applicable to such arbitration.

14.   In any action or proceeding arising out of this agreement, the prevailing party shall be entitled to reasonable attorney's fees and costs.

15.   Time is of the essence. All modification or extensions shall be in writing signed by the parties.

16.   This constitutes an offer to purchase the described property. Unless acceptance is signed by Seller and the signed copy delivered to Buyer, in person or by mail to the address below, within _____days, this offer shall be deemed revoked and the deposit shall be returned. Buyer acknowledges receipt of a copy hereof.

Real Estate Broker _____   Buyer _____

By _____   Buyer _____

Address _____   Address _____

Telephone _____   Telephone _____

ACCEPTANCE

The undersigned Seller accepts and agrees to sell the property on the above terms and conditions. Seller has employed _____

as Broker(s) and agrees to pay for services the sum of _____Dollars ($_____), payable as follows: (a) On recordation of the deed or other evidence of title, or (b) if completion of sale is prevented by default of Seller, upon Seller's default or (c) if completion of sale is prevented by default of Buyer, only if and when Seller collects damages from Buyer, by suit or otherwise and then in an amount not less than one-half of the damages recovered, but not to exceed the above fee, after first deducting title and escrow expenses and the expenses of collection, if any. In any action between Broker and Seller arising out of this agreement, the prevailing party shall be entitled to reasonable attorney's fees and costs. The undersigned acknowledges receipt of a copy and authorizes Broker(s) to deliver a signed copy to Buyer.

Dated _____ Telephone _____   Seller _____

Address _____   Seller _____

Broker(s) agree to the foregoing. Broker _____ Broker _____

Dated _____ By _____   Dated _____ By _____

To order, contact—California Association of Realtors®
525 S. Virgil Ave., Los Angeles, California 90020
Copyright© California Association of Realtors® (Revised 1984)   FORM D-11-2

Page _____ of _____ Pages

Exhibit 19.2

COUNTER OFFER

THIS IS INTENDED TO BE A LEGALLY BINDING AGREEMENT – READ IT CAREFULLY.
CALIFORNIA ASSOCIATION OF REALTORS® (CAR) STANDARD FORM

This is a counter offer to the: ☐ Real Estate Purchase Contract and Receipt for Deposit, ☐ Mobile Home Purchase Contract and Receipt for Deposit, ☐ Business Purchase Contract and Receipt for Deposit, ☐ Other _____

dated _____, 19___, on property known as: _____

in which _____ is referred to as Buyer

and _____ is referred to as Seller.

Seller accepts all of the terms and conditions in the above designated agreement with the following changes or amendments:

_____
_____
_____
_____
_____
_____
_____
_____
_____
_____
_____
_____
_____
_____
_____

The Seller reserves the right to continue to offer the herein described property for sale and accept any offer acceptable to Seller at any time prior to personal receipt by Seller or _____, Seller's authorized agent, of a copy of this counter offer, duly accepted and signed by Buyer. "Accept," as used herein, includes delivery in person, by mail, or by facsimile.

Unless this counter offer is accepted on or before _____, 19___ at _____AM/PM, it shall be deemed revoked and deposit shall be returned to the Buyer. Seller's acceptance of another offer shall revoke this counter offer. This counter offer and any supplement, addendum, or modification relating hereto, including any photocopy or facsimile thereof, may be executed in two or more counterparts, all of which shall constitute one and the same writing.

Receipt of a copy is acknowledged.

Date _____ 19_____ Seller _____

Time _____ Seller _____

☐ The undersigned Buyer accepts the above counter offer, **OR**
☐ The undersigned Buyer accepts the above counter offer with the following changes or amendments:

Unless the following changes or amendments are accepted and a copy duly accepted and signed by Seller is personally delivered to Buyer or _____, the agent obtaining the offer on or before _____, 19___ at _____AM/PM, it shall be deemed revoked and deposit shall be returned to Buyer. Receipt of a copy is acknowledged.

_____
_____
_____
_____

Date _____ 19_____ Buyer _____

Time _____ Buyer _____

Receipt of signed copy on _____, 19___ at _____AM/PM, by Seller _____ (Initials)

or Seller's authorized Agent _____ (Initials) is acknowledged.

THE FOLLOWING IS REQUIRED ONLY IF BUYER HAS MADE CHANGES OR AMENDMENTS ABOVE:
Seller accepts Buyer's changes or amendments to Seller's counter offer and agrees to sell on the above terms and conditions.
Seller acknowledges receipt of a copy and authorizes Broker(s) to deliver a signed copy to Buyer.

Date _____ 19_____ Seller _____

Time _____ Seller _____

THIS STANDARDIZED DOCUMENT FOR USE IN SIMPLE TRANSACTIONS HAS BEEN APPROVED BY THE CALIFORNIA ASSOCIATION OF REALTORS® IN FORM ONLY. NO REPRESENTATION IS MADE AS TO THE APPROVAL OF THE FORM OF ANY SUPPLEMENTS NOT CURRENTLY PUBLISHED BY THE CALIFORNIA ASSOCIATION OF REALTORS® OR THE LEGAL VALIDITY OR ADEQUACY OF ANY PROVISION IN ANY SPECIFIC TRANSACTION. IT SHOULD NOT BE USED IN COMPLEX TRANSACTIONS OR WITH EXTENSIVE RIDERS OR ADDITIONS.

A REAL ESTATE BROKER IS THE PERSON QUALIFIED TO ADVISE ON REAL ESTATE TRANSACTIONS. IF YOU DESIRE LEGAL OR TAX ADVICE, CONSULT AN APPROPRIATE PROFESSIONAL.

This form is available for use by the entire real estate industry. The use of this form is not intended to identify the user as a REALTOR®. REALTOR® is a registered collective membership mark which may be used only by real estate licensees who are members of the NATIONAL ASSOCIATION OF REALTORS® and who subscribe to its Code of Ethics.

REPRINTED BY PERMISSION CALIFORNIA ASSOCIATION OF REALTORS® . ENDORSEMENT NOT IMPLIED

————— OFFICE USE ONLY —————
Reviewed by Broker or Designee
Date

Copyright® 1986, 1987, CALIFORNIA ASSOCIATION OF REALTORS®
525 South Virgil Avenue, Los Angeles, California 90020
REVISED 4/89

CO-14

Exhibit 20

RELEASE OF CONTRACT

THIS IS INTENDED TO BE A LEGALLY BINDING CONTRACT. READ IT CAREFULLY.
CALIFORNIA ASSOCIATION OF REALTORS® STANDARD FORM

The undersigned Buyer and Seller, the parties to that certain: ☐ Real Estate Purchase Contract and Receipt for Deposit, ☐ Mobile Home Purchase Contract and Receipt for Deposit, ☐ Business Purchase Contract and Receipt for Deposit, ☐ other

_____

dated _____, 19_____, covering the following described property:

_____

_____

_____

_____

_____

_____

_____

_____

_____

_____

hereby mutually release each other from any and all claims, actions or demands which each may have up to the date of this Agreement

against the other by reason of said Contract.

It is the intent of this Agreement that all rights and obligations arising out of said Contract are declared null and void.

_____holding
(Name of Broker or Escrow Holder)

the deposit under the terms of said Contract is hereby directed and instructed to disburse said deposit in the following manner:

$_____ TO _____

$_____ TO _____

$_____ TO _____

$_____ TO _____

Dated_____   Dated_____

Buyer_____   Seller_____

Buyer_____   Seller_____

Dated_____   Dated_____

Broker_____   Broker_____

By_____   By_____

NO REPRESENTATION IS MADE AS TO THE LEGAL VALIDITY OF ANY PROVISION OR THE ADEQUACY OF ANY PROVISION IN ANY SPECIFIC TRANSACTION. A REAL ESTATE BROKER IS THE PERSON QUALIFIED TO ADVISE ON REAL ESTATE OR BUSINESS TRANSACTIONS. IF YOU DESIRE LEGAL ADVICE CONSULT YOUR ATTORNEY.

To order, contact California Association of Realtors®
525 S. Virgil Avenue, Los Angeles, California 90020
Copyright© 1974, 1978, California Association of Realtors® (Revised 1984)   FORM RC-11   TT-L5-FG

REPRINTED BY PERMISSION CALIFORNIA ASSOCIATION OF REALTORS®. ENDORSEMENT NOT IMPLIED

Exhibit 21

CLOSING PROCEDURES / ESCROW CHECK FORM

PROPERTY _____ PURCHASE PRICE _____
DEPOSIT _____ MLS # _____ DATE SOLD ___ CONTROL # ___

SELLERS _____ **BUYERS** _____
Address _____ Address _____
City _____ City _____
Res. Ph. _____ Bus. Ph. _____ Res. Ph. _____ Bus. Ph. _____
Source & Fee _____ Source _____

LISTING BROKER _____ **SELLING BROKER** _____
Address _____ Address _____
City _____ City _____
SALESPERSON _____ SALESPERSON _____
Bus. Ph. _____ Res. Ph. _____ Bus. Ph. _____ Res. Ph. _____

ESCROW
TITLE COMPANY _____   Date Opened _____
Address _____   Contract COE Date _____
Phone # _____ Escrow # _____   Estimated COE Date _____
Officer _____ Sect'y _____   Prelims Received _____

FINANCING
LENDER _____   Type _____
Address _____   Appraisal Amt. _____
Phone # _____ Points _____   Date Submitted _____
Representative _____ Res. Ph. _____   Date Approved _____

DEMAND
EXISTING LENDER(S) _____   Date Ordered _____
Address _____   Date Received _____

TERMITE
COMPANY _____   Date Ordered _____
Address _____   Work Auth. Date _____
Phone _____ Contract _____   Clearance _____

INSURANCE
COMPANY _____ Agent _____   Date Ordered _____
Address _____ Phone _____   Date Received _____

SIGN OFF
COMMISSION RECEIVED _____ $ _____   Sellers _____

MOVING DATES
COMMISSIONS PAID _____ $ _____   Buyers _____
_____ $ _____   Sellers _____
_____ $ _____   Buyers _____

MISC.
_____ $ _____   Lock Box _____
          Key _____
          Sign _____
Date Closed _____ Client Followup _____   Client Letter _____

Exhibit 22

Form Approved
OMB NO. 63-R-1501

A.

Lawyers Title of San Francisco

a division of First American Title Guaranty Company

B. TYPE OF LOAN

1. ☐ FHA	2. ☐ FmHA	3. ☐ CONV. UNINS.
4. ☐ VA	5. ☐ CONV. INS.	
6. File Number		7. Loan Number

8. Mortgage Insurance Case Number

C. NOTE: *This form is furnished to give you a statement of actual settlement costs. Amounts paid to and by the settlement agent are shown. Items marked "(p.o.c.)" were paid outside the closing; they are shown here for informational purposes and are not included in the totals.*

D. NAME OF BORROWER:

E. NAME OF SELLER:

F. NAME OF LENDER:

G. PROPERTY LOCATION:

H. SETTLEMENT AGENT:

I. SETTLEMENT DATE:

PLACE OF SETTLEMENT:

J. SUMMARY OF BORROWER'S TRANSACTION		K. SUMMARY OF SELLER'S TRANSACTION	
100. GROSS AMOUNT DUE FROM BORROWER:		**400. GROSS AMOUNT DUE TO SELLER:**	
101. Contract sales price		401. Contract sales price	
102. Personal property		402. Personal property	
103. Settlement charges to borrower *(line 1400)*		403.	
104.		404.	
105.		405.	
Adjustments for items paid by seller in advance.		*Adjustments for items paid by seller in advance.*	
106. City/town taxes to		406. City/town taxes to	
107. County taxes to		407. County taxes to	
108. Assessments to		408. Assessments to	
109.		409.	
110.		410.	
111.		411.	
112.		412.	
120. GROSS AMOUNT DUE FROM BORROWER:		**420. GROSS AMOUNT DUE TO SELLER:**	
200. AMOUNTS PAID BY OR IN BEHALF OF BORROWER:		**500. REDUCTIONS IN AMOUNT DUE TO SELLER:**	
201. Deposit or earnest money		501. Excess deposit *(see instructions)*	
202. Principal amount of new loan(s)		502. Settlement charges to seller *(line 1400)*	
203. Existing loan(s) taken subject to		503. Existing loan(s) taken subject to	
204.		504. Payoff of first mortgage loan	
205.		505. Payoff of second mortgage loan	
206.		506.	
207.		507.	
208.		508.	
209.		509.	
Adjustments for items unpaid by seller.		*Adjustments for items unpaid by seller.*	
210. City/town taxes to		510. City/town taxes to	
211. County taxes to		511. County taxes to	
212. Assessments to		512. Assessments to	
213.		513.	
214.		514.	
215.		515.	
216.		516.	
217.		517.	
218.		518.	
219.		519.	
220. TOTAL PAID BY/FOR BORROWER:		**520. TOTAL REDUCTION AMOUNT DUE SELLER:**	
300. CASH AT SETTLEMENT FROM/TO BORROWER:		**600. CASH AT SETTLEMENT TO/FROM SELLER:**	
301. Gross amount due from borrower *(line 120)*		601. Gross amount due to seller *(line 420)*	
302. Less amounts paid by/for borrowers *(line 220)*		602. Less reductions in amount due seller *(line 520)*	
303. CASH (☐ FROM) (☐ TO) BORROWER:		**603. CASH (☐ TO) (☐ FROM) SELLER:**	

Page 1

Exhibit 23.1

L. SETTLEMENT CHARGES		
700. TOTAL SALES/BROKER'S COMMISSION based on price $ @ %	**PAID FROM BORROWER'S FUNDS AT SETTLEMENT**	**PAID FROM SELLER'S FUNDS AT SETTLEMENT**
Division of Commission (line 700) as follows:		
701. $ to		
702. $ to		
703. Commission paid at Settlement		
704.		
800. ITEMS PAYABLE IN CONNECTION WITH LOAN		
801. Loan Origination Fee %		
802. Loan Discount %		
803. Appraisal Fee to		
804. Credit Report to		
805. Lender's Inspection Fee		
806. Mortgage Insurance Application Fee to		
807. Assumption Fee		
808.		
809.		
810.		
811.		
900. ITEMS REQUIRED BY LENDER TO BE PAID IN ADVANCE		
901. Interest from to @ $ /day		
902. Mortgage Insurance Premium for months to		
903. Hazard Insurance Premium for years to		
904. years to		
905.		
1000. RESERVES DEPOSITED WITH LENDER		
1001. Hazard Insurance months @ $ per month		
1002. Mortgage Insurance months @ $ per month		
1003. City property taxes months @ $ per month		
1004. County property taxes months @ $ per month		
1005. Annual assessments months @ $ per month		
1006. months @ $ per month		
1007. months @ $ per month		
1008. months @ $ per month		
1100. TITLE CHARGES		
1101. Settlement or closing fee to		
1102. Abstract or title search to		
1103. Title examination to		
1104. Title insurance binder to		
1105. Document preparation to		
1106. Notary fees to		
1107. Attorney's fees to		
(includes above items numbers:		
1108. Title insurance to		
(includes above items numbers:		
1109. Lender's coverage $		
1110. Owner's coverage $		
1111.		
1112.		
1113.		
1200. GOVERNMENT RECORDING AND TRANSFER CHARGES		
1201. Recording fees. Deed $: Mortgage $: Release $		
1202. City county tax/stamps: Deed $: Mortage $		
1203. State tax/stamps: Deed $: Mortage $		
1204.		
1205.		
1300. ADDITIONAL SETTLEMENT CHARGES		
1301. Survey to		
1302. Pest inspection to		
1303.		
1304.		
1305.		
1400. TOTAL SETTLEMENT CHARGES (enter on lines 103, Section J and 502, Section K)		

FORM 5000-LT (5/83)

Exhibit 23.2

190 *Closing the Sale and Escrow Procedure*

BUYER'S AFFIDAVIT

That Buyer is acquiring property for use as a residence and that sales price does not exceed $300,000.

CALIFORNIA ASSOCIATION OF REALTORS® STANDARD FORM

(FOREIGN INVESTMENT IN REAL PROPERTY TAX ACT)

1. I am the transferee (buyer) of real property located at _____

_____ .

2. The sales price (total of all consideration in the sale) does not exceed $300,000.

3. I am acquiring the real property for use as a residence. I have definite plans that I or a member of my family will reside in it for at least 50 percent of the number of days it will be in use during each of the two 12 month periods following the transfer of the property to me. I understand that the members of my family that are included in the last sentence are my brothers, sisters, ancestors, descendents, or spouse.

4. I am making this affidavit in order to establish an exemption from withholding a portion of the sales price of the property under Internal Revenue Code Section 1445.

5. I understand that if the information in this affidavit is not correct, I may be liable to the Internal Revenue Service for up to 10 percent of the sales price of the property, plus interest and penalties.

Under penalties of perjury, I declare that the statements above are true, correct and complete.

Date _____   Signature _____

Typed or Printed Name _____

IMPORTANT NOTICE:

An affidavit should be signed by each individual transferee to whom it applies. Before you sign, any questions relating to the legal sufficiency of this form, or to whether it applies to a particular transaction, or to the definition of any of the terms used, should be referred to an attorney, a certified public accountant, or other professional tax advisor, or to the Internal Revenue Service.

To order, contact—California Association of Realtors®
525 S. Virgil Avenue, Los Angeles, California 90020
Copyright© 1985, California Association of Realtors®

FORM AB-11

REPRINTED BY PERMISSION CALIFORNIA ASSOCIATION OF REALTORS®. ENDORSEMENT NOT IMPLIED

TT-L5-FG

Exhibit 24

1. The strategy for obtaining the offer suggests that you:

   (A) Wait for a buying signal before starting to close
   (B) Have your customer consider several properties at one time
   (C) Start closing from the very first customer contact
   (D) Have your buyers underbid the listed price

2. To avoid telling the seller the offering price over the telephone, it is best for you to:

   (A) Request an appointment by mail
   (B) Suggest that the offer is better than their asking price
   (C) Have a third party, who has no knowledge of the offer amount, arrange the appointment
   (D) Advise seller he or she must wait

3. The advantages of the assumption close include all of the following *except*:

   (A) It does not matter if the buyer is qualified
   (B) It is usable in every selling situation
   (C) It uses gentle persuasion
   (D) It uses low pressure tactics

4. Commingling of a principal's funds is:

   (A) An illegal act
   (B) The placing of a principal's funds in the licensee's personal account
   (C) The unlawful appropriation and use of a client's funds
   (D) Both A and B

5. California Real Estate Law allows licensees to do the following with buyer's funds submitted on an offer:

   (A) Give it all to the seller
   (B) Place it in the broker's trust account
   (C) Place it in escrow
   (D) Any of the above

6. Standard coverage title insurance protects against:

   (A) Zoning ordinances
   (B) Personal liability
   (C) Liens of record
   (D) Unrecorded easements

7. Which of the following is *not* true regarding a valid escrow?

   (A) Escrow is required by law
   (B) Escrow instructions are, in effect, a contract
   (C) It requires competent parties
   (D) It involves mutual agreement as to terms and conditions

8. Responsibilities of the escrowholder include all of the following *except*:

   (A) Ordering a preliminary title report
   (B) Negotiating with the parties and offering advice
   (C) Computing closing costs
   (D) Requesting closing funds from buyer

9. The buyer's remedy of specific performance for breach of contract by the seller would most likely be based on the fact that:

   (A) "Time is of the essence" was written in the contract
   (B) Each parcel of property is unique
   (C) Buyer did not meet escrow provisions
   (D) Seller did not meet escrow provisions

10. The deposit receipt becomes a legal and binding contract when:

    (A) The offer is accompanied by a deposit
    (B) The offer is accepted by the offeree
    (C) The earnest money deposit is accepted by the offeree
    (D) The acceptance of the offer is communicated to and acknowledged by the offeror

Chapter 11
Financing the Sale

REAL ESTATE AND THE MONEY MARKET

Financing is one of the most important factors in the real estate industry. Understanding real estate finance and effectively applying this knowledge to each transaction can often make the difference between failure and success of the sale.

Home Purchases Require Financing   For most people no other single transaction involves more money than the purchase of a home. Very few people can afford such a purchase without long-term financing.

The Money Supply   Money is a commodity, and the economic laws of supply and demand affect its cost and availability. The availability of money at affordable rates is vital to real estate activity.

The General Money Market   The licensee should have an understanding of the function and operation of the general money market which comprises the money, capital, and mortgage markets, and their interrelationship with governmental institutions, such as the U.S. Treasury and the Federal Reserve System.

Money Markets. This refers to the short-term credit and investment markets (less than one year maturities). Examples include 30, 60, and 90 day Treasury bills (T-bills), bankers' acceptances, federal funds, negotiable certificates of deposit, commercial paper, and Eurodollars.

Capital Markets. These trade longer-term (one year or more) securities (notes and bonds), corporate stock, and other instruments. Examples include U.S. Treasury notes and bonds, U.S. government agency bonds, state and local government bonds, corporate bonds, corporate stocks, and real estate mortgages.

Mortgage Market. The mortgage market is a segment of the capital market, which trades mortgage instruments of relatively long-term maturity and greater risk. Other capital markets compete with real estate for available money.

THE SOURCE OF FUNDS: SAVINGS

The ultimate source of all mortgage money is money which is available for loan because it is in the keeping of the lending party or institution, i.e., savings.

Types of Savings   There are two sources of savings, *personal* and *business*.

Individual Savings. Individuals put money into savings accounts, life insurance, pension funds, etc.

Business Savings. Businesses have savings in the form of corporate reserves, corporate pension funds, etc., as well as bank accounts.

Methods of Investment   There are two basic methods by which savings are invested in the real estate mortgage market:

Directly. Savings may be invested by the saver directly in mortgages, or by the seller who personally extends credit to the buyer for all or part of the purchase price.

Indirectly. Savers' deposits in banks, savings and loans, life insurance companies, mutual savings banks, and other financial intermediaries may be invested by those entities in the real estate mortgage market. These intermediaries may be classified as institutional lenders or noninstitutional lenders.

INSTITUTIONAL LENDERS

Institutional lenders are defined as financial depositories or intermediaries which pool depositors' money and invest it in real estate loans. They include banks, savings and loans, and insurance companies.

Savings and Loan Associations (S&Ls) Since their introduction, S&Ls have specialized in attracting savings for investment in real estate loans. They generally account for about half the real estate lending in California.

Organization. A savings and loan may be either a stock company or a mutual organization, and licensed or chartered by the state (stock or mutual companies) or the federal authorities.

Lending Characteristics. Savings and loans primarily deal in conventional loans on single family residences, with relatively high loan-to-value ratios. Interest rates, term, amount of loan, and points and fees vary, and are generally higher than those of other institutional lenders. S&Ls usually base the security of the loan on the property's value, not on the borrower's personal credit.

High Loan-to-Value Ratio. S&Ls usually lend 80% of sales price or appraised value, whichever is less. On 90% to 95% loans, taxes and insurance must be impounded.

Life Insurance Companies Although their primary business is to sell insurance, life insurance companies can market almost any type of real estate loan.

Organization. Life insurance companies may be either stock companies or mutual companies. They are licensed by the state in which they incorporate their lending activities, and are governed by both their state of incorporation and the states in which they do business.

Lending Characteristics. Insurance companies generally prefer long-term loans on large developments or other income producing property. They are limited to medium loan-to-value ratios, and usually have lower interest rates than the other institutional lenders. They are often represented and serviced by loan correspondents or mortgage companies.

Commercial Banks Commercial banks can make almost any type of loan on almost any type of reasonable collateral, as well as unsecured personal loans.

Organization. Commercial banks are stock corporations that operate under a charter or license from either state or federal authorities.

Lending Characteristics. Banks concentrate primarily on high interest, short-term loans to businesses, in which previous customer relationship is an important consideration. They generally prefer short-term construction or interim loans but make some residential mortgage loans. For most borrowers they usually require strong collateral or security. Interest rates are in the medium range of the marketplace.

Equity Loans. In response to the federal Tax Reform Act of 1986 and the Revenue Act of 1987, banks are marketing "lines of credit" corresponding to the federal tax classification of "home equity indebtedness." (See Chapter 13)

Mutual Savings Banks These are mutual companies with no capital stock or stockholders; depositors share in the bank's net earnings. They are found mainly in the northeastern United States, but state laws permit them to make FHA or VA loans anywhere in the country.

NONINSTITUTIONAL LENDERS

There are several sources of loans other than financial institutions. These lenders are not governed or regulated by state or federal authorities as closely as institutional lenders.

Mortgage Companies The mortgage companies are primarily representatives of the ultimate sources of money, such as life insurance companies, savings banks, trust or pension funds, or private parties. They are essentially money brokers who may or may not service the loans they originate.

Organization. Mortgage companies may take any legal form of business organization, such as a sole proprietorship, partnership, or corporation, and are the least regulated of California lenders. In California a real estate broker's license is required.

Representing Lenders. Many mortgage companies do not lend their own money, but negotiate loans for other institutions such as insurance companies, mutual savings banks, pension funds, and even for some individuals. However, some companies, called mortgage bankers, do make loans of their own funds. These loans are usually those readily salable in the secondary mortgage market.

Locating Funds. Mortgage companies seek out sources of funds, institutional and private, and act as "correspondents" in making loans.

Servicing. Mortgage companies not only initiate and process loan applications, they often service those loans.

Construction Loans. Mortgage companies also package permanent or "take-out" loans in combination with construction loans.

Market Activities. They arrange for loan sales in the secondary mortgage market with or without "warehousing." Warehoused loans are those assembled and held until the portfolio is complete before being sold to an investor.

Secondary Financing. Mortgage companies frequently arrange junior or "secondary" financing, usually from private sources.

Private Lenders Individuals may invest their savings directly in real estate loans, work through a mortgage company or a loan broker, or extend credit to the purchaser of their home based on their equity in the home.

Freedom of Choice. Private lenders fill some important gaps in the loan market. They often invest in higher-risk junior loans with relatively high interest rates; short-term, 3 to 5 year loans; partially amortized, balloon payment loans; and single-family residential loans in familiar locations.

Unregulated. Private lenders are not limited by any licensing or charter requirements.

Pension and Endowment Funds A great deal of money is held in pension funds and university endowments. Within limits imposed by their needs for safety, these represent a growing source of real estate financing. They generally operate through correspondents, mortgage companies, etc.

Bank Trust Departments Real estate funds are also potentially available from the trust departments of commercial banks. Under supervision of the trustees, these funds are often invested in first trust deeds for the administered estate.

GOVERNMENT PARTICIPATION

Three major sources of federal and state government-assisted financing of residential loans are the FHA, VA, and Cal-Vet programs.

Federal Housing Administration (FHA) The FHA was created by the National Housing Act of 1934 to insure loans made by approved financial institutions for home purchase, construction, or repair. Its programs are:

Title I. This program insures loans for the purchase of mobilehomes, and up to $15,000 for the repair, alteration, or improvement of a single-family home.

Title II (FHA 203b). This is the "FHA loan" most commonly encountered in real estate practice. It insures loans for the purchase or construction of 1 to 4 unit dwellings for the general public.

☐ *Maximum Loan Insurance.* For a single family home, the maximum is $124,875 (as of 1990). A nonoccupant mortgagor is limited to a 75% loan-to-value ratio. Different counties have differing loan insurance maximums. There is no maximum purchase price.

□ *Downpayment*. FHA loans are noted for their low downpayments, which are calculated as the sum of:

- 3% of first $25,000 of appraisal, plus
- 5% of excess over $25,000 of appraisal, plus non-recurring closing costs, plus
- 100% of selling price over appraisal.

□ *Interest Rate*. Interest is now negotiable (not set by FHA). If the loan is assumed, the interest rate remains at the original rate.

□ *Maximum Term*. 30 years

□ *Insurance*. Mutual Mortgage Insurance Premium (MMI, MIP) is now paid to FHA in advance in one lump sum, but may be added to the loan amount. Rates range from 2.34% to 3.8% depending on the term of the loan and the amount financed.

□ *Loan Fees and Charges*. Maximum 1% origination fee may be paid by borrower. Discount points and interest rates are negotiable. Prepayment penalty is not allowed. Impounds are required.

□ *Assumption*. All FHA loans are assumable, with no increase in interest rates or points charged.

Title II (FHA 245). The graduated payment mortgage program insures loans for owner-occupied single family residences and permits smaller initial monthly payments to help buyers qualify. Monthly payments gradually increase over the first 5-10 years until a constant level is reached. Interest is partially deferred, resulting in negative amortization.

Title II (FHA 234). The condominium housing program insures loans for the purchase or construction of condominiums. Terms and conditions are similar to FHA 203.

U.S. Department of Veterans Affairs (VA or GI Loans) Except in rare circumstances, the USDVA is not a direct lender, but guarantees the lender against partial loss caused by default of a veteran borrower on loans for a home (1 to 4 units), mobilehome with or without site, or a condominium.

Procedure. The GI loan program is administered by the U.S. Department of Veterans Affairs, formerly the Veterans Administration. The USDVA appraiser estimates value and issues a "Certificate of Reasonable Value" (CRV). The loan is then made by an approved lender.

Amount. The guarantee limit is 60% of the loan up to $46,000. This allows a qualified veteran to purchase up to approximately a $184,000 residence with no downpayment.

Eligibility. Minimum service requirement is 90 days in wartime (World War II or Korean War), or 181 days in peacetime or after January 1955.

Terms. Terms are partly set by VA regulations and partly left up to lender.

☐ *Maximum Loan Amount*. Loan cannot exceed CRV; vet pays excess in cash. There is no maximum purchase price.

☐ *Downpayment*. No downpayment is required by the USDVA except excess above CRV; however, the lender may require one.

☐ *Interest*. Interest must remain at the original loan rate except on adjustable rate mortgages (ARMs). Payments may be amortized or on a graduated payment plan.

☐ *Secondary Financing*. This is allowed if certain conditions are met; subject to USDVA review.

☐ *Loan Term*. Maximum repayment periods are:

House/condominium.........................30 years, 32 days

Double wide mobilehome.................20 years, 32 days

Single wide mobilehome...................15 years, 32 days

☐ *Loan Fees and Charges*. Seller must pay discount points, except on construction loans or refinancing. No prepayment penalty is allowed. Impounds are required.

☐ *Resale*. The loan may be taken over by anyone. If it is assumed the vet remains liable unless released from liability. If taken subject to, vet remains primarily liable.

☐ *Deficiency*. USDVA can make a claim against the vet even if the lender cannot under the California law.

Cal-Vet Under the California Veterans Farm and Home Purchase Act, the state sells bonds to raise funds to help veterans purchase a "farm or home," including mobilehome, townhouse, or condominium. The program is administered by the California Department of Veterans Affairs (DVA).

Eligibility. The veteran must be California born or a resident when entering service, and honorably discharged, with a minimum 90 days active duty in an authorized war, campaign, or expedition. Unremarried spouses of Cal-Vets killed in action, prisoners of war, or missing in action are eligible. Eligibility expires 25 years after discharge except that for prisoners of war, disabled veterans, and veterans wounded in action, eligibility lasts 30 years.

Title. The security device used for Cal-Vet financing is the land contract. The seller conveys title to the state and the state resells the property to the veteran under a land contract (conditional sales contract). The state holds title until the loan is repaid, and during that time certain restrictions on sale or transfer apply.

Terms. Except for the vesting of title under the land contract, terms are generally similar to other programs.

☐ *Maximum Loan*. Amount depends on the type of property.

    Home/townhouse/condominium $125,000

    Mobilehome: On owner's lot $90,000

                     In mobile park $70,000

    Working farm $200,000

☐ *Junior Loans*. Secondary financing is allowed, with DVA approval.

☐ *Purchase Price*. There is no maximum.

☐ *Downpayment*. Amount depends on the type of property, and its value.

    3% for home of $35,000 or less, or 5% on homes over $35,000

    5% for a farm

    100% of excess of purchase price over appraisal

☐ *Terms*. Interest rate and monthly payment are variable.

☐ *Prepayment Penalty*. Six months' interest may be charged on the amount prepaid in excess of 20% of the original loan amount, if prepaid during the first 5 years.

☐ *Insurance*. Life and disability insurance must be applied for by the veteran, and premiums are included in the monthly payment. Cal-Vet is the beneficiary for the unpaid balance.

☐ *Impounds*. Impounds are required for taxes and insurance.

☐ *Repayment*. Loan term is usually 25 years but cannot exceed 40 years.

THE SECONDARY MORTGAGE MARKET

The secondary mortgage market refers to the "market" where previously originated senior trust deeds and mortgages are bought and sold at a discount to obtain new funds to make new loans at current rates of interest. This is in contrast to the *primary* mortgage market, which *originates* trust deeds and mortgages, both senior (first) and junior (second, third, etc.).

Senior and Junior Financing   Senior or primary *financing* involves first trust deeds and first mortgages. Junior or secondary financing refers to second trust deeds and second mortgages, as well as those claims recorded after the second (thirds, fourths, etc.).

Secondary Mortgage Market Institutions Buyers include the Federal National Mortgage Association (FNMA or "Fannie Mae"), Federal Home Loan Mortgage Corporation (FHLMC or "Freddie Mac"), and Government National Mortgage Association (GNMA or "Ginnie Mae").

Federal National Mortgage Association. FNMA or "Fannie Mae" is the leading secondary mortgage market buyer of mortgages and trust deeds. It purchases approved existing FHA, VA, and conventional loans.

☐ *Origin.* FNMA was created as a government-owned corporation by the National Housing Act of 1934 to provide liquidity in the secondary mortgage market.

☐ *Present Structure.* This government-owned corporation was converted to an independent private corporation in 1968. Its stock is listed on the New York Stock Exchange.

Government National Mortgage Association. GNMA or "Ginnie Mae" is a federally-owned agency which purchases low-income housing loans and other special purpose government backed programs from approved real estate lenders.

☐ *Origin.* The Housing and Urban Development Act of 1968 created GNMA to assume some of FNMA's previous functions, notably management and liquidation of government-owned housing, and providing special assistance for federally-aided housing programs.

☐ *Function.* GNMA guarantees pass-through securities authorized by FNMA when the packages of securities are backed by FHA, VA, and the Farmers Home Administration.

Federal Home Loan Mortgage Corporation. FHLMC, or "Freddie Mac" buys conventional mortgages (not underwritten by any agency of the government) from primary lenders such as S&Ls, and then pools the mortgages and sells securities backed by the pool.

☐ *Origin.* FHLMC was established in 1970 by the Emergency Home Finance Act; it is the youngest of the three secondary market institutions. Owned by the Office of Thrift Supervision, formerly the Federal Home Loan Bank Board (FHLBB), FHLMC was established to increase credit in the secondary market by selling bonds and using the proceeds of the bond sales to purchase mortgages from member savings associations.

Uniform Practices. FHLMC and FNMA both have maximum dollar limitations for various types of loans. Loans written to conform to these standards are referred to as "conforming" loans. FNMA/FHLMC uniform instruments are encouraging uniformity of forms throughout the industry: note, deed of trust, mortgage, appraisal, residential loan application.

FINANCING INSTRUMENTS

The instruments (documents) involved in a real estate loan are the evidence of indebtedness (the note) and the security instrument (trust deed or mortgage).

Promissory Note The note is the borrower's written promise or obligation to repay a debt according to the specified terms and conditions. It is the *evidence of the debt*. The debt may be secured by real property and/or personal property.

Common Types. Notes can be classified according to their repayment schedule. The two basic types are *straight* and *installment*.

☐ *Straight Note or Interest Only.* The borrower makes periodic (usually monthly) payments of interest only, with the entire lump sum principal due at the maturity (due date) of the note.

☐ *Installment Note.* A fully or partially amortized, note is paid off in installments over the life loan.

☐ *Fully Amortized.* Each fixed payment includes principal and interest in amounts sufficient to pay off the loan in full with the last scheduled payment.

☐ *Partially Amortized.* The stated number of fixed payments of principal and interest are not adequate to pay off the full loan at maturity; therefore, a balloon payment is required on the note's due date to pay it off.

Terms. The specific provisions of promissory notes vary depending on the agreements between lender and borrower, but a note normally specifies the total amount of the loan, interest rate to be charged, precise due date, identification of the lender (payee) and borrower (payor), schedule of payments, and any special provisions such as prepayment privileges or penalties, penalties for late payments, or an acceleration clause. If the borrower fails to comply with the terms of the agreements, the loan is declared to be in *default*.

Deed of Trust The deed of trust is the instrument which pledges the property as the security or collateral for the promissory note. The effect is to create a lien on the property. Recording establishes the priority of the lien.

Compared to Mortgage. California lenders, by custom, prefer to use the trust deed instead of the mortgage contract (commonly used in many other states), because it is quicker and less expensive to foreclose in the event of default.

Terminology. In general practice, the terms "trust deed" and "mortgage" are used interchangeably even though they are distinctly different in rights and responsibilities.

Parties. There are three parties to a trust deed, the parties to the loan and an outside trustee. The borrower is called the *trustor*, the lender who is the beneficiary of the trust, and a *trustee* is the neutral third party who acts on behalf of both parties as stakeholder holding the legal title in trust.

Title. Legal title (a bare legal title, sometimes referred to as "naked title") rests in the trustee during the term of the loan, but the trustor holds equitable title and is the record owner, holding a title that is encumbered with the trust deed lien.

Foreclosure. The beneficiary may seek satisfaction or remedy for default by either a court action or a trustee's sale.

Right of Reinstatement. Regardless of foreclosure procedure, California law requires that the lender must permit the borrower to *reinstate* the loan (bring the account into good standing) at any time up to within five days prior to a scheduled foreclosure sale. (Civil Code § 2924c)

Right of Redemption. Depending on the remedy used by the lender, the trustor has various means of *redeeming* the property after defaulting.

☐ If the lender opts for a court action to remedy a default, the trustor may have an equity of redemption, a right to redeem the property.

☐ In a trustee's sale action, the trustor may *reinstate* by bringing the loan current within the three month period following the notice of default and up to five days prior to the scheduled sale. After the right of reinstatement terminates, the trustor may redeem only by paying the loan off in full. If a trustee's sale is held, the sale is final and there is no equity of redemption.

Deficiency Judgments. If the value of the security is insufficient to pay off an indebtedness, and if foreclosure is by court action, the lender may, in some situations, seek a deficiency judgment. If remedy is by trustee's sale, no deficiency judgment action is available to the lender.

Reconveyance. Upon payment in full, the lender must instruct the trustee to execute and record a "deed of reconveyance" in favor of the trustor.

Statute of Limitations. The promissory note will outlaw (expire) four years after its due date; however, the trust deed never outlaws. The trustee holds title and the lender can have the trustee sell the property to recover the unpaid balance.

Effect of Bankruptcy. When a debtor files a petition in bankruptcy, an automatic stay immediately goes into effect against all creditors of the petitioner. A stay means all foreclosure proceedings must stop immediately. Any foreclosure sale held after a petition has been filed is null and void unless the court grants the beneficiary relief from the stay.

Mortgage   The mortgage is a contract by which real property is hypothecated to secure a note, commonly used in many other states.

Parties. A mortgage has only two parties, the parties to the loan. The mortgagor is the borrower who gives the mortgage to the lender. The mortgagee is the lender who receives the mortgage from the borrower.

Title. Title remains with the mortgagor during the life of the loan.

Foreclosure. Foreclosure can only be by court action unless the mortgage contract contains a power of sale clause.

Rights of Reinstatement and Redemption. Before decree of foreclosure and at any time up to five days before a scheduled foreclosure sale, the mortgagor may reinstate at any time by bringing the loan current. After foreclosure sale, the mortgagor may have an "equity of redemption." If a deficiency judgment is possible against the defendant (mortgagor), the property is sold subject to a "right of redemption" lasting *three months* if the proceeds of the sale satisfy the secured debt with interest and costs of sale, or *one year* if the proceeds do not satisfy the debt with interest and costs of sale.

Payment in Full. The mortgagee executes and records a "satisfaction of mortgage" when the debt is fully paid.

Statute of Limitations. The mortgage note and contract both outlaw four years after the due date or date of default.

Deficiency Judgment   The lender (mortgagee or beneficiary) foreclosing in a judicial foreclosure may seek a deficiency judgment if the sale proceeds do not satisfy the debt, except that a deficiency judgment is *barred* on credit extended by a seller, and on hard money purchase money loans on owner-occupied homes of not more than 4 units.

QUALIFYING

Lenders establish their own criteria for evaluating prospective borrowers. In general, the specific criteria will involve the evaluation of the applicant's financial ability and credit history and the evaluation of the property. (See Exhibit 25, Residential Loan Application)

Borrower's Financial Ability   The borrower's financial standing is considered in terms of absolute income, relation of income to amount of loan and other obligations, and demonstrated ability to handle money.

Income. Stability and consistency of the borrower's primary full time income, generally for the past 2 to 3 years, is considered. Verification may be required. Consistent and verifiable overtime, bonus, part time, benefits, alimony and child support may be considered. Other income may include rental income, interest, stocks, and dividends.

Variables. Chapter 7 discusses qualifying in more detail. In general, a superior credit and employment record and/or a large downpayment may offset a higher expense to income ratio.

Credit History. Emphasis is placed on the applicant's ability to repay a loan. The applicant's history in the use of credit and the manner in which obligations were met are carefully evaluated.

Rejections. Reasons for negative decisions by lenders include incomplete credit application or one lacking required verifications, unfavorable credit information, temporary, irregular, or unstable employment, insufficient income for debt service, previous defaults, litigation, bankruptcy, or insolvency, unless applicant provides offsetting documentation, and new or temporary residence without demonstrated credit or employment at prior residence.

Unlawful Discrimination. The Federal Equal Credit Opportunity Act prohibits lenders from using sex, marital status, or family planning intention as a criterion of creditworthiness.

Property To insure security in the property's value over the term of the loan, the lenders also qualify the property. Lenders typically look at its location, age and condition, neighborhood (but "redlining" is prohibited), floor plan, design and materials, street design and traffic flow, access to employment, schools, shopping, and cultural activities, and harmonious land use.

Negatives. Possible negative influences are absence of normal utilities or fire and police services, exposure to excessive traffic or offensive land uses and pollutants, and presence of geological hazards, landslide, mudslide, or flood hazards.

ALTERNATIVE FINANCING METHODS

The traditional fully amortized, fixed-rate, long-term (25-30 year) mortgage pioneered by the FHA during the early 1930s now is being at least partially replaced. Lenders shy away from this type of loan during periods of tight money, high interest rates, inflation, or recession. Other methods now being utilized include the following.

Assumption of Existing Mortgage The buyer may assume primary liability for an existing loan.

Terms and Conditions. Terms may remain the same or may change, depending on the lender and type of loan. VA and FHA loans are assumable and pass on the same terms and conditions to qualified borrowers. Some fixed rate and variable rate mortgages are assumable. Read the existing mortgage agreement and seek legal advice if uncertain.

Due-on-Sale Clauses. In a mortgage or trust deed a due-on-sale clause may prohibit an assumption without the lender's consent by giving the lender the right to insist that the loan be paid off if the property changes hands.

☐ *Wellenkamp Interpretation.* In California, from 1978 to 1985, the State Supreme Court prohibited all lenders except federally chartered savings and loans from exercising the due-on-sale clause on their real estate loans, unless the lender could prove a threat to the loan security.

☐ *Garn-St. Germain Act.* This federal law, fully effective since October 15, 1985, makes all such state laws and rulings ineffective and due-on-sale clauses fully enforceable with very few exceptions.

Sale "Subject to" Existing Mortgages Property may be conveyed to the buyer with the buyer accepting title knowing that there is a mortgage lien on property, but the buyer does not personally assume the debt.

Seller's Liability. The seller remains primarily liable for any deficiency judgment which might be obtained in a judicial foreclosure.

Buyer's Liability. In the event of foreclosure, the buyer can lose only his equity in the property.

Due-on-Sale Clauses. Property can be sold "subject to" only if there is no enforceable due-on-sale clause in the mortgage instruments (e.g., FHA insured and VA guaranteed loans).

Seller Financing The seller may act as lender and carry back a first, second, or third mortgage from the buyer.

Terms. The terms and conditions are subject to seller and buyer negotiation, and exempt from usury limitations.

Flexibility. Seller financing is an advantageous alternative to an institutional loan because the seller may have less rigid qualifying requirements.

Disclosure. A seller financing disclosure statement may be required (Civil Code § 2956–2967) if an "arranger of credit" is involved (Exhibit 10, Chapter 4). An arranger of credit under this law is either:

☐ A person, other than a party to the transaction, who is involved for compensation in developing or negotiating credit terms or in any transaction or transfer of residential real property (up to 4 units) which is facilitated by the extension of credit, excluding attorneys, or

☐ A party to the transaction who is either a real estate licensee or an attorney.

Land Contract The real property sales contract, also called a land contract, agreement of sale, conditional sales contract, or contract for deed, is an agreement wherein the seller (vendor) extends credit for the purchase of the property but does not convey title to the buyer (vendee) until specified conditions have been satisfied.

Title. The buyer receives possession of the property and a promise of legal title later, but not legal title at inception.

Use. The land contract is considered by some to be advantageous to the buyer who does not have sufficient downpayment or credit to qualify for an institutional loan. However, there are disadvantageous to both parties because of greater risks.

All-Inclusive Trust Deed The AITD is also called a wraparound or wrap. It is a junior trust deed used to "wrap" the existing trust deed(s) into one package, with the buyer being charged one overall interest rate which calculates lower than the same amount financed at current market rates.

Seller's Role. The seller makes the existing trust deed payments from the buyer's AITD payments. The seller thus earns a higher interest on the amount of his equity.

Legal Implications. Because there may be legal pitfalls, most people should seek legal advice from an attorney when drawing up the necessary documents for an AITD.

Adjustable Rate Mortgage (ARM) With a fixed-rate mortgage, the interest rate stays the same during the life of the loan. With an ARM, an adjustable rate mortgage, the interest rate changes periodically, usually in relation to an index, and payments may go up or down accordingly.

Low Initial Rate. Lenders generally charge lower initial interest rates for ARMs than for fixed-rate mortgages. This makes the ARM easier on the pocketbook at first than a fixed-rate mortgage for the same amount. One may qualify for a larger loan because lenders sometimes make this decision on the basis of current income and the first year's payments. Moreover, an ARM can be less expensive over a long period than a fixed-rate mortgage—for example, if interest rates remain steady or move lower.

Higher Future Payments. Against these advantages, there is the risk that an increase in interest rates will lead to higher monthly payments in the future. The trade-off is a lower initial rate in exchange for assuming more risk. The borrower needs to consider future expectations of income, other debts, and how long he or she plans to own the home. (If one plans to sell soon, rising interest rates may not pose the problem they do if one plans to own the house for a long time.) Under some ARMs, payments can increase even if interest rates generally do not increase.

FEDERAL REGULATIONS

The principle of "caveat emptor" is no longer applicable to real estate, particularly as disclosure requirements expand in the interest of consumer protection. In the area of financing, the two major federal disclosure laws are Regulation Z (Truth in Lending) and RESPA, the Real Estate Settlement Procedures Act.

Truth in Lending Federal Reserve Regulation Z, which is enforced by the Federal Trade Commission (FTC), originated in 1969 as part of the Consumer Credit Protection Act and has been often revised since. The purpose is to insure that prospective buyers and borrowers know in advance what the cost of credit will be, and can compare the offerings of different lenders.

"Creditor." For application of this law a "creditor" is any person or firm that extends or offers to extend credit more than 25 times a year, or more than 5 times a year for transactions secured by a dwelling. The term "arranger of credit" is no longer used by Regulation Z. The effect of this change is to release real estate brokers from responsibility for providing Truth in Lending disclosures unless they are otherwise "creditors."

Application. The law applies to a "creditor" of real estate loans to natural persons for personal, family, or household purposes, including all owner-occupied dwellings. It does *not* apply to:

☐ Commercial loans to builders, developers, or for rental property on which the owner does not reside.

☐ Credit over $25,000 unless secured by real property or "personal property which is . . . the consumer's principal dwelling," e.g., a mobilehome.

Disclosure Requirements. The creditor must furnish the borrower with a disclosure statement (Exhibit 26) which must include:

☐ *Amount Financed*. This is the total amount of "credit extended," frequently less than the face amount of the note.

☐ *Itemization of the Amount Financed*. This is required except when estimates of settlement costs have already been supplied under RESPA.

☐ *Finance Charge*. The finance charge is the total dollar amount that the credit will cost. Included in the finance charge are:

• Interest

• Loan fees, assumption fees, finder's fees, and buyer's points

• Premiums for mortgage guarantee or similar insurance.

Not included in the finance charge in a transaction secured by real property are:

- Points paid by seller
- Fees for title examination, abstract of title, title insurance, property survey, and similar purposes
- Fees for preparing deeds, mortgages, reconveyance, settlement, and similar documents
- Notary, appraisal, and credit report fees.

☐ *Annual Percentage Rate*. The APR represents a relationship of the total finance charge and the total amount financed. The term "annual percentage rate" and/or the abbreviation APR must be used, together with a brief explanation such as "the cost of credit as a yearly rate." It must be accurate to within $\frac{1}{8}$% in most transactions.

Right to Rescind. The borrower may rescind before midnight of the third business day following consummation of the contract or delivery of the disclosure statement, whichever is later, if the security is the borrower's principal residence. This right applies only when *current* principal residences are used to secure a loan, not to purchase money loans secured by property *intended* to become the principal dwelling. Each consumer must be given two copies of the notice of right to rescind. Regulation Z provides (but does not mandate) a model form.

Advertising. Anyone placing an advertisement for consumer credit must comply with the advertising requirements of Regulation Z. Real estate brokers and home builders who place ads must comply even if they are not the "creditors" in the financing being advertised.

☐ If an advertisement contains any one of the following terms, the ad must also disclose other credit terms:

- Downpayment (includes value of any trade-in when a developer extends credit)
- Number of payments or period of repayment
- Amount of any payment
- Amount of any finance charge.

☐ If *any* of the above terms is used, then the following *three* disclosures must be given:

- Downpayment
- Terms of repayment
- The annual percentage rate, using that term spelled out in full or just the abbreviation APR.

ARM Disclosures The 1988 Regulation Z amendments are the first disclosures specifically designed for the increasingly popular variable rate instruments. Before 1988, only the standard Truth in Lending disclosures were made, and they came late in the financing process (when actual costs were fully known) and could not accurately reflect the effects of variable terms.

Content. The new disclosures, using a $10,000 model loan example and a historical summary of the index being used, are able to give the borrower a clear picture of how payments and loan balance may be affected by a variable interest rate. The essential features of an ARM are specifically addressed in these disclosures: the index used, how interest rate and payment are determined, frequency of adjustment, caps, and the possibility of negative amortization.

Requirements. The Regulation Z amendments require creditors to distribute to consumers an educational booklet about adjustable rate mortgages, and to provide a detailed description of the variable rate feature, along with a historical example.

Application. The amendments apply only to *closed-end* credit transactions secured by the consumer's *principal dwelling,* including both purchase money and non-purchase money, for terms of more than one year.

Timing. The information must be provided at the time an application form is given to the consumer *or* before the consumer pays a non-refundable fee, whichever is earlier. Disclosure at this time is possible under the amendments because the new rule requires that disclosure reflect ARM loan program *features,* but not the terms of individual transactions.

Two Disclosures. Under the new rule, the variable rate disclosures are given to consumers earlier than the standard Truth in Lending information. The later Truth in Lending disclosures must include a statement that an adjustable rate feature exists and that the variable rate disclosures have been provided to the consumer.

Educational Booklet. The Federal Reserve's *Consumer Handbook on Adjustable Rate Mortgages* or another booklet containing comparable information must be provided by the lender to a prospective borrower at the time an application form is given to the consumer or before the consumer pays a non-refundable fee, whichever is earlier.

ARM Features. Creditors are required to specify the following:

☐ The index to which interest rate changes are tied

☐ A source of information about the index

☐ An explanation of how the interest rate and payment will be determined, for example, a statement that the interest rate will be based on a specified index plus a margin and that the payment will be based on the interest rate, the loan balance, and the remaining loan term

☐ A statement that will alert consumers about a discount feature when the initial rate is discounted

☐ The frequency of rate and payment adjustments

☐ Rate and payment caps

☐ If the presence of rate or payment caps can result in negative amortization, a statement about those features

☐ The existence of a demand feature, if applicable

☐ A statement describing the type of information that will be contained in an adjustment notice

☐ When adjustment notices will be provided.

☐ It is now required that all dwelling-secured ARM loans contain the maximum interest rate that may apply during the loan term.

Historical Example. The disclosure must contain an example, based on a $10,000 loan, illustrating how payments and loan balance would have been affected by historical changes in the index to be used. Because the example is not based on the actual amount borrowed, creditors can pre-print the disclosures for each loan program and give them to consumers with the ARM handbook.

☐ *Index Values.* The index values used in the example begin with the value for 1977 (where data are available) and will be updated annually until a 15-year history is shown. For example, the disclosures for an ARM made in 1988 include index values for each year from 1977 through 1987. In each subsequent year until 1991, disclosures will include the index value for one more year. If the values for an index are not available back to 1977, creditors may start with the first year for which values are available.

☐ *Actual Payments.* The disclosure also explains to consumers how to calculate their actual monthly payment for a loan amount other than $10,000. The idea behind the example is that consumers can easily convert figures based on a $10,000 example to calculate their own monthly payments.

Real Estate Settlement Procedures Act (RESPA) Passed in 1974, RESPA is a federal law to protect and inform homebuyers by regulating unnecessary and excessive closing costs and disclosing settlement costs in advance so that borrowers can shop around for more economical loans.

Application. This law applies to first mortgage loans, made by federally regulated or insured lenders, secured by 1 to 4 family residences, including individual co-ops, condominiums, and mobilehomes sold with the land.

Exclusions. It excludes construction and home improvement loans, vacant lots, parcels of 25 acres or more, assumptions, property purchased for resale, land sales contracts, or any transaction in which title is not transferred

Disclosure Requirements. The lender must deliver to the borrower, without charge:

□ Not later than 3 business days after application is received, HUD's "Special Information Booklet" and good faith estimates of costs likely to be incurred.

□ "At or before settlement," a Uniform Settlement Statement (HUD-1 form) indicating all settlement costs. Buyer's and seller's costs must be itemized separately. If the borrower requests, he must be permitted to inspect the statement one business day preceding the date of settlement.

Prohibitions. RESPA prohibits various practices likely to inflate or manipulate settlement costs. Violations do not invalidate the sale but complaints may be filed with HUD and legal remedies may be pursued.

□ Giving or taking kickbacks for the referral of settlement connected business is prohibited. (This does not prohibit cooperative brokerage and referral arrangements of brokers and sales agents or fees for actual services rendered.)

□ The seller may not, as a condition of sale, insist that a buyer use a particular title company.

□ No charge may be made for the preparation of the Special Information Booklet or the Uniform Settlement Statement.

□ The lender may not collect from the borrower an initial deposit in excess of an accrued liability up to the date of the first mortgage installment, plus an additional amount for an accrual for future liabilities not in excess of two months' installments.

RESIDENTIAL LOAN APPLICATION

| MORTGAGE APPLIED FOR | ☐ Conventional ☐ FHA ☐ VA | Amount $ | Interest Rate % | No. of Months | Monthly Payment Principal & Interest $ | Escrow/Impounds (to be collected monthly) ☐ Taxes ☐ Hazard Ins. ☐ Mtg. Ins. ☐ |

Prepayment Option

SUBJECT PROPERTY

| Property Street Address | City | County | State | Zip | No. Units |

Legal Description (Attach description if necessary)

Year Built

Purpose of Loan: ☐ Purchase ☐ Construction-Permanent ☐ Construction ☐ Refinance ☐ Other (Explain)

| Complete this line if Construction-Permanent or Construction Loan ▶ | Lot Value Data | Original Cost | Present Value (a) | Cost of Imps. (b) | Total (a + b) | ENTER TOTAL AS PURCHASE PRICE IN DETAILS OF PURCHASE. |
| Year Acquired | $ | $ | $ | $ | |

Complete this line if a Refinance Loan	Purpose of Refinance	Describe Improvements [ ] made [ ] to be made
Year Acquired	Original Cost	Amt. Existing Liens
$	$		Cost: $

| Title Will Be Held In What Name(s) | Manner In Which Title Will Be Held |

Source of Down Payment and Settlement Charges

This application is designed to be completed by the borrower(s) with the lender's assistance. The Co-Borrower Section and all other Co-Borrower questions must be completed and the appropriate box(es) checked if ☐ another person will be jointly obligated with the Borrower on the loan, or ☐ the Borrower is relying on income from alimony, child support or separate maintenance or on the income or assets of another person as a basis for repayment of the loan, or ☐ the Borrower is married and resides, or the property is located, in a community property state.

BORROWER				CO-BORROWER		
Name		Age	School Yrs	Name		Age	School Yrs

Present Address	No. Years ☐ Own ☐ Rent		Present Address	No. Years ☐ Own ☐ Rent
Street			Street	
City/State/Zip			City/State/Zip	
Former address if less than 2 years at present address		Former address if less than 2 years at present address
Street			Street	
City/State/Zip			City/State/Zip	
Years at former address ☐ Own ☐ Rent		Years at former address ☐ Own ☐ Rent

| Marital Status ☐ Married ☐ Separated ☐ Unmarried (incl. single, divorced, widowed) | DEPENDENTS OTHER THAN LISTED BY CO BORROWER NO. AGES | Marital Status ☐ Married ☐ Separated ☐ Unmarried (incl. single, divorced, widowed) | DEPENDENTS OTHER THAN LISTED BY BORROWER NO. AGES |

| Name and Address of Employer | Years employed in this line of work or profession? ___ years Years on this job ___ ☐ Self Employed* | Name and Address of Employer | Years employed in this line of work or profession? ___ years Years on this job ___ ☐ Self Employed* |

| Position/Title | Type of Business | Position/Title | Type of Business |

| Social Security Number*** | Home Phone | Business Phone | Social Security Number*** | Home Phone | Business Phone |

GROSS MONTHLY INCOME				MONTHLY HOUSING EXPENSE**			DETAILS OF PURCHASE	
Item	Borrower	Co-Borrower	Total		PRESENT	PROPOSED		Do Not Complete If Refinance
Base Empl. Income	$	$	$	Rent	$		a. Purchase Price	$
Overtime				First Mortgage (P&I)		$	b. Total Closing Costs (Est.)	
Bonuses				Other Financing (P&I)			c. Prepaid Escrows (Est.)	
Commissions				Hazard Insurance			d. Total (a + b + c)	$
Dividends/Interest				Real Estate Taxes			e. Amount This Mortgage	( )
Net Rental Income				Mortgage Insurance			f. Other Financing	( )
Other† (Before completing, see notice under Describe Other Income below.)				Homeowner Assn. Dues			g. Other Equity	( )
				Other:			h. Amount of Cash Deposit	( )
				Total Monthly Pmt.	$	$	i. Closing Costs Paid by Seller	( )
				Utilities			j. Cash Reqd. For Closing (Est.)	$
Total	$	$	$	Total	$	$		

DESCRIBE OTHER INCOME

| ▷ B—Borrower C—Co-Borrower | NOTICE: † Alimony, child support, or separate maintenance income need not be revealed if the Borrower or Co-Borrower does not choose to have it considered as a basis for repaying this loan. | Monthly Amount $ |

IF EMPLOYED IN CURRENT POSITION FOR LESS THAN TWO YEARS COMPLETE THE FOLLOWING

B/C	Previous Employer/School	City/State	Type of Business	Position/Title	Dates From/To	Monthly Income
						$

THESE QUESTIONS APPLY TO BOTH BORROWER AND CO-BORROWER

If a "yes" answer is given to a question in this column, explain on an attached sheet.	Borrower Yes or No	Co-Borrower Yes or No			Borrower Yes or No	Co-Borrower Yes or No
Have you any outstanding judgments? In the last 7 years, have you been declared bankrupt?				Are you a U.S. citizen?		
Have you had property foreclosed upon or given title or deed in lieu thereof?				If "no," are you a resident alien?		
Are you a co-maker or endorser on a note?				If "no," are you a non-resident alien?		
Are you a party in a law suit?				Explain Other Financing or Other Equity (if any).		
Are you obligated to pay alimony, child support, or separate maintenance?						
Is any part of the down payment borrowed?						

*FHLMC/FNMA require business credit report, signed Federal Income Tax returns for last two years, and, if available, audited Profit and Loss Statements plus balance sheet for same period.

**All Present Monthly Housing Expenses of Borrower and Co-Borrower should be listed on a combined basis.   Conforms to FHLMC 65 and FNMA 1003. Rev. 10/86

***Optional for FHLMC

Exhibit 25.1

This Statement and any applicable supporting schedules may be completed jointly by both married and unmarried co-borrowers if their assets and liabilities are sufficiently joined so that the Statement can be meaningfully and fairly presented on a combined basis; otherwise separate Statements and Schedules are required (FHLMC 65A/FNMA 1003A). If the co-borrower section was completed about a spouse, this statement and supporting schedules must be completed about that spouse also.

☐ Completed Jointly   ☐ Not Completed Jointly

ASSETS		LIABILITIES AND PLEDGED ASSETS			
		Indicate by (*) those liabilities or pledged assets which will be satisfied upon sale of real estate owned or upon refinancing of subject property			
Description	Cash or Market Value	Creditors' Name, Address and Account Number	Acct. Name if Not Borrower's	Mo. Pmt. and Mos. left to pay	Unpaid Balance
Cash Deposit Toward Purchase Held By	$	Installment Debts (include "revolving" charge accts)		$ Pmt./Mos.	$
				/	
Checking and Savings Accounts (Show Names of Institutions/Acct. Nos.)				/	
				/	
Stocks and Bonds (No./Description)				/	
				/	
Life Insurance Net Cash Value Face Amount ($)		Other Debts Including Stock Pledges			
SUBTOTAL LIQUID ASSETS	$				
Real Estate Owned (Enter Market Value from Schedule of Real Estate Owned)		Real Estate Loans			
Vested Interest in Retirement Fund					
Net Worth of Business Owned (ATTACH FINANCIAL STATEMENT)					
Automobiles (Make and Year)		Automobile Loans			
Furniture and Personal Property		Alimony, Child Support and Separate Maintenance Payments Owed To			
Other Assets (Itemize)					
		TOTAL MONTHLY PAYMENTS		$	
TOTAL ASSETS	A $	NET WORTH (A minus B) $		TOTAL LIABILITIES	B $

SCHEDULE OF REAL ESTATE OWNED (If Additional Properties Owned Attach Separate Schedule)

Address of Property (Indicate S if Sold, PS if Pending Sale or R if Rental being held for income)		Type of Property	Present Market Value	Amount of Mortgages & Liens	Gross Rental Income	Mortgage Payments	Taxes, Ins. Maintenance and Misc.	Net Rental Income
	◇		$	$	$	$	$	$
TOTALS →			$	$	$	$	$	$

LIST PREVIOUS CREDIT REFERENCES

◇ B - Borrower C – Co-Borrower	Creditor's Name and Address	Account Number	Purpose	Highest Balance	Date Paid
				$	

List any additional names under which credit has previously been received _____

AGREEMENT   The undersigned applies for the loan indicated in this application to be secured by a first mortgage or deed of trust on the property described herein, and represents that the property will not be used for any illegal or restricted purpose, and that all statements made in this application are true and are made for the purpose of obtaining the loan. Verification may be obtained from any source named in this application. The original or a copy of this application will be retained by the lender, even if the loan is not granted.   The undersigned ☐ intend or ☐ do not intend to occupy the property as their primary residence.

I/we fully understand that it is a federal crime punishable by fine or imprisonment, or both, to knowingly make any false statements concerning any of the above facts as applicable under the provisions of Title 18, United States Code, Section 1014.

_____ Date _____   _____ Date _____
Borrower's Signature   Co-Borrower's Signature

INFORMATION FOR GOVERNMENT MONITORING PURPOSES

The following information is requested by the Federal Government for certain types of loans related to a dwelling, in order to monitor the lender's compliance with equal credit opportunity and fair housing laws. You are not required to furnish this information, but are encouraged to do so. The law provides that a lender may neither discriminate on the basis of this information, nor on whether you choose to furnish it. However, if you choose not to furnish it, under Federal regulations this lender is required to note race and sex on the basis of visual observation or surname. If you not wish to furnish the above information, please check the box below. [Lender must review the above material to assure that the disclosures satisfy all requirements to which the Lender is subject under applicable state law for the particular type of loan applied for.]

Borrower: ☐ I do not wish to furnish this information
Race/National Origin:
☐ American Indian, Alaskan Native ☐ Asian, Pacific Islander
☐ Black ☐ Hispanic ☐ White
☐ Other (Specify): _____
Sex: ☐ Female ☐ Male

Co-Borrower: ☐ I do not wish to furnish this information
Race/National Origin:
☐ American Indian, Alaskan Native ☐ Asian, Pacific Islander
☐ Black ☐ Hispanic ☐ White
☐ Other (Specify): _____
Sex: ☐ Female ☐ Male

TO BE COMPLETED BY INTERVIEWER

This application was taken by:
☐ face to face interview
☐ by mail
☐ by telephone

_____   _____
Interviewer   Name of Interviewer's Employer

_____   _____
Interviewer's Phone Number   Address of Interviewer's Employer

Conforms to FHLMC 65 and FNMA 1003   Rev. 10/86   **REVERSE**

Exhibit 25.2

FEDERAL REAL ESTATE LOAN DISCLOSURE STATEMENT

CALIFORNIA ASSOCIATION OF REALTORS® STANDARD FORM

Broker:

_____
(name)

_____
(address)

Creditor:

_____
(name)

_____
(address)

YOUR LOAN IN THE AMOUNT OF $ _____ IS TO BE SECURED BY A DEED OF TRUST IN FAVOR OF CREDITOR ON REAL PROPERTY LOCATED AT _____

_____ .

ANNUAL PERCENTAGE RATE The cost of your credit as a yearly rate.	FINANCE CHARGE The dollar amount the credit will cost you.	AMOUNT FINANCED The amount of credit provided to you or on your behalf.	TOTAL OF PAYMENTS The amount you will have paid after you have made all payments as scheduled.
_____%	$	$	$

YOUR PAYMENT SCHEDULE WILL BE:

Number of Payments	Amount of Payments	When Payments Are Due

ITEMIZATION OF THE AMOUNT FINANCED OF $_____

Amount given to you . $ _____

Amount paid on your account $ _____

Amount paid to others on your behalf:

1. Appraisal . . . . $ _____
2. Credit report . . . . $ _____
3. Notary . . . . $ _____
4. Recording . . . . $ _____
5. Title insurance . . . . $ _____
6. Document preparation . . . . $ _____
7. Property insurance . . . . $ _____
8. Other _____ (DESCRIBE) $ _____
9. Other _____ (DESCRIBE) $ _____

<u>Insurance:</u>
Property insurance may be obtained by Borrower through any person of his choice. If it is to be purchased through Broker or Creditor, you will pay $_____ .
Credit life and disability insurance are not required to obtain this loan.
<u>Late Charge</u>: If any payment is not made within _____ days after it is due, a late charge must be paid by Borrower as follows:

_____

<u>Prepayment</u>: If you pay off early, you ☐ MAY ☐ WILL NOT have to pay a penalty.
<u>Acceleration</u>: If the property securing this loan is sold or otherwise transferred, the Creditor ☐ HAS ☐ DOES NOT have the option to require immediate payment of the entire loan amount.
SEE YOUR CONTRACT DOCUMENTS FOR ANY ADDITIONAL INFORMATION ABOUT NONPAYMENT, DEFAULT, ANY REQUIRED REPAYMENT IN FULL BEFORE THE SCHEDULED DATE, AND PREPAYMENT REFUNDS AND PENALTIES.

I HAVE READ AND RECEIVED A COMPLETED
COPY OF THIS STATEMENT.

Date _____, 19 _____ .

Borrower_____

Borrower_____

*IMPORTANT NOTE:
Asterisk denotes an estimate.
To order, contact — California Association of Realtors®
525 South Virgil Avenue, Los Angeles, California 90020
Copyright ©1970, 1978, by California Association of Realtors®
(Revised, 1983)

FORM LD-11

TT-L5-FG

Exhibit 26

1. Second trust deed loans originate in the:

    (A) Primary mortgage market
    (B) Secondary mortgage market
    (C) Trust deed exchange
    (D) None of the above

2. Regulation Z in some situations provides for the following within 3 business days after the transaction is consummated:

    (A) Delivery of special information booklets
    (B) Delivery of good faith estimates
    (C) Right to rescind
    (D) All of the above

3. The ultimate source of all mortgage money is:

    (A) Federal government programs
    (B) State government programs
    (C) Local government programs
    (D) Individual and business savings

4. The _____ calls for the seller to take back a junior trust deed, earn interest on one overall interest rate, and make payments with the buyer's funds.

    (A) Land contract
    (B) Shared appreciation mortgage
    (C) All-inclusive trust deed
    (D) FNMA buydown

5. On an assumption of an existing mortgage:

    (A) The seller remains primarily liable for the existing loan
    (B) If an FHA or VA existing loan, the lender may change the terms
    (C) The buyer becomes primarily liable for the existing loan
    (D) The seller is automatically released from any liability

6. The Cal-Vet program obtains its funds from:

    (A) Corporate donors
    (B) California comptroller's office
    (C) Sale of bonds
    (D) FNMA

7. The two basic types of promissory notes are:

    (A) Straight note and interest only
    (B) Fully amortized and partially amortized
    (C) Straight note and installment note
    (D) Installment note and fully amortized

8. Three major sources of direct government assistance for residential loans are:

    (A) Fannie Mae, Ginnie Mae, Freddie Mac
    (B) Fannie Mae, Ginnie Mae, Cal-Vet
    (C) Cal-Vet, Ginnie Mae, VA
    (D) Cal-Vet, FHA, VA

9. RESPA applies to all of the following except:

    (A) First mortgages on 1 to 4 family residences
    (B) Home improvement loans
    (C) Mobilehomes sold with the land
    (D) Co-ops and condominiums

10. When a note is paid in full, the lender must instruct the trustee to execute and record in favor of the trustor a(n) _____ :

    (A) Equity of redemption
    (B) Payment in full
    (C) Deed of reconveyance
    (D) Notice of default

Chapter 12
Applied
Real Estate Math

MATH REVIEW

This chapter briefly reviews basic mathematical principles fundamental to real estate computations. The areas of basic importance are commissions, percentage returns on investments, interest rates on loans, documentary transfer tax, prorations at close of escrow, and square footage and area calculations.

Pocket Calculators   Modern real estate practice makes extensive use of financial calculators. Many models are available in the market, and the real estate professional should acquire and learn to use one of these valuable tools of the trade.

Advanced Functions. Such calculators perform not only the four basic arithmetic functions of adding, subtracting, multiplying, and dividing, but also do the mathematics of amortization, discounting, tax depreciation schedules, annual percentage rates, compounding, balloon payments, effective yield rates, etc.

Knowledge of Arithmetic Still Needed. The major problem that confronts the user of any calculator is that you cannot use the calculator to do arithmetic problems until you first decide what arithmetic to do. Remember, GIGO: garbage in, garbage out.

Integers This text assumes that you know how to perform the basic arithmetic functions with integers (whole numbers), or that you have a calculator that will do them quickly and easily for you. With the calculator it is very easy, for example, to divide 43,560 into 871,200 to determine the number of acres in a parcel of land that is 450 feet wide and 1936 feet deep.

Fractions Fractions are frequently used in the arithmetic of real estate, and it is assumed that, as with integers, you know how to do the four arithmetic functions. Practice with your calculator so that it is quick and easy to figure the number of square feet in 2/3 of an acre by multiplying 2/3 x 43,560.

Decimals Decimals present almost no special problems in arithmetic provided you remember to enter the decimal points properly. Practice with your calculator will greatly reduce common errors.

Percentages Percentages provide a special problem because percent is not really an arithmetic term but an expression of a ratio. Therefore, to do arithmetic with the calculator using percentage (usually denoted by %), the percentage must first be converted into either a decimal or a fraction. (Many calculators will do this for you.) Common equivalents are shown in the table below.

Percentage	Decimal	Fraction
100%	1.00	1/1
66 2/3%	.6667	2/3
50%	.50	1/2
33 1/3%	.333	1/3
16 2/3%	.1667	1/6
12 1/2%	.125	1/8
6 2/3%	.0667	1/15

Rounding Calculators can perform instant wonders at working problems out to as many decimal places as the display will permit. For example, 326 ÷ 77 = 4.233766234. Except in scientific calculations, however, such accuracy is rarely needed or appropriate, and numbers are rounded up or down, to the extent that the refinement is needed in the particular application.

Appraisal. An appraisal estimate that came out as $103,356 would most likely be rounded to $103,500. Precise appraisal figures suggest an accuracy and precision that professional appraisers do not claim.

Taxes. The IRS rounds income tax calculations to the nearest dollar. An interest income of $106.70 would be rounded to $107; a deduction of $102.20 would be rounded to $102. (.50 and above is rounded up to 1, and .49 and below is rounded down to 0.)

Lenders. Banks and lenders dealing with money must necessarily round up or down to the nearest cent and will, therefore, round their money calculations to two decimal places. The monthly payment on a $60,000 loan at $11\frac{3}{4}$% for 30 years would be $605.6458407. Clearly the lender would require a payment of $605.65.

Interest Rates. Annual interest rates in current money and capital markets frequently carry decimals to five or more places. For example, an annual interest rate of $10\frac{7}{8}$% expressed as a decimal would be .10875. The monthly rate entered into a financial calculator would be .0090625, and the interest portion of the first monthly payment on a $60,000 loan at $10\frac{7}{8}$ would be $543.75 ($60,000 x .0090625 = $543.75).

Varying Practices. Different rounding policies will produce slightly different results, and variations will be found among the financial institutions.

PERCENTAGE CALCULATIONS

Much of the business world operates on percentages; many business decisions are based on data that are usually expressed as percentages. The real estate licensee will frequently encounter percentages.

Basic Formulas   Most percentage problems involve multiplication or division using three common key elements: percent, total, and part.

$$\text{Percent} \quad \times \quad \text{Total} \quad = \quad \text{Part}$$
$$25\% \quad \text{of} \quad 1000 \quad = \quad 250$$

$$\frac{\text{Part}}{\text{Percent}} = \text{Total} \qquad \frac{\text{Part}}{\text{Total}} = \text{Percent}$$

$$\frac{250}{25\% \text{ or } .25} = 1{,}000 \qquad \frac{250}{1000} = .25 \text{ or } 25\%$$

Calculations   Commissions, price reductions, profits, tax rates, interest rates, and inflation are only a few of the percentages that affect real estate.

To Find Commission. *What is the dollar amount of commission the broker will receive if he sells a $132,000 home on a 6% commission basis?*

Calculation:

Percent	x	Total		Part
Commission Rate	x	Sales Price	=	Commission
6%	x	$132,000	=	$7,920.00

To Find Price Reduction. *An office recently sold a home for $120,000 which was considered to be 95% of its original listing price. What was the original listing price?*

Calculation:

$$\frac{\text{Part}}{\text{Total}} = \text{Percent}$$

$$\frac{\text{Selling Price}}{\text{Percent}} = \text{Listing Price}$$

$$\frac{\$120,000}{.95} = \$126,316 \text{ (rounded) Listing Price}$$

Check:

95% of $126,316 = $120,000

Allowing for rounding, the actual listing price was probably $126,500.

Profit. *A property recently sold for $165,000, and was originally bought for $95,000 three years ago. What is the percentage of profit?*

Calculation:

$$\frac{\text{Part}}{\text{Total}} = (\text{"Part" is the dollar profit.})$$

$$\frac{\text{Profit}}{\text{Investment}} = \text{Percent Profit}$$

$$\$165,000 \quad - \quad \$95,000 \quad = \quad \$70,000$$

$$\frac{\$70,000}{\$95,000} = 7368, \text{ or } 73.7\% \text{ Profit}$$

Check:

73.7% of $95,000 = $70,015 rounded to $70,000

INTEREST

Because of the large role of financing in today's real estate market, and the dramatic effects that interest rates have on monthly and total payments, interest calculations are of great importance.

Definitions Most real estate transactions involve the use of mortgage loans, and thus the need to understand their basic terminology:

Principal (P). The amount of money borrowed.

Interest (I). The dollar cost of using other people's money (OPM).

☐ *Simple Interest.* The most common method of calculating interest costs in real estate transactions. The interest is based on a percentage of the unpaid loan balance.

☐ *Compound Interest.* Calculated on the balance including the accrued interest. Compounding can be daily, monthly, quarterly, semiannually, or annually. This method is frequently used on savings accounts.

Rate of Interest (R). The annual percentage rate paid to use OPM.

Time (T). The term or duration of the loan.

Formula The four part formula for interest calculations is: **Interest** equals **principal** multiplied by the yearly percentage **rate** of interest by the amount of **time**:

$$\text{Interest} = \text{Principal} \times \text{Rate} \times \text{Time}$$

$$I = P \times R \times T \quad \text{or} \quad P = \frac{I}{R \times T} \quad \text{or} \quad R = \frac{I}{P \times T} \quad \text{or} \quad T = \frac{I}{P \times R}$$

All interest rates are related to a one-year period. Therefore, to find annual interest, simply calculate P x R. The time is always 1. For other time periods the formulas are:

$$\text{Monthly Interest} = \frac{\text{Annual Interest}}{12}$$

$$\text{Daily Interest} = \frac{\text{Annual Interest}}{365} \quad \text{or} \quad \frac{\text{Monthly Interest}}{\text{Days in Month}}$$

To Find Interest. *How much interest will be paid in 1 year on a straight loan of $100,000 at 10% for 3 years?*

$$
\begin{array}{ccccccc}
I & = & P & \times & R & \times & T \\
I & = & \$100,000 & \times & .10 & \times & 1 \\
I & = & \$10,000 & & & &
\end{array}
$$

To Find Rate. *What is the annual rate of interest on a straight loan with a principal amount of $1,200 on which $240 interest has been paid over a 2 years?*

$$R = \frac{I}{P \times T} \qquad R = \frac{\$240}{\$1200 \times 2} \qquad R = .10 \text{ or } 10\%$$

To Find Time. *For how many years is a note with a principal of $1,000, total interest of $360 paid at a rate of 12% annually?*

$$T = \frac{I}{P \times R} \qquad T = \frac{\$360}{\$1000 \times .12} \qquad T = 3 \text{ years}$$

To Find Principal. What is the principal amount of a straight note on which $5,750 of interest has been paid over 5 years at a rate of 11.5%?

$$P = \frac{I}{R \times T} \qquad P = \frac{\$5750}{.115 \times 5} \qquad P = \$10,000$$

DISCOUNTING AND POINTS

Most lenders require these initial fees to set up loan accounts. One point equals 1% of the loan amount, a nonrecurring cost (one time charge). An additional fee on certain loans is charged by a lender to offset the difference between the loan interest rate and the current discount rate (the percent subtracted from a loan to increase the profit to a purchaser of the loan), to make the loan competitive in the secondary market. The greater the demand in the secondary money market, the higher the discount points will be. One discount point is roughly equivalent to adding $\frac{1}{8}$% of prepaid interest to the nominal rate of 30 year period loan (based on a so-called "average" 8-year payoff of a loan). Discount points may also be paid to buy down interest rates or to buy down the terms of an adjustable rate mortgage.

Formula   The three part formula used for interest calculations applies: **Interest** equals **principal** multiplied by the **rate** (the number of points).

$$\text{Interest} = \text{Principal} \times \text{Rate}$$

To Find Interest. *What is the dollar amount of the loan origination fee if the lender charges 2 points on a $90,000 loan?*

$$
\begin{aligned}
I &= P \times R \\
I &= \$90,000 \times .02 \\
I &= \$1,800
\end{aligned}
$$

Discount Points   A mortgage discount is a one-time prepaid interest charge by a lender to increase the lender's effective yield. The difference between the amount of the note and the amount the investor pays for the note in relation to the full amount of the note is the discount.

To Find Discount. *What was the discount on a $10,000 note sold to an investor for $8,000?*

$10,000   Note
−8,000   Price of note to investor
$2,000   Discount

$$\frac{\$2,000}{\$10,000} = 20\% \text{ Discount or 20 points}$$

To Find Points Required To Equate Two Rates   Assume the current market rate of interest is 11.25%, the VA ceiling rate is 10.5%, and the proposed loan is $75,000. What are the required discount points to equate the VA and the market rates of interest? What is the amount of discount charged on the $75,000 loan? What will the lender's effective yield be?

To Calculate the Difference in the Two Rates. Take the current market rate minus the current VA rate:

11.25% − 10.5% = .75% or $\frac{3}{4}$%

Convert the difference to eighths of a percent: $\frac{3}{4}$% = $\frac{6}{8}$%

Convert the eighths to discount points ($\frac{1}{8}$ = 1 point):

$\frac{6}{8} \div \frac{1}{8}$ = 6 discount points required.

To Find Amount of Discount Charged. Convert the discount points to discount rate (1 point equals 1%): 6 points x 1% per point = 6%

Discount Rate   x   Total Loan Amount   =   Amount of Discount
.06   x $75,000   = $4,500 (cost to seller)

To Find Effective Yield to Lender. Convert discount points to percent of increase:

1 point = $\frac{1}{8}$% increase in effective yield to the lender
6 points x $\frac{1}{8}$% = $\frac{6}{8}$% or $\frac{3}{4}$% increase

Add the percent of increase to the contract rate:
$\frac{3}{4}$% + $10\frac{1}{2}$% = $11\frac{1}{4}$% effective yield to the lender.

YIELD CALCULATIONS

Owners and prospective buyers of income producing real estate are concerned with the yield or percentage of return on their investment. Yield is used for comparative purposes when they decide whether to invest, hold, sell, or exchange for another property.

Formulas   Yield is another concept expressed as a percentage, so the basic formulas of total, part, and percent again apply, where

Total = Amount of Investment

Part = Net Income from Investment

Percent = Yield or Rate of Return on Investment

Percent	x	Total	=	Part (i.e. Net Income)
Part	÷	Percent	=	Total (i.e. Cost or Investment)
Part	÷	Total	=	Percent (i.e. Rate of Return)

Again, given any two terms it is possible to find the third. Most often, cost and income will be known and the investor will want to find the rate of return.

Calculations   **Income Property.** *The data project $57,600 net income during the first year of ownership of a property that is priced at $576,000. What will be the rate of return on the property?*

Calculation: $\dfrac{\text{Part}}{\text{Total}}$ = Percent

$\dfrac{\text{Income}}{\text{Price}}$ = Rate of Return

$\dfrac{\$57,600}{\$576,000}$ = 10%

Securities. *An investor paid $18,000 for a note and deed of trust with a face value of $20,000 (a 10% discount) and an interest rate of 12%. The note was paid off in one year, giving the investor a profit of $4,400. What was the investor's yield on the investment?*

Calculation: $\dfrac{\text{Part}}{\text{Total}}$ = Percent

$\dfrac{\text{Amount of Profit}}{\text{Amount of Investment}}$ = Rate of Return

$\dfrac{\$4,400}{\$18,000}$ = .244 or 24.4%

COMMISSION

The formulas used to calculate commissions are further applications of the basic percentage formulas.

Formulas In commission calculations,

Total	=	Sales Price
Part	=	Commission Amount
Percent	=	Commission Rate

Calculations Knowing two terms, the third can be found. Commission calculations often have the additional step of splitting the commission amount, on a percentage basis, between broker and salesperson and/or between cooperating offices.

To Find Amount *What dollar amount of commission will the broker receive on a $92,000 sale, if the commission rate is 6%?*

Calculation:

Percent	x	Total	=	Part
Commission Rate	x	Sales Price	=	Commission Amount
.06	x	$92,000	=	$5,520

To Find Sales Price *What was your listing sold for if the 6% commission amounted to $6,900?*

Calculation:

$$\frac{\text{Part}}{\text{Total}} = \text{Percent}$$

$$\frac{\text{Commission Amount}}{\text{Commission Rate}} = \text{Sales Price}$$

$$\frac{\$6,900}{.06} = \$115,000$$

To Find Commission Rate *The broker received $12,500 commission on a property which sold for $250,000. What was the commission rate?*

Calculation:

$$\frac{\text{Part}}{\text{Total}} = \text{Percent}$$

$$\frac{\text{Commission Amount}}{\text{Sales Price}} = \text{Commission Rate}$$

$$\frac{\$12,500}{\$250,000} = 0.05 = 5\%$$

To Find Amount with Split *You sold one of your office listings for $165,000 for which you received a 65% split of your broker's 6% commission. What amount of commission did you receive?*

Calculation:

Percent	x	Total	=	Part
Commission Rate	x	Sales Price	=	Commission Amount
.06	x	$165,000	=	$9,900
Percent	x	Total	=	Part
Commission Rate	x	Commission	=	Your Commission
.65	x	$9,900	=	$6,435

Four-Way Split *You listed a property for $142,000 with a 6% commission rate. A salesperson from another office sold it for $140,000. The co-op office agreement is a 50/50 commission split. The split in your office is 65% to you and 35% to your broker. The selling salesperson's arrangement is 90% to selling salesperson and 10% to the broker. What did each person receive on the sale?*

Calculation:

Total Commission:

Percent	x	Total	=	Part
Commission Rate	x	Sales Price	=	Commission Amount
.06	x	$140,000	=	8,400

Each Office's Commission:

$$\begin{array}{ccccc}
\text{Percent} & \times & \text{Total} & = & \text{Part} \\
\text{Commission Rate} & \times & \text{Commission} & = & \text{Office's Commission} \\
.50 & \times & \$8,400 & = & \$4,200
\end{array}$$

Each Agent's Commission:

Listing Salesperson's Commission	.65	×	$4,200 =	$2,730
Listing Broker's Commission	.35	×	$4,200 =	$1,470
Selling Salesperson's Commission	.90	×	$4,200 =	$3,780
Selling Broker's Commission	.10	×	$4,200 =	$ 420
				$8,400

PRORATIONS

Proration refers to the division of expenses among the parties to the transaction. It takes place most commonly as part of the escrow process, to adjust income and expense items to the date of transfer of ownership.

Basic Concepts of Proration When property changes hands, prorations are made between buyer and seller so that each pays the expenses of the property (or receives income from it) for the time he or she owns it.

Prepaid Items. Such items as prepaid insurance or taxes are debited to the buyer and credited to the seller. (Seller is in effect reimbursed.)

Prepaid Rent. Rent paid in advance by the tenant to the owner for the time following close of escrow, is debited to the seller and credited to the buyer. (Income for period following transfer is passed along to buyer.)

Accrued Expenses. Expenses that are due, but not yet paid by the seller, such as unpaid mortgage interest or property taxes, are debited to the seller and credited to the buyer. (Buyer will be paying some of seller's taxes in a future tax bill. Seller reimburses buyer in advance through proration.)

"Banker's Rule." Prorations are usually calculated on a 360 day year, or 12 months of 30 days each.

"Buyer's Day." The property is considered to belong to the buyer on the day escrow closes.

Common Prorations Proration generally applies to charges which are paid periodically, such as taxes, rents, insurance, homeowners' association dues, etc. So that each party pays a fair share, the monthly or annual payment period must be converted to a daily figure.

Property Taxes Property taxes are paid on a fiscal year, July 1 to June 30, and are prorated on that basis. Taxes are usually paid in two installments during the tax year. The proration may be for either accrued or prepaid taxes, depending on when the transfer of property takes place.

Formula. Calculate the total unpaid or prepaid tax as of the closing date. The seller is to pay the accrued portion to the date of escrow closing, the buyer to pay from COE onward.

□ Unpaid taxes for the time the seller owned the property are debited to the seller and credited to the buyer.

□ For prepaid taxes, the debit is to the buyer and a credit is made to the seller.

Example. *The home you sold is to have an escrow closing date of April 1. The $1,620 tax bill for the year is paid through June 30. Prorate the taxes.*

Calculation:

Find the monthly tax charge, by dividing $1,620 by 12 = $135/month.

Calculate the months the buyer will own the home in the tax year. April 1 through June 30 = 3 months.

Multiply the 3 months by the monthly rate: 3 x $135 = $405 credit to seller.

Mortgage Interest Most amortized principal and interest mortgage payments include interest paid in arrears. This means that an April loan payment includes interest for March.

Formula. To prorate interest in arrears, compute the number of days of earned or accrued interest to be charged to the seller. Interest charges start with the day after the last interest payment date, to the date of closing, and the computed amount is credited to the buyer (who will be making the next payment).

Example. *The buyers close escrow on August 16 and are assuming the loan of $63,280 at 10 1/2% interest paid to and including August 3. How much interest should be credited to the buyers?*

Calculation:

Calculate the interest on the unpaid loan balance.
$63,280 x .105 = $6,644.40 per year

Divide the annual interest by 360 to determine the daily interest cost .
$6,644.40 ÷ 360 = $18.457

Determine the number of days of accrued interest.
        15 days elapsed - 3 days already paid = 12 days accrued
        (on the 16th the property belongs to the buyers)

    Multiply the daily charge by the number of days.
        12 days x $18.457 = $221.48 credit to the buyers

Insurance   Homeowners' insurance policies are usually written for periods of one to three years with the premium payable in advance. If the buyer chooses to assume the existing insurance policy, escrow practice is to prorate the premium on a 360-day per year basis and calculate the exact number of years, months, and days as of close of escrow.

Rents   Rents are usually collected in advance but may sometimes be collected in arrears. They are adjusted as of the date of escrow closing using the methods described above, on an actual day basis. Keep in mind that each party should receive the income for the days he or she owns the property.

AMORTIZATION

Amortization is a method designed to pay a debt in full during the life of the loan, by calculating the periodic payments so that both principal and interest are covered. (In tax accounting, amortization has a different meaning—the recovery of cost over a period of time, related to depreciation.)

Types of Amortization   A loan may be fully or partially amortized. In either case, part of the debt is liquidated with each periodic payment. This contrasts to a straight loan, where the entire amount is paid at the end of the loan term.

Fully Amortized. Most amortized trust deeds or mortgage loans are payable in equal or nearly equal monthly installments including both principal and interest (level payment plan). Each amortized payment will reflect an increasing amount of principal applied to reduce the loan together with a correspondingly diminished amount of interest. In a fully amortized loan, the last equal payment extinguishes the debt.

Partly Amortized. Payments are less than needed for full amortization. In an installment sale only the principal is amortized. Partial amortization results in a balloon payment at the end of the term, for the amount not amortized.

Negative Amortization. Graduated payment mortgages often begin with a period of negative amortization, where monthly payments are lower than interest so that the debt actually grows in the first years.

Amortization Tables

Amortization is not a simple percentage calculation, so it is normally derived from tables which summarize a complex arithmetic, or calculated using a computer or calculator with amortization capacity. The amortization table on pages 232-233 gives the numbers applicable to a $1,000 loan at various interest rates and various times. A full book of amortization tables would give the figures for loans of different amounts, making the loan amount the fourth variable.

Application. Typical uses of an amortization table include calculating monthly payment to pay off a loan in a desired time, the time needed to pay off with a given monthly payment, and lender's yield.

Procedure. The four variables used in compiling the tables are loan amount, interest rate, loan term, and monthly payment. Below is the procedure for finding one factor when the other three are known.

Examples

To Find Monthly Payment. *An $11,000 loan is to be amortized over a period of 18 years with 14% interest. What would be the approximate monthly payment?*

Solution: Using the amortization table:

Down "term of years" column to 18 (years)

Across to 14% (interest rate column) to $12.70 (per $1,000)

Multiply 11 (thousands) x $12.70 = $139.70 per month (fully amortized, principal and interest)

To Find Loan Period. *A $12,000 loan was paid off by a monthly payment of $168 which included principal and interest at a rate of 15%. How many years did it take to amortize?*

Solution: Convert $168 per $12,000 to payment per $1000

$168 ÷ 12 = $14 per $1,000

Down 15% interest rate column to $14

Across to term of years column = 15 years

To Find Interest Amount. *A $14,000 loan was amortized over 20 years with equal monthly payments which included 13% interest. Approximately how much interest was earned by the lender?*

Solution: Determine monthly amortization payment

Down term of years column to 20 (years)

Across to 13% (interest rate column) to $11.72

Multiply 14 (thousands) x $11.72 = $164.08 per month

Determine total interest paid

20 years x 12 months = 240 payments made

240 payments x $164.08/months	= $39,379.20	P + I
Less original loan	= $14,000.00	P
Approximate interest earned	$25,379.20	I

To Find Interest Rate. *A $10,000 loan is to be amortized over seven years with monthly payments of $176.60. What is the annual interest rate?*

Solution: Find the monthly payment per $1,000

Monthly payment of $176.60 ÷ 10 = $17.66

Down column to 7 years

Across to 17.66, and up to 12%.

To Find Cost of Credit. Knowing from the table the amount of the monthly amortized payments, it is possible to determine total interest paid over the term of a loan.

☐ Calculate the total number of monthly payments by multiplying the number of years x 12.

☐ Multiply the result times the dollar amount of the monthly payments, to find the total principal and interest paid during the life of the loan.

☐ Deduct the original loan amount (principal). The balance equals the total interest paid.

Table of Monthly Payments to Amortize a $1,000 Loan

(Including Principal and Interest)

Term of years	5%	5.5%	6%	6.5%	6.6%	7%	7.5%	8%	8.25%	8.5%	8.75%	9%	9.25%	9.5%	9.75%	10%
5	18.88	19.11	19.34	19.57	19.62	19.81	20.04	20.28	20.40	20.52	20.64	20.76	20.88	21.01	21.13	21.25
6	16.11	16.34	16.58	16.81	16.86	17.05	17.30	17.54	17.66	17.78	17.90	18.03	18.15	18.28	18.40	18.53
7	14.14	14.38	14.61	14.85	14.90	15.10	15.34	15.59	15.71	15.84	15.96	16.09	16.22	16.35	16.47	16.61
8	12.66	12.90	13.15	13.39	13.44	13.64	13.89	14.14	14.27	14.40	14.52	14.65	14.78	14.92	15.04	15.18
9	11.52	11.76	12.01	12.26	12.31	12.51	12.77	13.02	13.15	13.28	13.41	13.55	13.68	13.81	13.94	14.08
10	10.61	10.86	11.11	11.36	11.41	11.62	11.88	12.14	12.27	12.40	12.53	12.67	12.80	12.94	13.08	13.22
11	9.87	10.12	10.37	10.63	10.68	10.89	11.15	11.42	11.55	11.69	11.82	11.97	12.10	12.24	12.38	12.52
12	9.25	9.51	9.76	10.02	10.08	10.29	10.56	10.83	10.96	11.11	11.24	11.38	11.52	11.67	11.81	11.96
13	8.74	8.99	9.25	9.52	9.57	9.79	10.06	10.34	10.47	10.62	10.75	10.90	11.04	11.19	11.33	11.48
14	8.29	8.55	8.82	9.09	9.14	9.36	9.64	9.92	10.06	10.20	10.34	10.49	10.64	10.79	10.93	11.09
15	7.91	8.17	8.44	8.72	8.77	8.99	9.28	9.56	9.70	9.85	10.00	10.15	10.29	10.45	10.59	10.75
16	7.58	7.85	8.12	8.40	8.45	8.63	8.96	9.25	9.40	9.55	9.69	9.85	10.00	10.15	10.30	10.46
17	7.29	7.56	7.84	8.12	8.17	8.40	8.69	8.99	9.13	9.29	9.44	9.59	9.74	9.90	10.05	10.22
18	7.04	7.31	7.59	7.87	7.93	8.16	8.45	8.75	8.90	9.06	9.21	9.37	9.52	9.68	9.84	10.00
19	6.81	7.08	7.37	7.65	7.71	7.95	8.25	8.55	8.70	8.86	9.01	9.17	9.33	9.49	9.65	9.82
20	6.60	6.88	7.17	7.46	7.52	7.76	8.06	8.37	8.52	8.68	8.84	9.00	9.16	9.33	9.49	9.66
21	6.42	6.70	6.99	7.29	7.35	7.59	7.90	8.21	8.36	8.53	8.68	8.85	9.01	9.18	9.34	9.51
22	6.26	6.54	6.84	7.13	7.19	7.44	7.75	8.07	8.22	8.39	8.55	8.72	8.88	9.05	9.21	9.39
23	6.11	6.40	6.69	7.00	7.06	7.30	7.62	7.94	8.10	8.27	8.43	8.60	8.76	8.93	9.10	9.28
24	5.97	6.27	6.56	6.87	6.93	7.18	7.50	7.83	7.99	8.16	8.32	8.49	8.66	8.83	9.00	9.18
25	5.85	6.15	6.45	6.76	6.82	7.07	7.39	7.72	7.88	8.06	8.22	8.40	8.56	8.74	8.91	9.09
26	5.74	6.04	6.34	6.65	6.72	6.97	7.30	7.63	7.79	7.96	8.14	8.31	8.48	8.66	8.83	9.01
27	5.64	5.94	6.24	6.56	6.62	6.88	7.21	7.55	7.71	7.88	8.06	8.23	8.41	8.58	8.76	8.94
28	5.54	5.84	6.16	6.48	6.54	6.80	7.13	7.47	7.64	7.81	7.99	8.17	8.34	8.52	8.70	8.88
29	5.45	5.76	6.08	6.40	6.46	6.73	7.06	7.40	7.57	7.75	7.92	8.10	8.28	8.46	8.64	8.83
30	5.37	5.68	6.00	6.33	6.39	6.66	7.00	7.34	7.51	7.69	7.87	8.05	8.23	8.41	8.59	8.78
35	5.05	5.38	5.71	6.05	6.13	6.39	6.75	7.11	7.29	7.47	7.65	7.84	8.03	8.22	8.41	8.60
40	4.83	5.16	5.51	5.86	5.93	6.22	6.59	6.96	7.14	7.33	7.52	7.71	7.91	8.10	8.30	8.49

Table of Monthly Payments to Amortize a $1,000 Loan

(Including Principal Interest)

Term of years	10.25%	10.50%	10.75%	11%	11.25%	11.50%	11.75%	12%	12.25%	12.50%	12.75%	13%	13.25%	13.50%	14%	15%
5	21.37	21.49	21.62	21.74	21.87	21.99	22.12	22.25	22.37	22.50	22.63	22.75	22.88	23.01	23.27	23.79
6	18.65	18.78	18.91	19.04	19.16	19.29	19.42	19.55	19.68	19.81	19.94	20.07	20.21	20.34	20.61	21.15
7	16.73	16.86	16.99	17.12	17.25	17.39	17.52	17.66	17.79	17.92	18.06	18.19	18.33	18.47	18.74	19.30
8	15.31	15.44	15.57	15.71	15.84	15.98	16.12	16.26	16.39	16.53	16.67	16.81	16.95	17.09	17.37	17.95
9	14.21	14.35	14.49	14.63	14.76	14.90	15.04	15.19	15.33	15.47	15.61	15.75	15.90	16.04	16.33	16.92
10	13.35	13.49	13.63	13.78	13.92	14.06	14.20	14.35	14.49	14.64	14.78	14.93	15.08	15.23	15.53	16.13
11	12.66	12.80	12.95	13.09	13.24	13.38	13.53	13.68	13.83	13.98	14.13	14.28	14.43	14.58	14.89	15.51
12	12.10	12.24	12.39	12.54	12.68	12.83	12.98	13.14	13.29	13.44	13.59	13.75	13.90	14.06	14.37	15.01
13	11.63	11.78	11.92	12.08	12.23	12.38	12.53	12.69	12.84	13.00	13.15	13.31	13.47	13.63	13.95	14.60
14	11.23	11.38	11.54	11.69	11.85	12.00	12.16	12.32	12.47	12.63	12.79	12.95	13.11	13.28	13.61	14.27
15	10.90	11.05	11.21	11.37	11.52	11.68	11.84	12.00	12.16	12.33	12.49	12.65	12.82	12.98	13.32	14.00
16	10.62	10.77	10.93	11.09	11.25	11.41	11.57	11.74	11.90	12.07	12.23	12.40	12.57	12.74	13.08	13.77
17	10.37	10.53	10.69	10.86	11.02	11.18	11.35	11.52	11.68	11.85	12.02	12.19	12.36	12.53	12.87	13.58
18	10.16	10.32	10.49	10.65	10.82	10.98	11.15	11.32	11.49	11.66	11.83	12.00	12.18	12.35	12.70	13.42
19	9.98	10.14	10.31	10.48	10.64	10.81	10.98	11.16	11.33	11.50	11.67	11.85	12.03	12.20	12.56	13.28
20	9.82	9.98	10.15	10.32	10.49	10.66	10.84	11.01	11.19	11.36	11.54	11.72	11.89	12.07	12.44	13.17
21	9.68	9.85	10.02	10.19	10.36	10.54	10.71	10.89	11.06	11.24	11.42	11.60	11.78	11.96	12.33	13.07
22	9.55	9.73	9.90	10.07	10.25	10.42	10.60	10.78	10.96	11.14	11.32	11.50	11.69	11.87	12.24	12.99
23	9.44	9.62	9.79	9.97	10.15	10.33	10.51	10.69	10.87	11.05	11.23	11.42	11.60	11.79	12.16	12.92
24	9.35	9.52	9.70	9.88	10.06	10.24	10.42	10.61	10.79	10.97	11.16	11.34	11.53	11.72	12.10	12.86
25	9.26	9.44	9.62	9.80	9.98	10.16	10.35	10.54	10.72	10.90	11.09	11.28	11.47	11.66	12.04	12.81
26	9.19	9.37	9.55	9.73	9.91	10.10	10.28	10.47	10.66	10.84	11.03	11.22	11.41	11.60	11.99	12.76
27	9.12	9.30	9.49	9.67	9.85	10.04	10.23	10.42	10.60	10.79	10.98	11.17	11.37	11.56	11.95	12.73
28	9.06	9.25	9.43	9.62	9.80	9.99	10.18	10.37	10.56	10.75	10.094	11.13	11.32	11.52	11.91	12.70
29	9.01	9.19	9.38	9.57	9.75	9.94	10.13	10.33	10.52	10.71	10.90	11.09	11.29	11.48	11.88	12.67
30	8.96	9.15	9.33	9.53	9.71	9.90	10.09	10.29	10.48	10.67	10.87	11.06	11.26	11.45	11.85	12.64
35	8.79	8.98	9.18	9.37	9.56	9.76	9.96	10.16	10.35	10.55	10.75	10.95	11.15	11.35	11.76	12.57
40	8.69	8.89	9.08	9.29	9.48	9.68	9.88	10.09	10.29	10.49	10.69	10.90	11.10	11.30	11.71	12.53

BUILDING CALCULATIONS

Real property consists of land and structures which have physical dimensions of length, width, area, and volume. Appraisers, lenders, and investors require analysis and comparison of building content. For this purpose, exterior dimensions are used. The square foot system is probably the most popular and can be applied to residential, commercial and industrial structures. Gross floor area is computed excluding porches, garages and basements—which are treated separately. The cubic foot system is used to calculate total volume. It includes attics, basements, and dormer projections which the square foot system does not include. Basic formulas include:

$$A = L \times W$$

Area of a rectangle equals Length times Width

$$V = L \times W \times H$$

Volume equals Length times Width times Height

$$V = \frac{ba}{2} \times L$$

Area of a triangle equals Base times Altitude quantity divided by 2 times Length

$$D = \frac{square\ units}{width}$$

Depth equals square units divided by width

$$W = \frac{square\ units}{depth}$$

Width equals square units divided by depth

To Find Area of a Rectangle
Calculate the area of this house.

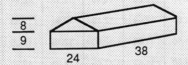

To Find Cubic Content of a Rectangle
Calculate the volume of the lower part of the house.

$$
\begin{array}{lllllll}
V & = & L & x & W & x & H \\
V & = & 24 & x & 38 & x & 9 \\
V & = & 8,208 \text{ cubic feet} & & & &
\end{array}
$$

To Find Cubic Content of a Triangle
Calculate the volume of the attic.

$$
\begin{array}{ll}
V & = \dfrac{ba}{2} \times L \\[2mm]
V & = \dfrac{24 \times 8}{2} \times 38 \\[2mm]
V & = 3,648 \text{ cubic feet}
\end{array}
$$

Area Calculations Result: 8,208 + 3,648 = 11,856 cubic feet

To Find Depth
Two-story row houses in a certain area have 18'6" fronts. These homes are sold for $16,650, which is equivalent to $12.50 a square foot. How deep are these houses?

$16,650	÷	$12.50	= 1,322 sq. ft.
1,322 sq.ft.	÷	2 floors	= 666 sq. ft. per floor
666 sq. ft. per floor	÷	18,5'	= 36 feet

MATHEMATICAL FORMULAS

Square

A side multiplied by 1.4142 equals diameter of its circumscribing circle.
A side multiplied by 4.443 equals circumference of its circumscribing circle.
A side multiplied by 1.128 equals diameter of an equal circle.
A side multiplied by 3.547 equals circumference of an equal circle.

To Find Side of an Equal Square

Multiply diameter by	0.8862
Or divide diameter by	1.1284
Or multiply circumference by	0.2821
Or divide circumference by	3.545

To Find Side of an Inscribed Square

Multiply diameter by	0.7071
Or multiply circumference by	0.2251
Or divide circumference by	4.4428

To Find Circumference

Multiply diameter by	3.1416
Or divide diameter by	0.3183

To Find Diameter

Multiply circumference by	0.3183
Or divide circumference by	3.1416

To Find Radius

Multiply circumference by	0.15915
Or divide circumference by	6.28318

To Find the Area of a Circle

Multiply circumference by one-quarter of the diameter	
Or multiply the square of diameter by	0.7854
Or multiply the square of circumference by	0.07958
Or multiply the square of 1/2 diameter by	3.1416

To Find the Square of a Sphere or Globe

Multiply the diameter by the circumference	
Or multiply the square of diameter by	3.1416
Or multiply four times the square of radius by	3.1416

To Find the Cubic Inches (Volume) in a Sphere or Globe

Multiply the cube of the diameter by	0.5236

1. A discount (mortgage discount point) is:

   (A) A one-time prepayment charge by a lender
   (B) Used to make a loan more competitive
   (C) Used to increase the lender's effective yield
   (D) All of the above

2. The interest method frequently used on savings accounts is:

   (A) Simple interest
   (B) Compound interest
   (C) Accrued interest
   (D) Prepaid interest

3. The _____ loan repayment plan is designed to pay a debt in full during the life of the loan.

   (A) Prorated
   (B) Discounted
   (C) Amortized
   (D) Subsidized

4. Which of the following is *not* true regarding a point?

   (A) May be a loan origination fee
   (B) Is a one-time charge
   (C) Is 1% of the loan amount
   (D) None of the above

5. 92.6 percent of 341 is:

   (A) 315.766
   (B) 31.567
   (C) 305.67
   (D) 315.676

6. A home's selling price of $137,250 was 95% of its original listing price. What was the original listing price?

   (A) $144,473.68
   (B) $1,444,736.80
   (C) $14,447.36
   (D) $130,387.50

7. What is the interest on a $29,000 loan at 16.75% for one year?

   (A) $485.75
   (B) $4,875.50
   (C) $48,575.50
   (D) $4,857.50

8. How long did a borrower have use of $129,500 if a 16.45% rate of interest cost him $12,475?

   (A) 213.5 days
   (B) 13 years
   (C) 21.35 months
   (D) 2135.5 days

9. What was your commission rate if you received $16,250 commission on a listing you sold for $302,000?

   (A) 5.5%
   (B) 5.58%
   (C) 5.83%
   (D) 5.38%

10. What was the listing broker's commission on a $179,000 sale at 6.5%, if the co-op office agreement is 50/50 split as follows: selling salesperson 75%, selling broker 25%, listing salesperson 75%, listing broker 25%?

    (A) $5,235.75
    (B) $4,363.13
    (C) $581.75
    (D) $1,454.37

Chapter 13
Tax Aspects of
Real Estate

PRINCIPLES OF TAXATION

The concept of taxes may be traced back to the earliest days of recorded history. Under our political and economic systems, the basic purpose of taxation has been to pay the cost of government services. An additional effect of taxation is a redistribution of the wealth of a nation because of the welfare transfers and subsidies paid to various sectors of the economy.

Basis of Payment The two broad principles of taxation widely recognized declare that taxes should be based on either of the following:

Ability to Pay. One of the earliest assumptions regarding taxes is that tax should be assessed according to one's ability to pay. This is called a progressive tax, in contrast to proportional and regressive taxes.

Benefits Received. It is also usually considered reasonable that taxes should be levied in proportion to the benefits received from government services, such as health and safety, parks, schools, street improvements, transit districts, etc.

Proportional Tax A tax in which the rate of tax remains constant "across the board," e.g., 10% of the individual's or business's income regardless of size of income or ability to pay, is classified as a proportional tax. The ad valorem ("according to value") real property tax and the sales tax are examples of this type of tax.

Progressive Tax A progressive tax employs increased rates of taxation as income increases. This is the basic structure of our income tax system, in which higher income levels pay higher income tax rates.

Regressive Tax A tax collected on a basis which results in a higher percentage at the lower income levels is a regressive tax. An example is the Social Security tax (FICA). Since the tax rate applies to income only up to a certain amount, persons with incomes above that amount pay an increasingly smaller percentage of their total income.

PROPERTY TAX

The "ad valorem" (according to value) tax system is generally applied to real property. The federal government has delegated property taxation to the states, which in turn delegate this authority to the local governments.

Taxable Property Taxes are levied on both real and personal property.

Real Property Taxes. Local city and county governments levy real property taxes on land and improvements within their jurisdiction; California homeowners, as well as businesses which own real property, pay this type of property tax.

Personal Property Taxes. Local governments levy personal property taxes on personal items such as business inventories and trade fixtures used in a business. In the past homeowners were assessed for pianos, livestock, etc.; today the vehicle license fee is the main personal property tax encountered in private life.

Assessments State law specifies assessment procedures voted into law by the electorate's approval of Proposition 13, known as the Jarvis-Gann initiative, in 1978. Under this law:

1% Limit. The maximum rate of any real property tax is limited by Proposition 13 to 1 percent of the assessed value, plus an amount to pay for voter approved bonds.

Base Year. Real property assessed values were rolled back to those of the March 1, 1975, lien date, subject to a maximum 2 percent annual inflationary increase.

Reassessment. On the sale of the real property, or when capital improvements are made, the assessed value is subject to an adjustment to full cash value (market value).

Tax Calendar The fiscal year for real property taxes runs from July 1 through June 30.

Lien Date. Taxes on real property become a lien against that specific property on March 1 prior to the fiscal year.

Installments. Taxes may be paid in two installments.

- One half of the tax is due on November 1. If not paid by 5 p.m. on December 10, the tax becomes delinquent and a 10 percent penalty and other miscellaneous charges are levied.

- The second installment, the remaining half of the tax, is due on February 1. If not paid by 5 p.m. on April 10, the tax becomes delinquent and a 10 percent penalty and other charges are levied.

- If either December 10 or April 10 falls on a Saturday, Sunday, or holiday, the tax is due by 5 p.m. the next business day.

Tax Stamp Sale If an owner fails to pay the property taxes on or before June 30 of the fiscal year, the property is "sold to the state" for unpaid taxes ("tax stamp sale"). This sale is referred to as a "book sale." It is not a conveyance of title and the delinquent owner remains in undisturbed possession of the property.

Redemption Period. The owner's name is entered in the delinquent account book which starts a five-year redemption period. If the taxes are not paid during the five-year redemption period, the delinquent property will be deeded to the state and the delinquent owner will be dispossessed. (Most counties will allow the former owner the privilege of reclaiming the property, and the title, as long as the state has not actually sold the property and conveyed the title to a new owner.)

Actual Sale After the five-year redemption period, the county tax collector, by law, has the right to sell the property to other governmental agencies or to any person at a public auction, and will establish a minimum bid approved by the Board of Supervisors and the State Controller.

Last-Minute Redemption. The owner may still redeem the property prior to auction by paying current taxes, delinquent taxes, penalties, interest, and administrative costs and receive a certificate of redemption.

Sale Procedure. Property tax sales are conducted on a cash basis with a tax deed to the successful bidder. Title companies may be reluctant to insure a title by tax deed for the first year because of possible litigation by the former owner.

REAL PROPERTY TAX EXEMPTIONS

The law requires that all real properties in California be assessed for tax purposes; however, certain property owners or renters receive partial or total exemption from property taxes.

Tax Exempt Property Most real property owned and occupied by governmental agencies, nonprofit educational institutions, certain nonprofit charitable organizations, and many church organizations is totally or partially exempt from property taxes in California.

Homeowner's Exemption Each California owner-occupied residential unit may receive a $7,000 annual tax exemption (deduction) from the full value of the property.

Qualifying Date. The owner must have owned and resided in the residence as of one minute past midnight on March 1 of the year preceding the fiscal year beginning July 1.

Filing Required. The owner must file by April 15 to be fully eligible for the exemption of $7,000, or by December 1 in order to receive 80 percent of the $7,000 exemption. Annual renewal is no longer required; once filed, the homeowner is entitled to the exemption as long as he or she remains the owner-occupant of that property.

Veteran's Exemption Certain California veterans may qualify for a $4,000 exemption on the assessed value of their property. However, the veteran may not claim both the homeowner's exemption and the veteran's exemption on the same property concurrently.

Disabled Veterans. The principal residence of a veteran who is blind, has lost the use of two or more limbs, or is totally disabled because of injury or disease incurred in military or naval service may be exempt to the amount of $40,000 market value ($60,000 if the household income does not exceed an amount determined yearly. The county assessor should be called to find out the amount).

Senior Citizens **Low-Income Refund.** A property owner 62 or older with a total household income of $12,000 or less may be eligible for a state-assisted refund on property taxes paid. The refund ranges from 4% to 96% of the taxes paid. The lower the income the greater the refund.

Deferral. Senior citizens (age 62 years or older) may qualify for deferral or postponement of property taxes on their residences.

Renter's Credit Under the California Renter Relief Act of 1973, the state extended a share of homeowners' tax benefits to residential renters. California residents who rent and occupy their principal residence as of March 1 each year may deduct a set dollar amount from their state tax liability.

SPECIAL ASSESSMENTS

Special local taxes may be levied on a specific property or area specifically benefiting from certain improvements or services. Examples of such improvements include streets, sidewalks, sewers, curbs, street lighting, etc.

Enforcement These special taxes are enforced in the same manner as general real property taxes. A special assessment becomes a lien on the specific property and may be foreclosed if not paid.

Federal Tax Treatment Special assessment taxes are not allowable deductions under the federal income tax laws, but add to cost basis of the property.

DOCUMENTARY TRANSFER TAX

The Documentary Transfer Tax Act of 1968 authorized individual counties and cities to place a transfer tax on the conveyance of real property. This replaced a former federal transfer stamp tax, discontinued in 1968.

Tax Rate The transfer tax rate is 55 cents for each $500 or fraction thereof, of taxable consideration. Taxable consideration means equity transferred. Assumed loans are not included in taxable consideration.

Example

A $130,000 transaction, where a $60,000 existing loan is assumed, would require $77 documentary transfer tax.

Calculations:

$130,000	− $60,000	=	$70,000	equity transferred
$70,000	÷ $500	=	140	units of $500
140	x $0.55	=	$77	tax

Payment The tax is usually paid by the seller at the time of recording.

INCOME TAX ASPECTS OF REAL ESTATE OWNERSHIP

The real estate licensee should understand the significant role of income tax planning in real estate transactions. Proper tax planning must begin before the taxpayer buys, sells, or exchanges, not after the transaction is completed. Advise your client or customer to consult a qualified tax accountant or lawyer, as needed.

Both the federal and state governments levy personal and business income taxes which, by and large, parallel each other. The discussion in this chapter is limited to federal income tax on real estate transactions involving individual ownership.

Tax Concepts The basic concept underlying the federal income tax is that most income is to be taxed, regardless of source. However, the U.S. Internal Revenue Code does allow certain income tax advantages with regard to real property ownership and sales, and makes other distinctions based on sources and amounts of income.

Classification of Income. Income from wages, commissions, interest, dividends, business profits, and the like is classified as ordinary income, distinguished from capital gains. Another set of classifications is active, passive and portfolio income.

Tax Brackets. Effective January 1, 1987, the number of tax brackets was reduced from 15 to 5. Since 1988 there are 3 brackets, with rates of 15%, 28%, and 33%.

Tax Rates. A *marginal tax rate* or tax bracket refers to the percentage at which the last dollar of income is taxed. An *effective tax rate* is the relationship between the total tax paid and the total taxable income.

Capital Gains Profits made from the sale of real estate, stocks, bonds, or other capital assets are classified as "capital gains."

Calculating Gain. Gain is the amount realized or value received in exchange, minus the seller's costs.

☐ The amount realized equals selling price minus selling expense

☐ The seller's cost equals original cost plus capital improvements minus allowable depreciation.

☐ The seller's basis is referred to as book value, cost basis, or adjusted cost basis. Maintenance and repair costs on business property are operating expenses, deductible when paid, and do not affect basis.

Tax Treatment. Currently both long and short term capital gains are taxed at the same rates as ordinary income. At present there is no tax advantage to holding assets for more than six months to qualify profit as "long term capital gain."

□ Long term capital gains realized through 1986 were given favorable treatment, and only 40% of the gain was taxed, at ordinary income tax rates. The maximum tax rate of 50% applied to 40% of the gain resulted in a maximum tax of 20%.

□ In 1987 the 60% exclusion of long term capital gains was eliminated. The rate on long term capital gain was capped at 28%. Since 1988, long term capital gains have been taxed at the same rates as ordinary income, the same as short term capital gains.

□ Several proposals have been placed before Congress to reinstate the favorable tax treatment of long-term capital gain, but none has been approved as of this writing.

Capital Loss. Before 1987, only 50% of net long term capital loss was deductible against ordinary income, to a maximum of $3,000 in any one year, with the balance of the deductible loss carried forward. Under current law, 100% of both short and long term capital loss is deductible, with the same $3,000 annual ceiling and carry forward.

New Categories of Income and Loss There are now three categories of income and loss, applicable both to ordinary income or loss and to capital gain or loss.

Active. Income (or loss) from business activity

Portfolio. Investment income (or loss)

Passive. Income (or loss) from a passive activity, including all income from rental real estate.

Passive Losses Passive losses can generally be offset only against passive income, with some exceptions. Unused or "suspended" passive losses are carried forward against future passive profits.

Exceptions. There are two exceptions to passive loss limitations, a temporary phase-in and an offset allowance for certain real property income.

□ For properties owned prior to enactment of the new law (October 16, 1986), the passive loss deduction limitation is phased in:

• 65% was allowed in 1987

• 40% in 1988

• 20% in 1989

• 10% in 1990

• None thereafter

□ For individuals who actively participate in management of the real property, up to $25,000 of passive losses may offset active or portfolio income. The $25,000 allowance is reduced, however, by

50% of any amount by which the individual's adjusted gross income exceeds $100,000. Thus, it is not available to individuals with adjusted gross incomes of $150,000 and over.

Owner-Occupied Residence

A basic premise of many federal programs is that homeownership is to be encouraged. Accordingly certain tax advantages are available for owner-occupied homes.

Deferred Gains Tax. Upon the sale of a personal residence, the tax law provides a grace period of 24 months for sellers to reinvest their gain in another home in which they plan to live without having to pay (recognize) a capital gains tax at the time of sale. To qualify, the new home purchase price must be equal to or greater than the sale price of the previous home. The tax is deferred until a later date.

Senior Exemption. A one-time, tax free capital gain exemption is allowed for taxpayers age 55 or older who sell their home which has been their principal residence 3 out of the last 5 years, up to a maximum of $125,000 of tax free exemption.

Income Tax Deductions. Allowable itemized expense deductions include: real property taxes, mortgage interest expenses (with some limitations), and limited uninsured casualty loss. (Depreciation, capital loss, and maintenance and repair are *not* deductible.)

☐ For 1987 only, mortgage interest deductibility was limited to loans up to the purchase price plus cost of improvements and loans for medical or educational expenses (except for mortgages in place before August 16, 1986).

☐ For 1988 and after, mortgage interest deductibility is limited to:

• Home acquisition indebtedness, up to $1 million. (Refinancing cannot increase home acquisition indebtedness.)

• Home equity indebtedness up to $100,000.

This provision is the source of the growing market in "home equity lines of credit" being offered by many banks and S&Ls.

Real Property Classifications

How the sale of a property is taxed depends on the purpose for which the seller holds the property.

IRS Categories. As classified by IRS, real property now falls into five classes. The classes include property held:

☐ *As Personal Residence*. Where the seller owns and lives. It may be a single-family residence, condominium, townhouse, yacht, apartment unit, or mobilehome.

☐ *For an Investment*. A non-income-producing unimproved property held for capital growth through appreciation.

244   *Tax Aspects of Real Estate*

□ *For the Production of Income*. Includes residential income, commercial, industrial, office, and other income-producing types of properties. It is property leased to someone else to use.

□ *For Use in Trade or Business*. Includes property used in the owner's own business operations, for example, a retail store, motel, industrial facility, medical office, other professional office or service facilities used by the owner.

□ *For Sale to Customers*. For example, real estate inventory or subdivided lands for sale to the public. Referred to as stock-in-trade.

Tax Effects. The old 60% deduction for "capital gains treatment" has been eliminated. There are, however, other tax applications that are specific for each class of property:

□ Rollover deferment applies only to personal residences.

□ Depreciation applies only to income-producing property.

□ Tax-deferred exchange applies only to investment, income, and trade or business property.

Law Changes   To meet changing revenue needs and because of its perceived usefulness as a tool for adjusting the economy and promoting social and political goals, the tax law is constantly changing.

Economic Recovery Tax Act of 1981 (ERTA). Tax cuts were instituted to encourage greater investment by business. The major tax cut for business involved faster and simpler depreciation. Depreciation was no longer based on the useful life of the asset; most depreciable real estate was placed on a 15-year basis (18 years if acquired after March 15, 1984, 19 years if acquired after May 8, 1985).

Tax Reform Act of 1986. This totally new law replaced the old Internal Revenue Code of 1954, which had been modified many times. The stated intent was to make the system fairer by reversing the trend toward using tax incentives and tax subsidies to cure social and economic problems. Many special tax incentives for real estate investment, enhanced by the 1981 ERTA, were reversed.

□ Accelerated depreciation of real estate was eliminated.

□ Long-term capital gains exclusions were eliminated.

□ Interest deductions became somewhat limited.

□ Real estate tax shelters became severely limited since the new law for the most part limits the amount of passive losses to the amount of income from passive investments, with some exceptions up to $25,000 and exceptions during a phase-in period through 1990.

□ The attractiveness of real estate as a tax shelter investment was replaced by its attractiveness as an economically profitable investment.

The Revenue Act of 1987. Modifications included new rules for deductibility of home mortgage interest and rules for installment sales. Further minor modifications were made in 1988 and 1989 to increase federal revenue without calling any change a "tax increase."

Depreciation Concepts and Techniques

For income tax purposes, depreciation is a bookkeeping entry, not an actual out-of-pocket expense or physical deterioration. It is a provision for the recapture of the depreciable portion of a capital asset out of income while the property is owned. This "theoretical depreciation" is allowed on (1) income-producing property or (2) property used in the operation of a trade or business. The IRS guidelines are:

Depreciable Real Property. This is defined as income producing improvements with limited useful life.

□ Includes not only structures, but orchards, groves, fruit and nut bearing trees, sidewalks, curbs, and gutters.

□ Includes additions to structures such as a patio, swimming pool, or rooms.

□ Excludes owner-occupied residences (not income-producing) and land (considered indestructible).

Calculating Depreciation. Depreciation laws changed several times in the 1980s. Properties will still be found where knowledge of earlier laws is important.

ADR Methods. For property placed into service through 1980, the Asset Depreciation Range (ADR) methods were applicable. If ADR election was in effect prior to 1981, the election continued on those properties.

□ *Straight-Line Method.* Allowance is prorated equally over the useful life after deducting salvage value, if any.

Formula: 100% ÷ Useful Life = Annual Depreciation Rate

Example: 100% ÷ 25 years = 4% Annual Depreciation Rate

□ *200% Declining Balance.* This method allows 2 times the straight-line rate. It is an accelerated method which allows the greatest amount of depreciation in the first year. The same rate is applied on the declining balance in each successive year. Variations:

150% Declining Balance: Allows $1\frac{1}{2}$ times straight-line rate

125% Declining Balance: Allows $1\frac{1}{4}$ times straight-line rate

☐ *Sum-of-the-Years' Digits.* An accelerated method in which the years of useful life are added and a fraction thereof is utilized each year.

Example

For a property with a 15-year useful life, the years' digits (1+2+3+...+14+15) add up to 120. Depreciation claimed is 15/120 the first year, 14/120 the second, and so on to 1/120 the fifteenth year.

ACRS. For property placed into service beginning January 1, 1981, the Accelerated Cost Recovery System (ACRS) was adopted to calculate depreciation. In addition to a 15-year straight-line depreciation schedule of 6.67% annually (later extended to 18 years, then to 19 years), other features included:

☐ The 175% declining balance method with a change to the straight-line method at a time which would maximize the deduction

☐ The 200% declining balance method with a switch to straight-line for low-income housing.

☐ Component depreciation was eliminated. Composite depreciation was required on the entire structure. However, a substantial improvement was treated as a separate building.

☐ Salvage value was no longer applicable.

☐ An optional extended recovery period of either 35 or 45 years could be elected instead of 15 years (or 18 years or 19 years).

☐ New and used property were treated the same.

TRA '86. The Tax Reform Act of 1986 maintains a modified ACRS structure, but makes significant changes in the way assets are classified and depreciation figured.

☐ Personal property assets are classified as 3, 5, 7, 10, or 15-year assets, and depreciation schedules use 200% or 150% declining balance methods.

☐ Real estate is depreciated over $27\frac{1}{2}$ years (residential) or $31\frac{1}{2}$ years (nonresidential), straight line only. In effect, accelerated depreciation is eliminated for nearly all real estate.

☐ An investor may elect a 40-year straight-line depreciation schedule if desired.

Installment Sales The Installment Sales Act of 1980 allows a seller to prorate tax on capital gain over the term of the installment contract. Before 1986-1987 this applied to any classification of property including "dealer" property and residences.

Eligibility. Most real property sales *except* dealer property now qualify for installment sales.

☐ Any portion of the sale price can be received in the year of sale with no limitation on the downpayment (formerly limited to 30% maximum).

☐ Election for installment treatment is automatic unless the taxpayer elects to the contrary.

☐ All of the purchase price can be deferred provided one payment was received after the tax year in which the sale occured.

Advantages. The primary attraction is that the seller pays tax on a prorated share of the first year's receipts. In addition,

☐ Part of each year's receipts are considered as gain, and the balance of the payment is return of investment.

☐ The seller can accept a small or no downpayment and thereby offer a more negotiable package.

☐ Property sold on a land contract qualifies, as title transfer is not a requirement.

Revenue Act of 1987. This law eliminated installment sale reporting for "dealer" property, but also eliminated a "proportionate disallowance rule" which reduced the benefits of installment sale reporting for many other properties. That rule applied for only one year, 1987.

Tax Reporting Two recent federal laws govern reporting of sellers' income from real estate transactions. These special reporting requirements are *in addition* to the normal inclusion of the income on the seller's tax return.

Form 1099-S. The Tax Reform Act of 1986 requires that all real estate transactions closing after January 1, 1987, must be reported to the IRS on a special Form 1099-S (Exhibit 27). The primary reporting responsibility falls to the person responsible for closing the transaction — the escrow agent, if there is one.

☐ *Responsible Party*. If no one is responsible for closing the transaction, the primary mortgage lender, or the seller's broker, or the buyer's broker, in that order, must forward copies of Form 1099-S to the buyer, seller, and IRS.

□ *Fees*. The '88 Act makes it unlawful for any real estate broker to charge a customer a separate fee for reporting the transaction to the IRS.

□ *Forms*. The form used to transmit the 1099-S to the IRS is the Form 1096, Annual Summary and Transmittal of U.S. Information Returns (Exhibit 28).

Foreign Investment in Real Property Tax Act (FIRPTA). This law requires that every buyer of U.S. real property must, unless an exemption applies, deduct and withhold from the seller's proceeds ten percent of the gross sales price. Withheld funds must be reported and paid to the IRS within 20 days after close of escrow. The primary exemptions are:

□ Seller's affidavit that the seller is not a "foreign person" (Exhibit 8, Chapter 4)

□ "Qualifying statement" from IRS specifying that no withholding is necessary

□ The buyer purchases the property for use as a personal residence and the purchase price is not over $300,000. (Exhibit 24, Chapter 10)

California Conformity In October 1987, California enacted the "California Personal Income Tax Fairness, Simplification, and Conformity Act of 1987," which brought California personal income tax and bank and corporation tax law into substantial conformity with new federal law in most respects effective January 1, 1987.

Brackets. The number of marginal tax rates (tax brackets) was reduced to 6, with a maximum rate of 9.3%.

Taxable Income. Calculations remain somewhat different from federal law. For example, unemployment and social security benefits and lottery winnings continue to be exempt.

Deductions. Base-broadening changes conform to those in the federal law, including passive loss limits, limitation on home mortgage interest deductibility, phase-out by 1990 of consumer interest deductions, and repeal of income averaging.

Capital Gains. The treatment of capital gains conforms to new federal treatment, with minor exceptions.

Forms. The new law instructs the Franchise Tax Board to make use to the maximum extent possible of the forms and procedures used by the federal government, dramatically simplifying the state return preparation process.

Type or machine print FILER'S name, street address, city, state, and ZIP code		OMB No. 1545-0997	**19****89** Proceeds From Real Estate Transactions
			Statement for Recipients of

Copy A For Internal Revenue Service Center

FILER'S Federal identification number	TRANSFEROR'S identification number	1 Date of closing (MMDDYY)	2 Gross proceeds $
Type or machine print TRANSFEROR'S name (first, middle, last)		3 Address or legal description	
Street address			
City, state, and ZIP code			
Account number (optional)		4 Check here if the transferor received or will receive property or services as part of the consideration ▶ ☐	

For Paperwork Reduction Act Notice and instructions for completing this form, see Instructions for Forms 1099, 1098, 5498, 1096, and W-2G.

Form **1099-S**   Department of the Treasury · Internal Revenue Service

---

☐ VOID   ☐ CORRECTED

FILER'S name, street address, city, state, and ZIP code		OMB No. 1545-0997	**19****89** Proceeds From Real Estate Transactions
			Statement for Recipients of

Copy B For Transferor

FILER'S Federal identification number	TRANSFEROR'S identification number	1 Date of closing	2 Gross proceeds $
TRANSFEROR'S name (first, middle, last)		3 Address or legal description	
Street address			
City, state, and ZIP code			
Account number (optional)		4 Check here if the transferor received or will receive property or services as part of the consideration ▶ ☐	

This is important tax information and is being furnished to the Internal Revenue Service. If you are required to file a return, a negligence penalty or other sanction will be imposed on you if this item is required to be reported and the IRS determines that it has not been reported.

Form **1099-S**   Department of the Treasury · Internal Revenue Service

---

Instructions for Transferor

Generally, persons responsible for closing a real estate transaction must report the real estate proceeds to the Internal Revenue Service and must furnish this statement to you. If the real estate transferred was your main home, file **Form 2119**, Sale of Your Home, with your income tax return even if you sold at a loss or you did not replace your home. If the real estate transferred was not your main home, report the transaction in the applicable parts of **Form 4797**, Sales of Business Property, **Form 6252**, Installment Sale Income, and/or **Schedule D** (Form 1040), Capital Gains and Losses.

Box 1.—Shows the date of closing.

Box 2.—Shows the gross proceeds from a real estate transaction. Gross proceeds include cash and notes payable to you and notes assumed by the transferee (buyer). This does not include the value of other property or services you received or are to receive.

Box 3.—Shows the address of the property transferred or a legal description of the property.

Box 4.—If you received or will receive property (other than cash) or services as part of the consideration for the property transferred, this box should be checked. The value of any property (other than cash) or services is not included in Box 2.

Copy C For Filer

Exhibit 27

6969   ☐ CORRECTED

| Form **1096** | **Annual Summary and Transmittal of** | OMB No. 1545-0108 |
| Department of the Treasury Internal Revenue Service | **U.S. Information Returns** | 19**89** |

⌐ Type or machine print FILER'S name (or attach label)   ⌐

Street address   PLACE LABEL HERE

City, state, and ZIP code
L   ⌐

| If you are not using a preprinted label, enter in Box 1 or 2 below the identification number you used as the filer on the information returns being transmitted. Do not fill in both Boxes 1 and 2. | Name of person to contact if IRS needs more information | **For Official Use Only** |
| | Telephone number ( ) | ☐☐☐☐☐☐☐ ☐☐ |

| 1 Employer identification number | 2 Social security number | 3 Total number of documents | 4 Federal income tax withheld $ | 5 Total amount reported with this Form 1096 $ |

Check only one box below to indicate the type of forms being transmitted.   If this is your FINAL return, check here . . . . . ☐

W-2G 32	1098 81	1099-A 80	1099-B 79	1099-DIV 91	1099-G 86	1099-INT 92	1099-MISC 95	1099-OID 96	1099-PATR 97	1099-R 98	1099-S 75	5498 28
☐	☐	☐	☐	☐	☐	☐	☐	☐	☐	☐	☐	☐

Under penalties of perjury, I declare that I have examined this return and accompanying documents and, to the best of my knowledge and belief, they are true, correct, and complete.

Signature ▶ .... Title ▶ .... Date ▶..........................

Please return this entire page to the Internal Revenue Service. Photocopies are NOT acceptable.

Instructions

Purpose of Form.—Use this form to transmit Forms W-2G, 1098, 1099, and 5498 to the Internal Revenue Service.

Completing Form 1096.—If you received a preprinted label from IRS with Package 1099, place the label in the name and address area of this form inside the brackets. Make any necessary corrections to your name and address on the label. However, do not use the label if the taxpayer identification number (TIN) shown is incorrect. If you are not using a preprinted label, enter the filer's name, address, and TIN in the spaces provided on the form. **The name, address, and TIN you enter on this form must be the same as those you enter in the upper left area of Form 1099, 1098, 5498, or W-2G.** A filer includes a payer, a recipient of mortgage interest payments, a broker, a barter exchange, a person reporting real estate transactions, a trustee or issuer of an individual retirement arrangement (including an IRA or SEP), and a lender who acquires an interest in secured property or who has reason to know that the property has been abandoned. Individuals not in a trade or business should enter their social security number in Box 2; sole proprietors and all others should enter their employer identification number in Box 1. However, sole proprietors who are not required to have an employer identification number should enter their social security number in Box 2.

Group the forms by form number and submit each group with a separate Form 1096. For example, if you must file both Forms 1098 and Forms 1099-A, complete one Form 1096 to transmit your Forms 1098 and another Form 1096 to transmit your Forms 1099-A.

In Box 3, enter the number of forms you are transmitting with this Form 1096. Do not include blank or voided forms in your total. Enter the number of correctly completed forms, not the number of pages, being transmitted. For example, if you send one page of three-to-a-page Forms 5498 with a Form 1096 and you have correctly completed two Forms 5498 on that page, enter 2 in Box 3 of Form 1096. Check the appropriate box to indicate the type of form you are transmitting.

No entry is required in Box 5 if you are filing Form 1099-A or 1099-G. For all other forms, enter in Box 5 of Form 1096 the total of the amounts from the specific boxes of the forms listed below:

Form W-2G	Box 1
Form 1098	Box 1
Form 1099-B	Boxes 2, 3, and 6
Form 1099-DIV	Boxes 1a, 5, and 6
Form 1099-INT	Boxes 1 and 3
Form 1099-MISC	Boxes 1, 2, 3, 5, 6, 7, 8, and 10
Form 1099-OID	Boxes 1 and 2
Form 1099-PATR	Boxes 1, 2, 3, and 5
Form 1099-R	Boxes 1 and 8
Form 1099-S	Box 2
Form 5498	Boxes 1 and 2

If you will not be filing Forms 1099, 1098, 5498, or W-2G in the future, either on paper or on magnetic media, please check the "FINAL return" box.

If you are filing a Form 1096 for corrected information returns, enter an "X" in the CORRECTED box at the top of this form.

For more information about filing, see the separate Instructions for Forms 1099, 1098, 5498, 1096, and W-2G.

For Paperwork Reduction Act Notice, see separate Instructions for Forms 1099, 1098, 5498, 1096, and W-2G.   Form **1096** (1989)

Exhibit 28

THE TAX-DEFERRED EXCHANGE - SECTION 1031

Section 1031 of the Internal Revenue Code states, "No gain or loss shall be recognized if property held for productive use in a trade or business or for investment . . . is exchanged solely for property of a like kind to be held either for productive use in a business or for investment."

Like-Kind Property One investment, income, or business property is exchanged for one to be held for the same purpose. In this context, "like-kind" does not suggest the necessity for the same quality, grade, or size of property.

Like in Character or Nature. An exchange may qualify for deferred treatment as long as the properties in the exchange fall into like-kind categories, i.e., the properties must be of a similar nature (real property) and must be given and received for investment, income, or for use in the taxpayer's trade or business.

Exclusions. Only three types of property—investment, income, and trade or business—may qualify for tax-deferred exchange. Neither personal residences nor dealer properties qualify for Section 1031 tax-deferred exchanges.

Requirements A completely tax-deferred exchange requires the taxpayer to exchange even or up in both value and equity. This means the exchanger must acquire property with an equal or greater equity and larger fair market value than the property exchanged. To qualify for favorable tax treatment under Section 1031, the like-kind property must be exchanged for like-kind property. No cash, no mortgage relief, and no other unlike property, such as personal property, securities, or non-qualifying real property may be received.

Definitions Equity is the basic commodity in all exchanges. For tax-deferred exchanges, three other essential concepts are basis, gain, and boot.

Basis. Basis is the book value of the property. It is cost plus capital improvements minus depreciation. It is *not* the same as equity. For properties acquired by gift or inheritance, special rules apply for determining basis.

☐ The basis of property received as a gift is the donor's basis or market value, whichever is lower.

☐ Inherited property's basis is its fair market value on the date of the decedent's death.

```
┌─────────────────────────────────────────────────────────────────┐
│                          Basis Example                          │
│                                                                 │
│  Your client paid $100,000 for a property. The land was valued  │
│  at $20,000 and the improvements were valued at $80,000 using   │
│  the assessor's ratio. During his ownership your client         │
│  replaced the roof at a cost of $2,000, a capital improvement,  │
│  and took $20,000 depreciation on the improvement. Calculate    │
│  the basis.                                                     │
│                                                                 │
│  Calculation:                                                   │
│                                                                 │
│        Cost                              $100,000               │
│                                                                 │
│        Plus: Capital Improvements        +  2,000               │
│                                                                 │
│        Less: Depreciation                 - 20,000              │
│                                                                 │
│        Equals:                           $ 82,000   Basis       │
└─────────────────────────────────────────────────────────────────┘
```

Gain. The gain (profit) upon sale is the difference between the basis and the amount realized from the sale. Selling expenses such as commission, advertising, attorney fees, etc., are deducted from the selling price to arrive at the amount realized in computing gain.

```
┌─────────────────────────────────────────────────────────────────┐
│                            Example                              │
│                                                                 │
│  If your client were to resell the above property with a basis  │
│  of $82,000 for $110,000, he would have a gain of $28,000,      │
│  classified as either "ordinary" or "capital" gain depending    │
│  upon the classification of the property.                       │
└─────────────────────────────────────────────────────────────────┘
```

Boot. Any "unlike" property involved in the exchange, normally to equalize the values of the equities being transferred, is classified as boot. Examples of boot include:

☐ Cash received though an exchange, either actually or constructively

☐ Net mortgage relief, which occurs when an exchange transaction party is relieved of a mortgage by an assumption, refinancing, or having the property taken subject to the remaining debt

☐ Other unlike property: personal property (boat, cars, etc.), installment notes, securities, livestock, mortgages assigned, junior trust deeds, and property held for purposes other than investment, income, or trade or business use.

Trading Up and Down. From a practical point of view, an investor who is "trading up" is in an advantageous position to exchange, where one who "trades down" can rarely avoid the receipt of boot and the consequence of taxable gain, although trading down is one way to spread recognized gain over a period of time.

General Tax Rule For income tax on an exchange or sale, the tax liability is based on the boot or the gain, whichever is less.

Example

Your client owns an apartment building with a basis of $230,000 and a $240,000 mortgage. In an exchange, he accepts a property worth $250,000 (mortgaged at $240,000) plus $20,000 cash.

Gain equals: sale price minus basis

($250,000 + $20,000) − $230,000 = $40,000 gain

Boot is the unlike property: $20,000 cash

Thus your client's tax will be based upon the boot of $20,000.

The remaining $20,000 gain will be deferred into the acquired building.

STARTING AN EXCHANGE PROGRAM

The real estate broker or office may find exchanges to be a desirable specialization or sideline.

Basic Rule Always be prepared to advise your clients and customers to seek specific tax and legal counsel.

Expertise While this text has discussed many facets of taxation and exchanging, it is not possible to become an expert in either area without considerable additional course work and practical experience. Suggested skills to acquire for a successful exchange program include:

Subject Knowledge. General expertise in real estate, plus special knowledge applicable to exchanges.

☐ Become knowledgeable in basic tax laws as they relate to the exchange and sale of real property.

☐ Become an expert in financing and the language of finance instruments such as notes, discounts, AITDs, "wraps," etc.

☐ Develop an awareness of property values; what causes changes in property values, how to take salable listings, and when to reject certain listings.

Counseling Skills. Even more than in an ordinary sale, the broker in an exchange is acting as a mediator and facilitator. Become a skillful interviewer by practice and conscious effort. Know your clients, their motivations, financial portfolio, tax situation, real estate needs, etc. The more information you gather about them, the better the chances are to succeed in the exchange.

Prospecting for Exchange Clients Earlier chapters on the listing process, advertising, and prospecting discussed prospecting methods in general, which are also applicable for exchange prospecting. Special suggestions for exchange prospecting include:

☐ Plan and write well-placed exchange property message ads.

☐ Inquire of owners of presently listed property as to their receptivity to exchange offers.

☐ Evaluate hard-to-sell properties and old and new listings for exchange potential.

☐ Participate in local, regional, and national Board meetings' exchange discussions.

☐ Solicit cooperation among fellow licensees and organized property exchange groups.

☐ Contact former buyers who may be ready for a change.

Fundamental Rules The following rules will help insure quality customer service.

Fair Market Value. All properties should be listed at fair market value; exchanges must be mutually beneficial to all parties.

☐ Cash price and exchange price should be the same. Only one price should be quoted for each property in the transaction.

☐ Equity should be measurable and workable (a fundamental requirement).

Written Contracts. Strive for long-term (6 months or more) exclusive listings (use a form like CAR's "Exclusive Employment of Broker to Exchange, Sell, Lease or Option," Exhibit 29), at least on one of the exchange properties. No oral agreements should be introduced in the exchange transaction.

Documentation. The licensee should research property thoroughly and prepare a form of property analysis.

Cooperation. All exchange licensees need the cooperation of their colleagues. Most successful exchanges involve two or more licensees. The "loner" licensee will find it difficult to succeed. Cooperating licensees must disclose all of the available essential facts to each other.

	Exchange properties and services must be marketed just like sales.
Develop a Marketing Plan	

Develop a Marketing Plan

Exchange properties and services must be marketed just like sales.

Promote the Property. Prepare a "property package" which consists of pertinent data regarding the property and the client, for presentations at various exchange group meetings.

Plan With Client. Meet regularly with the client to discuss marketing strategy, or to present exchange proposals.

Educate the Client. Provide the owner and client with a total picture of the property's exchange potential: basis, mortgage disposition, gain, etc.

THE EXCHANGE AGREEMENT

An exchange must be carefully planned so that each step in the transaction is legitimate and the intent of the parties is to structure an exchange and not to create a taxable sale. When properly executed, the exchange agreement is a legal and binding contract (Exhibit 30).

Equity-Based Transaction

Real estate practitioners are generally attuned to sales price or loan amount as the basis of the transaction. In the case of exchanges, equity becomes the basis of the transaction.

Exchange Escrow

A successful tax-deferred exchange escrow complies with the wishes of the exchangers, the licensees, the lenders, and the tax regulators. The exchange escrow form should conform with the licensees' exchange agreement form in all its details in order to avoid the transformation of an exchange transaction into a sale and purchase agreement.

Legal Aspects. Escrow processing cannot deal with the legal or tax aspects of this transaction. This is a job for legal professionals.

Structure. The device should be structured by the exchange specialist or legal counsel, not the escrowholder. The escrow is a repository for instructions, not the inventor. In taking the basic data, exchanges should be viewed as a series of sales which may, for simplicity's sake, be diagrammed to derive the net result.

Similarities to Sale

Whether or not this is technically considered a sale, sale related items such as funds clearance, retrofit matters, local ordinance requirements, and FIRPTA are issues that must be incorporated in the instructions, as applicable.

EXCLUSIVE EMPLOYMENT OF BROKER TO
EXCHANGE, SELL, LEASE OR OPTION
CALIFORNIA ASSOCIATION OF REALTORS® STANDARD FORM

THIS IS INTENDED TO BE A LEGALLY BINDING AGREEMENT—READ IT CAREFULLY.

1. The undersigned _____
(PRINCIPAL), hereby grants to _____
a licensed real estate broker, hereinafter called "agent," the EXCLUSIVE AND IRREVOCABLE RIGHT commencing on _____
_____ , 19 ___ and terminating at midnight on _____ , 19 ___ to advise, offer, solicit and negotiate for
the disposition of the Principal's right, title, and interest, through exchange, sale, lease or option on terms acceptable to Principal of the real and
personal property described as follows: _____
_____
_____
_____

SUBJECT TO: _____
_____
_____
_____

TERMS: _____
_____
_____

2. Agent is hereby authorized to accept and hold on my behalf a deposit from any offer or pending my acceptance. No offer shall be submitted to
me unless signed by the offeror or his authorized agent.

3. I warrant that I am the owner of or have the right to obtain and deliver marketable title to the property described above. Evidence of title of
the real property shall be in the form of a California Land Title Association Standard Coverage Policy of Title Insurance to be paid for
by _____

4. Agent may ☐ may not ☐ place a for sale or exchange sign on the property.

**5. Notice: The amount or rate of real estate commissions is not fixed by law. They are set by each broker
individually and may be negotiable between the seller and broker.**
Compensation to Agent: (a) I hereby agree to pay Agent a fee of $ _____ upon exchange, sale, lease or
exercise of an option which has been executed during the term hereof or any extension thereof by Agent, or through any other person, or by me, or if
said property is withdrawn from exchange, sale, lease or option without the consent of Agent, or made unmarketable by my voluntary act during the
term hereof or any extension thereof; or

(b) If within _____ days after expiration hereof, or any extension thereof, I enter into an agreement with anyone with whom
Agent has had negotiations prior to final expiration, provided I have received notice in writing thereof before or upon expiration of this agreement or any
extension thereof.

6. If any action or proceeding be instituted to enforce this agreement, the prevailing party shall receive reasonable attorney's fees and costs.

7. In the event of an exchange agent may represent all parties and collect compensation or commission from them provided there is full disclosure
to all principals of such Agency. Agent may cooperate with sub-agents and other agents and divide such compensation or commission in any manner
acceptable to them.

8. Other Provisions: _____
_____
_____

9. I acknowledge that I have read and understand this Agreement, and that I have received a copy hereof.
Dated _____ , 19 ___   _____ , California

_____   _____
PRINCIPAL   PRINCIPAL

_____   _____
ADDRESS   CITY—STATE—PHONE

10. In consideration of the above, Agent agrees to use diligence in the performance of his obligations.

_____   _____
AGENT   ADDRESS—CITY

By _____
                                          _____
                                          PHONE   DATE

NO REPRESENTATION IS MADE AS TO THE LEGAL VALIDITY OF ANY PROVISION OR THE ADEQUACY OF ANY PROVISION IN ANY SPECIFIC TRANSACTION. IF YOU DESIRE
LEGAL ADVICE, CONSULT YOUR ATTORNEY.

To order, contact—California Association of Realtors®
525 S. Virgil Avenue, Los Angeles, California 90020
Copyright © 1977, California Association of Realtors® (Revised 1980)   FORM EX-11

TT-L5-FG

Exhibit 29

EXCHANGE AGREEMENT

THIS IS INTENDED TO BE A LEGALLY BINDING CONTRACT. READ IT CAREFULLY.

CALIFORNIA ASSOCIATION OF REALTORS® STANDARD FORM

_____, California. _____, 19 _____

herein called _____, offers to exchange

the following described property, designated as Property No. _____ situated in _____;

County of _____, State of _____:

_____

_____

_____

_____

for the following described property of _____

herein called _____, designated as Property No. _____;

situated in _____;

County of _____, State of _____:

_____

_____

_____

Terms and Conditions of Exchange:

_____

_____

_____

_____

_____

_____

_____

_____

_____

_____

_____

_____

_____

_____

_____

_____

_____

_____

_____

The supplements initialed below are incorporated as part of this agreement.

Other

_____ Structural Pest Control Certification Agreement   _____ _____

_____ Special Studies Zone Disclosure   _____ _____

_____ Flood Insurance Disclosure   _____ _____

Both parties acknowledge receipt of a copy of this page. Page 1 of _____ pages.

To order, contact—California Association of Realtors®
525 S. Virgil Avenue, Los Angeles, California 90020
Copyright © 1978, California Association of Realtors®   FORM E-11-1

Exhibit 30.1

EXCHANGE AGREEMENT

The following terms and conditions are hereby incorporated in and made a part of the offer.

CALIFORNIA ASSOCIATION OF REALTORS® STANDARD FORM

1.   The parties hereto shall deliver signed escrow instructions to _____
_____, escrow holder, within _____ days from acceptance,
which shall provide for closing within _____ days from acceptance. Escrow fees shall be paid as follows: _____
_____
_____

2.   Title is to be free of liens, encumbrances, easements, restrictions, rights and conditions of record or known to the conveying party,
other than the following: _____
_____
_____

Each party shall provide the other with (a) a standard California Land Title Association policy, or (b) _____
_____, issued by _____
to be paid for as follows: _____ ,
showing title vested in the acquiring party subject only to the above and to any liens or encumbrances to be recorded in accordance with this
agreement. If the conveying party fails to deliver title as above, the acquiring party may terminate this agreement and shall be released from
payment of any compensation to broker(s) for services rendered.

3.   Unless otherwise designated in escrow instructions, title to the property acquired shall vest as follows: _____
_____

(The manner of taking title may have significant legal and tax consequences. Therefore, give this matter serious consideration.)

4.   Property taxes, premiums on insurance acceptable to the party acquiring the property insured, rents, interest and _____
_____ shall be prorated as of (a) the date of recordation of deed,
or (b) _____
Any bond or assessment which is a lien on a party's property shall be paid or assumed as follows: _____
_____

5 (A). Possession of Property No. _____ shall be delivered (a) on close of escrow, or (b) not later than _____ days after close of
escrow, or (c) _____
_____

5 (B). Possession of Property No. _____ shall be delivered (a) on close of escrow, or (b) not later than _____ days after close of
escrow, or (c) _____
_____

6.   If, as a part of this exchange, any property is to be sold to a third party, the original transferor shall indemnify and hold harmless
the party conveying the property to the third party from all claims, liability, loss, damage and expenses including reasonable attorneys' fees
and costs incurred by reason of any warranties or representations made by conveying party to the purchaser provided they conform to the
warranties and representations made by the original tranferor either by this agreement or in any statement made or document delivered to
the conveying party or to the designated escrow holder.

7.   Each party warrants that he has no knowledge of the existence of any notices of violations of city, county or state building, zoning,
fire and health codes, ordinances, or other governmental regulations filed or issued against his property.

8.   Each party represents to the other that no tenant, if any, is entitled to any rebate, concession or other benefit except as set forth in
rental agreements and leases, copies of which are to be exchanged or delivered within _____ days of acceptance. If such rental
agreements or leases are not disapproved in writing within _____ days of receipt thereof, this condition shall be deemed waived.

9.   Unless acceptance of this offer is signed by the other party hereto and the signed copy delivered to the undersigned, in person or by
mail to the address below, within _____ days, this offer shall be deemed revoked.

10.   Each party agrees that _____ broker
address _____ , California
telephone _____ can act as agent for, and may accept compensation for
services from, each party herein. Broker is authorized to cooperate with other brokers and to divide such compensation as agreed by them.

11.   It is the intention of the parties to the extent permitted by law, that the mutual conveyances agreed to herein will qualify as an
"exchange" within the meaning of Section 1031 of the Internal Revenue Code of 1954 and Section 18081 of the California Revenue and
Taxation Code. Failure to so qualify however, shall not affect the validity of this agreement.

12.   Each party agrees to execute and deliver to escrow any instrument or to perform any act reasonably necessary to carry out the
provisions of this agreement.

13.   In any action or proceeding arising out of this agreement, the prevailing party shall be entitled to reasonable attorneys' fees and costs.

14.   Time is of the essence of this agreement. All modifications or extensions shall be in writing signed by the parties.

Both parties acknowledge receipt of a copy of this page. Page 2 of _____ Pages.

_____   _____
_____   _____

To order, Contact—California Association of Realtors®
525 S. Virgil Avenue, Los Angeles, California 90020
Copyright © 1982, California Association of Realtors®

FORM E-11-2

Exhibit 30.2

EXCHANGE AGREEMENT

THIS IS INTENDED TO BE A LEGALLY BINDING AGREEMENT. READ IT CAREFULLY.

CALIFORNIA ASSOCIATION OF REALTORS® STANDARD FORM

If the other party hereto accepts the foregoing offer, I agree to pay to _____
as broker for services rendered as follows: _____
_____

payable (a) on recordation of deed or on delivery of a Real Property Contract as defined by Civil Code Section 2985; or (b) upon default if completion of the exchange is prevented by me; or (c) _____
_____

In any action or proceeding arising out of this agreement, the prevailing party shall be entitled to reasonable attorney's fees and costs.

Receipt of a copy hereof is hereby acknowledged. Page 3 of _____ Pages.

_____ , State _____ , Dated _____ , 19 _____

Address _____   _____

Telephone _____   _____

Broker(s) agree to the foregoing.

Dated _____ , 19 _____   Dated _____ , 19 _____

Broker _____   Broker _____

By _____   By _____

ACCEPTANCE

The foregoing offer and agreement to exchange the properties upon the terms and conditions stated is hereby accepted and I agree to pay _____
_____ ,
California, telephone _____ as broker(s) for services rendered as follows: _____
_____

payable as follows: (a) on recordation of Deed or delivery of Real Property Sales Contract as defined by Civil Code Section 2985; (b) upon default if completion is prevented by me; or (c) _____ .

Unless otherwise designated in the escrow instruction, title to the property acquired shall vest as follows: _____
_____

(The manner of taking title may have significant legal and tax consequences. Therefore, give this matter serious consideration.)
In any action or proceeding arising out of this agreement, the prevailing party shall be entitled to reasonable attorneys' fees and costs.

Receipt of a copy hereof is acknowledged and broker is authorized to deliver a signed copy to the other party named above. Page 3 of _____ Pages.

_____ , State _____ , Dated _____ , 19 _____

Address _____   _____

Telephone _____   _____

Broker(s) agree to the foregoing:

Dated _____ , 19 _____   Dated _____ , 19 _____

Broker _____   Broker _____

By _____   By _____

To order, contact—California Association of Realtors®
525 S. Virgil Avenue, Los Angeles, California 90020
Copyright© (1982), California Association of Realtors®   FORM E-11-3

Exhibit 30.3

Chapter 13 Quiz

1. The adjusted cost basis equals original cost
_____ capital improvements _____
allowable depreciation.

    (A)   minus; plus
    (B)   plus; plus
    (C)   plus; minus
    (D)   minus; minus

2. A $200,000 transaction in which the buyer
assumes an existing loan of $160,000 and pays
the balance as cash down requires documentary
transfer tax of:

    (A) $220.00
    (B) $176.00
    (C) $44.00
    (D)   None of the above

3. The California homeowner's exemption:

    (A)   Is $2,750
    (B)   Must be filed by February 1
    (C)   Applies to owners age 55 or older
    (D)   Applies to owner-occupied residences

4. Which of the following cannot be depreciated
by income property owners for income tax
purposes?

    (A)   Paved sidewalk
    (B)   Storage lockers
    (C)   Fences
    (D)   Land

5. Boot in a Section 1031 exchange could be:

    (A)   Cash
    (B)   Mortgage relief
    (C)   A note secured by a deed of trust
    (D)   Any of the above

6. Delinquent property tax regulations in
California provide a redemption period of:

    (A)   One year
    (B)   Five years
    (C)   Three years
    (D)   Seven years

7. Your client asks you to estimate the basis on a
property he has just purchased for $200,000
with a $150,000 assumable loan. He paid
$50,000 cash down and made $25,000 of major
long-lived repairs necessary to make the
property rentable. What is the basis of this
property?

    (A) $200,000
    (B) $225,000
    (C) $175,000
    (D) $75,000

8. To build a successful exchange program the
licensee should do all of the following, except:

    (A)   Develop an awareness of property values
    (B)   Become knowledgeable in basic tax laws
    (C)   Accept all listings offered
    (D)   Become knowledgeable in customer
          psychology

9. Advantages of the Installment Sales Act of
1980 include the following:

    (A)   No limitation on the downpayment
    (B)   Applicable to land contracts
    (C)   Seller pays tax on only a prorated share
          of the first year's receipts
    (D)   All of the above

10. Under the Revenue Act of 1987, home
mortgage interest:

    (A)   Is not deductible
    (B)   Is deductible on acquisition indebtedness
          up to $1 million plus home equity
          indebtedness up to $100,000
    (C)   Is limited to one principal residence
    (D)   Is always deductible without limitation

Chapter 14
Income Property Investment

BASIC REASONS FOR INVESTING IN REAL ESTATE

Knowing why investors are attracted to real estate should help you to better serve your clients and customers and to achieve your own personal goals and objectives. Sales strategies should be planned to demonstrate to prospective investors how ownership of a particular investment property will satisfy their basic reasons for investing in real estate.

Income Tax Benefits
Operating expenses, mortgage interest payments, and depreciation allowance deductions may offset other earned income, thereby reducing the taxpayer's liability. Real estate investments can produce tax-free income, tax-deferred income, and tax-sheltered income.

Leverage
Real estate makes it possible to use OPM: other people's money. Real estate investments need not require a 100% cash purchase; buyers may obtain relatively high loan-to-value loans and increase the percentage yield on their invested downpayment.

Tax-Free Refinancing
Property owners may borrow on their equity without paying income tax on the amount obtained. The IRS considers refinancing to be a withdrawal of capital invested and not taxable income.

Hedge Against Inflation
Because property values usually rise with or above reported inflation rate levels, real estate may act as a hedge against the ill effects of inflation. Repayment of existing loans with inflated or "soft" dollars further serves as an inflation hedge.

Building an Estate Many investors regard their real estate investments as the foundation for an estate, with assistance from their rent-paying tenants in covering expenses and mortgage payments.

Pride of Ownership The ownership of real property provides a psychological benefit to the investor.

Investment and Consumption Recreational properties, second homes, time-share ownership, etc., may be purchased both for vacation use and with the hope for increased value (appreciation) over time.

High Yields Real estate investments continue to generate relatively high rates of return (yield) on cash invested.

Cash Flow Real estate investments can produce a net spendable cash flow to increase disposable income.

REAL ESTATE INVESTMENT TERMINOLOGY

Sales strategy can be more effective if you know appropriate real estate investment terminology. Exhibit 31 outlines investment terms and their relationships in graphic form.

Income and Expense Terms The following terms are presented in a suggested analytical sequence, that is, the outline follows the steps of a property analysis (Exhibit 32, 33), which is prepared by the licensee and used as a sales aid.

Annual Gross Revenue (Gross Scheduled Income). This is an estimate of the total receipts in each future year if all the rentable spaces are rented (at the adjusted rent schedule) without any collection losses; a hypothetical base figure used in estimating what actual receipts will be.

Vacancy and Collection Loss Allowance (Vacancy Factor). This is usually expressed as a percentage of annual gross revenue and is a deduction from the estimate of the annual gross revenue to allow for:

☐ Vacancies

☐ Variations from adjusted rent schedule

☐ Losses in collection.

Effective Annual Gross Revenue (Gross Operating Income, Effective Gross Income). This is an estimate of what the actual receipts will be in each future year, calculated by subtracting the vacancy allowance from the annual gross revenue.

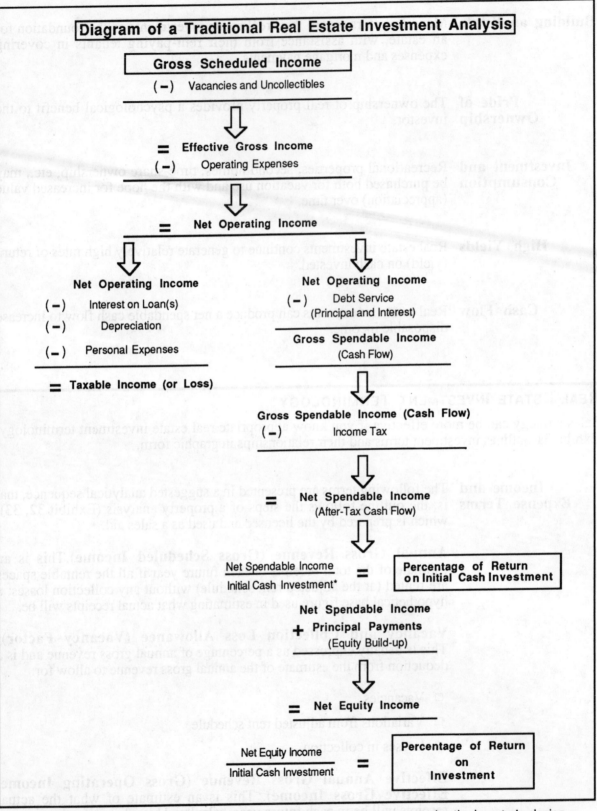

Diagram of a Traditional Real Estate Investment Analysis

Gross Scheduled Income

(–) Vacancies and Uncollectibles

= **Effective Gross Income**

(–) Operating Expenses

= **Net Operating Income**

Net Operating Income

(–) Interest on Loan(s)

(–) Depreciation

(–) Personal Expenses

= **Taxable Income (or Loss)**

Net Operating Income

(–) Debt Service
(Principal and Interest)

Gross Spendable Income
(Cash Flow)

Gross Spendable Income (Cash Flow)

(–) Income Tax

= **Net Spendable Income**
(After-Tax Cash Flow)

$$\frac{\text{Net Spendable Income}}{\text{Initial Cash Investment*}} = \boxed{\begin{array}{c}\textbf{Percentage of Return}\\\textbf{on Initial Cash Investment}\end{array}}$$

Net Spendable Income

+ **Principal Payments**
(Equity Build-up)

= **Net Equity Income**

$$\frac{\text{Net Equity Income}}{\text{Initial Cash Investment}} = \boxed{\begin{array}{c}\textbf{Percentage of Return}\\\textbf{on}\\\textbf{Investment}\end{array}}$$

* Some consider the initial cash investment to consist of the downpayment plus the investor's closing costs. But most brokers use only the downpayment as the initial cash investment, noting that closing costs are frequently deducted as an expense in the first year.

Exhibit 31

Annual Operating Expenses (Operating Expenses). These vary with type of property. Typical items are property taxes, insurance, etc. Depreciation, interest, loan payments, and income tax are not operating expenses as such, but are considered personal expenses of the owner.

Annual Net Income (Net Operating Income, NOI). This is the annual effective gross revenue less annual operating expenses.

Taxable Income. Annual net income less interest on loan payment, depreciation, and personal expenses produces a taxable income for the investor, a figure usually quite different from the property's net operating income.

Gross Spendable Income (Cash Flow or Before-Tax Cash Flow). Annual net income less annual debt service (ADS), which is the principal and interest payment.

Net Spendable Income (After-Tax Cash Flow). Gross spendable income less income tax due on taxable income.

Profit Terms There are several ways of expressing the profitability of an income property, so that various properties can be compared as investments.

Expense Ratio. The ratio of annual operating expenses to effective annual gross revenue, expressed as a percentage.

Earning Expectancy. A year by year forecast of the future net income of the property for its remaining economic life. (In the case of the land portion of real property owned in fee, the remaining economic life is infinite.)

Percentage of Cash Return On Initial Investment (Cash-on-Cash Return). Calculated by dividing net spendable income by the initial cash investment.

Percentage Return On Initial Investment. Obtained by dividing the net equity income (net spendable income plus principal payments, i.e., the equity buildup) by the initial cash investment.

CASH FLOW VS. TAX FLOW ANALYSIS

One major objective of investors has traditionally been to develop allowable deductions which are greater than the cash flow to create a tax loss on paper, thereby reducing tax liability.

Income Tax Benefits Real estate investment has made it possible to reduce tax liability by excluding or sheltering from taxable income a certain amount of cash flow from the investment.

Pre-1986. Prior to the Tax Reform Act of 1986, for many investors tax shelter was more important than the actual cash flow.

From 1987. Starting in 1987, because of severe limitations placed on deductiblity of "paper losses," a positive cash flow and appreciation became far more significant investment objectives in real estate.

Depreciation The principal source of tax shelter in real estate investments is depreciation. While operating expenses can also be significant, they are usually actual out-of-pocket expenses, whereas for tax purposes, depreciation is a bookkeeping deduction, not an out-of-pocket expense.

Advantage of Depreciation. Because depreciation is a bookkeeping deduction, as such it does not reduce the actual cash flow to the investor.

IRS Schedules. Theoretical depreciation schedules allowable by the IRS provide for the recapture of the depreciable portion of property over a period set by law. It is not related to depreciation as used in appraisal (actual loss of value), but is a "capital cost recovery" system. For property acquired on or after January 1, 1987, a depreciation period of:

- $27\frac{1}{2}$ years applies to residential property, and

- $31\frac{1}{2}$ years to nonresidential property.

The 1981 tax law provided accelerated depreciation periods of

- 15 years on property acquired from January 1, 1981, through March 15, 1984,

- 18 years on property acquired from March 16, 1984, through May 8, 1985, and

- 19 years on property acquired from May 8, 1985, through December 1986.

Depreciation schedules set up during these earlier periods are retained for properties still owned. The chart below displays in graphic form the number of years required to depreciate based on when the property was acquired.

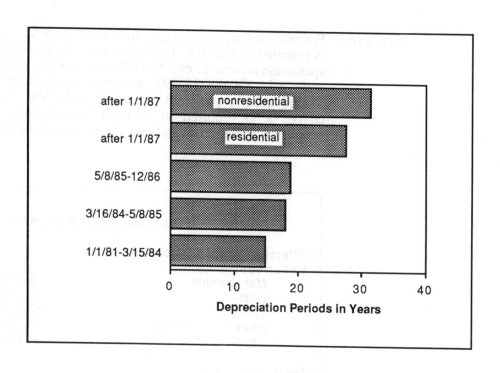

after 1/1/87 — nonresidential
after 1/1/87 — residential
5/8/85-12/86
3/16/84-5/8/85
1/1/81-3/15/84

0   10   20   30   40

Depreciation Periods in Years

Cash Flow   Gross spendable income or before-tax cash flow is the amount of cash left after all operating expenses and mortgage payments are paid. A simplified annual cash flow statement may be shown as:

Cash Flow Statement		
Effective Annual Gross Revenue		$10,000
Expenses:		
Management	$ 600	
Utilities	$1,100	
Taxes	<u>$2,300</u>	
Total Expenses		<u>− 4,000</u>
Annual Net Income		$ 6,000
Mortgage Payment		<u>− 5,000</u>
Cash Flow		$ 1,000

Tax Flow For income tax purposes the profit and loss (P&L) statement information is reported to the IRS. The above cash flow statement reported $1,000 spendable income after a $5,000 mortgage payment and other expenses were paid. Of the $5,000 mortgage payment, $4,000 is interest and $1,000 goes to principal reduction. A $2,500 allowable depreciation charge is not reported on the cash flow statement but appears on the simplified annual profit and loss statement as follows.

Profit and Loss Statement

Effective Annual Gross Revenue		$10,000
Expenses:		
Management	$ 600	
Utilities	$1,100	
Taxes	$2,300	
Interest on Mortgage	$4,000	
Depreciation	$2,500	
Total Expenses		– $10,500
Loss		($ 500)

The $500 loss reported on the profit and loss statement for tax purposes is the amount of shelter available to reduce the investor's tax liability within the passive loss limitations.

INCOME PROPERTY INVESTMENT ANALYSIS

Real estate competes against numerous other investment opportunities such as stocks, bonds, mutual funds, money market certificates, savings accounts, T-bills, oil, movies, gold and other metals, and many other investment media. Analysis enables the investor to choose the best investment to meet that investor's objectives.

Fixed Investments vs. Equity Investments One way of classifying competing investments is as fixed or equity investments.

Fixed Investments. Fixed dollar amounts are invested over a period of time (which may be definite or indefinite) at a fixed rate of return.

- ☐ Fixed investments with a definite time period, which may become less valuable as a result of inflation, are bonds, trust deeds, life insurance policies, and CDs.

- ☐ A passbook savings account is an example of a fixed investment for an indefinite period, which also may be affected by inflation.

> A $50,000 investment in a $50,000 bond yielding 10% will provide a return limited to $5,000 per year during the predetermined time period.

Equity Investments. Fixed dollar amounts are invested for indefinite periods of time where the equity value may increase or decrease over time. Equity investments have, in the past, been excellent hedges against inflation. Examples are well-located real estate investments and, to a lesser extent, common stock investments.

> A $50,000 investment in a $200,000 income-producing property whose value increases 10% per year will increase the equity to $70,000 in one year, or an increase of 40%.

Investment Income Analysis

An investment may be evaluated according to the quantity, quality, and durability of the income it provides.

Quantity Of Income Stream may be determined by evaluating the:

☐ Volume (total and net dollar amount) of income

☐ Relationship of volume of income to amount invested

☐ Relationship of expenses to spendable income

☐ Relationship of rate of return to interest cost of loan on property

☐ Predictability of income stream (Can it be increased or is it likely to decrease in the future?)

Quality Of Income Stream refers to the following business, management, and marketing considerations:

☐ Basis of income stream. Residential-income, commercial, retail, professional, or industrial tenants

☐ Extent of management required to develop and maintain the desired quantity and quality of income stream

☐ Present and forseeable vacancy factor

☐ Composition or mix of tenants, compatibility or lack of compatibility, potential for future problems.

Durability Of Income Stream involves the following economic and financial considerations:

☐ Income stream derived from month-to-month, short- or long-term lease tenants

☐ Financial and credit ratings of national, regional, and local tenants

☐ Competitive rent levels. Is the competition likely to attract away present tenants?

☐ Diversification of use. Single-use vs. multi-use tenants, one vs. many tenants.

Other Factors of Investment Analysis Besides production of income, investors look for appreciation, liquidity, and acceptable levels of risk. These factors should also be included in an investment analysis.

Risk. This is the chance of receiving return of and promised return on investment.

☐ *Purchasing Power Risk*. During periods of inflation the yield on an investment may be greatly reduced by a loss of real purchasing power.

☐ *Market Risk*. There can be fluctuations in the market prices of securities and other investments from causes beyond the control of the investor. For example, competitors may build a more accessible, modern shopping center or apartment complex causing a decline in the investor's income stream which consequently lowers the value of the property.

☐ *Interest Rate Risk*. Trust deed investors may make loans at below-market rates of interest which become less marketable as interest rates continue to rise to higher levels.

☐ *Business Failure or Earning Power Risk*. This is brought about by either poor management or changes in marketplace conditions.

Liquidity. There is a risk of losing money as the result of having to convert an asset into cash quickly. The more liquid an asset, the more readily it can be monetized and the less the sacrifice upon conversion to cash. Accordingly, investors often are concerned with:

☐ How quickly the real estate can be sold without great sacrifice

☐ How quickly a loan can be obtained using the property as security for the loan.

Appreciation. This refers to increase in the market value of the property due to any inherent or external cause.

- ☐ Inflation

- ☐ Improved management practice

- ☐ Ability to increase rent schedules or reduce expense levels

- ☐ Growth area location and other marketplace conditions

- ☐ Combination of one or more of the above.

Management. Success or failure of an investment may be directly attributable to the quality of management. There is always a cost of management even though the investor-owner carries out the management function at no charge in the profit and loss statement. The owner-investor must still consider the opportunity costs of his or her management time and efforts, i.e., self-management means foregoing the earning of income from other sources of employment.

INVESTMENT STRATEGIES

Investment strategies vary depending on the goals or objectives to be realized.

Determining Goals Frequently you will have clients or customers who are not sure what their goals or objectives are with respect to real estate investment or personal financial planning. You will be able to make effective use of your time and energy if you can help them identify their goals or objectives and thereby make it possible for investment decisions to be made. To be effective, a goal must be:

Measurable. A goal cannot be abstract. "Being happy" is a relative condition, not a concrete, measurable objective capable of definition. Examples of definable or measurable goals are:

- ☐ "I want to list three new properties and make one sale a month."

- ☐ "I want to earn an additional $1,000 a month for my own personal investment program."

- ☐ "I want to find an investment property which yields 10% on cash invested."

Realistic. Goals must be capable of attainment within a definite time period. Generally speaking, a one year goal is realistic. If a goal cannot be attained within the set time period, the goal or the time period should be changed.

☐ Long range goals are those attainable in a 10 to 15 year period.

☐ Medium range goals are those attainable in 5 to 10 years.

☐ Less than one year goals are often really time management or scheduling matters.

In Writing. Unwritten goals are easily forgotten, and even though vague or ambiguous, may go unchallenged. Written goals provide a reminder of their existence and a basis for critical examination.

Evaluated Periodically. Priorities change from time to time and attained goals should be replaced with new realistic, attainable, and written goals.

Goals and Methods

Basic investment goals or objectives may include appreciation, income, depreciation, or a combination of these. In order to best serve your client's or customer's needs, it is advantageous to determine which of these basic investment goals is or are their motivating priorities.

Appreciation (Equity Build-Up). While not immediately spendable or realized until the property is sold, this is an increase in both the value of the property and the equity in the property, caused by one or more of the following:

☐ Increase in market value due to favorable market conditions

☐ Inflation

☐ Increase in equity as the principal loan balance is reduced with the periodic payments

☐ Capital improvements adding to the value of the improvement.

Income (Gross Spendable Income or Cash Flow). The residual net income less annual debt service equals income. For net spendable income, calculate gross spendable income less taxes due on taxable income.

Depreciation. Depreciation provides a tax shelter by providing tax-free income to the investor. A part of each year's annual income is set aside as tax-free income to provide a capital cost recovery of the depreciable asset investment.

If the depreciation taken creates a "paper loss"—the books on property show a loss—the loss offsets profits shown by other investments, within the passive loss limitations. Passive losses can offset only passive profits, except:

☐ Up to $25,000 of passive losses can offset active or portfolio income if the owner actively participates in the management of the property. (The $25,000 is reduced for individuals with adjusted gross incomes in excess of $100,000. See Chapter 13.)

☐ For properties acquired before August 16, 1986, the passive loss limitation is phased in.

Investor Techniques Investors are able to attain their goals or objectives most frequently by techniques or methods known as leverage, pyramiding, refinancing, and combinations of these methods.

Leverage. This is the use of other people's money (OPM) which costs less in interest than what it can earn for the investor. Basic to this method is the ability to control a parcel of real estate with less than an all-cash purchase and a relatively high loan-to-value ratio loan.

☐ *Example.* An 80% loan at 10% interest which is yielding 17% on the client's cash investment gives the investor leverage.

☐ *Caution.* While leverage is great on the upside, it can be devastating on the downside when it results in a negative leverage position requiring the investor to pay more for the borrowed money than it is earning.

Pyramiding. Equity is "traded up" into larger properties. As investment property increases in value, either a new loan is obtained and its proceeds invested in additional properties, or second or third trust deeds are obtained for reinvestments in additional properties.

Refinancing. As discussed earlier, the tax-free transaction of withdrawal of capital from an investment property gives the investor cash for other investments.

INCOME PROPERTY CLASSIFICATIONS

Real property acquired for income or investment may be categorized as residential income, commercial, or industrial property.

Residential Income Property Properties range in size from single family homes to massive apartment complexes, all of which fill the needs of some investors.

Single-Family Residences. Houses or individual condominium units may be acquired as rental property for investment or speculation.

Multiple Units. Two to eight unit structures, including duplexes, triplexes, fourplexes, etc., are generally not considered true investment type properties. They may not generate sufficient income for allocation according to generally acceptable accounting practices, and efficient management practices are limited with fewer units. The rationale for investment in these units may be one or more of the following:

□ To build an equity which can be used to trade up into larger properties.

□ To provide future large investors with experience in property management at the smaller level.

□ For liquidity, since smaller units may, under certain market conditions, be more marketable than either single-family houses or larger units.

□ For personal and financial security. Older adults and retirees may want their own home, yet welcome the rental income and the limited companionship of tenants, and enjoy the limited management and maintenance duties.

□ For income tax advantages which are available to owners of residential income properties.

Apartments. Investment-size properties are multifamily dwellings ranging from eight to several hundred units. Generally speaking the true investment category requires a minimum of 12 to 16. California law requires that there be an on-site resident manager for buildings of 16 or more units if the owner does not reside on the premises.

Commercial Property   Investments are available in many types of business properties such as banks, theaters, shopping centers, hotels, motels, retail stores, office buildings, parking lots, and restaurant buildings.

Industrial Property   There is a market for investments in properties used for manufacturing and industrial uses on industrially zoned land. Large-scale investment in industrial property today is likely to focus on industrial parks.

Industrial Parks. The modern industrial park is a planned development in an exclusive type of industrial subdivision developed according to a comprehensive plan to provide serviced sites for a community of compatible industries.

Advantages. Under continuous management, the industrial park provides control of the tract and buildings through restrictive covenants and/or zoning, maintaining aesthetic value throughout the development.

PROPERTY ANALYSIS

Purpose: _____ Date: __/__/__   List Price $ _____   Market Value $ _____

Name: _____   Loans $ _____   Loans $ _____

Location: _____   List Price Equity $ _____   Market Value Equity $ _____

Type of Property: _____

Assessed Value: Existing Financing: Annual Payment   Interest

Land	$ _____ _____ %.	1st $ _____ _____ _____ %
Improvement	$ _____ _____ %	2nd $ _____ _____ _____ %
Personal Property	$ _____ _____ %	3rd $ _____ _____ _____ %
TOTAL	$ _____ 100%	Potential 1st $ _____ _____ _____ %

Adjusted Cost Basis as of _____ $ _____   2nd $ _____ _____ _____ %

		%	2	3	Comments	
1	SCHEDULED GROSS INCOME					1
2	Less: Vacancy and Credit Losses					2
3	GROSS OPERATING INCOME					3
4	Less: Operating Expenses					4
5	Taxes					5
6	Insurance					6
7	Utilities					7
8	Licenses, Permits, Advertising					8
9	Management					9
10	Payroll, Including Payroll Taxes					10
11	Supplies					11
12	Services					12
13	Maintenance					13
14	Other					14
15						15
16						16
17	TOTAL EXPENSES					17
18	NET OPERATING INCOME Cap Rate List Price ___ % Cap Rate Market Value ___ %					18

ESTIMATE OF MARKET VALUE

				4	5	
19	INCOME APPROACH: Estimated Value Capitalized at Rate of ___ %					19
20	Cost Approach:					20
21	Sq. Ft. @ ___ Per Sq. Ft.					21
22	Sq. Ft. @ ___ Per Sq. Ft.					22
23	Sq. Ft. @ ___ Per Sq. Ft.					23
24	Less: Estimate of Accumulated Depreciation ___ %					24
25	Depreciated Value of Improvements					25
26	Plus: Site Improvements					26
27	Plus: Land Sq. Ft. @ ___ Per Sq. Ft.					27
28	ESTIMATE OF MARKET VALUE BY COST APPROACH					28
29	MARKET DATA APPROACH: @					29
30	FINAL ESTIMATE OF MARKET VALUE (CORRELATED)					30

INCOME ADJUSTED TO FINANCING

		1	2	3	4	5	
31	NET OPERATING INCOME (Line 18)						31
32	Less: Loan Payments	3rd Loan	2nd Loan	1st Loan	Total		32
33	Interest						33
34	Principal						34
35	Total Loan Payment						35
36	GROSS SPENDABLE INCOME	Rate: ___ % (Line 36 ÷ MV Equity)					36
37	Plus: Principal Payment						37
38	GROSS EQUITY INCOME	Rate: ___ % (Line 38 ÷ MV Equity)					38
39	Less: Depreciation Personal Property		Improvements				39
40	REAL ESTATE TAXABLE INCOME						40

Exhibit 32

COMPARATIVE INVESTMENT ANALYSIS
CALIFORNIA ASSOCIATION OF REALTORS® STANDARD FORM

NAME: _____ DATE ____ / ____ / ____

PURPOSE: _____

LINE No.		(1) PRESENT POSITION		(2) PROPERTY		(3) PROPERTY		(4) PROPERTY		(5) PROPERTY		(6) PROPERTY		No.
1	List Price													1
2	Market Value													2
3	Less: Total Loans													3
4	Equity													4
5	Plus: Available Cash													5
6	Total Effective Equity													6
7	Less: Transaction Costs													7
8	NET EFFECTIVE EQUITY													8

CASH POTENTIAL

9	Cash From Owner													9
10	Plus: Cash from Potential Loan													10
11	Total Cash Available													11
12	Less: Transaction Costs													12
13	NET CASH AVAILABLE													13

PROPERTY INCOME ANALYSIS

14	Gross Scheduled Income													14
15	Less: Vacancy & Credit Losses													15
16	Gross Operating Income													16
17	Less: Operating Expenses													17
18	NET OPERATING INCOME													18
19	Capitalization Rate													19

OWNERSHIP ANALYSIS OF PROPERTY INCOME: TAXABLE INCOME

20	Net Operating Income													20
21	Less: Interest Payments													21
22	Less: Depreciation													22
23	TAXABLE INCOME													23

SPENDABLE INCOME

24	Net Operating Income													24
25	Less: Principle & Interest Payments													25
26	GROSS SPENDABLE													26
27	Less: Income Tax													27
28	Less: Capital Improvements													28
29	NET SPENDABLE ANNUALLY													29
30	Per Month													30

EQUITY INCOME

31	Net Operating Income													31
32	Less: Interest on Loans													32
33	Less: Income Tax													33
34	NET EQUITY INCOME													34
35	Net Equity Income Rate	%		%		%		%		%		%		35
36	Plus: Equity Growth Rate %	%		%		%		%		%		%		36
37	TOTAL EQUITY RATE	%		%		%		%		%		%		37

The statements and figures presented herein, while not guaranteed, are secured from sources we believe authoritative.

Exhibit 33

Chapter 14 Quiz

1. As an investment, a bond is classified as:

    (A) A collateralized obligation
    (B) An equity investment
    (C) A fixed investment
    (D) A hedge against inflation

2. In a tax-flow analysis of an income property, which is not an allowable item?

    (A) Interest
    (B) Principal
    (C) Property taxes
    (D) Operating expenses

3. The _____ is an estimate of the total receipts to be received in each future year if all rentable units are rented without any vacancy or collection loss.

    (A) Effective annual gross revenue
    (B) Gross spendable income
    (C) Annual gross revenue
    (D) Annual net income

4. The principal source of tax shelter in real estate investments is:

    (A) Interest
    (B) Principal
    (C) Property taxes
    (D) Depreciation

5. The quantity of income stream may be determined by evaluating the:

    (A) Volume of income
    (B) Volume of income related to amount invested
    (C) Expenses related to spendable income
    (D) All of the above

6. The _____ reported on the profit and loss statement for tax purposes is the amount of shelter available to reduce the investor's tax liability.

    (A) Income
    (B) Expense
    (C) Loss
    (D) Profit

7. Investment goals and objectives should be:

    (A) Kept flexible
    (B) In writing
    (C) Measurable
    (D) All of the above

8. In addition to the risk factor, the following are considered in an investment analysis, except:

    (A) Liquidity
    (B) Appreciation
    (C) Management
    (D) Fixed rate returns

9. An example of an equity investment is:

    (A) A bond
    (B) Trust deeds
    (C) Real estate
    (D) A real estate loan

10. "Risk" in an investment analysis includes:

    (A) Market risk
    (B) Purchasing power risk
    (C) Interest rate risk
    (D) All of the above

PREVIEW

Introduction

Business Opportunity Defined

Business Opportunity Transactions

Financial Statement

Broker's Role

The Uniform Commercial Code (U.C.C.)

California Sales and Use Tax

Alcoholic Beverage Control Act

Franchise Investment Law

Property Management

Common Interest Developments

Mobilehomes

Subdivisions

Real Property Loan Brokerage

Real Property Securities Dealer

International Real Estate Transactions

INTRODUCTION

The real estate field is so wide-ranging that many areas of specialization have developed to serve the specific needs of clients and customers. Each has its own distinctive regulations, business practices, and skills. Among the growing number of other specializations are the types briefly described in this chapter. Each is worthy of an entire chapter or course; this chapter is only an introduction.

BUSINESS OPPORTUNITY DEFINED

The Business and Professions Code (§ 10030) defines "business opportunity" as including "the sale or lease of the business and goodwill of an existing business enterprise or opportunity."

Licensing and Regulation

The rules, laws, and regulations governing transfer of chattels apply as well as certain sections of the Real Estate Law.

Real Estate License Required. A valid California real estate license is required to act as an agent, for compensation, to sell, solicit, lease, and transact other business opportunity activities.

No Specialized License. The special classification of business opportunity license no longer exists. In 1966, separate real estate and business opportunity licenses were merged by an act of the legislature.

Personal Property (Chattels or Choses)

The sale of a business opportunity involves the sale of personal property (chattels).

Definition. Personal property is that which is movable and is not real property. In a business opportunity sale, it includes tangible trade fixtures and stock-in-trade, as well as intangible goodwill.

Bill of Sale. The transfer instrument for personal property is the bill of sale (the transfer instrument for real property is generally the deed). Under the Statute of Frauds (UCC § 2201), a contract for the sale of goods of $500 or more must be in writing to be enforceable.

Security Agreement. The encumbering instrument for a debt on personal property is the security agreement (Exhibit 34) which replaces the earlier chattel mortgage.

Taxation. Personal property is divided into two categories for tax purposes, depending on where it is located.

☐ *Secured.* Secured personal property is that which is located in or on the real property of the same owner. It is assessed and the taxes are paid with the real estate taxes.

☐ *Unsecured.* Taxes on unsecured personal property (located in or on the real property of another owner) are due on the lien date, March 1, and become delinquent on August 31. Unsecured personal property includes stock-in-trade, fixtures, and furniture in rented or leased premises.

Goodwill The expectation of continued public patronage is a valuable asset; it has been described as what makes people return where they were well treated. Goodwill rarely exceeds the value of the physical stock-in-trade, furniture, fixtures, and equipment, but it may do so in a business with an extremely popular name and reputation.

BUSINESS OPPORTUNITY TRANSACTIONS

Typical business opportunity sales involve the stock-in-trade, fixtures, furniture, goodwill, and sometimes business name and/or lease, of operating businesses such as grocery stores, liquor stores or bars, bakeries, drugstores, service stations, restaurants and fast food places, rooming houses, hotels, and motels.

Sale with Real Estate When a buyer is purchasing both a business and the real estate housing the business, the licensee usually treats the transaction as two separate and concurrent sales, which may be completed through two concurrent and contingent escrows.

Parties Most business opportunity transactions involve the principal who is seeking to buy, sell, lease, or exchange a business opportunity, the licensee who is the agent of the principal, and a third party.

Agent and Principal. The laws of agency require that the licensee exercise the utmost good faith, loyalty, and honesty in all relationships with the principal, a fiduciary obligation.

Third Party. The agent is also duty bound to deal fairly and honestly with the third party, regardless of their actual positions of buyer or seller.

Sales Commissions Commissions are based on the sale price of the furniture, fixtures, equipment, and goodwill. Commissions are not charged against inventory, or stock-in-trade. To do so would limit the buyer's ability to conduct the business profitably because the profit margin would be lowered by the commission.

Listing The usual document for listing a business opportunity is the Exclusive Authorization and Right to Sell a Business (Exhibit 35).

Termination Date. If an exclusive listing agreement is obtained, it must have a definite termination date.

Oral Listing. The Statute of Frauds (CC § 1624) does *not* require that a listing for the sale of personal property be in writing. Therefore, while an oral listing is not good business practice, it is enforceable. However, the Real Estate Law requires that the broker must have written authority from the owner before issuing a sendout slip to a prospect.

Sendout Slip. A sendout slip is a form signed by the prospect to protect the broker's commission. The prospect agrees that if he buys any property on the list, he will buy through that broker.

Deposit Receipt. There is also a special Business Purchase Contract and Receipt for Deposit form (Exhibit 36).

FINANCIAL STATEMENT

Buyers, lenders, and investors evaluate a business by looking at its financial statement. A complete financial statement consists of two major parts: the balance sheet and the profit and loss statement.

Balance Sheet One of the two major documents forming a full financial statement is the balance sheet, which shows assets, liabilities, and net worth (equity) of a business as of a specific date. It is a picture of the financial status of the firm at a specific point in time.

Assets. Anything of value owned by the firm is an asset, shown on the left of the balance sheet.

Liabilities. The right of the balance sheet shows anything owed, including claims of creditors.

Net Worth. Owner's equity, or what is owned free of debt, is the owner's net worth. It is the difference between the assets and the liabilities.

Formulas					
Assets	−	Liabilities	=	Net Worth
Assets	=	Liabilities	+	Net Worth
Liabilities	=	Assets	−	Net Worth

Profit and Loss Statement The second major document forming the full financial statement of a business is the profit and loss (P&L) statement, also called the income statement. It is a statement showing gross income, expense of operation, and net profit (or loss) for a given period of time.

Gross Profit. Gross sales less cost of goods sold. The cost of goods sold is the beginning inventory, plus purchases, less the ending inventory.

Operating Expenses. Deducted from gross profit to find net profit.

Net Profit (or Loss). Gross profit less expenses.

BROKER'S ROLE

Although no special business opportunity license is required, business opportunity brokerage places special requirements on the broker's knowledge and communication skills.

Responsibility to Buyer and Seller The broker has great responsibilities to a buyer even though the seller is the principal in most business opportunity transactions. The broker must provide both with full information, and often guide them in detail through an unfamiliar process.

Meeting of Minds. Exercise care in negotiating the sale to assure the compatibility of the buyer's motives to buy and the seller's motivation to sell.

Evaluation by Buyer. Give the buyer the opportunity to evaluate properly all material aspects of the business; often the buyer is investing a major portion of his or her life savings.

Accurate Information. Verify the accuracy of listing information. If it cannot be verified, the listing form should indicate "Not Verified By Agent." Advise the owner that nondisclosure of any material fact concerning the business constitutes fraud.

Working Equipment. Obtain the seller's certification that all equipment used in the operation of the business will be in working condition on the buyer's possession date.

Clearances. Obtain assurance that all government agency clearances required for the legal transfer of the business will be obtained.

Permits. Advise the seller that the sale will be subject to receipt of all required permits and/or licenses in the buyer's name.

Financial Records. Suggest that the sale be made subject to the buyer's inspection and approval of the seller's financial and other pertinent records.

Lease. Verify the acceptability of the lease, if a leased premise is part of the transaction.

Regulations. Be sure the purchaser is aware of the various federal, state, and local government agencies which must issue approvals for the business.

Successor's Liability. If sales taxes or social security and unemployment taxes are involved, remind the seller that no funds are to be released from escrow until the seller provides clearances from the State Board of Equalization and the Employment Development Department. Under the doctrine of "successor's liability," the buyer may be held responsible for the seller's unpaid taxes.

Sales Tax. Advise buyers that they are responsible for payment of a sales tax on the acquired furniture and fixtures; the state will collect it from the seller.

Costs. Inform the buyer and the seller of escrow costs and legal fees each is expected to pay.

Attorney's Role   The broker should never offer legal advice, but should advise both buyer and seller to seek legal counsel as necessary. Appropriate roles for an attorney include advice and representation, as well as:

Escrow. An attorney may hold the sale escrow.

Document Preparation. An attorney can help prepare bills of sale and other pertinent documents such as financial statements and reports required by regulatory agencies.

THE UNIFORM COMMERCIAL CODE (U.C.C.)

Shortly after 1900, many separate acts (the Uniform Sales Act, the Uniform Negotiable Instruments Act, and others) were simplified, updated, and combined into this one new code. In 1965, California adopted the modern version. The U.C.C. is designed to protect buyer, seller, and creditor alike in personal property transactions.

Secured Transactions, U.C.C. Division 9   A secured transaction is any one in which the creditor is protected (secured) by an interest in something of value. (In real property transactions, a mortgage or trust deed creates a security interest.)

Application. Division 9 applies to any transaction intended to create a security interest in any personal property including goods, documents, trade fixtures and equipment, instruments, etc. Exceptions covered by other provisions of the code include motor vehicles and farm and construction equipment.

Principal Instruments. These generally parallel the instruments used in real property transactions, though the names and exact functions are different.

☐ The promissory note is given to the lender as evidence of the debt.

☐ A security agreement (Exhibit 34) is used to secure a promissory note. This document has replaced the chattel mortgage in California. The parties are debtor (borrower) and secured party (lender).

☐ A financing statement., known as form UCC-1 (Exhibit 37), filed to "perfect" the security interest.

   • The Secretary of State receives and files most financing statements.

- The county recorder files (does not record) financing statements covering crops or timber to be cut and consumer goods.

☐ Multipurpose form. UCC-2 (Exhibit 38, Financing Statement Change Form) is used for any change or subsequent development. It serves as an amendment statement, continuation statement, termination statement, release statement or assignment statement.

Bulk Sales Law, U.C.C. Division 6

A bulk sale is defined as a transfer in bulk, and not in the ordinary course of business, of a substantial part of the equipment, supplies, inventory, etc., of an enterprise. Its purpose is primarily to protect creditors, but also buyers of businesses, against sellers' leaving unpaid debts on departure from the business.

Application. Compliance with the Bulk Sales Law is required in the sale of most business opportunities.

Notice Required. The transferee (buyer) must record and publish a Notice to Creditors of Bulk Transfer ("Notice of Intention to Sell"), recording the notice in the county and publishing it in a newspaper of general circulation in the judicial district 12 business days before closing date of sale. Notice is also sent by certified mail to the county tax collector 12 business days before closing date of the sale.

Escrow. If the U.C.C. provides for an escrow, the law requires the buyer/transferee to deposit the full purchase price with the escrowholder. A distribution of the cash consideration in strict compliance with the law will be made by the escrowholder.

☐ If at close of escrow, the deposited money is not sufficient to pay in full all the creditors' claims, the escrowholder cannot close the escrow and must report the deficiency to the creditors.

☐ Section 6106.1 of the law prohibits payments from the escrow for fees and/or commissions prior to the close of escrow.

☐ If escrow is not required under the U.C.C., the buyer/transferee must apply the cash consideration as required by law.

Effect of Compliance. By following the procedures of the Bulk Sales Law, the vendee (buyer) is released from any liability to creditors of the seller.

Effect of Noncompliance. The sale is valid as between buyer and seller but is presumed fraudulent and void against existing creditors of the seller. Creditors will therefore be able to reach the merchandise now in the possession of the new owner of the business.

CALIFORNIA SALES AND USE TAX

Because business opportunity sales involve transfer of personal property, state sales and use tax laws apply.

Administration The State Board of Equalization is the agency which administers these tax laws.

Board's Functions. The Board of Equalization takes its name from another of its three main functions:

- ☐ Equalizes tax assessment ratios among counties
- ☐ Assesses public utility properties in all counties
- ☐ Enforces, collects, and apportions sales and use tax

Pertinent Documents. The Board of Equalization regulates businesses by issuing:

- ☐ *Seller's Permit.* Required of all retail or wholesale establishments.
- ☐ *Certificate of Clearance (Clearance Receipt).* Shows that seller has paid all sales taxes owed, relieving buyer of successor's liability.

Sales Tax A consumer's tax, the sales tax consists of a state sales tax plus a local tax which may be split between city and county. Some counties impose an additional $\frac{1}{2}$% for public transportation.

Consumer Sales. The tax is paid by the consumer, collected by the seller (retail or wholesaler) on goods sold to consumers rather than for resale.

Tangible Goods. The tax is due on most tangible goods sales; it does not apply to intangibles such as goodwill, accounts receivable, or goods purchased for resale by a merchant who holds a seller's permit.

Business Opportunity Sales. Sales tax is due on furniture, equipment, fixtures, etc., in a business opportunity sale, but not on inventory which is for resale.

Use Tax The use tax is assessed at the same rate as the sales tax. Called an "excise tax," it is an alternative to a sales tax in certain situations.

For Use in California. Use tax is assessed on personal property included in the sale of a business, and on goods sold in this or in another state for storage, use, or other consumption in California.

Sales Tax. Property covered by sales tax is exempt from use tax.

Out-of-State Purchases. New or used vehicles bought outside California usually require use tax before registration is issued. Use tax also applies to mail orders.

ALCOHOLIC BEVERAGE CONTROL ACT

The state Department of Alcoholic Beverage Control (ABC) administers this law, which regulates the manufacture and sale of alcoholic beverages in California.

Licensing Licenses or permits are required for sale of alcoholic beverages in any manner. Licenses are classified according to:

Beverage Type. Beer, beer and wine, and general licenses are issued.

Premises. A license may be issued for liquor to be sold for consumption on or off the premises. An on-sale license is for beverages to be consumed on the premises, e.g., a bar or restaurant. An off-sale license is for beverages to be consumed off the premises, e.g., a package store or grocery store.

How Obtained. Licenses are either original (newly issued by the ABC) or transferred. Fees for original licenses issued by ABC:

☐ On-Sale: General $6,000

General for seasonal business $4,500

Beer and wine $300

Beer $200

☐ Off-Sale: General $6,000

Beer and wine $100

Transfer or Resale of Licenses **Price.** For the first 5 years from the original date of issue, the sale price of on-sale or off-sale general licenses shall not exceed $6,000. After that there is no purchase price restriction.

Escrow. Escrow is required.

Transfer of General Licenses **Notice.** Notice of Intended Transfer is always required. Before the filing of a transfer application with the ABC Department for a retail license, the applicant and licensee must file a notice of intended transfer with the county recorder and establish an escrow.

Posting and Publication. Notice must be posted on the premises and (for on-sale licenses) published in a newspaper of general circulation.

Protests. Private parties and/or public officials may protest the transfer within 30 days of the first posted notice of application to sell alcoholic beverages on the premises. A valid protest can delay approval while pending or on appeal.

Approval of Transfer. No funds may be paid out of escrow before approval of transfer, and the transfer of title to the licensed business must coincide with the license transfer.

Refusal to Transfer. The ABC Department may refuse to transfer a license while disciplinary action is being taken against the license holder.

FRANCHISE INVESTMENT LAW

The Corporations Code regulates transactions in franchises, which form a growing segment of the business opportunity market.

Definition A franchise is an agreement between two or more persons involving:

- ☐ *A Marketing Plan*. The franchisee is allowed to sell goods or services under a marketing plan prescribed in substantial part by the franchisor.

- ☐ *A Trademark*. The franchisee's business is substantially associated with the trademark, trade name, logotype, or advertising of the franchisor.

- ☐ *A Fee*. The franchisee is required to pay a franchise fee.

Intent of the Law A disclosure law on franchises has a threefold purpose:

- ☐ To compel the franchisor to furnish a full and adequate disclosure statement of the material terms to the franchisee.

- ☐ To protect the franchisee against fraud or unfulfilled promises of the franchisor.

- ☐ To protect the franchisor by providing a better understanding of the business relationship between the franchisor and the franchisee.

Exemption A major exemption exists which allows the franchisor not to register under this law if the franchisor meets three qualifications.

- ☐ *Net Worth*. Franchisor has a net worth of not less than five million ($5,000,000) dollars, or has a net worth of one million ($1,000,000) dollars and is more than 80% owned by a corporation with a net worth of not less than $5,000,000.

- ☐ *Established Franchises*. Franchisor has had at least 25 franchisees conducting business at all times during the five year period immediately preceding the offer.

- ☐ *Disclosure*. Franchisor makes a written disclosure incorporating 14 items prescribed by this law.

PROPERTY MANAGEMENT

Owners of income property often employ professional managers, particularly if their holdings are extensive or at a distance. Management includes day-to-day administration, maintenance, accounting, and planning.

Types of Property Managers
Two general classifications of property managers may be identified. Owner's employees may be on a straight salary, or a salary plus incentive bonus to induce successful performance. Agents, for a fee, manage one or more properties for various property owners.

Agent. The property manager, who is subject to the legal principal-agency relationship, may be associated with a real estate brokerage firm (with or without a formal structured property management department) or a professional property management agency, managing properties for a fee based on performance. Because of the agency relationship, the property manager is required to have a real estate broker license.

Building Manager. As an employee of the building owner or the property management agency, this person manages a single large property, most often on a straight salary basis. A prime qualification for building managers is the ability to manage the property successfully with little or no direct supervision by the owner or management agency.

Resident Manager. The manager lives on the property and oversees the day-to-day on-site operations, and may be employed by either the owner or the property manager who supervises the work. The resident manager is not required to have a real estate license.

Building Superintendent. A building superintendent may be employed to supervise a large building's maintenance, operation, and the hiring, firing, and supervision of janitors and maintenance persons.

California Law
A resident manager, agent, custodian, or other responsible person must live on the premises if the owner of an apartment building containing 16 or more units does not reside there. For smaller properties:

5 to 15 Units. Apartments containing less than 16 units, but more than 4 units, must have a conspicuously posted notice stating the name and address of the owner or owner's agent if neither the owner nor the agent resides on the premises.

Under 5 Units. Apartments of less than 5 units are exempt from the residency and posted notice requirements.

Property Manager Functions
The job of the professional property manager can be described in terms of general responsibilities and specific duties.

Responsibilities to Owner. The manager's basic responsibility as an agent is to represent the owner's best interests. This includes:

- Maximizing the net income from the managed property in order to obtain the highest return commensurate with its highest and best use.
- Maintenance of cash flow (total income less total expense) against rising costs.
- Enhancing and maintaining the physical value of the property.
- Enhancing and maintaining the prestige and image of the property.

Responsibilities to Tenant. The tenant is the third party in the agency relationship. Accordingly the manager must deal fairly and honestly and disclose all material facts about the property that would reasonably influence the tenant's decisions about the property, and provide for safe conditions for the tenants and their guests.

Professional Competence. The manager should develop, improve, and maintain a practical knowledge or understanding of:

- Merchandising rentable space
- Leases and leasing
- Maintenance
- Cost accounting and accounting procedures
- Housing and antidiscrimination laws
- Psychology and human relations
- Fair employment laws
- Property insurance
- Market research to evaluate social, political, and economic trends and economic rents
- Real estate law and credit practices.

Specific Duties. These include, but are not limited to:

- Establishing a rent schedule based on a complete market area analysis of social, political, and economic factors, such as:
  - Character of buildings and amenities of market area
  - Economic and demographic characteristics
  - Employment, shopping, educational, religious, recreational, and cultural facilities
- Merchandising the units, which includes:
  - Advertising vacancies through the media and cooperating brokers
  - Qualifying and screening prospective tenants
  - Preparing and executing leases.

- Maintaining records (payroll, expenses, receipts, bank accounts)
- Supervising all purchasing, maintenance schedules, and repairs
- Employing, supervising, and retaining competent personnel
- Developing management, employee, and tenant policies
- Auditing and paying bills, insurance premiums, and property taxes
- Preparing reports and communicating with the principal(s).

Professional Designations
The Institute of Real Estate Management (IREM), an affiliate of the National Association of Realtors®, has promoted the professional growth of its membership through its code of ethics and educational programs. Qualified individuals may use the designation Certified Property Manager (CPM) or Accredited Resident Manager (ARM) after their names. Qualified property management firms may use the designation Accredited Management Organization (AMO).

CPM Qualifications. To qualify for this designation, a Realtor® must:

- Be actively employed in property management.
- Provide evidence of a minimum three years experience in real property management under the direct supervision of a CPM, or have the equivalent of five years effective management experience, or have three full years of experience coupled with a four year degree in business administration, real estate, economics, or law.
- Have an established reputation for integrity and ethics.
- Subscribe to the IREM By-Laws, Pledge, and Code of Ethics.
- Satisfy the educational and examination requirements of IREM.
- Be a member in good standing of the local Board of Realtors® or of the National Association of Realtors®.
- Be approved by the membership standards committee and governing council of IREM.

ARM Qualifications. On-site apartment managers must:

- Meet certain educational requirements, standards of experience, and professional qualifications.
- Be approved by a local chapter or committee of IREM.

AMO Qualifications. To qualify for this designation (not CPM, which is for individuals only), a property management firm must:

- Have at least one key executive qualified as a CPM.
- Meet experience and integrity requirements, as well as subscribe to the IREM By-Laws, Pledge, and Code of Ethics.
- Meet certain standards of fiscal and operational liability and obtain specified types of insurance coverage.

COMMON INTEREST DEVELOPMENTS

Condominiums and cooperatives are the most frequently encountered types of common interest developments (CIDs), an increasingly important form of ownership characterized by common ownership of certain areas or aspects of the property, and governance by an owners' association.

Condominiums A condominium is defined as an estate in real property consisting of an undivided interest in common in a portion of a parcel of real property together with a separate interest in space in a residential, industrial or commercial building, such as an apartment, office, or store. Condominiums are vertical subdivisions in concept.

Nature of Ownership. The condominium buyer:

☐ Owns in fee simple the space in a particular unit

☐ Holds a tenancy in common interest in the common areas

☐ Receives a deed

☐ Receives a separate tax assessment

☐ May apply for and receive a title insurance policy on the unit

☐ Receives the same "bundle of rights," within certain prescribed limitations, as the buyer of any real property.

Governance. Rights and limitations are prescribed and administered by the condominium owners' association which, by law, must be established by the original developer for the administration, maintenance, and enforcement of the rules set forth in the condominium declaration. The elected governing board may perform the management function itself or hire professional property managers to do so.

Regulation of Sales. Projects having five or more condominium units are regulated under the Subdivided Lands Act as subdivisions and must comply with its provisions. For subsequent sales:

☐ The condominium declaration may or may not provide that in the event the condominium owner decides to sell his unit, the other owners in the project have the right of first refusal.

☐ The declaration may or may not establish the price to other owners, such as market value or prior acquisition cost, whichever is the lesser of the two.

Financing. Each individual condominium purchaser decides upon the type of financing used to buy each unit, and in other respects is treated as an individual property owner.

☐ Each individual's default can be subject to foreclosure proceedings.

□ Each unit receives its own property tax assessment and bill and property insurance bill.

□ The management association has the right to assess owners for their share of the operating, maintenance, and insurance expenses of the common areas.

□ Each unit owner who itemizes deductions for income tax purposes may deduct loan interest and property taxes paid.

Stock Cooperatives A stock cooperative is defined in Business and Professions Code §11003.2 as a corporation formed primarily for the purpose of holding title to improved real property, with the essential element that each shareholder of the corporation receives a right of exclusive occupancy of a portion of the real property, title to which is held by the corporation. Right of occupancy is transferable only concurrently with the transfer of the share of stock in the corporation.

Regulation. Projects with five or more shareholders are within the definition of a subdivision, under the jurisdiction of the Real Estate Commissioner.

Financing. The corporation holding title to the property arranges for construction financing and permanent "take-out" financing in its own name. Individual unit owners purchase shares of stock or an investment certificate valued in proportion to the value of their unit. Financing for the shares of stock may be arranged by the corporation or the individual. Buyers invest in a share of the project and become members of the shareholders' association, which manages the property.

Taxes and Insurance. Management normally pays all taxes and related fees from the assessment fees collected. Unless a written request is received by the assessor for separate assessments, the corporation receives and pays the single property tax bill and insurance premium on the property from the assessments on the stockholders.

Defaults. Nonpayment of assessments by any stockholder may require other stockholders to take responsibility for payments to avoid foreclosure or canceled insurance policies. Unpaid assessments for payments on the single mortgage, which is the obligation of the corporation, could lead to foreclosure of the entire property.

Sales Limitations. As with a condominium, a real estate broker or sales license is required for an agent to list and sell a stock cooperative for a fee or a commission. Special provisions in some co-op agreements include:

□ Right of first refusal to the other owners in the corporation, or the corporation itself, when a cooperative shareholder decides to sell his or her stock.

□ Selling price limited to the market value or acquisition cost, whichever is less.

MOBILEHOMES

A mobilehome is a structure (no longer a vehicle), transportable in one or more sections, designed and equipped to contain not more than two dwelling units, to be used with or without a foundation system. A mobilehome does not include a recreational vehicle, commercial coach, or factory built housing as defined in the Health and Safety Code.

Characteristics One of the fastest growing segments of the housing market is the mobilehome market, which is increasingly referred to as the "manufactured homes" market. Reasons for the growing popularity and acceptability include:

Cost. Manufactured housing is relatively inexpensive compared to traditional "site-built" housing

Financing. Many of the same financing terms as for site-built homes are being made available by Congress, Federal Home Loan Bank Board, Federal National Mortgage Association, state legislatures, and courts.

Zoning. The California Legislature has established (Government Code §65852.3) that communities cannot prohibit manufactured housing from being located on lots zoned for single-family residences.

Construction. Because of improved quality of construction, more comfortable, spacious interiors, and often the placing of the unit on a permanent foundation, the Manufactured Housing Institute reports that only four percent of these homes are moved after factory delivery.

Sales Regulations on sales and on licensing of sellers, and specialized sale and escrow documents, reflect the dual nature of a mobilehome as both real and personal (movable) property.

Under Real Estate License. A licensed broker may sell, or offer to sell, buy or offer to buy, solicit prospective purchasers of, solicit or obtain listings of, or negotiate the purchase, sale, or exchange of any mobilehome only if the mobilehome has been registered with the Department of Housing and Community Development for at least one year.

Dealer's License. No real estate broker may maintain a place of business where two or more mobilehomes are displayed and offered for sale unless the broker is also licensed as a dealer with the Department of Housing and Community Development.

Specialized Procedures. The documents involved in transfer of a mobilehome, including listing agreement, deposit receipt, escrow instructions, etc., provide for information and compliances unique to mobilehomes: make and model, identification of park, license or registration number, etc. (Exhibits 39 and 40).

Financing   Most government-related home financing programs also make provision for mobilehomes.

FNMA. The Federal National Mortgage Association will buy mortgages on manufactured housing on the same basis as site-built housing. That is, if a borrower buys a lot as part of a financing package and does not move the home from the lot, it can be conventionally financed.

FHA Title I. FHA insures loans to finance alterations, improvements, and repairs to existing mobilehomes, and insures loans to purchase new and resale mobilehomes.

FHA Title II. FHA insures loans for the purchase of mobilehome lots or a combination of home and lot purchase, and also insures loans made to finance construction of mobilehome parks.

VA. The VA guarantees lenders against loss by a defaulting borrower on a mobilehome and/or site. There are maximum loan guarantees which are changed from time to time.

Cal-Vet. Cal-Vet loans are available for financing for single-family occupancy only. There are maximum loan limits set by the California Department of Veterans Affairs.

SUBDIVISIONS

Subdivisions are defined as those divisions of real property for the purpose of sale, lease, or financing which are regulated by law.

California Subdivision Laws   In California two major laws govern the legal and physical aspects of subdivisions.

The Subdivided Lands Act. Under the jurisdiction of the Real Estate Commissioner, this law covers the legal and financial aspects of the division of land into 5 or more lots, 5 or more units in a condominium project, community apartment project, or stock cooperative project, and 12 or more timeshare interests.

The Subdivision Map Act. This law gives control of the "physical aspects" to local government and applies to the division of land into two or more parcels, and to condominiums, community apartment projects, or the conversion of five stock cooperatives.

Consumer Protection   Because the purchaser of property in a new subdivision is in a particularly vulnerable position, state and federal laws place extensive regulations on subdivision sales and offerings. Many consider the federal law to be more lenient than the California laws.

California Law. The basic purpose of the Subdivided Lands Act is to protect consumers from fraud, deceit, or misrepresentation, through disclosure and procedural requirements. The act also regulates the advertising and financing methods used by the developer.

Public Report. A Public Report is required to indicate that all parcels can be used for the purpose for which they are offered. Costs of investigations leading to a Public Report are borne by applicant fees collected by the Commissioner.

Out-of-State-Sales. Sale of out-of-state subdivisions in California requires a:

☐ Real Property Securities permit, and a

☐ Public Report before offering for sale in California.

Interstate Land Sales Full Disclosure Act. This federal law has had a great impact in states with lenient state subdivision controls. The ILSFDA:

☐ Declares it unlawful to sell or lease certain subdivided lands interstate without registration with the Office of Interstate Land Sales Registration, a division of HUD. This regulation applies to subdivisions containing 100 or more unimproved lots sold in interstate commerce.

☐ The law requires that a purchaser or lessee must receive a copy of the HUD report or, in California, a copy of the Commissioner's Public Report before a sale or lease can be made.

The Subdivision Market The market for lots in standard subdivisions is generally found among people interested in building their own homes and among building contractors who purchase a number of lots for building purposes. Many subdividers develop subdivisions and construct the dwellings themselves, offering house and lot packages complete with financing arranged for purchasers.

REAL PROPERTY LOAN BROKERAGE

Under California law any person who negotiates a loan secured by real property for another and for compensation must be licensed as a real estate broker or salesperson. Numerous changes have been made in the governing law since it was passed in 1955. At the present time, Chapter 3, Article 7 of the Real Estate Law (Broker's Loan Law) covers the licensee's activities as an arranger of loans. The specialist in this field must keep abreast of current developments.

Purpose The California Legislature passed the Real Property Loan Brokerage Law in 1955 because of the borrowing public's complaints of hidden charges and exorbitant commission fees being charged by certain brokers. In its current form the law protects the borrower by:

Disclosure. The loan broker is required to provide the borrower with a Mortgage Loan Disclosure Statement (Exhibit 41) containing complete loan information. The disclosure statement is to contain estimated loan costs, expenses, and commissions to be paid by the borrower.

Timing. The borrower is to be given the disclosure statement before being obligated to complete the loan.

Limits on Costs. On loans below certain limited amounts, there are limits on commissions and other costs and expenses. These limits apply to hard money loans secured by:

☐ First trust deeds under $20,000

☐ Junior trust deeds under $10,000.

Balloon Payments   The Broker's Loan Law prohibits balloon payments under the following circumstances:

Borrower's Home. If the term of the loan is six years or less and the borrower's home is used as the security for the loan.

Short-Term Loans. Any property loan to which the law applies, if the term of the loan is less than three years.

Seller Credit Exempted   The limitations of the Broker's Loan Law (Article 7) do not apply to credit extended by a seller.

REAL PROPERTY SECURITIES DEALER

A "real property securities dealer" is defined as a principal or agent engaged in the secondary market in the sale of trust deeds under a dealer-guaranteed trust deed investment contract. This specialization is also closely regulated.

Governing Law   Chapter 3, Article 6, of the Real Estate Law regulates the activities of real property securities dealers. A dealer is required to comply with the regulations of the Business and Professions Code and the regulations of the Real Estate Commissioner.

Applicability   The law regulates any person who acts as a principal or agent in the business of selling "real property securities" to the public or offers to accept funds for continual reinvestment in real property securities.

Covered Transactions. Securities within the meaning of Article 6 include:

☐ Guaranteed notes and sales contracts

☐ Out-of-state subdivision units offered for sale in California

☐ "Promotional notes" (unseasoned) on new subdivisions.

Licensing and Disclosure. The broker must be licensed, and each security offering must be authorized.

☐ When any real property security is to be guaranteed by a broker, the broker's license must be endorsed as Real Property Securities Dealer after the broker has posted bond and paid fees.

☐ A permit from the Real Estate Commissioner is required for each security or series of securities sold.

☐ A Real Property Securities Disclosure Statement must be given to each investor.

INTERNATIONAL REAL ESTATE TRANSACTIONS

The field of international real estate transactions offers expanding opportunities for specialization, particularly in California.

Expanding Market U.S. real estate continues to be attractive to foreign investors for several reasons, including:

Prices. Acquisition at relatively attractive prices compared to property in many other countries

Stability. The relatively stable U.S. political economy

Tax Structure. Income tax advantages for real property ownership.

The International Real Estate Federation This organization, which has an NAR affiliate American Chapter, has as its purpose the promotion of high professional standards and improved relations throughout the professional real estate world.

Extent. Approximately 35 countries are represented and annual meetings are held throughout the world.

Membership. Membership in the Federation is open to all Realtors® and the American Chapter has more than 2,000 active members.

WOLCOTTS FORM 1095—SECURITY AGREEMENT (Personal Property)—With Interest Included Note—Rev 1-85 (Price class 1)

SECURITY AGREEMENT

(PERSONAL PROPERTY)

THIS SECURITY AGREEMENT is made this ______ day of ______ 19__

by and between ______ of ______,

County of ______, State of California, (hereinafter "Debtor")

and ______ of ______,

County of ______, State of California, (hereinafter "Secured Party").

Debtor hereby grants to Secured Party a security interest in all that certain personal property (hereinafter "Security"), now owned or hereafter acquired (except consumer goods acquired more than ten (10) days after the Secured Party gives value, unless those goods are installed in or affixed to such property), and the proceeds and products thereof, described and situated as follows:

as security for the payment to Secured Party of

($ ______) Dollars,

according to the terms and conditions of a certain Promissory Note, of even date herewith, in substantially the following form:

Exhibit 34.1

INSTALLMENT NOTE—INTEREST INCLUDED

$_____ _____, California, _____, 19____

In installments as herein stated, for value received, the undersigned maker(s) promise(s) to pay to _____

_____, or order,

at _____

the sum of _____

_____ DOLLARS,

with interest from _____

_____ on the unpaid principal at the rate of

_____ per cent per annum; principal and interest payable in installments of

_____ Dollars

or more on the _____ day of each _____ month, beginning

on the _____ day of _____

_____

_____

_____

_____ and continuing until said principal and interest have been fully paid.

Each payment shall be credited first to interest then due, and the remainder applied to principal; and interest shall thereupon cease upon the principal so credited. Should default be made in payment of any installment when due, the whole sum of principal and accrued interest shall become immediately due, without notice, at the option of the holder of this note. Interest after maturity will accrue at the rate indicated above. Principal and interest are payable in lawful money of the United States. Each maker will be jointly and severally liable, and consents to the acceptance of security or substituted security for this note, and waives presentment, demand and protest and the right to assert any statute of limitations. A married person who signs this note agrees that recourse may be had against his/her separate property for any obligation contained herein. If any action be instituted on this note, the undersigned promise(s) to pay such sum as the Court may fix as attorney's fees. This Note is secured by a Security Agreement (Personal Property) of even date herewith.

_____   _____

_____   _____

This Security Agreement also secures: (a) any and all extensions or renewals of said promissory note; (b) the repayment of all sums, including but not limited to legal expenses, that may be advanced or incurred by Secured Party for the maintenance, protection or preservation of the Security, or any part thereof; (c) any and all other sums that may hereafter be advanced by Secured Party to or for the benefit of Debtor; (d) any and all other expenditures that may hereafter be made by Secured Party pursuant to the provisions hereof; and (e) any and all other debts and obligations of Debtor to Secured Party that may hereafter be incurred.

Debtor shall execute such Financing Statements and other documents and do such other acts and things as Secured Party may from time to time require to establish and maintain a valid, perfected security interest in the Security; and Debtor shall permit Secured Party and Secured Party's representatives to inspect the Security and/or the records pertaining thereto from time to time at any reasonable time.

Debtor shall keep the Security in good condition and repair, and shall not use it for any unlawful purpose; and shall not remove, nor permit to be removed, any part of the Security from the above premises without the prior written consent of Secured Party, which shall not be unreasonably withheld; and shall provide, maintain and deliver to Secured Party physical damage and loss insurance policies covering the Security in amounts and with insurance companies satisfactory to Secured Party, naming Secured Party as loss payee, as Secured Party's interest may appear.

Debtor hereby declares and warrants to Secured Party that Debtor is the absolute and sole owner, and is in possession of all of the Security, and that the same is free and clear of all liens, encumbrances, adverse claims, and any other security interests. Debtor shall not sell or offer to sell or otherwise transfer the Security or any interest therein without the prior written consent of Secured Party; nor shall Debtor sell, assign or create or permit to exist any lien on or security interest in the Security in favor of anyone other than Secured Party, unless Secured Party consents thereto in writing. Debtor shall, upon Secured Party's request, remove any unauthorized lien or security interest on the Security, and defend any claim affecting the Security; and Debtor shall pay all charges against the Security, including but not limited to taxes, assessments, encumbrances and insurance, and upon Debtor's failure to do so, Secured Party may pay any such charge as it deems necessary and add the amount paid to the indebtedness of Debtor secured hereunder.

Exhibit 34.2

If Debtor fails to make payment of any part of the principal or interest as provided in said promissory note at the time and in the manner therein specified, or if any breach be made of any obligation, promise or warranty of Debtor herein contained, then the whole principal sum unpaid on said promissory note. with accrued interest thereon, shall immediately become due and payable, without notice, at the option of Secured Party, and Secured Party, at its option, may: (a) sell. lease or otherwise dispose of the Security at public or private sale; unless the Security is perishable and threatens to decline speedily in value or is a type customarily sold on a recognized market, Secured Party will give Debtor at least ten (10) days prior written notice of the time and place of any public sale or of the time after which any private sale or any other intended disposition may be made: (b) retain the Security in satisfaction of the obligations secured hereby, with notice of such retention sent to Debtor as required by law: (c) notify any parties obligated on any of the Security consisting of accounts, instruments, chattel paper, choses in action or the like to make payment to Secured Party and enforce collection of any of the Security herein; (d) require Debtor to assemble and deliver any of the Security to Secured Party at a reasonably convenient place designated by Secured Party; (e) apply all sums received or collected from or on account of the Security, including the proceeds of any sales thereof, to the payment of the costs and expenses incurred in preserving and enforcing the rights of Secured Party, including but not limited to reasonable attorneys' fees, and the indebtedness secured hereby in such order and manner as Secured Party in its sole discretion determines; Secured Party shall account to Debtor for any surplus remaining therefter, and shall pay such surplus to the party entitled thereto, including any second secured party who has made a proper demand upon Secured Party and has furnished proof to Secured Party as requested in the manner provided by law; in like manner, Debtor agrees to pay to Secured Party without demand any deficiency after any Security has been disposed of and proceeds applied as aforesaid. Secured Party shall have all the rights and remedies of a secured party under the Uniform Commercial Code in any jurisdiction where enforcement is sought. Debtor agrees to pay all costs incurred by Secured Party in enforcing its rights under this Security Agreement, including but not limited to reasonable attorneys' fees. All rights, powers and remedies of Secured Party hereunder shall be cumulative and not alternative. No delay on the part of Secured Party in the exercise of any right or remedy shall constitute a waiver thereof, and no exercise by Secured Party of any right or remedy shall preclude the exercise of any other right or remedy or further exercise of the same remedy.

It is further agreed, subject to applicable law, that upon any sale of the Security according to law, or under the power herein given, that Secured Party may bid at said sale, or purchase the Security, or any part thereof at said sale.

Debtor warrants that if Debtor is a business entity, the execution, delivery and performance of the aforesaid promissory note and this Security Agreement are within its powers and have been duly authorized.

If more than one Debtor executes this Security Agreement, the obligations hereunder are joint and several. All words used herein in the singular shall be deemed to have been used in the plural when the context and construction so require. Any married person who signs this Security Agreement expressly agrees that recourse may be had against his/her separate property for all of his/her obligations to Secured Party.

This Security Agreement shall inure to the benefit of and bind Secured Party, its successors and assigns and each of the undersigned, their respective heirs, executors, administrators and successors in interest. Upon transfer by Secured Party of any part of the obligations secured hereby, Secured Party shall be fully discharged from all liability with respect to the Security transferred therewith.

Whenever possible each provision of this Security Agreement shall be interpreted in such manner as to be effective and valid under applicable law, but, if any provision of this Security Agreement shall be prohibited or invalid under applicable law, such provisions shall be ineffective only to the extent of such prohibition or invalidity, without invalidating the remainder of such provisions or the remaining provisions of this Security Agreement.

IN WITNESS WHEREOF, Secured Party and Debtor have executed this instrument.

_____   _____

_____   _____

_____   _____
      Secured Party   **Debtor**

Exhibit 34.3

EXCLUSIVE AUTHORIZATION AND RIGHT TO SELL A BUSINESS
THIS IS INTENDED TO BE A LEGALLY BINDING AGREEMENT—READ IT CAREFULLY.
CALIFORNIA ASSOCIATION OF REALTORS® STANDARD FORM

1. **Right to Sell.** I hereby employ and grant _____
hereinafter called "Agent" the exclusive and irrevocable right commencing on _____ , 19 _____ , and expiring at midnight on
_____ , 19 _____ , to sell the business known as _____ situated
in _____ , County of _____ , California at _____ .
2. **Terms of Sale.** The purchase price shall be $ _____ to be paid in the following terms:
_____
_____
_____

(a) The following items of personal property are to be included in the above-stated price:
_____
_____
_____

(b) Agent is hereby authorized to accept and hold on my behalf a deposit upon the purchase price.

(c) Title to the Business shall be by Bill of Sale and other instruments of transfer or assignment necessary to carry out the Purchase Agreement.

(d) I warrant that I am the owner of the business or have the authority to execute this agreement. I authorize the Agent named herein to cooperate with sub-agents.

3. Compensation to Agents. I hereby agree to compensate Agent as follows:

(a) _____ % of the selling price, or the fee of $ _____ if the business is sold during the term hereof, or any extension thereof, by Agent, on the terms herein set forth or any other price and terms, I may accept, or through any other person, or by me, or _____ % of the price shown in 2 or the fee of $ _____ , if said business is withdrawn from sale, transferred, conveyed, leased without the consent of Agent, or made unmarketable by my voluntary act during the terms hereof or any extension thereof.

(b) the compensation provided for in subparagraph (a) above if the business is sold, or otherwise transferred within _____ days after the termination of this authority or any extension thereof to anyone with whom Agent has had negotiations prior to final termination, provided I have received notice in writing, including the names of the prospective purchasers, before or upon termination of the agreement or any extension thereof. However, I shall not be obligated to pay the compensation provided for in subparagraph (a) if a valid listing agreement is entered into during the term of said protection period with another licensed real estate broker and sale is made during the term of said valid listing agreement.

4. If action be instituted to enforce this agreement, the prevailing party shall receive reasonable attorney's fees and costs as fixed by the Court.

5. I agree to save and hold Agent harmless from all claims, disputes, litigation, and/or judgments arising from any incorrect information supplied by me, or from any material fact known by me concerning the business which I fail to disclose.

6. Other provisions:
_____
_____
_____

7. I acknowledge that I have read and understand this Agreement, and that I have received a copy hereof.
Dated _____ 19 _____   _____ California

_____   _____
OWNER   OWNER

_____   _____
ADDRESS   CITY-STATE-PHONE

8. In consideration of the above, Agent agrees to use diligence in procuring a purchaser.

_____   _____
AGENT   ADDRESS-CITY

BY _____
                                          _____   _____
                                          PHONE   DATE

To order, contact—California Association of Realtors®
525 S. Virgil Avenue, Los Angeles, California 90020
California Association of Realtors®   FORM BA-11

Exhibit 35

BUSINESS PURCHASE CONTRACT AND RECEIPT FOR DEPOSIT

This is more than a receipt for money. It is intended to be a legally binding contract. Read it carefully.

CALIFORNIA ASSOCIATION OF REALTORS® STANDARD FORM

_____, California. _____, 19 _____

Received from _____

herein called Buyer, the sum of _____ Dollars $ _____

evidenced by cash ☐, cashier's check ☐, or _____ ☐, personal check ☐ payable to _____

_____, to be held uncashed until acceptance of this offer, as deposit on account of purchase price of

_____ Dollars $ _____

for the purchase of the business known as _____

and situated in _____, County of _____, California,

located at _____

1.   Buyer will deposit in escrow with _____ the balance of purchase price as follows:

_____

_____

_____

_____

_____

_____

_____

_____

_____

_____

_____

_____

_____

_____

_____

_____

_____

_____

_____

Set forth above any terms and conditions of a factual nature applicable to this sale, such as financing, liabilities to be assumed by buyer, the assistance to be provided by seller to buyer after sale and if the sale includes real property whether a separate Real Estate Purchase Contract is to be executed by the parties.

2.   Deposit will ☐ will not ☐ be increased by $ _____ to $ _____ within _____ days of acceptance of this offer.

3.   The supplements *initialled* by buyer below are incorporated as part of this agreement:

Other

_____ Inventory of personal property included in purchase price	_____ Allocation of purchase price	_____ _____
_____ Financial Statements for the years _____ and _____ .	_____ Agreement not to compete	_____ _____
_____ Schedule of accounts receivable	_____ Copy of lease	_____ _____

4.   Buyer and Seller acknowledge receipt of a copy of this page, which constitutes Page 1 of _____ pages.

Buyer_____   Seller_____

Buyer_____   Seller_____

A REAL ESTATE BROKER IS THE PERSON QUALIFIED TO ADVISE ON REAL ESTATE AND BUSINESS TRANSACTIONS. IF YOU DESIRE LEGAL OR TAX ADVICE CONSULT A COMPETENT PROFESSIONAL.

THIS STANDARDIZED DOCUMENT FOR USE IN SIMPLE TRANSACTIONS HAS BEEN APPROVED BY THE CALIFORNIA ASSOCIATION OF REALTORS® IN FORM ONLY. NO REPRESENTATION IS MADE AS TO THE APPROVAL OF THE FORM OF SUPPLEMENTS, THE LEGAL VALIDITY OF ANY PROVISION OR THE ADEQUACY OF ANY PROVISION IN ANY SPECIFIC TRANSACTION. IT SHOULD NOT BE USED IN COMPLEX TRANSACTIONS OR WITH EXTENSIVE RIDERS OR ADDITIONS.

To order, contact—California Association of Realtors®
525 S. Virgil Ave., Los Angeles, California 90020
Copyright © 1981, California Association of Realtors®   FORM BPC-11-1

Exhibit 36.1

BUSINESS PURCHASE CONTRACT AND RECEIPT FOR DEPOSIT
The following terms and conditions are hereby incorporated in and made part of the offer.
CALIFORNIA ASSOCIATION OF REALTORS® STANDARD FORM

5A.   Salable merchandise for resale, stock in trade, work in progress on hand at time of physical possession to be transferred to Buyer shall be purchased by Buyer at (a) current wholesale price, or (b) _____

5B.   Assets to be transferred to buyer are the business, goodwill, fixtures, furniture and furnishings, equipment, supplies, tools, leasehold improvements, telephone number, lists of customers, trade names, signs, all transferable permits, franchises, leases, customer deposits, accounts receivable and all other property listed in any supplement hereto except the following: _____

_____

_____

_____

_____

_____

6.   Buyer and Seller shall deliver signed escrow instructions to escrow holder within _____ days from Seller's acceptance which shall provide for closing within _____ days from Seller's acceptance. Escrow fees to be paid as follows: _____

7.   Personal property taxes, business taxes, rents, interests, insurance acceptable to Buyer, prepaid deposits shall be prorated as of (a) close of escrow or (b) _____

8.   Seller shall furnish Buyer with bills of sale and other instruments of transfer or assignment necessary to carry out this agreement. If assignment of existing lease is made part of this agreement, Seller shall deliver assignment of such lease together with lessor's consent to such assignment.

9.   If transfer of liquor license is included in this sale, Seller shall comply with the Alcoholic Beverage Control Act concerning such transfer. Escrow shall not close and no funds shall be transferred to Seller until escrow holder is advised by the State Department of Alcohol Beverage Control that the license transfer has been approved. The costs of such transfer shall be paid by _____

10.   Seller shall deliver to escrow holder clearances from the State Board of Equalization and the Department of Benefit Payments and no funds shall be released from escrow before such delivery.

11.   Seller shall comply with the Bulk Sales Provisions of Division 6 of the Uniform Commercial Code and instruct Escrowholder to publish and record such notices as required under the Code.

12.   Seller represents that to the best of Seller's knowledge no notices of violations of federal, state or local statute, law or regulation including any such notices regarding the real property in which the business is situated exist or are filed or issued affecting the operation of the business.

13.   Seller shall furnish or cause to be furnished to Buyer or Buyer's representatives all data and information concerning the business that may reasonably be requested by Buyer. Within _____ days from Seller's acceptance Buyer and his counsel, accountants or other designated representatives shall be given access to Seller's original books, records and tax returns. Seller represents that the books and records are those maintained in the ordinary and normal course of business and used by Seller in the computation of federal and state income tax returns. If examination of the books and records discloses conditions or information unsatisfactory to Buyer, Buyer may cancel this agreement. If not disapproved in writing within _____ days of receipt of books and records this condition shall be deemed waived.

14.   Seller shall carry on the business diligently and substantially in the same manner as previously until date of close of escrow.

15.   Seller's representations and warranties set forth herein or in any written statements delivered to Buyer shall be true and correct at date of closing and shall survive the passing of title to the business.

16.   Possession shall be delivered to Buyer (a) upon close of escrow or (b) _____

17.   Buyer shall not be liable for any obligation of the business which is not set forth in this agreement. Liabilities to be assumed by Buyer

_____

_____

_____

_____

_____

_____

_____

_____

_____

_____

_____

_____

18.   Buyer shall pay any sales or use tax under the laws of the State of California or under any local ordinances payable as a result of this sale and shall furnish Seller with resale certificates for any items bought for resale.

Buyer and Seller acknowledge receipt of a copy of this page, which constitutes Page 2 of _____ pages.

To order, contact—California Association of Realtors®
525 S. Virgil Avenue, Los Angeles, California 90020
Copyright © 1981, California Association of Realtors®   FORM BPC-11-2

Exhibit 36.2

19.   If Buyer fails to complete said purchase as herein provided by reason of any default of Buyer, Seller shall be released from the obligation to sell business to Buyer and may proceed against Buyer upon any claim or remedy which Seller may have in law or equity provided, however, that by placing their initials here Buyer: (   ) Seller: (   ) agree that Seller shall retain the deposit as his liquidated damages, and that it would be impractical or extremely difficult to fix the actual damages suffered because of such default; that the amount paid by Buyer as deposit constitutes a reasonable estimate and agreed stipulation of such damages.

20.   If the only controversy or claim between the parties arises out of or relates to the disposition of the Buyer's deposit, such controversy or claim shall at the election of the parties be decided by arbitration. Such arbitration shall be determined in accordance with the Rules of the American Arbitration Association, and judgment upon the award rendered by the Arbitrator(s) may be entered in any court having jurisdiction thereof. The provisions of Code of Civil Procedure Section 1283.05 shall be applicable to such arbitration.

21.   If the leasehold property in which the business is situated is destroyed or materially damaged prior to close of escrow, then, on demand of Buyer, any deposit made by Buyer shall be returned to Buyer and this contract thereupon shall terminate. Any controversy or claim arising out of, or relating to this part of this agreement shall at the election of the parties be settled by arbitration in accordance with the rules of the American Arbitration Association, and judgment upon the award rendered by the Arbitrator(s) may be entered in any court having jurisdiction thereof. The provisions of Code of Civil Procedure Section 1283.05 shall be applicable to such arbitration.

22.   In any action or proceeding arising out of this agreement, the prevailing party shall be entitled to reasonable attorney's fees and costs.

23.   Time is of the essence. All modifications or extensions shall be in writing signed by the parties.

24.   This constitutes an offer to purchase the described business. Unless acceptance is signed by Seller and the signed copy delivered to Buyer, in person or by mail to the address below, within _____ days, this offer shall be deemed revoked and the deposit shall be returned. Buyer acknowledges receipt of a copy hereof.

Real Estate Broker _____   Buyer _____

By _____   Buyer _____

Address _____   Address _____

Telephone _____   Telephone _____

ACCEPTANCE

The undersigned Seller accepts this offer and agrees to sell the business on the above terms and conditions. Seller has employed
_____
as Broker(s) and agrees to pay for services the sum of _____
Dollars ($ _____), payable as follows: (a) On closing of escrow, or (b) if completion of sale is prevented by default of Seller, upon Seller's default or (c) if completion of sale is prevented by default of Buyer, only if and when Seller collects damages from Buyer, by suit or otherwise and then in an amount not less than one-half of the damages recovered, but not to exceed the above fee, after first deducting escrow expenses and the expenses of collection, if any. In any action between Broker and Seller arising out of this agreement, the prevailing party shall be entitled to reasonable attorney's fees and costs. The undersigned acknowledges receipt of a copy of this agreement consisting of _____ pages and authorizes Broker(s) to deliver a signed copy to Buyer.

Dated: _____ Telephone _____   Seller _____

Address _____   Seller _____

Broker(s) agree to the foregoing. Broker _____   Broker _____

Dated: _____ By _____   Dated: _____ By _____

Exhibit 36.3

STATE OF CALIFORNIA
UNIFORM COMMERCIAL CODE - FINANCING STATEMENT - FORM UCC-1 (REV. 1/76)
IMPORTANT - Read instructions on back before filling out form
This FINANCING STATEMENT is presented for filing pursuant to the California Uniform Commercial Code.

QUAD

1. DEBTOR (LAST NAME FIRST - IF AN INDIVIDUAL)	1A. SOCIAL SECURITY OR FEDERAL TAX NO.	
1B. MAILING ADDRESS	1C. CITY, STATE	1D. ZIP CODE
2. ADDITIONAL DEBTOR (IF ANY) (LAST NAME FIRST - IF AN INDIVIDUAL)	2A. SOCIAL SECURITY OR FEDERAL TAX NO.	
2B. MAILING ADDRESS	2C. CITY, STATE	2D. ZIP CODE
3. DEBTOR'S TRADE NAMES OR STYLES (IF ANY)	3A. FEDERAL TAX NUMBER	

4. SECURED PARTY

NAME

MAILING ADDRESS

CITY   STATE   ZIP CODE

4A. SOCIAL SECURITY NO., FEDERAL TAX NO. OR BANK TRANSIT AND A.B.A. NO.

5. ASSIGNEE OF SECURED PARTY (IF ANY)

NAME

MAILING ADDRESS

CITY   STATE   ZIP CODE

5A. SOCIAL SECURITY NO., FEDERAL TAX NO. OR BANK TRANSIT AND A.B.A. NO.

6. This FINANCING STATEMENT covers the following types or items of property (include description of real property on which located and owner of record when required by instruction 4).

7. CHECK IF APPLICABLE ☒ 7A. ☐ PRODUCTS OF COLLATERAL ARE ALSO COVERED

7B. DEBTOR(S) SIGNATURE NOT REQUIRED IN ACCORDANCE WITH INSTRUCTION 5(A) ITEM:
☐ (1) ☐ (2) ☐ (3) ☐ (4)

8. CHECK IF APPLICABLE ☒ ☐ DEBTOR IS A "TRANSMITTING UTILITY" IN ACCORDANCE WITH UCC § 9105 (1) (N)

9.   DATE:

▶

SIGNATURE(S) OF DEBTOR(S)

TYPE OR PRINT NAME(S) OF DEBTOR(S)

▶

SIGNATURE(S) OF SECURED PARTY(IES)

TYPE OR PRINT NAME(S) OF SECURED PARTY(IES)

CODE
1
2
3
4
5
6
7
8
9
0

10. THIS SPACE FOR USE OF FILING OFFICER (DATE, TIME, FILE NUMBER AND FILING OFFICER)

11. Return copy to:

NAME

ADDRESS

CITY

STATE

ZIP CODE

(1) FILING OFFICER COPY

FORM UCC.1 - FILING FEE $ 3.00
Approved by the Secretary of State

REDIFORM 5S801

Poly Pak (50 sets) 5P801

carbonless

Exhibit 37

IMPORTANT—Read instructions on back before completing form

This **STATEMENT** is presented for filing pursuant to the California Uniform Commercial Code

1. FILE NO. OF ORIG. FINANCING STATEMENT	1A. DATE OF FILING OF ORIG. FINANCING STATEMENT	1B. DATE OF ORIG. FINANCING STATEMENT	1C. PLACE OF FILING ORIG. FINANCING STATEMENT

2. DEBTOR (LAST NAME FIRST)		2A. SOCIAL SECURITY NO., FEDERAL TAX NO.

2B. MAILING ADDRESS	2C. CITY, STATE	2D. ZIP CODE

3. ADDITIONAL DEBTOR (IF ANY) (LAST NAME FIRST)		3A. SOCIAL SECURITY OR FEDERAL TAX NO.

3B. MAILING ADDRESS	3C. CITY, STATE	3D. ZIP CODE

4. SECURED PARTY		4A. SOCIAL SECURITY NO., FEDERAL TAX NO. OR BANK TRANSIT AND A.B.A. NO.
NAME		
MAILING ADDRESS		
CITY	STATE	ZIP CODE

5. ASSIGNEE OF SECURED PARTY (IF ANY)		5A. SOCIAL SECURITY NO., FEDERAL TAX NO. OR BANK TRANSIT AND A.B.A. NO.
NAME		
MAILING ADDRESS		
CITY	STATE	ZIP CODE

6.

A ☐ CONTINUATION—The original Financing Statement between the foregoing Debtor and Secured Party bearing the file number and date shown above is continued. If collateral is crops or timber, check here ☐ and insert description of real property on which growing or to be grown in Item 7 below.

B ☐ RELEASE—From the collateral described in the Financing Statement bearing the file number shown above, the Secured Party releases the collateral described in Item 7 below.

C ☐ ASSIGNMENT—The Secured Party certifies that the Secured Party has assigned to the Assignee above named, all the Secured Party's rights under the Financing Statement bearing the file number shown above in the collateral described in Item 7 below.

D ☐ TERMINATION—The Secured Party certifies that the Secured Party no longer claims a security interest under the Financing Statement bearing the file number shown above.

E ☐ AMENDMENT—The Financing Statement bearing the file number shown above is amended as set forth in Item 7 below. (Signature of Debtor required on all amendments.)

F ☐ OTHER

7.

8.		CODE	9. This Space for Use of Filing Officer (Date, Time, Filing Office)
(Date)_____ 19___		1	
		2	
By:_____		3	
SIGNATURE(S) OF DEBTOR(S)	(TITLE)	4	
		5	
By:_____		6	
SIGNATURE(S) OF SECURED PARTY(IES)	(TITLE)		

10. **Return Copy to**

```
NAME
ADDRESS
CITY AND
STATE
```

	7
	8
	9

(1) FILING OFFICER COPY
STANDARD FORM — FILING FEE $3.00   UNIFORM COMMERCIAL CODE— FORM UCC-2
Approved by the Secretary of State

Exhibit 38

EXCLUSIVE AUTHORIZATION AND RIGHT TO SELL
THIS IS INTENDED TO BE A LEGALLY BINDING AGREEMENT. READ IT CAREFULLY.
CALIFORNIA ASSOCIATION OF REALTORS® STANDARD FORM

(MOBILEHOME registered at least one year under Vehicle Code Div. 3 or Part 2 of Division 13 of Health and Safety Code)

1. **RIGHT TO SELL.** I hereby employ and grant _____
hereafter called "Agent", the exclusive and irrevocable right commencing on _____
19 ___ , and expiring at midnight on _____
19 ___ , to sell or exchange the mobilehome situated at _____

_____ County, California in _____ Mobilehome Park.
Space # _____ described as follows: Make _____ Model _____ Year _____
Net Length _____ Expando _____ Width _____ Class _____
Type _____ Bedrooms _____ Baths _____ Exterior _____ Roof _____ Skirting _____

Serial #'s: CAL. HCD #'s: HUD #'s: 19 ___ License #'s:
_____ U   (A) _____   _____   _____
_____ X   (B) _____   _____   _____
_____ XX (C) _____   _____   _____
_____ XXX (D) _____   _____   _____

together with all built in appliances, heating units and water heater and the following equipment:
Refrigerator _____ Range _____ Oven _____ Washer _____ Dryer _____
Disposal _____ Dishwasher _____ Air Conditioner—Serial #—Tonnage _____
Carport Awning _____ Patio Awning _____ Porch _____ Screen Rm. _____
Wheels _____ Tires _____ Other _____

Park Information
Type _____ Clubhouse _____ Swimming Pool _____ Space Rental _____
Gas _____ Electricity _____ Guests _____ Children _____ Pets _____ Cable TV _____
Name of Manager _____ Phone No. _____ Sign _____ Caravan _____
Has seller obtained written agreement from Park Management permitting overage mobilehome to remain? _____ Yes _____ No

2. **TERMS OF SALE.** The purchase price shall be $ _____, to be paid on the following terms:
_____
_____

(a) The following items of personal property are to be included in the above-stated price:
_____
_____

(b) Agent is hereby authorized to accept and hold on my behalf a deposit upon the purchase price. (c) I agree to deliver the above described mobilehome and personal property, if any is included, free of liens, encumbrances, recorded, filed or registered, or known to me. (d) Evidence of title shall be in form of a duly endorsed, dated and delivered Certificate of Ownership or mobilehome and delivery of current Registration Certificate, as required by the Vehicle Code. (e) I warrant that I am the owner of the mobilehome or have authority to execute this agreement. I warrant that the above described mobilehome complies with equipment requirements of Division 12 (commencing with section 24000) of the Vehicle Code. (f) I warrant that the above described mobilehome conforms to the requirements of the Health and Safety Code and the regulations of the Department of Housing and Community Development, HUD Regulations, and any applicable local ordinances and is either 1) located within an established mobilehome park as defined in Section 18214 of the Health and Safety Code and that advertising or offering for its sale is not contrary to any items of any contract between myself and the mobilehome park owner, or 2) located pursuant to a local zoning ordinance or permit, on a lot where its presence has been authorized or its continued presence and such use would be authorized for a total and uninterrupted period of at least one year. (g) I agree to deliver as soon as possible to Agent for submission to buyer a copy of my lease or rental agreement and all current park rules and regulations and inform agent of any changes occurring during the term hereof.

3. **Notice: The amount or rate of real estate commissions is not fixed by law. They are set by each broker individually and may be negotiable between the seller and broker.**

COMPENSATION OF AGENT. I hereby agree to compensate Agent as follows: (a) ___ % of the selling price if the mobilehome is sold during the term hereof, or any extension thereof, by Agent, on the terms herein set forth or any other price and terms I may accept, or through any other person, or by me, or ___ % of the price shown in 2), if said mobilehome is withdrawn from sale, transferred, or leased without the consent of Agent, or made unmarketable by my voluntary act during the term hereof or any extension thereof. (b) The compensation provided for in subparagraph a) above if the mobilehome is sold or otherwise transferred within ___ days after the termination of this authority or any extension thereof to anyone with whom Agent has had negotiations prior to final termination, provided I have received notice in writing, including the names of the prospective purchasers, before or upon termination of this agreement or any extension thereof.

4. If action be instituted to enforce this agreement, the prevailing party shall receive reasonable attorney's fees and costs.

5. I authorize the Agent named herein to cooperate with sub-agents.

6. The mobilehome is offered in compliance with state and federal Anti-Discrimination Laws.

7. In the event of an exchange, permission is hereby given Agent to represent all parties and collect compensation or commissions from them, provided there is full disclosure to all principals of such agency. Agent is authorized to divide with other agents such compensation or commissions in any manner acceptable to them.

8. I agree to hold Agent harmless from any liability arising from any incorrect information supplied by me, or from any material fact known by me concerning the mobilehome, the park or other location in which it is located, which I fail to disclose.

9. Other provisions: _____

10. I acknowledge that I have read and understand this Agreement, and that I have received a copy hereof.
DATED: _____ , 19 ___   _____ , California
Owner _____   Owner _____
Address _____   City, State, Phone _____

11. In consideration of the above, Agent agrees to use diligence in procuring a purchaser.
Agent _____   Address, City _____
By _____   Phone, Date _____

NO REPRESENTATION IS MADE AS TO THE LEGAL VALIDITY OF ANY PROVISION OR THE ADEQUACY OF ANY PROVISION IN ANY SPECIFIC TRANSACTION.

Exhibit 39

MOBILEHOME PURCHASE CONTRACT AND RECEIPT FOR DEPOSIT

THIS IS INTENDED TO BE A LEGALLY BINDING CONTRACT. READ IT CAREFULLY.
CALIFORNIA ASSOCIATION OF REALTORS® STANDARD FORM

(Mobilehome Registered at Least One Year Under Vehicle Code Div. 3
or Part 2 of Division 13 of Health & Safety Code)

THIS IS MORE THAN A RECEIPT FOR MONEY. IT IS INTENDED TO BE A LEGALLY BINDING CONTRACT. READ IT CAREFULLY.

_____ , California _____ , 19_____

Received from _____

herein called Buyer, the sum of _____ Dollars $ _____

evidenced by cash ☐, cashier's check ☐, or _____ ☐ personal check ☐ payable to _____

_____ , to be held uncashed until acceptance of this offer, as deposit on account of purchase price of

_____ Dollars $ _____

for the purchase of mobilehome situated at _____

County of _____ , California in _____

Mobilehome Park, Space # _____ , described as follows: Make _____

Model _____ Year _____ Net Length _____ Expando _____ Width _____

Serial #'s: CAL. HCD #'s: HUD #'s: 19   License #'s:

	U (A)		
	X (B)		
	XX (C)		
	XXX (D)		

together with all built-in appliances, heating units and water heater and the following additional equipment:

_____
_____
_____
_____
_____

1.   Buyer will deposit in escrow with _____ the balance of purchase price as follows:

_____
_____
_____
_____
_____
_____
_____
_____
_____
_____

(Set forth above any terms and conditions of this sale, such as financing, repairs and personal property to be included in the sale.)

2.   Deposit will ☐ will not ☐ be increased by $_____ to $_____ within _____ days of
acceptance of this offer.

3.   The supplements initialed below are incorporated as part of this agreement.   Other

_____ HCD certification of purchase price   _____ Occupancy Agreement   _____ _____

_____ Structural Pest Control Certification Agreement _____ VA Amendment   _____ _____

_____ Special Studies Zone Disclosure   _____ FHA Amendment   _____ _____

4.   Buyer and Seller acknowledge receipt of a copy of this page, Page 1 of _____ Pages.

Buyer _____   Seller _____

Buyer _____   Seller _____

Exhibit 40.1

MOBILEHOME PURCHASE CONTRACT AND RECEIPT FOR DEPOSIT

The following terms and conditions are hereby incorporated in and made a part of Buyer's Offer.

CALIFORNIA ASSOCIATION OF REALTORS® STANDARD FORM

5.   Title is to be free of liens, encumbrances, recorded, filed or registered, or known to seller except as set forth above.

6.   Unless otherwise designated in the escrow instructions of Buyer, title shall vest as follows: _____
_____

(The manner of taking title may have significant consequences. Therefore, give this matter serious consideration.)

7.   Evidence of title shall be in form of a duly endorsed, dated and delivered Certificate of Ownership and delivery of current Registration Certificate, as required by the law. If seller fails to deliver title as herein provided, Buyer may terminate this agreement and the deposit shall thereupon be returned to Buyer.

8.   Buyer acknowledges that present or any future movement of the mobilehome may be limited by law and is subject to the regulations current at that time by the Department of Transportation.

9.   Buyer acknowledges that Seller hereby is not assigning or subletting the space the mobilehome occupies in its present location unless such letting is specifically made part of this agreement. If the described mobilehome is located in a mobilehome park in which it is to remain, the buyer by his signature below represents that he has agreed to the terms of a rental agreement for the space involved.

10.   Possession shall be delivered to Buyer (a) on close of escrow, or (b) not later than _____ days after closing escrow, or (c) _____

11.   Escrow instructions signed by Buyer and Seller shall be delivered to the escrow holder within _____ days from the Seller's acceptance hereof and shall provide for closing within _____ days from the Seller's acceptance hereof, subject to written extensions signed by Buyer and Seller.

12.   If the mobilehome is destroyed or materially damaged prior to close of escrow, then, on demand by Buyer, any deposit made by Buyer shall be returned to Buyer and this contract thereupon shall terminate.

13.   If Broker is a participant of a Board multiple listing service ("MLS"), the Broker is authorized to report the sale, its price, terms and financing for the information, publication, dissemination, and use of the authorized Board members.

14.   **If Buyer fails to complete said purchase as herein provided by reason of any default of Buyer, Seller shall be released from the obligation to sell the mobilehome to Buyer and may proceed against Buyer upon any claim or remedy which Seller may have in law or equity provided, however, that by placing their initials here Buyer: ( ) Seller: ( ) agree that Seller shall retain the deposit as Seller's liquidated damages, and that it would be impractical or extremely difficult to fix the actual damages suffered because of such default; that the amount paid by Buyer as deposit constitutes a reasonable estimate and agreed stipulation of such damages.**

15.   If the only controversy or claim between the parties arises out of or relates to the disposition of the Buyer's deposit, such controversy or claim shall, at the election of the parties, be decided by arbitration in accordance with the Rules of the American Arbitration Association, and judgment upon the award rendered by the Arbitrator(s) may be entered in any court having jurisdiction thereof. The provisions of Code of Civil Procedure Section 1283.05 shall be applicable to such arbitration.

16.   In any action or proceeding arising out of this agreement, the prevailing party shall be entitled to reasonable attorney's fees and costs.

17.   Time is of the essence. All modifications or extensions shall be in writing signed by the parties.

18.   This constitutes an offer to purchase the described mobilehome. Unless acceptance is signed by Seller and the signed copy delivered to Buyer, in person or by mail to the address below, within _____ days, this offer shall be deemed revoked and the deposit shall be returned. Buyer acknowledges receipt of a copy hereof.

Real Estate Broker_____   Buyer _____

By_____   Buyer _____

Address_____   Address _____

Telephone_____   Telephone _____

ACCEPTANCE

The undersigned Seller accepts and agrees to sell the mobilehome on the above terms and conditions. Seller has employed_____

_____ as Broker(s) and agrees to pay for services the sum of

_____ Dollars ($_____) , payable as follows:

(a) On close of escrow, or (b) if completion of sale is prevented by default of Seller, upon Seller's default or (c) if completion of sale is prevented by default of Buyer, only if and when Seller collects damages from Buyer, by suit or otherwise and then in an amount of one-half of the damages recovered, but not to exceed the above fee after first deducting escrow expenses and the expenses of collection, if any. In any action between Broker and Seller arising out of this agreement, the prevailing party shall be entitled to reasonable attorney's fees and costs. The undersigned acknowledges receipt of a copy and authorizes Broker(s) to deliver a signed copy to Buyer. Page 2 of _____ Pages.

Dated _____ Telephone _____   Seller _____

Address_____   Seller _____

Broker(s) agree to the foregoing. Broker_____   Broker _____

Dated _____ By_____   Dated _____ By _____

To order, contact—California Association of Realtors®
525 S. Virgil Avenue, Los Angeles, California 90020
(Revised 1982)   FORM MHD-11-2

Exhibit 40.2

MORTGAGE LOAN DISCLOSURE STATEMENT (BORROWER)

CALIFORNIA ASSOCIATION OF REALTORS® STANDARD FORM

_____
(Name of Broker/Arranger of Credit)

_____
(Business Address of Broker)

I. SUMMARY OF LOAN TERMS

    A. PRINCIPAL AMOUNT OF LOAN . . . . $ _____

    B. ESTIMATED DEDUCTIONS FROM PRINCIPAL AMOUNT

        1. Costs and Expenses (See Paragraph III-A) . . . . $ _____

        2. Commission/Loan Origination Fee (See Paragraph III-B) . . . . . . $ _____

        3. Liens and Other Amounts to be Paid on Authorization of Borrower
           (See Paragraph III-C) . . . . $ _____

    C. ESTIMATED CASH PAYABLE TO BORROWER (A less B) . . . . $ _____

II. GENERAL INFORMATION ABOUT LOAN

    A. If this loan is made, you will be required to pay the principal and interest at _____ % per year, payable as

       follows: _____ _____ payments of $ _____
              (number of payments)   (monthly/quarterly/annually)

       and a FINAL/BALLOON payment of *$ _____ to pay off the loan in full.

             ***CAUTION TO BORROWER:** If you do not have the funds to pay the balloon payment
             when due, it may be necessary for you to obtain a new loan against your property
             for this purpose, in which case you may be required to again pay commissions,
             fees, and expenses for arranging a new loan. Keep this in mind in checking upon
             the amount and terms of the loan that you obtain at this time.

    B. This loan will be evidenced by a promissory note and secured by a deed of trust in favor of lender/creditor on
       property located at (street address or legal description):

       _____

       _____

       _____

    C. Liens against this property and the approximate amounts are:

       Nature of Lien   Amount Owing

       _____   _____

       _____   _____

       _____   _____

       CAUTION TO BORROWER: Be sure that the amount of all liens is stated as accurately as possible. If you
       contract with the broker for this loan, but it cannot be made or arranged because you did not state these lien
       amounts correctly, you may be liable to pay commissions, fees, and expenses even though you did not obtain
       the loan.

    D. If you wish to pay more than the scheduled payment at any time before it is due, you may have to pay a
       PREPAYMENT PENALTY computed as follows:

       _____

       _____

       _____

    E. The purchase of credit life or credit disability insurance is not required of the borrower as a condition of
       making this loan.

    F. The real property which will secure the requested loan is an "owner-occupied dwelling"*   YES ____ NO ____
                                                 (Borrower initial opposite
                                              YES or NO)

       *An "owner-occupied dwelling" means a single dwelling unit in a condominium or cooperative or a residential
       building of less than three separate dwelling units, one of which will be owned and occupied by a signatory
       to the mortgage or deed of trust for this loan within 90 days of the signing of the mortgage or deed of trust.

Exhibit 41.1

III. DEDUCTIONS FROM LOAN PROCEEDS

    A.   ESTIMATED MAXIMUM COSTS AND EXPENSES to be paid by borrower out of the principal amount of the loan are:

	PAYABLE TO	
	Broker	Others
1. Appraisal fee	_____	_____
2. Escrow fee	_____	_____
3. Fees for policy of title insurance	_____	_____
4. Notary fees	_____	_____
5. Recording fees	_____	_____
6. Credit Investigation fees	_____	_____
7. Other Costs and Expenses:		
	_____	_____
	_____	_____
TOTAL COSTS AND EXPENSES	$ _____	

    *B.   LOAN BROKERAGE COMMISSION/LOAN ORIGINATION FEE . . . . $ _____

    C.   LIENS AND OTHER AMOUNTS to be paid out of the principal amount of the loan on authorization of the borrower are estimated to be as follows:

	PAYABLE TO	
	Broker	Others
1. Fire or other property insurance premiums	_____	_____
2. Credit life or disability insurance premium (see Paragraph II-E)	_____	_____
3. Beneficiary statement fees	_____	_____
4. Reconveyance and similar fees	_____	_____
5. Liens against property securing loan:		
	_____	_____
	_____	_____
6. Other:		
	_____	_____
TOTAL TO BE PAID ON AUTHORIZATION OF BORROWER	$ _____	

If the loan to which this disclosure statement applies is a loan secured by a first deed of trust in a principal amount of less than $20,000 or a loan secured by a junior lien in a principal amount of less than $10,000, the undersigned certifies that the loan will be made in compliance with Article 7 of Chapter 3 of the Real Estate Law.

*This loan ☐ may/☐ will/☐ will NOT (check one) be made wholly or in part from broker-controlled funds as defined in Section 10241(j) of the Business and Professions Code.

*NOTICE TO BORROWER: This disclosure statement may be used if the broker is acting as an agent in arranging the loan by a third person or if the loan will be made with funds owned or controlled by the broker. The broker must indicate in the above statement whether the loan "may" be made out of broker-controlled funds. If broker-controlled funds are then used to make this loan, the broker must notify the borrower of that fact before the close of escrow.

_____   _____
(Name of Broker)   (Name of Designated Representative)

_____   _____
(License Number)   (License Number)

                                OR

_____   _____
(Signature of Broker)   (Signature)

NOTICE TO BORROWER

DO NOT SIGN THIS STATEMENT UNTIL YOU HAVE READ AND UNDERSTOOD ALL OF THE INFORMATION IN IT. ALL PARTS OF THE FORM MUST BE COMPLETED BEFORE YOU SIGN.

Borrower hereby acknowledges the receipt of a copy of this statement.

DATED: _____   _____
                                      (Borrower)

_____
(Borrower)

Approved DRE 3/10/83

Exhibit 42.2

Chapter 15 Quiz

1. The document used for the transfer of ownership of personal property is the:

   (A) Security agreement
   (B) Financing statement
   (C) Chattel mortgage
   (D) Bill of sale

2. Which formula is *incorrect*?

   (A) Assets = Liabilities plus Net Worth
   (B) Liabilities = Assets minus Net Worth
   (C) Assets = Liabilities minus Net Worth
   (D) Net Worth = Assets minus Liabilities

3. The tax assessed on personal property included in the sale of a business, on goods sold in this or another state for storage or consumption in California, is known as:

   (A) Personal property tax
   (B) Income tax
   (C) Franchise tax
   (D) Use tax

4. The parties to a security agreement are:

   (A) Mortgagor and mortgagee
   (B) Debtor and secured party
   (C) Trustor and beneficiary
   (D) Vendor and vendee

5. Under the Uniform Commercial Code, in California the function of the chattel mortgage is now filled by the:

   (A) Deed of trust
   (B) Security agreement
   (C) Financing statement
   (D) Financial statement

6. The Real Property Securities Law regulates the sale of:

   (A) Out-of-state notes and trust deeds
   (B) Unseasoned promotional notes
   (C) All notes secured by liens on real property
   (D) All of the above

7. A separate interest in a certain space in a building, combined with an undivided interest in common in certain common areas, is known as a:

   (A) Leasehold
   (B) Mobilehome
   (C) Condominium
   (D) Stock cooperative

8. The basic purpose for regulating the sale of subdivided land by the California Department of Real Estate is to:

   (A) Control the "physical aspects"
   (B) Regulate the physical design
   (C) Prevent fraud
   (D) Control the environment

9. A real estate broker's license is required of:

   (A) An owner-manager of an apartment building with 16 or more units
   (B) A resident manager of an apartment building with 16 or more units
   (C) An agent who manages a 16 unit apartment building for the owner
   (D) All of the above

10. The activities of loan brokers are regulated by the:

   (A) Real Property Securities Law
   (B) Broker's Loan Law
   (C) Real Estate Law
   (D) Both (B) and (C)

Index

Regulation Z, 115, 208-210
Reinstatement and redemption, 203-204, 239
Relocation, 72, 122, 148, 151
Rent, 101, 227-229, 289
Rent-a-desk, 33
Rental real estate, 243, 273
Renter's credit, 241
REO, 132
Replacement cost, 98
Rescission, 153, 171, 173, 209
Resident manager, 274, 288
Residential loan application, 214-215
RESPA, 175, 208, 211, 213
Return, 224, 265
Revenue Act of 1987, 196, 246, 248
Right of first refusal, 291
Risk, 197, 270
Rollover, 245
Rounding, 218-219
Rule 41C, 94
S corporation, 31
Sales and use tax, 285
Sales associates, 37-41
Sales contract, 172
Sales manager, 37, 39
Sales meetings, 41
Sales portfolio, 154
Sales process, 142-149
Sales tax, 238, 283, 285
Salesperson, 1, 2, 29, 33, 46, 59
Satisfaction of mortgage, 204
Savings, 194, 268
Savings and loans, 194-195
Secondary financing, 197, 199
Secondary market, 196, 200-201, 222
Secretary of State, 283
Secured personal property, 279
Secured transaction, 283
Securities, 21, 224
Security agreement, 279, 298-300
Security instrument, 202
Seller financing, 74, 151, 206, 296
Seller financing disclosure, 75, 87-89
Seller's agency, 52, 54, 131
Seller's Affidavit of Nonforeign Status, 75, 84-85
Seller's permit, 285
Selling agent, 51, 57, 60, 62, 132, 167
Sendout slip, 281
Senior exemption, 240, 244
Servicing, 75, 101
Settlement statement, 189-190, 213
Shelter, 268
Shopping centers, 4-5
Showing, 76, 123, 151-152
Signs, 23, 40, 109, 111, 121, 123
Social Security, 238
Sources of listings, 70
Special assessments, 241
Specialization, 1, 3, 16, 118, 254, 278
Specific performance, 171, 173
Speculation, 148, 273
Square foot system, 234

SREA, 13
Standard coverage, 178
Standards of Practice, 26
State Board of Equalization, 282, 285
Statute of Frauds, 76, 279
Statute of limitations, 203, 204
Stock cooperative, 292, 294
Stock-in-trade, 245, 279-280
Storage, 5
Straight-line, 247
Straight loan, 202, 229
Structural pest control, 175
Subagency, 25, 47-50, 55, 132
Subdivided Lands Act, 3, 291, 294
Subdivision Map Act, 3, 294
Subdivisions, 3, 10, 116, 132, 291-295, 297
Subject to, 174, 206
Subjective value, 92
Successor's liability, 282, 285
Sum-of-the-years' digits, 247
Supply and demand, 93
Suspended passive losses, 243
Take-out financing, 196, 292
Tax advantages, 262, 274, 297
Tax benefits, 262
Tax brackets, 242, 249
Tax calendar
Tax deed, 239
Tax-deferred exchange, 245, 252, 262
Tax exemptions, 240
Tax flow, 266, 268
Tax Reform Act of 1986, 196, 245, 247, 266
Tax reporting, 164, 248
Tax shelter, 245-246, 262, 266, 272
Tax stamp sale, 239
Taxes, 30, 32, 94, 218, 227, 237
Telephone prospecting, 70, 121
Telephone, 34-35, 70, 120-121, 167
Tenants, 269, 289
Termination date of listing, 77
Testimonial close, 163
Third parties, 58, 60, 129-131, 280
Tight money, 151, 205
Time management, 8, 118, 149
Timeshare, 294
Title companies, 172, 175, 213
Title insurance, 176-178
Title report, 174, 177
Tombstone ads, 110
Trademark, 32, 35, 287
Trading up, 253, 273
Training, 33, 36-39
Transferees, 72, 122, 148, 151
Treasury bills, 194
Trial closes, 74, 160
Trust deed, 202, 203, 273, 296
Trust funds, 22, 166, 173
Trustee's sale, 203
Truth in Lending, 115, 208, 210
Unethical conduct, 16
Uniform Commercial Code (U.C.C.), 283-284

Uniform Residential Appraisal Report, 96, 103-105
Uniform Settlement Statement, 175, 189-190, 213
Unlawful conduct, 14
Unlisted properties, 132
Unsecured, 279
Use tax, 285
Usury, 206
Utility, 91-92, 98
VA (USDVA), 196-198, 205, 223, 294
Vacancy factor, 263, 269
Valuation, 95-96
Value, 19, 92-96
Variable rate disclosures, 210
Vendee, 207
Veteran's exemption, 240
Warehousing, 5, 196
Wraparound, 207
Written contract, 76
Yield, 230, 262-263
Zoning, 92, 119, 178, 293